WRITING AND PRODUCING TELEVISION NEWS

Second Edition

WRITING AND PRODUCING TELEVISION NEWS Second Edition

Eric K. Gormly

Blackwell
Publishing

This book is dedicated to the memory of Travis Brooks Linn, a truly great journalist, writer, teacher, mentor and friend. He cared passionately about life and the people around him, and he touched the lives of everyone he met. He taught me much. I am grateful to have known him, and I shall miss him.

©2004 Blackwell Publishing
All rights reserved
Cover photo by Maike Rode; with permission

Blackwell Publishing Professional
2121 State Avenue, Ames, Iowa 50014, USA

Orders: 1-800-862-6657
Office: 1-515-292-0140
Fax: 1-515-292-3348
Web site: www.blackwellprofessional.com

Blackwell Publishing Ltd
9600 Garsington Road, Oxford OX4 2DQ, UK
Tel.: +44 (0)1865 776868

Blackwell Publishing Asia
550 Swanston Street, Carlton, Victoria 3053, Australia
Tel.: +61 (0)3 8359 1011

Authorization to photocopy items for internal or personal use, or the internal or personal use of specific clients, is granted by Blackwell Publishing, provided that the base fee of $.10 per copy is paid directly to the Copyright Clearance Center, 222 Rosewood Drive, Danvers, MA 01923. For those organizations that have been granted a photocopy license by CCC, a separate system of payments has been arranged. The fee code for users of the Transactional Reporting Service is 0-8138-1299-2/2004 $.10.

Printed on acid-free paper in the United States of America

First edition, ©1997, Iowa State University Press
    (*Writing News for Television: Style and format*)
Second edition, 2004

Library of Congress Cataloging-in-Publication Data
Gormly, Eric K.
   Writing and producing television news / Eric K. Gormly—2nd ed.
      p. cm.
Rev. ed. of: Writing news for television / Victoria McCullough Carroll.
1st ed. 1997
   ISBN 0-8138-1299-2 (alk. paper)
1. Television broadcasting of news. 2. Broadcast journalism—Authorship.
3. Report writing. / Carroll, Victoria.
Writing News for television. II. Title.
   PN4784.T4C37 2004
   808'06607—dc22   2003022614

The last digit is the print number: 9 8 7 6 5 4 3 2 1

About the Author

Dr. Eric Gormly is a former television news reporter. He began his career in radio at KOKE-FM & AM in Austin, where he wrote, reported, produced and anchored. He took his first job in television at KZTV-TV in Corpus Christi, Texas, where he worked as a reporter, editor, producer, videographer and fill-in anchor. He worked as a reporter, editor and fill-in anchor at KENS-TV in San Antonio, after which he worked as a reporter for KHOU-TV in Houston and KMOV-TV in St. Louis. He also worked as an anchor/host, interviewer, and producer for public affairs programs at KNPB-TV in Reno.

Dr. Gormly has taught a range of broadcast news and mass communication courses at the University of Nevada-Reno, Trinity University in San Antonio, the University of Texas at Austin, and Arizona State University. He currently is on faculty in the Department of Journalism at the University of North Texas in Denton, where he teaches the television news and media criticism courses and conducts research in the area of religion in media and culture. He received his bachelor's degree in journalism from the University of Texas at Austin, a master's degree in journalism from the University of Missouri-Columbia and a doctorate in radio-television-film studies from the University of Texas at Austin. He lives in Dallas with his wife Leah and their two cats, Athena and Vesta.

Contents

Preface   ix

Acknowledgments   xiii

1 Television News: An Introduction   3

2 Television Newswriting: A Different Style   11

3 A Brief Review of Grammar   17

4 Some General Rules for Television Newswriting   35

5 Usage   53

6 Approaching the Television News Story   69

7 Story Formats: Some Basics   101

8 The Voice Over: VO   137

9 Sound on Tape: SOT   165

10 The Voice Over/Sound Bite: VO/SOT   187

11 Putting the Formats Together   211

12 Interviewing: Conversation with a Goal   223

13 The Package   235

14 An Interview with Deborah Potter   271

15 The Live Shot   275

16 An Interview with Beverly White   285

17 Producing the Newscast   295

18 The Station and the Newsroom   321

19 A Look Inside: WFAA-TV, Dallas   331

20 Finding a Job   365

Index   387

Preface

Writing Is the Key

When working journalists prepare lists of tips for beginning television writers, almost without fail they top their lists with "Learn to write well." Writing is the key to a successful and solid news operation. Solid writing is the foundation on which reporting, news gathering, producing and anchoring skills are built. Without writing skills, students cannot hope to compete in this industry. This text develops the key skills need for writing and producing television news. It also provides a good introduction to how writing relates to the reporting, shooting and editing process. The book enables the student to become proficient and competent in writing television news scripts and provides the foundation for later courses in electronic production, news gathering, producing and so on.

Examples, Summaries and Exercises

Throughout the following chapters, scripts and wire copy from commercial newsrooms illustrate key points. The stories are timely and offer students as realistic a learning experience as possible. Each chapter provides numerous examples of key points. Many of the points are illustrated in detail through comparisons of weak and better writing samples for greater student comprehension. Key points are further reinforced in summaries at the end of each chapter.

The exercise sections in each chapter have been rated by reviewers as among the book's strongest points. All exercises have been used and tested in classrooms. They are not ideas that should work. They are student assignments that have worked.

Wire Copy

Many students want to jump into television news writing "from scratch." It is not the purpose of this book to dampen their enthusiasm, but television news writing is a discipline. Students are encouraged to concentrate their efforts on developing a writing style and leave electronic news gathering skills for later study. Thousands of working journalists have developed their writing skills by using wire copy as a source. Television script examples and assignments in the exercises provided rely on wire copy—a tested and proved successful teaching and learning method.

Script Formats

There is little standardization among television news departments around the country. The scripts presented in this book as examples adopt as standardized a format as possible. They accurately reflect script formats used by some, but not all, newsrooms. However, students will benefit from mastering the formatting skills described in this book. It is essential to have some mastery of script writing and formatting before walking into a station for an internship or a job. Once a student thoroughly learns one approach to writing and formatting scripts, it becomes much easier to adapt to another style. Someone without a base from which to work will have a difficult time succeeding in a newsroom.

Chapter Organization

Chapter 1 is an overview of the industry and a discussion of what it takes to work as a television journalist and the role of writing.

Chapter 2 deals with the difference in writing for television news as opposed to other news media. Television news takes a very different approach because it is written for the ear and must fit within the constraints of a news telecast.

Chapter 3 reviews basic rules of grammar. For some classes, this may seem unnecessary. However, most will find that a quick review of grammar as well as doing the exercises can be quite helpful and will improve the quality of writing later.

Chapter 4 focuses on specific rules for television newswriting. The characters on the page or TelePrompTer must conform to a particular style, and the phrasing and choice of words must demonstrate both good journalism and good television news writing, which the journalist must deliver orally to be heard—rather than read—by the audience.

Chapter 5 takes the student through language usage for television, looking at simpler, shorter words, phrases and sentences. The chapter emphasizes clarity in writing, active voice, present and future tense, literary devices and stronger writing.

Chapter 6 exposes the student to how a basic television news story is constructed. After reviewing newsworthiness criteria, the chapter turns to creating leads, describing different types of leads, developing the body of the story, concluding the story and putting it all together.

Chapters 7 to 13 and 15 represent the core of the book. These chapters develop the various story formats, showing step-by-step how to turn basic information, visuals and sound into solid stories that are properly scripted.

Chapter 7 introduces basic television news story formats and scripting. The chapter then turns to the reader and the reader with graphics, detailing how to script these two formats and discussing what the viewer will see and hear.

Chapter 8 brings in the visual element and shows how to write and script a voice over. As with the reader and every other format covered in this book, the chapter discusses what the viewer will see and hear. The chapter emphasizes logging video and writing to pictures and use of natural sound.

In Chapter 9, the student reads about use of primary sound in the form of sound bites, or sots. The chapter discusses how to recognize good sound bites, how to place them in a story, how to write into and out of them and a few cautions.

Chapter 10 shows how to put vos and sots together in the same story.

Chapter 11 provides practice in various combinations of the format elements covered in the previous chapters.

Chapter 12 gives an in-depth discussion of how to conduct an interview in terms of both content and technical considerations. Although this is not a textbook on reporting or interviewing, the student needs to have a basic understanding of how the process of getting sots on tape should work.

Chapter 13 deals with the reporter's package. This is a markedly different format because the reporter's voice tracks are edited onto the finished story. The chapter is divided into two parts, the first of which takes the student through the process of writing and scripting a reporter's package. Whereas this first part shows the writer's perspective, the second part takes a deeper look into the reporter's process of developing the various elements that will go into the package: the research, gathering the visuals and sound, laying the voice tracks and so on. Given the complexity, the instructor might want to extend discussion and exercises from this chapter into an additional class session or two.

Chapter 14 consists of an interview with former network correspondent Deborah Potter on the writing process. She gives good insight on some key issues writers should keep in mind.

Chapter 15 details the live-shot format, which is a very different approach to writing. This is a much looser endeavor and requires great flexibility and thinking on one's feet. Given the importance of live reports in today's television newscasts and the need for reporters to be able to do a live remote, I believe it important to devote a chapter to how to set up and execute one.

Chapter 16 features an interview with major-market reporter Beverly White. Beverly is a live-shot specialist and discusses several aspects of live reporting in the interview.

Many who go into television news and develop into good writers should and will become producers. Newsrooms are demanding good producers, and it represents a great job choice for skilled students. Chapter 17 details the producing process from start to finish, helping to prepare the student for that career path.

Chapter 18 provides a generic introduction to newsroom structure and the various roles involved.

Chapter 19 shows a detailed look at the newsroom of a major market television station, WFAA in Dallas. The chapter focuses in particular on one producer and one reporter, following each of them through an entire day.

Finally, Chapter 20 gives an in-depth discussion of the job-search process, providing specific strategies for each major step and element the job seeker will need to know.

Options for Lesson Plan Organization

The chapters flow into one another for optimal student comprehension, but the organization also allows instructors to tailor the curriculum to meet their particular classroom needs. For example, some instructors may want to spend substantial time on the grammar chapter, others may want to skim through it, still others may want to assign the reading and exercises as homework only without spending time in class.

Acknowledgments

There are many who contributed to the writing of this book. I wish to thank Alan Albarran, chair of the fine Department of Radio-Television-Film at the University of North Texas, who informed me that Blackwell Publishing was looking for an author for this text. Mark Barrett and Cheryl Garton on the editorial staff at Blackwell Publishing were most helpful. Thanks also to the Associated Press and the Dallas Morning News, both of which allowed me to use their stories as examples in this book.

I'm extremely grateful to the Belo Corporation in Dallas for their cooperation and the many people at WFAA-TV news who were critical to sections of this book: Nann Goplerud, David Duitch, Katharyn DeVille, Brad Watson, Brad Hawkins, Don Smith, Connie Howard, Jack Beavers, Mike Coscia, Danny Manley and a host of others. They were extremely gracious, open and cooperative.

In addition, Jed Gifford and Sandra Connell at Talent Dynamics were quite helpful in my research.

I want to thank my colleagues in the Department of Journalism at the University of North Texas. They have given me tremendous support in a range of areas, including the writing of this text. I work in an outstanding, high-quality department with outstanding, high-quality colleagues, and I am grateful for both.

Finally, I would like to thank my family: Donna, Paul, Robin, Tim and, most of all, my beloved wife Leah, who has patiently and lovingly supported me through this process and so many others.

Thank you all.

WRITING AND PRODUCING TELEVISION NEWS

Second Edition

1

Television News: An Introduction

It is 15 minutes to air, and the scene resembles quiet chaos. Desks are piled high with books, tapes and files; police scanners are crackling and television monitors blaring in the background. Some people are holding animated conversations on the phone; others are calling across the giant room; still others are pounding away at their computers, watching video images fly by at an editing station, or hustling through the area clutching scripts and tapes. But in the midst of the clamor, those crazed people are taking part in a constantly changing but carefully orchestrated process. This is a television newsroom, and each of the players has a specific role in assembling what, in a quarter of an hour, will go on the air as a live newscast.

Television news is a key source of information for the American public. It's also an extremely tough, competitive business. Working in television news strikes many people as a glamorous way to make a living. And it is. For about a week and a half. Once the glamour has worn off, what remains is an incredibly difficult job. It's challenging and filled with stress, each person charged with tasks that must be executed well and precisely and on deadline. There is no time for lapse. Mistakes can be catastrophic. And when someone does the job poorly, it becomes evident not just to a few, but to the entire viewing audience—which could number from a few thousand to more than a million people, depending on the size of the market. Anyone going into this business must understand that this is not an easy job. The hours are long, the pay early in the career is poor, and a television journalist never leaves the job at the newsroom. It's tough to land a position, tough to keep it once you're there, and tough to enterprise good stories, tell them well and air them before your competition does.

Working in television news is not simply a job, it's a lifestyle. You will work holidays and birthdays and anniversaries. During your time off, you'll be looking for and developing story ideas, reading and viewing the competition, and critiquing your own work to see where you can improve. It is filled with pressure, and it never ends.

However, television news can be an exciting and rewarding way to make a living—meeting and interviewing a range of people you would otherwise never know, gaining exposure to the major issues of your community, finding and telling the stories that mean something to your viewers, and having a chance to make a difference. It's an important role, and with the tremendous responsibilities can come great satisfaction in doing the job and doing it well.

What follows are, in no particular order, some aspects to keep in mind as you are moving toward a career in television news.

Skills—Learn to master the basic skills that go into television news, and know that writing is at the base of everything a television newsroom produces. Your writing must be clear, well-structured and interesting. Writing is key to this business, and that holds for reporters, producers and anchors. Assignment editors, videographers, tape editors and everyone else involved are part of the writing process in one way or another and need to understand good writing to do their jobs well.

Another point to keep in mind is that good writing depends first on good reporting. This is not a text on reporting, but any reporter, writer, producer or assignments editor must know how to track down information. You must know how things work and who potential contact people are. Know how to work the phones. Know what reference materials are out there. Take a class or two on basic reporting skills. Get a good text on basic reporting and get some practice doing it. A text on beat reporting or in-depth reporting wouldn't hurt. Also, know how to use a critical research tool that's at your disposal: the Internet. Get a good book or take a class on precision on-line journalism and develop your on-line research skills.

Good vocal delivery is also a part of good writing for a reporter or anchor. This is not a text on developing delivery skills, but a reporter or anchor must be able to orally communicate the scripted words. If this is your career path, develop those skills early. Take a class in oral delivery. Get some experience doing debate or theatre. Learn how to orally interpret the words on the page so that your meaning is clear and you give the viewer a sense of the event or issue you're covering.

Education—It never stops, and you need a solid foundation before getting your degree. As will be discussed later, television news journalists absolutely must have a broad education. They have to know enough about the world and how it functions to even recognize a good story, let alone know what questions to ask or where and how to find the answers. Then, you as the writer must be able to explain the issue or situation in an understandable and interesting way. All of this depends on knowledge. You must have a basic understanding of literature, science, business, economics, government, history, art appreciation . . . it's starting to read like the litany of required liberal arts courses, isn't it? Well, there's a reason those courses are required. You will be applying all of it and then some if you're going to be successful in television news.

Plus, the knowledge you'll need doesn't just come from college classes or official sources. What you learn from traveling, unrelated work experience and social time with a range of people will broaden you and your ability to make sense of the world. It all comes into play in this job.

Curiosity and Power of Observation—You need both in ample quantities, and one feeds the other. It never ceases to amaze me how many students say they want to work in television news but rarely read a newspaper, or worse still, watch a newscast. If you are not insatiably curious about the world around you, *change majors now*. This is *not* the career for you. You should read your local newspaper each day (skim most of it, read for detail on what interests you), a national newspaper regularly and two or three major news magazines each month and watch a lot of television news. This is one of the few professions in which good (as well as bad) examples of work done by others are readily available. Watch carefully to see how they do what they do, mentally file what you think is good, and discard the rest. Get to know the styles of presentation; which stations tend to lead with what kinds of stories and which stations typically beat the others; who the better writers, reporters, videographers and editors are—watch with a critical eye, and you will learn from those who are already doing what you want to build your career around.

At the same time, be curious about the people and events you find in your personal contacts. Enjoy talking with people and finding out about them. I've been told I never met a stranger, and that's largely true. It should be true of you, as well. You'll learn a lot more, you'll improve your interviewing skills and you just may come across a terrific story that way. I can't count the number of good stories I found because I was curious about something and asked, or simply struck up a conversation with someone.

Mechanical Skills and Technology—I'm not talking about changing the oil in the car. You must be able to type. You must be able to compose at a computer. You must know how to work with a computer in using basic programs, on-line resources, networking and the like. You also should have a basic grasp of video and audio technology, and how visuals and sound are captured and edited into a finished piece.

Television newsroom technology has changed dramatically over the past several years. Newsrooms are fully computerized, enabling reporters, writers and producers to check rundowns, write their copy, view video and send scripts to others for approval or directly to a TelePrompTer. Reporters and videographers travel with cell phones and laptop computers, and they do so in trucks equipped to enable them to live from virtually anywhere. The technology provides a set of tools with which the television journalist works. Do not be intimidated. Learn the tools and how to use them.

Roles—You need to understand how every role in the newsroom functions and how each fits into the larger scheme of things. You will do your job better and will make a greater contribution to the final news product.

Pressure—It's a way of life, so get used to it. The best television journalists are those who can shut out distractions—which are many—and focus on the task at hand. Deadlines are constant, and you may be juggling several at once. As a deadline approaches, do not panic—stay calm and confident, and concentrate on what you need to do. It doesn't hurt to find healthy ways to cope with pressure, such as meditation or exercise. However, it's best to wait until after the deadline has passed before assuming the lotus position or engaging in calisthenics.

People—Work well with them. People can be annoying and irritating, and if they'd just do the job the way you think they should, life would be so much better—right? Forget it. Deal with their idiosyncrasies, get along with them, treat them with respect, and do your job. Develop a solid work ethic and contribute wherever and whenever you can. Above all, do not burn bridges. I'll say it again: *Do not burn bridges.* This is a tough business to break into, and a tough business in which to advance. Get to know people in the business, and maintain contact with them. A friend or acquaintance whom you treat well now might well be the contact who gets you a choice job later.

In addition, thousands of stories are floating around the industry about people whose careers have been damaged or derailed because they mistreated someone else earlier in their career. The people whose positions are below or equal to yours this year may well be the people who can fire you or promote you two years from now. I know of no one whose career has suffered as a result of respectful treatment of others.

Criticism and Ego—Deal with both in a positive manner. A healthy ego is essential to surviving in television news (or in life, for that matter). Being egotistical, however, will not serve you well. The key here, along with the aforementioned respect for others, is to have confidence in yourself. You will have to learn many things the hard way, and you'll make a lot of mistakes. It's best to keep them minimal, but it's going to happen. It's part of the process. When you make a mistake or do a mediocre or poor job at something—especially if a dose of criticism from someone is included—don't beat yourself over it. Accept it, learn from it, and go forward with the confidence that you can do better. Believe in yourself and focus on doing the best job you can.

Health—Maintain it. Get exercise, eat well, get enough sleep, and if you drink, do it in moderation. Your job performance will suffer otherwise. Even making sure you eat properly during the day is key. Early in my career, I would alternate between having terrific live shots during which I was articulate and on top of it, and live shots in which I had trouble pronouncing my own name. Finally, I realized that the live shots that crashed and burned were a result of my system crashing and burning—it only happened if I hadn't eaten lunch or dinner, which meant my blood sugar would dive, and my brain went along with it. Once I made the connection, I made sure I had some snack bars (or, better still, that I'd eaten a proper meal when I should), and my live shots went off beautifully. Also, part of health is mental health. Stay optimistic and enjoy the work and find a way to diminish stress.

Initiative—You should look forward to doing news every waking moment. Look for ways to enterprise stories, look to work with others on stories, pick peoples' brains about how they do what they do and be the first to answer the newsroom phone when it rings. Two aspects should be driving you—you should love being involved in the process, and you should be competing against everyone else while trying to further your career. By competing, I don't mean that you need to resort to being underhanded, I mean you need to work that much harder to become better and show others your value. The more enterprise and initiative you show—and the more you produce as a result—the more you'll learn and the faster you'll advance.

Professionalism—In your actions, in your appearance, in your attitude. Commit fully to doing this and doing it well.

Writing and Language—A *love* of these is *critical*. Words are the most basic tool you have. Finding just the right phrases, rhythms or sounds can mean the difference between a fair story and one that really cooks. Without writing—good writing—television journalism doesn't exist.

To carry this statement a step further, writing is at the heart of any news operation, and television is no exception. In TV, the writing process encompasses a great deal more than the time you spend pounding out a script in front of your computer. Writing begins the moment you develop or receive a story idea and ends only when the story has aired. Gathering the information; gathering visuals and sound; conceptualizing the story; building a stand-up choosing opening and closing shots; and weaving the narration, visuals, sound bites and natural sound together in the editing process—all of this and more are part and parcel of the writing process. Your task and challenge is to combine some or all of these elements into a finished story that is fair, balanced, accurate and well written. Everything that happens in a television newsroom, either directly or indirectly, ultimately comes down to writing.

Televisual news is dynamic. The techniques are ever-changing, and so the learning process is constant. The other constant is writing. If you are an outstanding writer, you have a good future in television news. This book will help you achieve that goal.

Summary

Television is a primary source of news and information for Americans. Television news is a competitive business in which newsroom staffers compete to get and keep jobs and television stations compete for viewers and advertisers. News is specialized, personalized, sophisticated and flexible and appears destined to become even more so.

Technological developments have changed and continue to change the way broadcasters do business. Beginning broadcasters should learn everything they can about new technology and its uses, but many basic skills required for a news writing career are still those fundamentals taught long before the introduction of high-tech computers, video cameras, editing systems and the like.

Your first job probably will be the toughest to get. The pay most likely will be low and the work demanding, but you will get that job as the result of hard work and preparation.

Personal habits you want to develop now in preparation for a career in broadcasting include learning to work under pressure, working with people, accepting criticism, looking at the world around you, taking initiative and taking care of your health. In addition, you can prepare yourself to compete for a job in television news by acquiring writing skills, a broad education, a broad range of experiences and office skills.

Writing is the foundation for many newsroom jobs. This book encourages you to be disciplined about learning to write well. It also encourages you to establish a strong writing foundation on which you can build.

Exercises

1. Keep a log for one day that lists your viewing of television news. Note the source and time and recap the news events you saw reported.

2. Familiarize yourself with the top international, national and local news stories of the day. Recap the top stories for each.

3. Honestly evaluate the personal habits you now possess to determine areas that need work as you prepare yourself for a career in television news. Do you work well under pressure? Do you work well with people? Do you accept criticism well? Are you curious about and interested in the world around you? Do you know how to take the initiative? Do you take care of your health?

4. List ways you can prepare yourself academically for a career in television news. How can you broaden your education? How can you broaden your range of experiences? Where can you acquire needed job skills?

5. Read a biography about or autobiography by a member of the broadcast media. Some reading suggestions follow.

Autobiography

This Just In: What I Couldn't Tell You on TV, by Bob Schieffer (Putnam Publishing Group, 2003).

Roone: A Memoir, by Roone Arledge (HarperCollins, 2003).

A Long Way from Home: Growing Up in the American Heartland, by Tom Brokaw (Random House, 2002).

Everyone is Entitled to My Opinion, by David Brinkley (Random House Value Publishing, 1998).

A Reporter's Life, by Walter Cronkite (Ballantine Books, 1997).

Mr. President, Mr. President!: My Fifty Years of Covering the White House, by Sarah McClendon with Jules Minton (General Publishing Group, 1996).

David Brinkley: A Memoir, by David Brinkley (Alfred A. Knopf, 1995)

David Brinkley: 11 Presidents, 4 Wars, 22 Political Conventions, 1 Moon Landing, 3 Assassinations, 2000 Weeks of News and Other Stuff on Television and 18 Years of Growing Up in North Carolina, by David Brinkley (Alfred A. Knopf, 1995)

The Camera Never Blinks Twice: The Further Adventures of a Television Journalist, by Dan Rather (W. Morrow, 1994)

A Bus of My Own, by Jim Lehrer (G. P. Putnam's Sons, 1992)

Fighting for Air: In the Trenches with Television News, by Liz Trotta (Simon & Schuster, 1991)

Hold On, Mr. President! by Sam Donaldson (Random House, 1987)

I Never Played the Game, by Howard Cosell with Peter Bonventre (Morrow and Company, 1985)

Live from the Battlefield, by Peter Arnett (Simon & Schuster, 1994)

Word for Word, by Andrew A. Rooney (G. P. Putnam's Sons, 1984)

Biography

Women in Television News Revisited: Into the Twenty-First Century, by Judith Marlane and Howard Rosenberg (University of Texas Press, 1999).

Almost Golden: Jessica Savitch and the Selling of Television News, by Gwenda Blair (Simon and Schuster, 1988)

Anchors: Brokaw, Jennings, Rather, and the Evening News, by Robert Goldberg (Carol Publishers, 1990)

Connie Chung: Broadcast Journalist, by Mary Malone (Enslow Publishers, 1992)

Edward R. Murrow: An American Original, by Joseph E. Persico (Dell Publishing, 1988)

Murrow: His Life and Times, by A. M. Sperber (Freudlich Books, 1986)

The Murrow Boys: Pioneers on the Front Lines of Broadcast Journalism, by Stanley Cloud and Lynne Olson (Houghton Mifflin, 1996)

2

Television Newswriting: A Different Style

Television news is often—sometimes in a disparaging way—referred to as a headline service. The reality is, that's basically what we are—we provide headlines with some additional supporting information and typically some visuals and sound. Your task is to take the day's events and issues and boil them down as succinctly as possible, providing a fair, accurate, balanced and interesting account. Because of this as well as other demands and constraints inherent in the medium, you'll need to write in a different style.

First, let's look at some of the differences between broadcast and print news. Television news is far more immediate than a newspaper, although newspapers typically have an on-line presence that enables them to post a story in a much more timely presence. Television can go live from nearly anywhere in the world, however, allowing the viewer to see and hear the event instantaneously. The downside is that full understanding of the story's implications can suffer without the time it takes to develop context.

Another difference, to expand on the point just made, is that television carries the sights and sounds of the event. This can be an advantage if the reporter or videographer is able to capture compelling video and sound. It can be a real disadvantage if no interesting visuals can be found or developed. Nothing is duller than watching video of a school board or city council meeting. In fact, the absence of good video might persuade the producer to move a story lower in the newscast or to drop it altogether.

Because of the existence of sights and sounds, television carries more emotionalism than print. Again, this can be good and bad—a compelling scene captured on video can help tell a story in dramatic fashion, but the compelling nature of a piece of video can also shift focus from the story or, worse still, entice you into running a story that would not be considered newsworthy otherwise.

Typically, television stations hire a fraction of the number of journalists you'd find at a newspaper. A major metropolitan daily might keep more than 200 reporters and editors on staff. In contrast, a television station in the same market might employ fewer than 40 reporters, anchors, producers and writers. As a result, unlike print, few television news reporters are assigned to cover one specific beat. Most reporters in television are called general assignment reporters, which actually means they have to be able to cover any beat reasonably well. It's much more difficult to develop and cultivate sources or get to know the inside of a particular beat area, so the TV reporter has to have enough general knowledge and contacts to do a competent job, no matter what the story.

Time is an issue. In television, a reporter or producer has much less time to prepare a story. Given that television newsrooms employ fewer reporters, each one often is responsible for more content on a given day, meaning that less time is available to spend on each story.

Another difference is the structure of the story. In a newspaper story, you will typically read the lead and perhaps the next few paragraphs. If it's interesting, you read on. If it's not, you stop and move to the next story. Not so for television. TV news stories are designed to be viewed and heard from beginning to end.

There is substantially less material in a typical newscast than in a newspaper, and the stories are shorter. Two reasons come into play here. First, there is a fixed amount of time allowed for news, and it's not much. Take the typical 30-minute newscast. About eight minutes generally will go to commercials, perhaps another seven to sports and weather, and another two minutes or so to what are called production elements—video teases of upcoming stories, the open and close of the newscast, and transitions from one segment to another. That 30-minute newscast has now left you with about 13 minutes for straight news—a mere 780 seconds in which to tell all the day's stories you believe are important to your audience. As I said, it's not much. So each story must be boiled down to its absolute bare essence. There is no time to waste a phrase or even a single word in television news, and because there are so many stories to tell in such a short time, stories are markedly briefer than you would find in print. Walter Cronkite once remarked that the entire transcript of one CBS Evening News program would fit on the front page of the New York Times with plenty of room to spare.

The other reason stories are shorter deals with the way the ear processes information. When you're hearing a story instead of reading it, it's more difficult to remember detail—especially detail that's not critical to the story. Plus, the story has to be built in a very logical, understandable way. For that reason, you'll write television news in a more simple and conversational style. That's simple, not simplistic—we're often accused of dumbing down a story, but that's generally not the case. Instead, we're breaking it down into a more understandable story that will be read aloud.

Try this. Read the following example aloud to a few friends or classmates who are not reading along, and put a stopwatch to it. Once you're done, note how long the story took, then ask your friends what they remember about it and how interesting they found it—but don't tell them you're going to test them on it ahead of time.

MOSCOW—Russia, saying it will push for a central U.N. role in Iraq, began consulting Saturday with other Security Council members over a proposed U.S. plan that relegates the United Nations to a largely advisory position.

Russia and France—two leading opponents of the U.S.-led invasion of Iraq—have said they had questions about Washington's proposal for a U.N. resolution on ruling postwar Iraq.

Deputy Foreign Minister Yuri Fedotov said that the draft, "fails to provide a clear picture of the transition from the U.N.'s oil-for-food program to the lifting of international sanctions against Iraq."

During discussions of the U.S. proposal, Moscow will again "underscore the need for the United Nations' central role in this process," Mr. Fedotov said, according to the Interfax news agency.

But objections have so far been muted, with the council's 15 members hoping to avoid the bitterness that broke out in the debate over the war.

The U.S. draft, introduced Friday, would give the U.N. stamp of approval to a U.S.–British occupation of Iraq for at least a year and give the Americans and British control of the country's oil wealth for rebuilding the country.

Under the plan, the United Nations would appoint a coordinator to work with the U.S.–British alliance, but the world body would have an advisory role, its influence limited mostly to humanitarian issues. Spain and Britain cosponsored the resolution.

Mr. Fedotov discussed the situation in Iraq and the U.N. role there Saturday with French Ambassador Claude Blanchemaison and Chinese Ambassador Zhan Deguag, the Foreign Ministry said. The three countries all hold veto powers on the council and opposed the U.S.-led war.

Chinese Deputy Foreign Minster Yang Wenchang will visit Moscow on Thursday to coordinate action on Iraq, the ministry said in a prepared statement.

On Saturday, the 15 ambassadors of the Security Council joined U.N. Secretary-General Kofi Annan for an annual retreat in upstate New York, where they were to discuss the U.S. proposal for a special U.N. coordinator.

Experts from Security Council member missions were to study the draft at a closed meeting Monday. The council will begin to debate Wednesday.

Main points to consider about this story:

Very long. With 13 minutes available, you just took up a quarter of your newscast. Consider that this is not a particularly long story by newspaper standards.

Too much detail. Do we care about the name or title of Chinese Deputy Foreign Minister Yang Wenchang? If we use this fact at all, couldn't we have simply called him a member of the Chinese government? Is it essential to the story that we discuss the fact that 15 ambassadors of the Security Council met with

Annan on Saturday in upstate New York for an annual retreat? If we used it at all, couldn't we have simply said Annan met with U.N. Security Council members over the weekend?

Difficult to pronounce. Names such as Claude Blanchemaison or Zhang Deguang are not only unnecessary to a television news story, they're extremely hard to say.

Stiff style. Although this story's style may work perfectly well for print, it works poorly for broadcast. It's not conversational. It's not how we talk. It's harder to understand.

Long sentences. In several instances, there is so much packed into a sentence that it's difficult to remember what was said at the beginning of the sentence by the time we reached the end. In addition, several of those sentences exceed the lung capacity of most readers.

Now try reading the following aloud to others:

> Russia says it has a problem with America's plan for postwar Iraq.
> The U-S offered the plan to the United Nations Friday.
> The resolution calls for the U-N to support a year-long American–British occupation of Iraq.
> It would also give Americans and the British control of Iraq's oil wealth to rebuild the country.
> However, the plan would limit the U-N's power.
> Its role in Iraq?
> Giving humanitarian advice and little else.
> Russia is pushing for a more central role for the U-N.
> Debate on the plan begins later this week.

Hear the difference? All but the most critical details have been cut. It's easier to read in terms of pronunciation. It's much more conversational and is laid out more logically. And it should have taken you about 27 seconds to read it. The second version was not dumbed down—those who had a tough time understanding the first story are likely college students like yourself, which means they're likely to have above-average intelligence. It is simply that we process words differently when we hear them rather than read them.

As a result, good broadcast news writing includes the basic elements of all good writing but also has its own style and set of conventions. In television, the story must be understood clearly the first time through. There is no chance to reread or relisten. There can be no lapse, no problem in understandability—if there is, if you lose the viewer even once, you risk losing that viewer for the rest of the story, meaning you've failed as a television writer. You may even lose the viewer from that newscast—it's way too easy to change a channel with the remote control. Your task, then, is to lay the story out logically using straight-line meaning. You will build the story bit by digestible bit so the audience can immediately grasp that point, see how it fits with the rest of the story, and be ready to hear your next point.

Another aspect to keep in mind concerns the sounds of the words you write. First, you want the words to have an interesting sound and rhythm to them so the viewer will be more interested in hearing them. Second, the words must be reasonably easy to pronounce for whoever will be reading those words. Sometimes difficult pronunciations are unavoidable, but keep them to an absolute minimum whenever possible.

Finally, you need to write the story in human terms, using descriptions, explanations and examples to which the audience can immediately relate. More on that shortly.

Summary

Here are the main points to review:

Simpler phrasing, simpler words—Break it down so that it's immediately understandable.

Shorter—You have little time for the story. Although you want to include critical detail, you will include only the most critical detail—only the detail that will advance the story. Also, shorter sentences are more easily understood.

Human terms—Use verbal images with which your audience will connect.

Progressively structured—You must achieve straight-line meaning, building the story bit by digestible bit. Never make your audience think back.

One main idea—Your story typically will focus on one main idea, communicating what is interesting and significant about that issue, event or person.

Another issue to keep in mind is that the majority of the time, you will write to visuals and sound.

In addition, your story must be **accurate**, **fair**, **balanced**, **thorough enough**, **interesting**, full of **imagery**, and **easily understandable**.

Remember:

The audience has one chance. Make it count.

Exercise

Collect three days' worth of your local newspaper. Videotape a particular newscast from the same three days. Find the stories covered by both, and pick three of them. Read one of the newspaper stories aloud, then watch that story on the newscast. Do the same with the other two stories, each in turn. After reading and watching each story, note the difference in the time it takes. Note what information is included in the television version, and what is left out. Note how the information is phrased in the television story. Note also how the anchor or reporter delivers the story verbally, and what difference that makes.

A Brief Review of Grammar

Basics must come first in any endeavor, and television news writing is no exception. Good grammar is essential to good writing. Yes, you can break a few rules from time to time, especially in the conversational style of television news—more on that later—but you must first know what the rules are and why they exist.

American English follows standardized rules, and although some of those rules shift over time with common usage, you need to have a good understanding of what those rules are and how they translate into the written and spoken word. Clarity is one reason to use good grammar. With standardized usage comes standardized meaning—you want to make sure your audience clearly understands what you are trying to say. Beyond accuracy, clarity is the chief goal of a television news writer. You should always strive to be clear in your writing, and good grammar is a key element of that.

Credibility is another reason for paying attention to grammar. Your audience has to believe you know what you're talking about and are giving an accurate representation of the day's events and issues. You're judged by the way you present your information. When you use lousy grammar, the viewer will quickly lose faith in you and what you have to say.

The rules in grammar are not etched in stone. Occasionally bending or breaking some of those rules is justified. However, you have to have a good framework from which to work. All too many people in broadcast news do not, and it shows. Like anyone else, if I hear lousy grammar coming out of some reporter's mouth, I tend to lose faith in that reporter's ability to accurately cover a story. Your reputation is on the line every time you write a story, and now is the time to solidify your grammar.

By this time, you should have a sense of the parts of speech and how they function. If you do not, get yourself a good grammar and usage text now. One good reference for journalists is *When Words Collide: A Media Writer's Guide to Grammar and Style, 5th edition,* by Lauren Kessler and Duncan McDonald (Wadsworth Publishing Company, 2000).

Another valuable addition to your shelf is *The Elements of Style, 4th edition*, by William Strunk Jr., E.B. White and Roger Angell (Allyn & Bacon, 2000).

You absolutely must get a current broadcast style guide. There are several of them out there, two of which are *The Associated Press Broadcast News Handbook: Incorporating the AP Libel Manual, 2nd edition*, by Brad Kalbfeld and James R. Hood (Associated Press, 1998), and *Broadcast News Writing Stylebook, 2nd edition,* by Robert A. Papper (Allyn & Bacon, 2002).

With any reference book, you want to get the latest edition available. In the meantime, let's review some basics.

Parts of Speech

First, it's helpful to know what words are—nouns or pronouns, adjectives or adverbs, and so forth. Once you identify a word as an adverb, for example, you know that the rules that apply to adverbs apply to that word. Understanding the parts of speech allows you to better follow the rules that govern speech. Understanding what words are helps you put them together better for grammatically correct sentences.

Nouns are people, places and things. *Mike* is a noun, *Detroit* is a noun, *desk* is a noun.

Pronouns replace nouns. *I, you, he, she, it, we* and *they* are all pronouns.

Verbs describe what nouns (or pronouns) are doing or being. *Sleep, reads, is* and *walks* are verbs.

> Mike *reads*.

The verb *reads* describes the action of the noun *Mike*.

> I *am*.

The verb *am* describes the state of being of the pronoun *I*.

Adjectives describe nouns or pronouns.

> A *smart* girl, a *fast* car, a *purple* shoe.

Smart, fast and *purple* are adjectives that describe the nouns *girl, car* and *shoe*.

Adverbs describe verbs, adjectives and other adverbs. Adverbs often, but not always, end in *-ly*.

> He walks *quickly*.

The adverb *quickly* describes the verb *walks*; it describes *how* he walks.

> She wore an *incredibly* pretty dress.

The adverb *incredibly* describes the adjective *pretty*, which describes the noun *dress*.

> She *very rarely* cries.

The secondary adverb *very* describes the primary adverb *rarely,* which describes the verb *cries.*

Conjunctions link words to words, phrases to phrases, and sentences to sentences. *And*, *yet*, *since*, *but*, *either*, *or*, *neither* and *nor* are conjunctions.

> The Japanese flag is red *and* white.

And is a conjunction that links the words red and white.

Prepositions connect nouns and pronouns to other elements in sentences, including verbs, other nouns and adjectives. *In*, *by*, *for*, *with* and *to* are all prepositions.

> He went *to* the beach.

To connects the noun *beach* to the verb *went.*

> I like the sound *of* laughter.

Of connects the nouns *laughter* and *sound.*

> Fruit is good *for* her.

For connects the pronoun *her* to the adjective *good.*

Parts of a Sentence

Now look at the roles that parts of speech play in building sentences. Subjects, verbs (or predicates), objects, clauses and phrases are parts of sentences.

Subjects of a sentence are the nouns or pronouns that act or are in a sentence. Ask "who?" or "what?" (usually before the verb) to find the subject.

> The judge made her ruling.

Who made the ruling? The *judge* did. The *judge* is the subject of the sentence.

> The car went over the embankment.

What went over the embankment? The *car* did. The *car* is the subject of the sentence.

"Predicate" is another way of saying verb. A simple predicate is the verb alone—the word or words that express action or being. A complete predicate is the verb and other associated words.

> The judge made her ruling.

Made is the verb, or simple predicate, expressing action. *Made her ruling* is the complete predicate.

Objects are the receivers of the action in a sentence. Ask "whom?" or "what?" (usually after the verb) to find the object.

> The judge made her ruling.

The judge made what? The judge made her *ruling*. *Ruling* is the object of the sentence.

Clauses are groups of related words within sentences; clauses always have a subject and verb (phrases are also groups of related words, but they do not have a subject or verb). Sometimes a clause can stand alone as a sentence (an independent clause). Other times, a clause must join a sentence to be a complete thought (a dependent clause).

> The business records are lost, and no one remembers how the company was founded.

The sentence above is made up of two independent clauses. Each of them—*the business records are lost* and *no one remembers how the company was founded*—has a subject and a verb.

Independent clauses often are joined by conjunctions, such as *and* in the example above. Dependent clauses also can begin with conjunctions, such as *although, as, because, since, until, whether* and *while*. They can also begin with pronouns, such as *who, whom, whose, which* and *that*.

> Although John Smith is 14 years old, he is a hero in this small town.

> John Smith, who is 14 years old, is a hero in this small town.

The first sentence uses the conjunction *although* to introduce the dependent clause: *Although John Smith is 14 years old.* The dependent clause in the second sentence begins with the pronoun *who*. Neither clause can stand on its own: It is *dependent* on the rest of the sentence to convey a complete thought.

Phrases are groups of words without a subject or a verb. Prepositional phrases begin with prepositions, such as *in, by, for, with* and *to*.

> Bob went to the store.

To the store is a prepositional phrase introduced by the preposition *to*.

> Steve looked for the tape.

For the tape is a prepositional phrase introduced by the preposition *for*.

Rules

What follows is a collection of some of the most commonly broken rules of grammar. I'll try to make it as painless as possible.

Subject–Verb Agreement

Subject–verb agreement problems are among the most common grammatical errors in broadcast writing. The rule is simple: Singular subjects use singular verbs and plural subjects use plural verbs. But subject–verb agreement can be more confusing than the simplicity of the rule suggests.

The first step in checking for an agreement problem is to identify the subject and the verb.

> Rescue workers pull victims from the icy water.

The subject is *rescue workers*. The most common way to make a noun plural in English is to add "s" to the end, so the "s" at the end of *workers* alerts you to a plural subject. The verb is *pull*. The most common way to make a verb plural in English is to omit the "s" at the end, so the lack of "s" at the end of the verb suggests to you that it is in its plural form. In the sentence, the plural subject takes a plural verb.

> **Right:** Rescue workers pull victims from the icy water.
> **Wrong:** Rescue workers pulls victims from the icy water.

Subject–verb agreement gets confusing when phrases and clauses separate subjects from their verbs.

> The file with all its folders and loose papers is heavy.

The temptation may be to think: The plural subject is *folders and loose papers;* the plural verb is *are,* but the subject of the sentence is not *folders and loose papers.* The subject is *file.* The words *with all its folders and loose papers* make up a prepositional phrase introduced by the preposition *with.* The verb must agree with the subject: The singular subject is *file,* and the singular verb is *is.*

Collective nouns can create confusion for a lot of writers who are trying to maintain subject–verb agreement. In American English, collective nouns are singular nouns that describe a group and that may seem plural as a result. *Family* is a collective noun. *Family* most often describes more than one person, but *family* uses a singular verb.

> **Wrong:** The *family are* going to the park.
> **Right:** The *family is* going to the park.

Other collective nouns are *team, group, class, committee, staff, faculty* and *company.* In addition, the proper names of most associations (the National Organization for Women), companies (IBM), boards (city council), and so forth are considered collective nouns.

> **Right:** The National Organization for Women is supportive of
> equal rights for women.
> **Right:** IBM is located in Armonk, N.Y.
> **Right:** The City Council is going to vote tomorrow.

So just remember, a company is an "it," not a "they," and the same goes for a team, a company board, and any other collective noun.

You should keep some additional points in mind. The words *anybody, each, every, everybody, nobody* and *either* are always singular collective nouns and take a singular verb. *Neither* and *none* are singular unless they link to plural nouns.

> **Right:** Neither the Americans nor the Chinese are going to vote
> for the measure.

To make matters more confusing, some collective nouns can be either singular or plural, depending on the sense:

> **Right:** The faculty is voting unanimously.

and

> **Right:** The faculty are listed in the campus directory by department.

Pronouns and Noun–Pronoun Agreement

In general, avoid pronouns, especially if the pronoun is far from the antecedent. For example,

> The union representative challenged the company spokesman on pay, health benefits and work hours. He said the whole meeting was worthless.

In the second sentence, who is *he*, the union representative or the company spokesman?

The function of the pronoun determines its case. **Case** refers to whether the form is nominative (the subject), objective (the object), or possessive: *he, him* or *his*, respectively. In addition, as you might have surmised from the previous section, it's not enough that subjects and verbs agree. Nouns and the pronouns that replace them must agree, too.

> **Wrong:** The *family* says *they* are going to the park
> **Right:** The *family* says *it* is going to the park.

The collective noun *family* is replaced by a pronoun after the verb *says*. The pronoun must agree with the singular noun, so the pronoun must be the singular *it*. If the sentence sounds awkward, rewrite it. Make the noun plural so that you can use the plural pronoun.

> **Right:** *Family members* say *they* are going to the park.

A frequent noun–pronoun error stems from the best of intentions. Television news writers trying to avoid sexism in their scripts do terrible things to grammar.

> **Wrong:** The head of a household typically spends 11 hours a day away from their home.

The noun *head* is singular. The pronoun *their* is plural. The writer needs the singular pronoun *his* or *her*, but which one?

> **OK:** The head of a household typically spends 11 hours a day away from *his* home.

This sentence is grammatically correct, but by assuming that the head of a household is male, the writer is being sexist and inaccurate because many heads of households are women. This sentence is offensive to some viewers and erodes the credibility of the writer because it may be untrue.

> **Better:** The head of a household typically spends 11 hours a day away from *his or her* home.

This sentence is grammatically correct, but wordy. *His or her* can bog down sentences and become tiresome to viewers.

> **Best:** Head*s* of household*s* typically *spend* 11 hours a day away from *their* home*s*.

The writer makes the noun plural, alters the verb for subject–verb agreement and uses the plural pronoun. The sentence is grammatically correct and easy to understand.

There is an easier solution: Omit the pronoun altogether.

> **Also Good:** The head of a household typically spends 11 hours a day away from home.

The example sentence works without the pronoun. This solution won't work always, but it does here. In striving for proper grammar, don't overlook an easy fix.

If a pronoun must be used, the appositive must agree with the word it references:

> **Wrong:** He handed the award to both recipients, Michael and I.
> **Right:** He handed the award to both recipients, Michael and me.

Michael and *me* refer to the *recipients*, the object of the preposition. It takes the objective case.

> **Wrong:** The two recipients, Michael and me, took the award.
> **Right:** The two recipients, Michael and I, took the award.

Michael and *I* refer to the *recipients*, in this case the subject, so you would use the subjective case.

If a pronoun is the object of a preposition, it takes the objective case.

> **Wrong:** The announcer handed the award to I.
> **Right:** The announcer handed the award to me.

You will also use the possessive case for a pronoun modifying what is called a gerund. A gerund is an –ing verb that functions as a noun.

> **Wrong:** The committee appreciates you accepting the award.
> **Right:** The committee appreciates your accepting the award.

Note the correct usage is *your*, the possessive form, not *you*, because it modifies the gerund *accepting*.

Reflexive Pronouns

Myself is a seemingly harmless word that is moving into everyday language in harmful ways (harmful to grammarians, anyway). *Myself* is a reflexive pronoun, along with *yourself, itself, herself, himself, ourselves, themselves* and *yourselves*.

Use reflexive pronouns when the noun acts on itself: *I bathed myself. She hurt herself. They fed themselves.*

In each sentence, the noun is doing something for or to itself. It seems simple enough, but look at the ways some writers are using *myself*.

> **Wrong:** For the rest of the crew and myself, good night.
> **Wrong:** Join Adrienne Scott and myself tonight at 11.
> **Wrong:** We asked the ticket taker to give the stub to Mr. Wilson or myself.

"Why? Why do writers do this?" grammarians ask. Do people believe *myself* sounds formal and educated? Have people been so bombarded with problems over *I* versus *me* (see below) that they're afraid to use *me* at all? In each of the example sentences, *me* instead of *myself* is correct.

> **Right:** For the rest of the crew and me, good night.
> **Right:** Join Adrienne Scott and me tonight at 11.
> **Right:** We asked the ticket taker to give the stub to Mr. Wilson or me.

I versus Me and Other Pronoun Problems

Since the *I* versus *me* controversy has been raised, note that *I* is used as a subject of a sentence, clause or phrase, and *me* is used as an object of a sentence, clause or phrase.

Subject of a Sentence.

> **Right:** I went to the store.
> **Wrong:** Me went to the store.

Therefore,

> **Right:** John and I went to the store.
> **Wrong:** John and me went to the store.

Object of a Sentence.

> **Right:** You can see me at 11.
> **Wrong:** You can see I at 11.

Therefore,

> **Right:** You can see John and me at 11.
> **Wrong:** You can see John and I at 11.

Subject of a Clause.

> **Right:** She is more sunburned than I.
> **Wrong:** She is more sunburned than me.

> **Right:** She is more sunburned than Melissa and I.
> **Wrong:** She is more sunburned than Melissa and me.

Note that the word *than* leads to the implied clause *than I am sunburned*, of which *I* is the subject. At first glance, *me* may look like the object of a prepositional phrase *than me*. But *than* is not a preposition. *Than* is a conjunction.

Object of a Prepositional Phrase.

> **Right:** They borrowed the pen and paper from me.
> **Wrong:** They borrowed the pen and paper from I.
> **Right:** They borrowed the pen and paper from her and me.
> **Wrong:** They borrowed the pen and paper from she and I.

The last two examples show that the *I* versus *me* rule applies to other pronouns too. Note the pronouns listed in the box that function as subjects and objects (Fig. 3.1).

Pronouns as Subjects	Pronouns as Objects
I	me
we	us
he	him
she	her
they	them

FIGURE 3.1

In the examples below, pronouns serve as subjects of sentences. Use pronouns from the "Pronouns as Subjects" list.

> **Right:** He and I met at the reunion weekend.
> **Wrong:** Him and I met at the reunion weekend.
> **Wrong:** Him and me met at the reunion weekend.

In the next examples, pronouns serve as objects of the preposition *to*. Use objects from the "Pronouns as Objects" list.

> **Right:** Before Marty left, he gave the phone number to him and me.
> **Wrong:** Before Marty left, he gave the phone number to him and I.
> **Wrong:** Before Marty left, he gave the phone number to he and I.

Ending Sentences with Prepositions

While we're on the subject of prepositions, don't use a preposition to end a sentence with. Of course, the phrasing of the rule breaks the rule. The correct way to express this thought is to drop the unnecessary preposition *with*. Simply say, "Don't use a preposition to end a sentence."

If there is no way to avoid the preposition, insert it before its object. For example,

> Whom are you giving it to?

is correctly stated,

> To whom are you giving it?

However, on occasion, ending on a preposition is acceptable to avoid carrying the rule to extremes. Winston Churchill, as the story goes, decided to have some fun with the stiff formality in the use of the English language by so many of his peers when he declared,

> "Ending a sentence with a preposition is something up with which
> I will not put."

Starting Sentences with Conjunctions

Composition writing discourages the use of conjunctions, such as *and* or *but*, at the start of sentences. Many computerized grammar checkers now isolate conjunctions at the start of sentences and advise computer composers to use them sparingly. *But* people commonly use conjunctions to link sentences when they speak. *And* it's natural that television news writers would use them to start sentences in their stories. In television news, it is acceptable, even desirable, to start sentences with conjunctions.

Adverb or Adjective?

There is a real problem afoot in broadcasting. Too many television news writers seem unable to distinguish between adverbs and adjectives. Most often, writers use adjectives where there should be adverbs.

> **Wrong:** Time went *quick*.
> **Wrong:** She dressed *sensible* for the weather.
> **Wrong:** Because of the ice, they drove *careful*.

Quick, *sensible* and *careful* are adjectives, and as such, they need to describe nouns or pronouns. But the writer isn't describing the noun *time*, the pronoun *she* or the pronoun *they*. The writer is describing the verbs *went*, *dressed* and *drove*. The sentences require adverbs, which describe the verbs in the sentence. So the writer needs adverbs:

Right: Time went *quickly*.
Right: She dressed *sensibly* for the weather.
Right: Because of the ice, they drove *carefully*.

Adverbs modify or describe verbs, adjectives and other adverbs. The examples above show adverbs describing verbs. Adverbs also describe adjectives.

Wrong: She wore a *real* wild hat to the party.
Right: She wore a *really* wild hat to the party.

The adverb *really* describes the adjective *wild*, which describes the noun *hat*. To test whether *real* is an adjective describing *hat* or an adverb describing the adjective *wild*, try omitting *wild*.

She wore a *real* hat.

It doesn't make sense. You know, then, that *real* isn't in the sentence to describe *hat*. It's in the sentence to describe *wild*. Its role is that of an adverb (*really*) describing an adjective (*wild*).
Adverbs also describe other adverbs.

Wrong: He ran *awful quick* after lighting the firecracker's fuse.
Wrong: He ran *awful quickly* after lighting the firecracker's fuse.
Right: He ran *awfully quickly* after lighting the firecracker's fuse.

The first sentence uses two adjectives, *awful* and *quick*, to describe the verb *ran*, but adjectives describe nouns, not verbs. The second sentence properly uses the adverb *quickly* to describe the verb *ran*, but it uses an adjective, *awful*, to describe the adverb *quickly*. Adjectives do not describe adverbs. Adverbs describe other adverbs. The third sentence properly uses the adverb *quickly* to describe the verb *ran*, and it properly uses the adverb *awfully* to describe the adverb *quickly*. Adverbs describe verbs and other adverbs.

Adverbs and adjectives should be as close as possible to the words they describe.

Yellow and red, fans' eyes caught the colorful flag.

The writer separates the adjectives *yellow* and *red* from the noun they describe, *flag*. The placement causes confusion. Are the fans' eyes yellow and red? Probably not. The sentence should be rewritten,

Fans' eyes caught the colorful yellow and red flag.

The same rule applies to adverbs.

Quickly and quietly along the second story balcony, the jewel
thief crept.

People cannot be expected to file away in their minds the adverbs *quickly* and *quietly*, saving them for the moment the writer finally presents them with the verb those adverbs describe, *crept*.

The jewel thief crept quickly and quietly along the second story balcony.

Good versus Well

Because *good* and *well* are so often misused, the words deserve a short section of their own. *Good* is an adjective, so it describes a noun or a pronoun.

> **Right:** It is a good cake.
> **Right:** It was a good night.
> **Right:** We had a good time.

Good is not an adverb, so it does not describe verbs.

> **Wrong:** He ran good.
> **Wrong:** She did good on her exam.

The confusion about *good* comes when it follows a linking verb. Linking verbs are words such as *appear, be, become, feel, look* and *seem*. They serve as equals signs in sentences, linking subjects with pronouns or adjectives.

> She is good.
> He looks good.

In the first example, *she* is the subject; *is* is a linking verb that links *she* and *good* (she = good). The linking verb is followed by the adjective *good*. In the second example, *he* is the subject. *Looks* is a linking verb that links *he* and *good* (he = good). The linking verb is followed by the adjective *good*. The adjective *good* describes him, or his appearance. The adjective does not describe the way he performs the act of looking. The writer is not saying that he has keen eyesight or is alert and watchful. If the writer wanted to describe his skills of looking or watching, he or she would use the adverb *well*.

But hold on, because the confusion continues. *Well* can be an adjective or an adverb. *Well* as an adjective means the opposite of ill.

> She is well.
> He seems well.

In the first sentence, the writer is saying *she is not ill*. The writer is using *well* as an adjective after a linking verb (she = well). In the second sentence, the writer is saying *he looks healthy*. The writer uses *well* as an adjective after the linking verb (he = well).

Well is also an adverb that describes how one does something.

> She swims well.
> He plays well.

In the first sentence, the adverb *well* describes how she performs the action of the verb, how she *swims*. If the opposite were true, she would swim *poorly* (again, an adverb). In the second sentence, the adverb *well* describes how he *plays*.

Now consider the following sentence:

> She feels well.

What is the writer saying? Is *well* used as an adverb or an adjective? *Well* as an *adjective* means *not ill*. The writer is reporting that the subject is in good health. *Well* as an *adverb* describes how the subject performs the action of the verb. Here, the subject *she* performs the act of *feeling* (maybe distinguishing between a rough texture and a soft one?) in a satisfactory way, or *well*. Without hearing the sentence in context, you don't know what it means. You don't know whether the writer is using *well* as an adjective or an adverb.

Linking verbs cause confusion for writers using the words *bad* and *badly*, too.

> I feel bad.

Bad is an adjective used after the linking verb to describe the pronoun *I*. *Bad* means the opposite of good. It describes the subject's (*I*) spirits or mental disposition (I = bad).

> I feel badly.

Badly as an adverb describes the way the subject (*I*) performs the act of *feeling*. Maybe frigid temperatures have numbed the subject's fingers so that he or she cannot feel a soft kitten or burning stove. The subject who *feels badly* cannot distinguish between textures. The subject who *feels badly* does not feel sorry or ill.

That

If the meaning is clear without *that*, drop it.

> The president has decided that he will take his case to the nation.

Drop *that*, and you have,

> The president has decided he will take his case to the nation.

It works just as well.
However, if "that" is necessary for clarity, use it.

> He felt his secretary was doing her job well.

Even the slightest pause after the word *secretary* could lead the listener to a problematic—and incorrect—conclusion. Insert *that* at the appropriate place and the problem is solved:

> He felt that his secretary was doing her job well.

That versus Which versus Who

That is used in a restrictive clause, whereas *which* is used in a nonrestrictive clause and is typically set off by commas:

> The truck that is parked out back is leaking oil.

The clause *that is parked out back* is restrictive, meaning it is necessary to the meaning of the sentence. Which truck is leaking oil? The one that is parked out back, which also means that no other trucks are parked there.

> The truck, which is parked out back, is leaking oil.

Here, the clause *which is parked out back* is nonrestrictive, meaning it is not necessary to the meaning of the sentence and is there to add description or information. The truck is leaking oil. It happens to be parked out back. There may be other trucks parked out back, as well.

Who, used to refer to people or objects to which you give human qualities, can be used in either restrictive or nonrestrictive clauses.

Using short introductory phrases is far better than parenthetical ones, and be cautious of introducing more than one point to a sentence:

> The state legislature, reacting to budget shortfalls, will be cutting funding to higher education, sparking protests from educators around the state.

There are two problems here—the parenthetical phrase, and that there are two points in the sentence. Rephrase and boil it down or break it down:

> Reacting to budget shortfalls, the state legislature will be cutting funding to higher education, sparking protests from educators around the state.

Or, better still:

> The state legislature says a budget shortfall means funding cuts for higher education. Educators around the state are protesting the move.

Placement

Placement of a phrase can substantially alter the meaning.

> The state legislature agreed today to take up the matter.

is not the same as

> The state legislature agreed to take up the matter today.

Spelling

A quick note about spelling: Always spell correctly, for several reasons. Clarity comes into play—if someone reading your copy comes across a misspelled word, there's a good chance the reader will stumble or pause to take a split second to make sure they know what you meant. Different spellings can also mean different pronunciations, which is another issue. Also, how much credibility will the reader of the copy put in your story if you can't even spell right?

In addition, you often will have to submit names, locations and so forth for the character generator, which will appear on the screen during the running of your story. If you misspell someone's name and he or she is the only one to catch it, it's bad enough. If you misspell a name and much of your audience catches it, it's not just your credibility that goes out the window—the whole station suffers. Trust me, that's not a conversation you want to have with your news director.

Summary

Use of good grammar is essential to be both clear and credible. Parts of speech define what words are. Nouns are people, places and things. Pronouns replace nouns. Verbs are action words that describe what nouns or pronouns are doing or being. Adjectives describe nouns or pronouns. Adverbs describe verbs, adjectives and other adverbs. Conjunctions link words to words, phrases to phrases, and sentences to sentences. Prepositions connect nouns and pronouns to other elements in sentences, including verbs, other nouns and adjectives.

Parts of a sentence define the role words play in sentences. The noun or pronoun that acts or is serves as the subject of a sentence. The verb alone is the simple predicate of a sentence. The verb and accompanying words are the complete predicate. The receiver of an action is the object of a sentence. Clauses are groups of related words within sentences that have a subject and verb. An independent clause can stand alone as a sentence. A dependent clause relies on the rest of the sentence to convey a complete thought.

Words and sentences are governed by traditional rules of grammar. Subject–verb agreement problems are among the most common grammatical errors in broadcast writing. Singular subjects use singular verbs, and plural subjects use plural verbs. Collective nouns are singular nouns that seem plural and use singular verbs. Nouns and the pronouns that replace them must agree, too.

In particular, writers also need to pay attention to the correct usage of reflexive pronouns and *I* versus *me* in sentences. They should try not to end sentences with prepositions. They should be able to distinguish correctly between adjectives and adverbs. They should also know the difference between *good* and *well*, and when to use *that* or *which*.

Exercises

1. Circle the sentences below that use incorrect subject–verb agreement.
    (a) A trial lawyer's skills are honed in the courtroom.
    (b) It was a rousing game, and the team was excited about the victory.
    (c) A new magazine written on campus by college students and their professors are capturing readers of all ages.
    (d) The City Council say the new law will help get more police on the streets.
    (e) The company, including most of the employees, disagree with new, tougher hiring guidelines that make it harder to hire locals for upper-level jobs.

(f) The National Organization for Women holds its annual rally today and expects as many as 5,000 participants to march on the state legislature.

(g) The bus load of victims were transported from the crash scene to a terminal, where emergency workers stood by to help them with their injuries.

(h) If the weather clears, Mary Grace's family and mine is going sailing tomorrow.

2. Supply the missing pronoun in the sentences below. Make sure the pronoun you choose agrees with the noun it replaces. Rewrite the sentence, if necessary, to select the best pronoun.

Example: The team celebrated <u>its</u> victory at a pizza party after the championship tournament.

(a) The umpires made _____ call after watching the replay tape.

(b) Seven sheriffs filed suit against the Department of Corrections, claiming _____ failed to remove state prisoners from crowded local jails.

(c) The president and first lady, debarking Air Force One, made _____ way down the steps and onto the runway.

(d) A woman who claimed she witnessed the car accident told the jury _____ was looking out the window just when it happened.

(e) Most of the company's CEOs started _____ careers in the sales department.

(f) The NFL star developed _____ love of the game as a child.

(g) The typical secretary starts _____ day at 8 a.m

3. Circle the sentences below that use *me* or *I* incorrectly.

(a) She is so much smarter than me, but she still gets the answers wrong.

(b) She gave him and I $5 each.

(c) He and I gave the $5 back to her.

(d) She and I traveled through Europe together but never really came to know each other.

(e) Since they were responsible for training the horse, I asked them to join me in the winner's circle.

(f) If you want to know for whom the bell tolls, it tolls for I.

4. Decide whether adjectives and adverbs in the sentences below are used correctly or incorrectly. Rewrite the sentence if it's incorrect.

Example: Everyone had a real good time.
__Correct <u>X</u> Incorrect Rewrite? *Everyone had a really good time.*

(a) She tried to use correct English.
___Correct ___Incorrect ___Rewrite?

(b) She tried to speak correct.
___Correct ___Incorrect ___Rewrite?

(c) Let's face it, you and I do things different.
___Correct ___Incorrect ___Rewrite?

(d) She was depressed because she did so bad on her final exam.
___Correct ___Incorrect ___Rewrite?

(e) Everyone agreed, she ran the race beautifully.
___Correct ___Incorrect ___Rewrite?

(f) The play was great and everyone said the actor did real good.
___Correct ___Incorrect ___Rewrite?

(g) I feel badly about the mistake.
___Correct ___Incorrect ___Rewrite?

(h) The restaurant guests agreed theirs was an awful good meal.
___Correct ___Incorrect ___Rewrite?

(i) The bank robbers were strangely in their decision not to take all the money.
___Correct ___Incorrect ___Rewrite?

(j) It was a real oddity that the dog never barked.
___Correct ___Incorrect ___Rewrite?

4

Some General Rules for Television Newswriting

Because television news is written to be read aloud, there are some special rules about how to type the copy into your computer and some general guidelines concerning your approach to writing the story. We'll cover actual scripting later in the book, once we've discussed story formats.

Symbols and Abbreviations

Don't use them. Instead of writing "%," write "percent." Instead of writing "$" before a dollar figure, write the word "dollar" after the figure.

Get into the habit of never abbreviating. Does "Dr." refer to "doctor" or "drive?" Does "St." refer to "saint" or "street?" When someone is reading copy aloud, you don't want to risk a problem such as, "He made the statement to Rev Al Sharpton . . ." The statement might be accurate—the unknown speaker may have wanted to get a rise out of Sharpton—but I doubt that's the meaning the writer intended. Never allow for any question—spell out the word and you'll always be safe.

Numbers

One through eleven are spelled out, and 12–999 are written numerically. With ordinals, it doesn't really matter—"1st" or "first" would be fine. Use the words "million," "thousand," and so on for large numbers, and combine alpha-numerics using dashes. For example, "1200" becomes either "one-thousand-200" or "12-hundred," "14,500" becomes "14-thousand-500," and so on. There are exceptions to this—street addresses, highways, phones numbers and years (to name a few) are all written numerically, because that's how we're used to seeing them.

Avoid decimals and "point," and use fractions or ratio comparisons instead, unless convention dictates otherwise. For example, if a well-known sports figure is arrested for driving under the influence, and he blew a 1.2 on the breathalyzer, you would write that police say he had "a blood alcohol content of one-point-two." However, a mortgage rate of "six-and-seven-eighths" is easier to understand than one of "six-point-eight-seven-five."

The best general rule to keep in mind is to avoid numbers if possible and to simplify them always. You want to round numbers into general percentages or comparisons if it won't alter the accuracy or sense of the story. For example, if 52.7 percent of the electorate showed up to vote, you should write "just more than half."

One great example of bogging down viewer consciousness and glazing over eyes occurs in smaller markets during elections. Election returns can be deadly—deadly boring, and deadly to the ratings. How to fix that?

Let's say you've thrown up a graphic that shows the race for State Senate District 12. The numbers look like this:

> Precincts reporting:
>   73% (11 of 15)
> Vote tally:
>   Herbert Schmootz   3,429
>   Millard Floobotz   6,997

You might want to put this on a graphic, but heaven help the audience who has to slog through listening to it. Instead, put it in understandable terms, such as fractions, ratios or comparisons. You might come up with something like:

> With nearly three-quarters of the precincts reporting, Floobotz
> leads Schmootz in the tally by about two-to-one.

It's better written, and you've avoided putting your viewer into a coma.

Continuing this idea of understandable terms, always try to translate large numbers into examples to which your audience can relate. Use comparisons or analogies from everyday life, things that will immediately connect with your audience. If your community has seen a decrease in the number of homicides, and that level dropped to 49 last year, you might say "that's fewer than one murder a week." Of course, if the count leapt from 32 to 49 murders, you'd phrase it, "that's nearly one murder a week." As another example, let's say your state spent two-billion dollars on highway construction and repairs. You check and find that there are 14 million vehicles in your state. You could say that the state spent 200 dollars per vehicle on its highways.

As one final example, on occasion you'll deal with some incomprehensibly large number in a story. The national debt is but one example, and there are countless others. I once wrote a series of science pieces, one of which dealt with the phenomenon of lightning. Several aspects struck me, one of which was way the charge of electricity superheated the air and caused thunder. I found that a lightning bolt heats up to around 50-thousand degrees Fahrenheit. But I wanted to put this in more understandable terms and find a comparison to which my audience could relate, something out of human experience. The image that occurred to me was molten lava, something much more tangible to the viewer. I learned that lava flows at 1,600 to 2,200 degrees Fahrenheit. Now I had my comparison: "The lightning bolt superheats the air to 50-thousand degrees Fahrenheit, about 25 times hotter than molten lava." Make it understandable to your viewers by using real-life examples to which they can relate.

Names

Write names as they are spoken. George W. Bush's vice-president goes by Dick Cheney, not Richard Cheney, and the two former Democratic presidents were called Bill Clinton and Jimmy Carter, not William Jefferson Clinton and James Carter. The Democratic advisor to Clinton, in contrast, went by James Carville, not Jim Carville.

Another rule of thumb dictates you not use a middle name or initial—with two exceptions. One concerns controversy or crime stories—you may want to include the middle name, especially if the surname is a common one, so the audience will not confuse the person involved in the crime with someone else who has the same name. The other exception involves common usage. The former lead singer for Van Halen is David Lee Roth, the poet went by e.e. cummings, the actor with the magnificent voice is James Earl Jones, and there is a HUGE difference between Jerry Lewis and Jerry Lee Lewis. Enough said.

Initials and Acronyms

Certain groups and objects are known by their initials. Use all capitals and separate the letters with hyphens.

> The Internal Revenue Service is known as the I-R-S.
> The Federal Bureau of Investigation is known as the F-B-I.

If the organization's acronym is not that well known or there's a chance for confusion, use the full name of the organization on first reference, then the initials thereafter.

> The Irish Republican Army, or I-R-A, is declaring a cease-fire.

Acronyms, which are words formed from initials and are spoken that way, are spelled out in all caps. NATO (pronounced NAY-toh) is the acronym formed from the North Atlantic Treaty Organization. Self-Contained Underwater Breathing Apparatus is called SCUBA, and the Mothers Against Drunk Drivers is designated MADD.

On occassion, you'll find a more complex situation. The National Association for the Advancement of Colored People, for example, would be written "the N-double-A-C-P." In some parts of the country, the National Collegiate Athletic Association would be written "the N-C-double-A."

While we're on the subject, writers use hyphens liberally in television news copy. It's a good way to show connection while separating the component parts.

Always substitute a hyphen for a period in initialed designations, such as "U-S policy" or "F-M radio."

Contractions

We use contractions in conversational language, so use them in television news copy. However, be careful of contracting the word "not"—if the contracted "not" will get lost, you may want to change it. Try saying the phrase, "He said he can't take it." For some of you, the "n't" will get lost because of the "t" sound in "take," so it might be better to write, "He said he cannot take it." Also, you might want to use the word "not" for emphasis, such as when someone is emphatic about a policy statement:

> Senator Kennedy said he would not stand by if the education budget were cut.

Punctuation

End a sentence with a period. If you have a soft pause, use a comma, but if you have a hard pause—or need to set off a phrase—use a dash. Two hyphens will substitute.

Question marks are permissible, but use them rarely. Will you be answering questions rather than posing them? Yes, most of the time.

Often, television writers will use ellipses . . . and these can work for many writers . . . one advantage is they are easier to see on the TelePrompTer . . . but sometimes . . . writers overuse them . . . to the point that ellipses become . . . the only punctuation they use . . . result . . . whoever is reading the copy . . . may lose a sense of what the ellipses stand for. My advice . . . if you like them and are certain you're the only one reading the copy . . . go ahead . . . otherwise . . . don't— at least, not for now. Use periods, commas and dashes instead—all three are quite clear in what they mean.

A few other notes on punctuation. Do not use quotation marks. They carry no meaning in broadcast copy. I have used them to set off examples for this book, but they simply don't belong on a television script page or in the TelePrompTer. If you are quoting someone (more on that in a minute), phrase it that way in the copy, but do not use quote marks.

Do not use a colon or semicolon. If you need a semicolon in your sentence, that's a sure sign the sentence is too long—break up the sentence instead. Instead of a colon, use a comma or dash.

From time to time, you will need to include in your copy information for the reader that should not be read aloud, such as a cue to tell which anchor is reading the story, or a pronouncer that follows a difficult-to-pronounce word. Set it off with parentheses:

> (Michelle – On Camera)

> The mayor of Verdi (ver-die) Nevada is taking aim at gun users.

Quotes

Never quote a source unless it's absolutely necessary. If the quote is compelling enough to use, your first choice will be tape. You'll take a segment of the statement, typically called a sound bite, and edit it into the story. If what the source says is fairly good but not necessarily worth a sound bite—or, if the tape didn't turn out, which happens occasionally—then paraphrase. Generally, you as the writer can boil down the essence of the statement more clearly and concisely than the person you interviewed. If you absolutely must use a quote in the reader's copy, then set it off with a phrase that lets the audience know, such as "using the governor's words," or "in what she called," or "as he put it." Avoid saying something like, "The vice-president said—quote—I will fight it every step of the way—end of quotation." It sounds stiff.

Another point to keep in mind about paraphrasing is: Don't be hesitant to use the word "says." We all use it, it doesn't get in the way, and it's perfectly acceptable. If you do feel "says" is getting repetitious, you can substitute another verb that accurately describes the nature of the statement, such as argued, responded, explained or asserted. However, be careful of red-flag words that might editorialize or be perceived as biased, such as claimed, denied or charged. Often, use of the first two implies some reason to doubt the credibility of the statement, and the third often implies reason to believe the receiver of the "charge" is guilty of something.

Pronouncers

As a reporter, anchor or writer, never assume you know how something is pronounced. Always—always—verify the pronunciation if the word is unfamiliar. Never assume. This is especially true for geographically specific names, such as counties, cities and streets, and names of individuals.

For example, how do you pronounce "Nevada?" It depends. The mountain range (Sierra Nevada) is (neh-VAH-duh), the state is (neh-VA-duh), and the town in Missouri is (nuh-VAY-duh). El Dorado? If it's the town in Arkansas, it's (EL-doh-RAY-doh). San Antonio, Texas, is located in Bexar County—that's (BEHR). Yep. And while we're in Texas, let's move up to Austin, where one major road, Manor, is pronounced (MAY-nohr) and another, Manchaca, is pronounced (MAN-SHACK). You never know, so don't ever assume. If, as you're writing a story, you have a question, ask someone. If it's an unknown town, call the sheriff's office or one of the local television or radio stations and ask. This is especially true about names of streets in your market—nothing marks a newcomer like mispronouncing the name of a local street.

As you're writing the copy, write the word followed by the pronouncer in parentheses. If the copy is already written and you need to insert it on hard copy, pencil it in above the word. Emphasized syllables are written all caps. A rough pronouncer guide follows. It's not the international phonetic alphabet, but it's easy to learn and it will work.

Pronouncer Guide

Vowels

AY	=	blame
AH	=	father
A	=	bat
AI	=	blare
AW	=	balk
EE	=	greet
EH	=	let
UH	=	the
IH	=	pretty
YEW	=	few
EYE	=	sight
EE	=	Claudine
IH	=	city
OH	=	float
OO	=	school
U	=	brook
AH	=	slot
AW	=	bought
OW	=	now
YEW	=	fuel
OO	=	sue
U	=	push
UH	=	cut

Consonants

K	=	cat (hard C)
S	=	brace (soft C)
CH	=	batch (hard CH)
SH	=	chaise (soft CH)
Z	=	fleas (S sounded as Z)
J	=	George (soft G)

Clichés

Do not allow these to slip into your work—it's lazy and it's poor writing. Every Memorial Day, at least one report will follow the same tired pattern: the service at the military cemetery, the laying of the wreath, the sound of taps on a bugle, and a closing with the phrase, "Gone but not forgotten." Please. Come up with something fresh, something new that tells the story in a different way. Some examples of other clichés you want to expunge from your writing:

last but not least
few and far between
a foot in the door
jumpstart the _____
when all is said and done
at the end of the day
in the final analysis
remains to be seen
only time will tell
hail of bullets
barrage of bullets
. . . and the list goes on.

In fact, the executive director of NewsLab, Deborah Potter, has compiled a list of nearly a hundred clichés she collected while a correspondent with CBS and CNN. You might do well to go to the NewsLab website (http://www.newslab.org), read through them, and strive to avoid them.

Other Problem Words and Phrases

Alleged

This has become the most overused term in journalism, with "alleged" being tossed in a various points to cover the reporter legally. Find another way to put it. "Canwell allegedly entered the bank with a shotgun" should be "Police say Canwell entered the bank with a shotgun." Don't make the problem worse by combining the two: "Police say Canwell allegedly entered the bank with a shotgun." The police are the ones making the allegation. This next example is inexcusable, and is taken from a real-life example of a reporter trying a tad too hard: "The bank was allegedly robbed by a masked gunman, who entered the bank and allegedly demanded money from the three tellers, captured here on videotape." Unless the entire event was a cleverly staged stunt (which is possible, I suppose), there's a serious problem with the phrasing, "The bank was allegedly robbed." Folks, a man with a mask on, carrying a shotgun, walked into the bank, demanded money and, with money in hand, left the bank. That, by definition, is a robbery—no allegation to it. The allegation is not whether the bank was robbed—it was robbed. The allegation would be who police believe made off with the money.

Suspect

Another overused term. You will often hear a phrase along the lines of, "The suspect made off with about five-thousand dollars."

No. The robber made off with about five-thousand dollars. When police think they know the identity of the robber, the person accused then becomes the suspect.

Reportedly and Officials Say

Although it's usually better to generalize when attributing, don't overdo it. Officials of which agency are saying this? Who or what group is reporting this reported information?

Responsible Writing and Related Issues

Accuracy

The rule concerning accuracy is simple: Be accurate. Check and double-check facts. Don't include information in a story that you sort of remember. Don't include unconfirmed information. Don't make assumptions about the facts of a story, no matter how safe those assumptions may seem. Don't draw conclusions that you can't back with facts. Inaccuracy leads to a loss of credibility. A loss of credibility leads to a loss of viewers. And both losses can lead to the loss of your job. Be accurate.

Television news writers look for "warning words" when testing their scripts for accuracy. *Always* and *never* are two of them. As with much of life, the extremes of *always* and *never* are rarely true or rarely accurate. The same goes for the extremes expressed with words such as *all*, *none*, *everybody* and *nobody*. Many beginning television news writers fall into the "A-good-time-was-had-by-all," or "Everyone-supports-this-worthwhile-cause" traps. Is either of these statements accurate? Probably not. Even at the best party, someone has a bad time. Even the most seemingly charitable cause can find opposition. "All" and "everyone" sentences may seem to be safe assumptions. They may be the exact words organizers of events or supporters of causes use. But they are most likely inaccurate. As such, they diminish a television news writer's credibility when they appear in a news script.

Superlatives also are warning words. Superlatives are "-est" words, such as *largest*, *smallest*, *oldest*, *youngest*, *fastest*, *slowest*, *richest* and *poorest*. If a public relations firm invites you to watch the building of the world's largest ice cream sundae for charity, you don't accept the fact that it's the "world's largest." Unless the PR firm offers proof that you are witnessing the building of the world's *largest* sundae or unless you have personal knowledge of the size of all the sundaes ever built (the Guinness Book of World Records might actually have that), you will attribute (see below) or omit the superlative.

Inaccuracy occurs also when television news writers use words they don't understand. If you have any question about what a word means, spend the few minutes it takes to look it up. Those minutes could save you hours spent explaining and issuing corrections later. Ask the Georgia television news writer who, in a feature about the mayor's attractive, energetic and much-loved wife, reported that guests commented on her "gauche" look in her inaugural gown. Gauche means lacking grace, awkward and tactless. There's no rule that bans you from reporting that guests believe a mayor's wife looked gauche. But it wasn't what the Georgia reporter meant to say. The writer made a mistake by using a word he did not understand. His mistake confused viewers. The writer made his round of apologies and explanations—and he learned to look up words he wasn't confident he could define. Again, the rule here is simple: Be accurate.

Fairness

An important part of accuracy is fairness. As a television news writer, you are an impartial storyteller. News scripts have no room for your opinions. Keep editorial bias out of your stories. Do not slant your stories. Be fair. Be impartial. Be objective. As a refresher, look at how *Webster's New World Dictionary* (Second College Edition) defines some words that describe a good television news writer.

> **fair** *adj.* 6. just and honest; impartial; unprejudiced; specif., free from discrimination . . .
> **impartial** *adj.* favoring no one side or party more than another; without prejudice or bias; fair; just.

A lack of fairness can be very subtle. It can happen unwittingly to television news writers who aren't careful about word selection. Words such as *still*, *just* and *only* introduce bias.

> The Department of Transportation *still* hasn't finished work on Route 6.

The sentence implies that the Department of Transportation should have completed the road work. It expresses the news writer's disapproval of a job that's taken too long.

> City Council's plan for a new conference center would cost *only* $400,000.

The sentence implies that the cost is affordable and reasonable, even insignificant. It expresses the news writer's value judgment about the cost of the project.

> *Just* 14 people showed up to work at the volunteers' tables.

The sentence implies that there were too few volunteers and expresses the writer's dissatisfaction with the volunteer turnout.

Balance

A television news writer balances stories with all available sides of the arguments. It's not enough to write that a local pro-life advocate calls the town

Planned Parenthood physician a "killer." The television news writer includes a response from Planned Parenthood or the physician. It's not enough to write that Republicans are complaining about the "tax and spend" policies of the Democrats. The television news writer includes the Democrats' defense against the charge and their counter-charge that the Republicans are the party of "borrow and spend." Or the television news writer makes clear that the charge is not necessarily fact by writing "Republicans are complaining about *what they see as*" or *"what they call* 'tax and spend' policies of the Democrats." This brings us to the next point.

Attribution

Broadcast generally requires quite a bit less attribution than print, but more on that in a moment. You must always attribute when you need to for clarity, credibility or legal reasons. Always attribute information in a story that, first, is opinion; second, you neither see for yourself nor know to be true; or third, comes from someone else.

Opinion. Attribute anything that even remotely sounds like an opinion, even if you believe that opinion is based on fact. In the example above, the Republicans' description of Democrats' policies as "tax and spend" is an opinion. You do not report it as fact. You attribute the opinion to those who expressed it—the Republican spokespeople. A militia member's assertion that all federal agents are jackbooted thugs out to enslave America must be attributed to the militia member. It is an opinion rather than fact, and viewers need to know that. The beautification board president who calls the city's new library an eyesore is expressing an opinion, not a fact. The statement must be attributed to the beautification board president.

You Neither See for Yourself nor Know to Be True. If something truly can be considered common knowledge—you don't have to cite the election board as the source when you refer to the governor, or cite an astronomer if you reference the sun rising in the East—you can leave out the attribution entirely. However, if you do not witness something or personally know it to be true, attribute the source.

Suppose you're writing a story about the geyser Old Faithful. The story is that the famous and usually timely geyser has failed to spout for the past three days. If you witness the disappointing event, you can write

> A crowd of tourists waited for hours but left disappointed when
> Old Faithful failed to perform for the third straight day.

But if you didn't see tourists waiting and the geyser failing, you must attribute.

> Disappointed tourists say they waited for hours while Old Faithful
> remained quiet.
> Park officials say it's the third straight day the famous geyser has
> failed to perform.

Attribution protects you. Hundreds of unexpected things can happen. Maybe the tourists you talked with left just moments before the geyser went off. Maybe that "crowd" of tourists was just two people. It's unlikely, but you don't know for sure. By attributing the information to the tourists and to park officials, you tell viewers where you received the information. You let your viewers know who's behind the assertions in the story.

In 1995, a news story in South Carolina reminded (the hard way) more than a few reporters about the need to attribute story information. When a young mother reported that her two boys were kidnapped, some journalists reported the kidnapping as fact. They failed to attribute the details of the kidnapping to the mother. They failed to attribute the information to police investigators. They told viewers there *was* a kidnapper. They told viewers *the kidnapper took the children.* Then the mother admitted that there was no kidnapper. There was no kidnapping. She admitted to drowning her children. Reporters who'd failed to use attribution appeared, and were, irresponsible. They lost, and deserved to lose, credibility with their viewers.

Comes from Someone Else. If a competing medium or station generates newsworthy information that you can't independently verify, you give the competitor credit. Television newscasts, radio programming, newspaper stories and magazine articles all are copyrighted. Media sources legally own the scripts, stories and articles they run, so using information from a copyrighted source is stealing. It is unethical and illegal. You can follow up on copyrighted information to generate your own stories and original scripts, but you cannot take (steal) information from other sources and present it as your own. You must attribute the information to its source. If a major newspaper uncovers evidence that the president of the United States knew about, approved of and directed a cover-up of a break-in at the opposition party's headquarters, you as a news writer must attribute the information to that newspaper.

> *The Washington Post* is reporting that President Nixon helped
> cover up illegal and covert political activities.

The story was called Watergate. It was widely reported. But the story belonged to two journalists working with the backing of their newspaper. Bob Woodward, Carl Bernstein and *The Washington Post* owned the story. Their work, when reported elsewhere, was attributed to them.

Failing to provide attribution could land you in court. Get in the habit now of attributing everything that is opinion, that you neither witness nor know to be true or that comes from someone else. An exception (there's always one!) is wire copy.

Television news writers get information from wire services such as The Associated Press (AP), United Press International (UPI) and Reuters. They don't always attribute information in the wire copy stories. Television stations pay for wire copy services. They buy the information, so it belongs to them.

A station and its news writers trust the information from wire services. Television news writers can use much of the information contained in wire copy without attribution and with confidence, keeping in mind two general guidelines. First, if the wire copy writer uses attribution, the television news writer, too, must attribute the information. If the wire copy says, "FBI agents say they shot the man in self-defense," the television news writer does not need to write

> The Associated Press reports that FBI agents say they shot the man in self-defense.

But neither can the television news writer's script read

> FBI agents shot the man in self-defense.

The television writer includes the attribution as it appears in the wire copy. Here, the television writer (like the wire copy writer) attributes the information to FBI agents. If the wire copy relies on attribution for accuracy, the television news writer requires attribution too.

> FBI agents say they shot the man in self-defense.

The second guideline is this: If there's a question or if the wire service story seems outlandish, television news writers may decide to attribute the information to the wire service that is reporting the story until they can obtain independent verification.

> **Probably Safe:** Representative Lyle says the federal budget must be balanced.

The television news writer most likely doesn't require attribution in this sentence. He or she trusts the information from the wire service. Because the station is paying for the wire service information, there is no strong argument for giving the wire service credit through attribution for the information.

> **Probably Unsafe:** Representative Lyle will give the country $4 trillion to pay off the national debt.

In this instance, the television news writer would want to get independent verification. The news writer may not be willing to put his or her reputation for accuracy on the line for a story that doesn't "ring true." He or she most likely will want to attribute.

> The Associated Press is reporting that Representative Lyle will give the country $4 trillion to pay off the national debt.

How do you know if a story "rings true?" It's a call each television news writer makes for himself or herself. It comes with understanding news and following current events so that an outlandish story will raise a red flag. It also comes with experience.

To expand on a point made earlier, attribution is especially important in crime stories. Police may tell you, "John Smith robbed the bank." It is acceptable for them to say it, but it is unacceptable for you to write it. You must write

> Police say John Smith robbed the bank.

Chances are, you didn't see John Smith rob the bank. Even if you did, the U.S. Constitution protects the accused. Every person is innocent until proven guilty in court. If you fail to attribute the information in a crime story, you could end up doing the court's job of convicting the accused. You also could open yourself up to a lawsuit. Courts commonly use the term *libel* to refer to all broadcast defamation. *Defamation* means attacking or injuring a person's reputation or honor by false or malicious statements.

As you attribute information, remember this important consideration: The source of information must be reliable. Police officers working a crime are reliable sources. Witnesses to the crime may be reliable sources. Friends and relatives of the alleged criminal may be reliable sources. (How many times have you seen neighbors of a crazed gunman interviewed on television?) But a person who has something to gain by what he or she says may not be a reliable source. A person who heard about the crime and wants to comment may not be a reliable source. A bank teller not on duty at the time of a robbery but who's eager to talk and apparently full of information may not be a reliable source.

Often, it's easy to identify an unreliable source. Someone with an ax to grind, someone who benefits from the information he or she gives you, someone speaking on behalf of a cause in which he or she is involved—these people all have reasons to give you biased, and even false, information. Other times, it's not so easy to spot those who might mislead you. It's not always intentional on their part—they may believe what they're telling you. You may report that they believe it by attributing it to them, but you may not report it as fact unless you know it to be so, no matter how convincingly your sources make their statements.

How to Attribute

When attributing, use some form of title or identifier at the beginning of the statement. This is the reverse of what you'll often see in print, but it better matches the way we think and the way we speak. For example, in print you might see

> President Bush will veto any military budget that does not include funding for a missile defense system, White House sources indicated today.

That doesn't work for broadcast because it's a bit stiff, and because the source is identified at the end, forcing us to think back. Plus, it's not conversational. A better way to phrase might be

> The White House says President Bush will veto any military
> budget that doesn't include funding for a missile defense system.

Also, when you attribute up front, you avoid the hyped-up "teaser" attribution such as the following:

> This nation has become morally bankrupt—that comment from
> Attorney General John Ashcroft . . .

Don't do it. It's a cheap gimmick used to get attention.

On the subject, always use at least some of the title or identifier in front of the name. For example, instead of saying

> John McCain, the Republican senator from Arizona, says that . . .

you would say,

> U-S Senator John McCain, an Arizona Republican, says that . . .

The idea is to get enough of a basic title or identifier in front of the name that the viewer/listener knows who the person is. Not everyone follows the news closely enough to immediately recognize John McCain's name, so a bit of identification just before makes it clear. Plus, the title is usually more important to the story and gives some sense of the role that person is playing, so the audience will understand the significance more.

In broadcast, you can often generalize the source without impairing the understanding of the story. Shorten titles if it will enhance the copy and the meaning or effect is not changed. For example, rather than write, "Lieutenant William Colby, public information officer for the Gang Task Force of the Dallas Police Department, provided statistics that show gang activity has decreased," you likely could substitute, "Dallas police say gang activity is down."

While we're on the topic of attribution, there are a few other caveats. One involves unidentified sources: It's always best to identify sources as fully as possible, even if you have verified the information through a dozen independent sources. Your credibility rises with full source identification, and sometimes even trusted sources can get it wrong. You also avoid something called a trial balloon that way. What's a trial balloon? It works like this:

The mayor wants to push through a redistricting plan that would allow a major manufacturer to build a factory on the south side of town. On the plus side, the factory could boost the economy and bring manufacturing jobs to the area. On the minus side, it would greatly increase air and noise pollution and traffic, and likely decrease home values. The issue gets even touchier when considering that the area in question is a racially minority area, and this administration has a history of trying to build factories in lower socioeconomic minority populated parts of town.

So the mayor gives you a call. He tells you that he loves your work, and is going to give you an exclusive on this plan. The only catch is that you cannot attribute it to him or his office. Being the ambitious reporter you are, you agree and run with the story. Once your story, "sans attribution," runs, the mayor tests the political winds to see where that "trial balloon" sails. If reaction is positive, the mayor holds a news conference taking credit for the plan. If the reaction is negative, the mayor holds a news conference emphatically stating that no one in his office would support any such plan and he has no idea where you, the irresponsible reporter, got the story. Without attribution, it can happen. Don't let it happen to you.

Degrees of Attribution

There are various designations for levels of attribution.

On the Record—For Direct Quotation. You can fully identify the source and quote him or her (which typically would mean a sound bite).

On the Record—Not for Direct Quotation. You can fully identify the source, but must paraphrase any comments.

On Background. You cannot fully identify the source but may indirectly describe the source's relationship to the story, such as, "a source in the police department told us." The words used for this sort of attribution must be negotiated with the source.

On Deep Background. You can use the information but cannot identify the source in any way. This can be dangerous territory.

Off the Record. You cannot use the information in the story unless you can develop that information from another source.

Rather than go into this complicated formula with your source, simply negotiate both what information you can use and how you can phrase the attribution of the source. Make sure that's clear, and don't worry about the terminology.

One final note, though. You will dig into stories in which and from which lives are affected in a major way. Some secretary may be blowing the whistle on her company's waste-dumping practices. At the same time, that secretary may be the single mother of three in a bad economy, so if she gets fired, they could all be out on the street. Even if she supports getting the information out, can you ensure her that no one would be able to trace her as the source? Never lose sight of the fact that what you write and report can have a profound and long-lasting effect on people's lives.

Summary

News writers must produce copy that can be easily understood and read by an anchor or reporter. Substitute words for symbols and abbreviations. Review the rules for writing numbers. Simplify and translate numbers into easily understandable terms, rounding and using examples and comparisons. Review the rules for writing names. Review the rules for writing acronyms and initials. Use contractions. Know which punctuation to use and which not to use. For quotes, use a sound bite or paraphrase. Include pronouncers in your copy, and never assume you know the correct pronunciation of an unfamiliar name or place. Avoid clichés and problem words and phrases.

News writers accept responsibility for producing not only understandable but accurate scripts. Responsible television news writing relies on four key guidelines:

1. **Accuracy**
2. **Fairness**
3. **Balance**
4. **Attribution**

Exercises

1. Rewrite the following in broadcast news style.

   (a) The Rev. Billy Graham
   (b) Pres. George Walker Bush
   (c) $6,000.00
   (d) $17,001.03
   (e) Organization of Petroleum Exporting Countries
   (f) Central Intelligence Agency
   (g) She said she could not find the key. (Think conversational).
   (h) He said, "I'll see you in prison first." (Assume you don't have a sound bite, but need to use the quote).

2. Come up with five streets in your town, and write pronouncers for them. Do the same for five well-known people in your community.

3. Read the story below. Assume it is accurate. Then read the list of statements. Mark the statements *T* (true) if it's a statement you know to be true based on information provided in the story, *F* (false) if it's a statement you know to be false based on information provided in the story or *U* (unknown) if the statement is not addressed or remains unanswered in the story.

   > As jury selection was about to begin in Middlesex Circuit Court, John VanFleet decided to plead guilty to charges he murdered 15-year-old Jamie Lee Thomas. The 22-year-old VanFleet faces a maximum of 68 years in prison for his guilty pleas yesterday to first-degree murder

and use of a firearm in the commission of a felony. After entering his pleas to the two counts, VanFleet pleaded innocent to one count of attempted murder, two counts of malicious wounding and three related firearms' charges. His trial on the remaining six charges was to begin today.

(a) A 22-year-old man was murdered.
(b) The killer used a gun to commit the murder last year.
(c) John VanFleet pleaded guilty to two charges.
(d) VanFleet pleaded guilty to six more charges.
(e) The victim was male.
(f) VanFleet will be sentenced to 68 years in prison.
(g) VanFleet pleaded innocent to three firearms' charges but guilty to one.
(h) A jury had been selected prior to VanFleet's pleas.
(i) The victim's family is relieved not to have to go through trial.
(j) VanFleet pleaded guilty first to two charges and then innocent to six charges.

4. Circle the sentences below for which you, as a television news writer, might want to use attribution.

(a) Fifty million Americans are overweight.
(b) People from many parts of the country travel to the Northeast in autumn to watch the leaves change color.
(c) Exposure of pregnant women to cats can cause birth defects to their unborn children.
(d) More American teenage boys are becoming involved in Nazi skinhead activities.
(e) John Doe kidnapped and raped a local woman.
(f) Republican policies are stifling this country's economy.
(g) Independence Day in the United States is a summer holiday.
(h) The state will ask the federal government to lift smog regulations for two major cities.
(i) When rain and freezing temperatures mix, it can cause snow.
(j) At age 16, teenagers are allowed to get their drivers' licenses.

Usage 5

Now that you're familiar with some of the basic rules of writing television news copy, let's turn to usage—how to word and phrase the information you're trying to get across. First and foremost, you must write conversationally. To put it another way, write the way you speak. As we've already discussed, you are writing words to be heard, not seen. You are telling a story. And although you've been speaking nearly your entire life, mastering this conversational style of writing takes some adjustment. Four general guidelines to keep in mind:

1. **Words**: Think small and simple and clear.
2. **Sentences**: Think short and simple and clear.
3. **Voice**: Write in active, not passive.
4. **Tense**: Use present or future when possible, but use them accurately.

Words

Use common, everyday, easily understandable words. Choose the simplest words that best describe and express—but this doesn't mean be imprecise. A "burglary" and a "robbery" are not the same thing, and you may need to identify the "gun" as a "large caliber semiautomatic." Be appropriate. You're not writing for 12-year-olds, and if the correct word is more complicated but still well understood, use it. Generally speaking, however, simpler is better. To "extinguish a conflagration" is to put out a fire. A "flaxen-haired woman" is blonde. A region's "flora and fauna" are its plants and animals.

Use informal language, but stay away from slang. Write a story in the same voice (word usage and so on) that you might use in describing something to your parents or a professor—casual, but not slang-ridden. The following, for example, would not cut it:

> So, like, the Mayor, he goes, like, It's happenin', and the
> city manager dude is like, No way, and the mayor's like, Way,
> and the CM is like, As if, and the mayor is like, Hey dude, Word.

You get the point.

Words and Sentences: Simplify and Clarify

Look for ways to trim down your copy, substituting simple phrases and—above all—cutting down on euphemisms and bureaucratic language. Take this example.

> In an effort to clear the excessive amount of unsightly trash from roadsides, the city council has expressed a desire to adopt a proposal to hire more sanitation workers to address the problem.

There are all kinds of problems here.

"In an effort to" translates very simply to, "To."

"Clear the excessive amount of unsightly trash from roadsides" is an excessive amount of copy—instead, you would write, "pick up roadside trash." Plus, most people think any roadside trash is excessive.

"The city council has expressed a desire to adopt a proposal to" becomes, "the city council wants to."

"Hire more sanitation workers to address the problem" can be rewritten simply as, "hire more workers." The phrase "address the problem" is superfluous—it's already implied in the previous copy.

So, let's compare the two.

> In an effort to clear the excessive amount of unsightly trash from roadsides, the city council has expressed a desire to adopt a proposal to hire more sanitation workers to address the problem.

becomes

> The city council wants to hire more workers to pick up roadside trash.

The second version is simpler, shorter and easier to understand. If you need an alternative lead, you can still get a bit creative by rephrasing somewhat:

> The city council says the amount of roadside trash has gotten out of hand—so it wants to hire more workers to clean up the litter.

This version is still shorter, still simpler, and still clearer. That's what you're looking for.

To restate, avoid euphemisms. Workers are not "right-sized," "streamlined" or "strategically restructured"—they are laid off or fired. It's not a "revenue enhancement," it's a tax. People do not "pass on to their eternal reward," they die.

In an airport recently, I heard the following announcement on the public address system:

> Please take precautions to secure and maintain consistent control over your luggage at all times so as to avoid the unlawful introduction of illegal or dangerous items.

Give me a break. Native English speakers would have to take a moment to decipher this code. How about,

> Please watch your luggage to make sure that no stranger puts
> something in your bags that doesn't belong.

Also, avoid what I call (with apologies to Firesign Theatre) Products of the Department of Redundancy Department. Some examples:

> The tornado destroyed office structures and decimated buildings.

> The committee voted to begin reconstruction and renovation in
> the historic district.

And, while we're at it, avoid PIN number, ATM machine, the Rio Grande River, the Sierra Nevada mountain range—all of these, all of these, are Products of the Department of Redundancy Department. Get rid of them.

Whenever possible, use words instead of phrases. Examples:

> "Prior to" becomes "before"
> "Subsequent to" becomes "after"
> "In the near future" becomes "soon"
> "Is of the opinion that" becomes "believes"
> "At this point in time" becomes "now"
> "At this particular point in time" becomes "now"

and my favorite,

> "At this particular juncture in time" becomes—you guessed it—
> "now."

The English language is filled with these kinds of phrases. I'm not saying they never have any use. I'm saying they rarely serve a purpose in television news writing.

Translate jargon into common English. You'll find a lot of jargon coming from professions such as science, medicine or law that use highly specialized language. Often this simply takes asking the scientist, doctor or lawyer to put the explanation into lay terms. If you do have to use an uncommon term, use it—but explain its meaning clearly.

Some sources such as the police are notorious for using heavy jargon, even in public statements. Take the following example:

> At approximately 7:57 a.m. in the morning on this date, I espied
> the subject traversing the lawn area in front of said subject's domicile.
> Upon arriving at the portal, the subject effected egress into the
> domicile.

What did he just say?

> At about eight this morning, the man walked across his lawn and
> went into the house.

You must translate this stuff into conversational English, usually through paraphrasing.

Caveats

Use race or age only when it's essential to the story. Some years back, the Ku Klux Klan filed a lawsuit to force the local cable company to air a program it created. The attorney who eventually represented them happened to be African American. That was an interesting twist to the story—in fact, failure to include race would have been a dereliction of duty on the part of the writer. Likewise, if one of the runners who finished the Boston Marathon also happened to be 87 years old, that's a fact you not only would want to include, but perhaps even lead with.

However, racism, ageism and any other negative –ism must be avoided. That includes sexism—you are journalists, not newsmen; positions are staffed, not manned; and those folks who hand out undersized snacks and overpriced drinks on airplanes are flight attendants, not stewardesses. Negative stereotypes are already entirely too plentiful out there. You don't want to play a role in perpetuating them. Along the same vein, be careful for potential pejoratives such as little, so-called or any other descriptor that could be interpreted as insulting or demeaning.

Finally, say what you mean and don't use judgments.

> Fortunately, only six people were killed in the train crash.

Not too fortunate for the six!

> The law would force California to return to Arizona only 20-percent of the water Arizona says it has rights to.

You think this writer has a position on this water thing?

Sentence Length and Structure

Some place great emphasis on sentence length falling within set limits. I don't. The length of a sentence in television news depends primarily on audience understanding and the lungs of the reader. The second issue is self-explanatory—if the reporter or anchor runs out of air while trying to complete a single sentence, that's a pretty good sign it's running a tad long.

Regarding the first point, remember that a listening viewer can only take in a certain amount of information at a time. You want to write one key idea per sentence, and only one. You may have supplemental information to support that one point, but don't load your sentence down with multiple ideas that require the viewer go through a mental juggling act to keep up. Usually, from ten to fifteen words will do it—an alarm should go off if you write more than a basic subject–verb–object sentence with an additional phrase here or there.

Take the following example.

> In the face of growing criticism over her handling of the budget, the mayor has decided to resign.

What's your main point? The mayor's resigning.

What additional information shores up that main point? Critics say she mishandled the budget. Criticism is growing.

Look at the following lead sentence from a newspaper story.

> The AIDS scare sweeping Germany worsened Friday with the announcement that at least 50 babies received AIDS-tainted plasma during treatment in Bavarian clinics, despite evidence that only a small number of the country's 60,000 people infected by the AIDS virus got it from tainted blood.

This newspaper lead has too much information for television news writing. It includes four separate thoughts. The television news writer breaks the information into four separate sentences. Each sentence serves as its own paragraph.

> The AIDS scare sweeping Germany worsened Friday.
> Officials say at least 50 babies at a Bavarian clinic received AIDS-tainted blood.
> Government figures estimate 60-thousand Germans are infected with the virus.
> Evidence shows only a small number of them got it from tainted blood.

If your sentence feels too complex—especially after reading it aloud—simplify the one sentence or break it down into two. You will rarely go wrong with simple, declarative sentences. Make certain that every word is critical to the story—words are your best resource, so don't waste them. Make your critical point creatively but clearly and efficiently. Also, a waste of airtime will lose viewers and gain the ire of producers. Neither is a positive event in your life.

At the same time, make sure you vary the length and structure of your sentences. If your entire story consists of sentences of identical length, it will sound choppy and boring. Variety is critical to many aspects of television news—variety of story length and formats (more on that later), variety of voices reading the stories, variety of visuals and sound included in the stories—and sentence length is no exception. It keeps the story interesting.

Finally, try to keep the verb close to the subject. You'll find that the closer a subject and verb are to each other in the sentence, the easier the sentence will be for TV viewers to understand.

> **Sentence 1:** The masked *thief ran* quickly down a nearby alley.
> **Sentence 2:** The *thief*, who wore a mask, quickly *ran* down a nearby alley.

Sentence 1 places the verb *ran* immediately after the subject *thief*. The result is conversational. It is clear. It is strong television news writing. The second sentence separates the subject and verb for a confusing and disjointed sentence that challenges viewers to keep up.

A third option for writing this sentence limits it to a single thought.

Sentence 3: The thief ran down an alley.

If the information that the thief wore a mask is important to the story, the writer may include it in a separate sentence.

Sentence 2 also highlights the damage dependent clauses can do to television news scripts. In this example, *who wore a mask* is the dependent clause. Dependent clauses are the enemies of simple sentence structure. They can separate subjects from their verbs.

> Seventeen people, *who are screaming and crying out for help,*
> remain trapped in the burning building.

The dependent clause (in italics) separates the subject and verb, making the sentence wordy and detracting from viewers' understanding. Viewers hear "seventeen people" but have to wait through the dependent clause to find out what's happening to them. Dependent clauses can bog down sentences to make them less clear and less conversational. They can take away from the effect the story has on viewers.

> As they scream and cry out for help, seventeen people remain
> trapped in the burning building.

The information that people are screaming and crying out for help has less effect on viewers when they don't know why. The power of this sentence is in the horror of being trapped in a burning building, but the writer makes viewers wait to hear about it. The dependent clause at the beginning of the sentence lessens the effect of the story.

Some television news writers check for dependent clauses in their writing by looking for commas. If you see a comma, chances are there is a dependent clause tacked onto, hanging onto or bogging down the sentence. Or you may have linked two independent clauses, which can be just as damaging to viewers' understanding of a script.

> Seventeen people are trapped in the burning building, and they are
> screaming and crying out for help.

In this example, the writer offers too much information for viewers to absorb at once. The sentence contains two separate thoughts (as two independent clauses). It is long. It may be difficult for a news anchor to read. It certainly will be difficult for viewers to understand quickly and easily.

In the three examples above, the clauses are separated by commas. Remember that commas are the news writer's warning signs that a rewrite may be necessary. If information in clauses is essential or interesting enough to include in the story, allow it its own sentence or incorporate the information in other sentences. By eliminating the commas, the writer eliminates the dependent and independent clauses. The result: Two sentences, each one thought, that the anchor can easily read and viewers can easily understand.

Seventeen people remain trapped in the burning building.
They are screaming and crying out for help.

Voice

Voice is often confused with tense—it is not the same thing. Voice refers to whether the sentence is active or passive. Read the following:

The car struck the tree.

Now, identify the verb, the subject and the object:

The verb? *struck*
The subject? *car*
The object? *tree*.

This sentence follows a classic S–V–O pattern: the subject is followed by the verb is followed by the object. This is a basic example of a sentence written in active voice.

Now, read the following:

The tree was struck by the car.

Once again, identify the verb, subject and object. The verb is *was struck*. The *subject* is the *car*, not the *tree*. The *car* is performing the action. The *tree* is receiving the action, so your *subject* is still *car* and your *object* is still *tree*. In this case, however, the order is reversed (object–verb–subject), rather than subject–verb–object. The second sentence is an example of passive voice.

Generally speaking, active voice is stronger, clearer and shorter. It makes for better writing. It carries better straight line meaning and gives more information. In a passive sentence, you don't necessarily have to name the subject/actor: "The tree was struck." Thus, an active sentence forces the writer to know the subject performing the action and include it in the sentence.

Always use active voice unless there is a compelling reason to use passive voice. Some of those compelling reasons follow.

First, when the person acted on is the focus of the story:

President Bush has been shot but his wound is not life-
threatening. It happened this afternoon . . .

Obviously, the most important aspect is the shooting of the president, not the person who did it. That information comes later.

Second, when the doer is unknown:

A police officer was beaten to death this afternoon . . . Police are
still searching for the attacker.

One could make the "focus of story" argument, as well. Even here, though, some would argue for active:

> An unidentified man beat a police officer to death . . .

Third, when active voice sounds awkward:

> A man was pinned between his car and the garage
> door . . .

Using the active voice, you get

> A car pinned a man against the garage door.

Unless your follow-up is about a priest exorcising a possessed car, you should probably go with passive voice.

Finally, when passive usage is common:

> I was born in Texas.

What would the active be? "I birthed in Texas?" It just doesn't work.

Actively seek out examples of passive voice and rewrite them to active. If you want to leave a sentence in passive, make certain you have a compelling reason to do so and can defend it.

Strong Verbs and Nouns, Few Adverbs and Adjectives

The best television news writing uses strong, colorful nouns and verbs. If you must use adjectives or adverbs, use them sparingly. Avoid piling modifiers on to give greater weight:

> All the people who anxiously stood by watching say it was an
> extremely tense and very frightening event.

versus

> The witnesses say it was terrifying.

Overwriting is like overacting. You don't want to be known as the Sarah Bernhardt of the television news writing world. In writing, like acting, little is much—pack power into a compact space—and the way to do that is through strong verbs and nouns.

While we're on the subject, let's discuss the verb "to be." To be is not to be. Get rid of it whenever possible. You want to write in terse, compelling phrasing, and the verb "to be" simply states existence. Find a stronger, more colorful verb.

For example,

> Texas is still in a drought.

Clear, to the point, and boring. Find a more active verb.

> A drought continues to beat down on Texas.

or

A drought continues to bake Texas.

Find something that implies more action than "to be."
Now read the following passage:

> People in the town said they could press their hands against the levy walls and feel the river's force pounding from the other side. Like the rumbling of a monster pushing to break free, one said. As the residents fled overnight, the river continued rising, carving away more of the levy's banks. Just after sunrise, those banks finally ruptured. Millions of tons of water spilled through the breach, spreading across the town and devouring all in its path. Buildings, vehicles, livestock— the water spared nothing.

Remember, you want to use strong nouns and verbs, and trim out adverbs and adjectives. This passage achieves that, using modifiers sparingly and relying on forceful verbs and nouns.

Tense

Write in present or future tense whenever possible, especially in a lead. Your next choice is present perfect or past perfect, and past tense is the least desirable. In television, we are dealing with immediacy, and your writing needs to reflect that. But use it accurately. Find the latest aspect that is occurring now or soon will be.

> Yesterday, Congress voted in a bill that will lower subsidies for dairy products. The president said he will sign the bill into law when it reaches his desk next week.

How might you shift this into present or future tense?

> A bill to cut dairy subsidies is heading to the president for approval. Congress passed the bill yesterday, and the president says he'll sign it into law once it reaches his desk.

or

> Dairy farmers may soon be getting less federal money. Congress passed . . .

or

> President Bush says he'll sign into law a bill to cut dairy subsidies. Congress passed . . .

Look at what is happening now, and write the lead (and as much else of the story as possible) that way.

Also, use present tense if it is an ongoing policy:

President Bush said he will press for a diplomatic solution with
North Korea.

He might have made the statement in a news conference last week, but so long as that policy is still in effect, present tense is accurate:

President Bush says he will press for a diplomatic solution with
North Korea.

Be careful, however, that you don't overdo present tense. As mentioned earlier, it has to be accurate. Look again at the AIDS story from Germany as it was rewritten for television.

The AIDS scare sweeping Germany worsened Friday.
Officials say at least 50 babies at a Bavarian clinic received
AIDS-tainted blood.
About 60-thousand Germans are infected with the virus.
Evidence shows only a small number of them got it from tainted
blood.

The story uses the past tense verb *worsened* in its first sentence. The news sounds old. Try rewriting the sentence with the present tense.

The AIDS scare *is growing* in Germany.

Now, the story takes on a feel of immediacy. It meets viewers' expectations of television to provide up-to-the-minute news. The writer also moved the subject and verb closer together for a clearer, more conversational first sentence.

The second sentence of the television story includes a present-tense verb.

Officials *say* at least 50 babies at a Bavarian clinic received
AIDS-tainted blood.

The verb *say* is one of the television news writer's best friends. It often can be used to introduce present tense into a story. But beware! In our example, you must leave the verb *received* in the past tense because the babies received the blood in the past. Suppose a news writer, striving for present tense, changes the tense:

Officials say at least 50 babies at a Bavarian clinic *are receiving*
AIDS-tainted blood.

This sentence is not accurate. Viewers get the impression that German officials are, at this moment (at present), pumping babies full of AIDS-tainted blood. This is not true. The present tense, used here, affects the accuracy of the writing.

Also, do not use what I refer to as false or pseudopresent tense. It's a storytelling technique used by some news operations to impart a sense of immediacy throughout the story. The following is an example:

As the robber is walking out of the store, police arrive. The man
runs down the street with the police in hot pursuit. The man ducks into
a store, and police follow him in. The robber opens fire on the two
cops, then runs out the back door into the alley.

You get the picture. Unless you are narrating the event live as it happens, this style is inappropriate.

Even worse:

> A man rams his car into the front of a jewelry store this morning.

Rams? No—it happened this morning. It's gimmicky and it's not conversational. People don't talk that way. Present tense used this way is inappropriate. Instead, find out the current situation:

> Cleanup continues this evening at a local jewelry store where a
> man rammed his car through the front windows. Police say the man
> was trying to rob the store when . . .

As mentioned, however, some news operations insist on this style of writing past events as if they are occurring now. If you happen to be working for one of them, do as you're told—jobs are hard enough to get and keep in this business. Otherwise, avoid it. I don't wish to step on toes, but it's a lazy way to make the copy sound more immediate without doing the hard work involved in writing present tense accurately.

Furthermore, while on the subject of tense and time reference, do not overuse the word "today." We'll discuss this in more detail in the next chapter. For now, suffice it to say that opting for time lapse (less than an hour ago) or day part (late this afternoon) generally is better writing. Also, use a comparative reference or day of the week (tomorrow night, early next week, this Friday) rather than a date. If it's the last week of March, put it that way.

Another point—it's generally best to put the time reference close to the verb it modifies:

> The mayor made the announcement at the opening of the south-
> side factory last week.

should be

> The mayor made the announcement last week at the opening of
> the southside factory.

I will end this section with a critical point to keep in mind: Much of good writing is good editing. Rewrite. Then rewrite again. Go back through your copy and edit ruthlessly. If it's unclear or complex, clarify, simplify and break it down. If it's wordy, trim it and tighten it. If it's not essential to the story, strike it. If the writing fails to be concise and to the point, make it so. Be able to defend every word.

A Literary Approach

Good television news writing uses many of the same literary techniques and devices great writing has historically employed, but with the added element of copy being written to be read aloud. Therefore, read your copy aloud—always.

Remember this example from earlier?

> People in the town said they could press their hands against the levy walls and feel the river's force pounding from the other side. Like the rumbling of a monster pushing to break free, one said. As the residents fled overnight, the river continued rising, carving away more of the levy's banks. Just after sunrise, those banks finally ruptured. Millions of tons of water spilled through the breach, spreading across the town and devouring all in its path. Buildings, vehicles, livestock—the water spared nothing.

First, think back to the earlier section on using strong nouns and verbs, and trimming out adverbs and adjectives. This passage achieves that, using modifiers sparingly and relying on forceful verbs and nouns.

Now, let's turn to the literary device called alliteration—the repeating of sounds. Used sparingly, the device works well. Read through aloud and listen for how certain sounds—F, P and L, R and K—repeat and weave their way through the segment. The key is to find words that work well for sound and meaning, keeping in mind the need for clarity and brevity. With this or any other device, however, never use it to the point that you call attention to it.

Next, consider the use of metaphor and simile. One of the townspeople described the river's force against the levy as being like the rumbling of a monster. Metaphor and simile work well to lend good description, to give examples that connect with the audience.

The passage also uses personification—giving human or lifelike qualities to something—when explaining the river was "devouring all in its path," and concluding, "the water spared nothing."

Onomatapeia—words that sound like what they describe—can be heard in the words "pounding," "rumbling" and "ruptured."

The passage employs the use of "threes" in the phrase, "buildings, vehicles, livestock." Something about a trinity gives a sense of completion in the human mind—physical space is perceived in three dimensions, three points establish a plane in geometry, our government has three branches, and so on. We hear it in our language, as well: past, present and future; yes, no and maybe. Giving three examples seems to substantiate a point. It's part of our psyche, so use it in your writing.

Finally, listen to the rhythm of the passage. It has a sort of movement, ebbing and flowing but always moving forward. Rhythm is especially important in broadcast news copy because it is performed for the audience—the sounds of the words make a difference.

To repeat an earlier point, these devices can serve you well, but use them sparingly. Don't overwrite. The idea is to describe creatively and clearly but efficiently. You should focus the viewer's attention on the story, not on your own writing.

And most important, read copy aloud—always. I realize it may seem a bit strange at first, reading aloud in a newsroom, but anyone who's any good does it. I promise they won't suspect you suffer from schizophrenia. Read aloud and listen to the sound of the copy, the sounds of the words. Listen for effect. And rely on literary devices.

One final point: Good writing depends on good journalism. The most well-turned phrases will fail to salvage a story that lacks interesting, compelling and essential information. If the reporting isn't there, neither is the story.

Summary

Simplify, clarify and trim down your writing. Edit out excess. Avoid judgmental or biased language. Keep sentences to one main point, and keep them short, but vary the length. Keep the verb close to the subject. Use active voice unless a compelling reason dictates using passive. Look for strong nouns and verbs, and use few adverbs and adjectives. Use present or future tense whenever possible, but use them accurately and appropriately. Avoid false present tense. Keep time references close to the verbs they modify. Edit ruthlessly. Use literary devices, but don't overdo.

Remember the four general guidelines:

1. **Words:** Think small and simple and clear.
2. **Sentences:** Think short and simple and clear.
3. **Voice:** Write in active, not passive.
4. **Tense:** Use present or future when possible, but use them accurately

Exercises

1. Supply a conversational, appropriate-for-television word or words for each noun, verb, adjective and adverb below.

(a) puissant	(f) occupation
(b) prevaricate	(g) jocularity
(c) resident	(h) loquacious
(d) benevolence	(i) harbinger
(e) swimmingly	(j) culpable

2. Rewrite the following sentences to rid them of dependent clauses. In the rewrite either incorporate the information in the clause into the rewritten sentence or create another sentence using the information included in the clause.

> Example: The 14-car pileup, officials say caused by slick roads after yesterday's ice storm, stalled traffic for three hours.

> Rewrite: The 14-car pileup stalled traffic for three hours. Officials blame slick roads after yesterday's ice storm.

or

> Rewrite: Officials blame icy roads for a 14-car pileup that stalled traffic for three hours.

(a) The president, who was speaking at a party fund-raiser, said the federal budget must be balanced.

Rewrite:

(b) Although supply centers have been set up, hurricane relief workers are still having trouble getting essential items to those in need.

Rewrite:

(c) The crime lab, which was set up in the late 1970s, is using out-of-date methods to analyze blood samples.

Rewrite:

(d) The bodies of two American balloonists, who were shot down earlier this month by a military helicopter, are being flown home from Belarus today.

Rewrite:

(e) Lawyers for the death row inmate, who is scheduled to die next week in the state's electric chair, have filed affidavits seeking a plea for a hearing on what they say is new evidence.

Rewrite:

3. Identify the sentences below as active voice or passive voice. Rewrite the passive voice sentences using active voice.

Example: A good time was had by many.
___Active   X Passive   Rewrite? Many had a good time.

(a) The paper was handed in on time by the student.
___Active   ___Passive ___Rewrite?
(b) A witness says three gunmen robbed the bank.
___Active   ___Passive ___Rewrite?
(c) Police were told by clerks the robber wore a mask.
___Active   ___Passive ___Rewrite?
(d) Investigators say the fire was started by an arsonist.
___Active   ___Passive ___Rewrite?
(e) A rapist struck again in the small community.
___Active   ___Passive ___Rewrite?
(f) The woman was accosted by a man with a beard.
___Active   ___Passive ___Rewrite?
(g) The clerk told reporters she could identify the thief.
___Active   ___Passive ___Rewrite?
(h) The victim was rushed to a hospital by bystanders.
___Active   ___Passive ___Rewrite?

    (i) Students were ordered by security to clear the parking lot.
         ___Active   ___Passive ___Rewrite?

    (j) Sellers said fans bought more peanuts than ever.
         ___Active   ___Passive ___Rewrite?

6

Approaching the Television News Story

We've talked about usage and how you should approach television news writing generally. Now, we turn to how to incorporate that usage into a basic television news story. I'll be repeating some of the points I made earlier to show how they fit into the story's lead, body and conclusion.

A television news story must answer the same questions as any news story: who, what, where, when, why and how. But the way you approach this process is decidedly different in television news than in print. Chances are you've heard of the inverted pyramid style of writing. In this approach, every essential fact is stuffed into one long, run-on lead paragraph that is then followed by more detail that expands on and explains all those essential facts. This story structure also has the advantage of being easily edited to fit the length available in that edition of the newspaper.

Forget the inverted pyramid—for a host of reasons. This antiquated approach to writing stories for newspapers was born during the Civil War. It should have died there. It served the purpose of getting key facts of stories over telegraph wires before others had a chance to cut the wires and keep that information from going out. We no longer face that problem.

Instead, if using a geometrical model is important to you, think about a television news story as being more of a diamond (Figure 6.1). One or two short, conversational sentences introduce the story. A body follows that broadens and develops the story, citing some illustrative examples and some background. The story then carries the viewer to a conclusion of a sentence or two that wraps things up. In a television news story, there is a beginning, a middle and an end. That's how we tell stories to each other, and that's how you'll tell stories to a television audience.

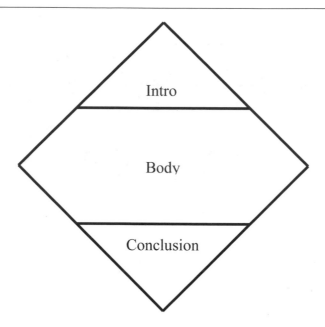

FIGURE 6.1

Before writing the lead (or the rest of the story), you need to consider what the story is about. Make certain you thoroughly understand the story before even beginning to write your script. Many reporters and writers will tackle a story they don't entirely understand. Rather than learning enough about the story to write an interesting, understandable and comprehensive piece, they decide that whoever is interested enough in the story will figure it out.

Read the next statement carefully. If you don't get it, they won't get it. Period. If you do not understand a story well enough to write it, do some more research. Call some sources and have them explain it to you. Ask someone else in the newsroom who may have covered a related story. Check on-line or check the library's resources. If all else fails, write around the problem or see whether you can hand off the story to someone else.

Next, remind yourself why this is a story in the first place. What makes this story worth covering on your newscast? All the main elements of newsworthiness you covered in your basic journalism class come into play:

Timeliness: What happened today is more newsworthy than what happened last month, unless we're just finding out about it.

Proximity: What happened nearby is more newsworthy than what happened elsewhere, all else being equal; also, what happens to local people in faraway locales is more newsworthy than what happens to people who live in those faraway locales, all else being equal.

Significance/Importance: What has a direct effect on us—financially, legally, emotionally, governmentally—is more newsworthy than the alternative. For example, an increase in the price of gasoline will have more significance to most people than a hike in the price of titanium or ostrich meat. What happens to children typically matters more than the same events happening to adults. A trend showing higher incidence of breast cancer is more newsworthy than evidence of a higher incidence of bird feeders being raided by squirrels.

Confrontation/Conflict: When two forces are in conflict, be they a person or people against others (such as a union strike against a company, or two teams battling it out at a sporting event), against oneself (overcoming a physical disability to achieve something great), against nature (a community's need to increase sources of fresh water in the face of a dwindling supply) or against fate (people having to put off retirement because of the drop in the stock market), the conflict or the struggle makes for news.

Prominence: Things that happen to someone with great stature or notoriety matter more to the community overall than the same thing happening to a relatively unknown person who lives a block over. If some guy chokes on a pretzel and loses consciousness but survives without serious injury, it's not news—unless the guy choking on the pretzel is the president of the United States. The same is true for prominent places and prominent things. A small plane crashing into an abandoned warehouse along the Mississippi River is not as newsworthy as its crashing into St. Louis' Gateway Arch.

Unusualness or Change: Unless there's an interesting trend at work, we do not do stories about the status quo. It's the unusual, the change, the break from status quo that interests most people and warrants a story. As the adage goes, thousands of airplanes taking off and landing safely each day isn't news. The one that crashes is.

Human Interest/Humor: Human interest may involve trends engaged in by entire cultures or details of one person's daily life, or just something funny that happened that day. It may not belong in the first two segments of the newscast, but if it's interesting to people, it's worth a story.

Now you're ready to tackle the first four steps of writing any television news story, irrespective of story format (more on that later). The four steps are:

1. **Read**: Read the information carefully.

2. **Comprehend**: Make certain you understand all the information as well as the context—how do various facts relate to each other, how does the information relate to what came before, how does it relate to the people involved?

3. **Sort, Arrange, Simplify**: Note which facts are essential, important or interesting, and which are relatively unimportant, keeping in mind the audience, the amount of time allotted for the story (more on that later) and what visuals and sound are available (more later on that, as well).

4. **Think**: Distill this story to its bare essentials to tell the story in the most simple, understandable way without sacrificing interesting detail. Think about the best way to tell the story.

We aren't dealing with visuals or sound as yet. Those will become part of the process later.

With all this in mind, you will

5. Only then begin to **write:**
   - Create a lead
   - Consider potential story structure outline
   - Consider potential conclusions
   - Write the story (reading it aloud)
   - Rewrite the story (reading it aloud).

As you gain more experience, this process will become much more organic, with steps shifting in order and overlapping. However, this is a good general model with which to begin. Let's turn now to creating the lead.

The Lead

The lead is the most important part of the news story in any medium, and television is no exception. The lead simultaneously must accomplish two equally important goals: First, pique the interest of the viewer, and second, lay a foundation for understanding the story.

With the advent of the remote control, many viewers demonstrate great ease in pointing, pressing and surfing on if they aren't interested. In television news, this means you must immediately capture the attention and interest of the viewers or you risk losing them. Not a good option. One job of the lead is to tell the viewers why they should care, why this story matters to them—get them curious to know more.

At the same time, you need to frame the story, giving a sense of some of the story's important elements. You set an understandable base from which to build. To do this, you first must organize the information in your mind, always considering your audience. What will the viewers find important or interesting? What will have the greatest appeal or greatest effect on their lives? It's important to find an audience connection or hook for your lead—phrasing the lead to relate or connect the story to the viewer, to include that bit of information that makes the lead (and the story, as a result) more relevant to their lives and their interests.

Length of Leads

Do not attempt to tell the entire story in the lead. In fact, you should include only a few major aspects of one key point in the lead—remember, one main thought per sentence. If the lead sentence is too long, break it down into two sentences. In fact, in television news, you can often consider the first two sentences together to represent the lead of the story.

> A man crossing a downtown street today miraculously escaped injury when he was struck by an empty cab that had slipped into reverse when the driver left the engine running to mail a letter at a curbside mailbox.

This lead is so overloaded it will never get off the ground. The writer tried to tell most of the story in the first sentence. That's the wrong approach in television. Break it down into two or three sentences, remembering to give only one main point per sentence.

> A man crossing a downtown street today is lucky to be alive and unhurt following a bizarre accident.
>
> The man was walking to his office this morning when a taxi traveling backwards slammed into him.
>
> No one was driving the cab.
>
> Police say the driver . . .

Do you see the difference? Set up the story with the lead, then use the lead as a springboard to tell the rest of the story.

Story Focus and Leads

The focus of your television news story is the point or points you want viewers to understand. If you are using wire copy as a source of information for a story, your job is to cull from the wire copy the information that will interest your viewers. You put that information into context by defining a focus. Let's see how the focus plays into how you might structure the story, and how you might approach the lead. Here's a wire copy story from Capitol Hill.

> (WASHINGTON)—The fight over Medicare may be the biggest and most controversial ever seen in Congress. That's what House Minority Leader Nancy Pelosi is promising. But House Speaker Dennis Hastert says the Republican mission is to preserve, protect and strengthen the health program for the elderly.
>
> House Republicans released a 59-page summary of their plan this morning. They offered no detailed accounting on whether their figures add up, but they promise the numbers in a few days.
>
> The Republican outline does include some details—such as a provision designed to eliminate fraud in the Medicare system. Also the summary says that premiums for all seniors will rise faster than under current law—and will triple for those whose income exceeds 100-thousand dollars.

Identify the wire copy writer's focus. The first sentence seems to focus on the controversy ahead that will pit Republicans and Democrats in a political battle over Medicare. The story begins with a political angle about the anticipated fight on Capitol Hill. The writer then introduces the Republican Medicare plan summary and its details. It's a fine story aimed, perhaps, at those political junkies who enjoy watching Congress slug it out, but it's too long and too detailed for television news. The television news writer must cut some information to focus the story for his or her viewers. But which information? It will depend on the audience.

Suppose the audience were elderly. The news writer would look for a lead that would appeal to elderly viewers interested in Medicare but perhaps not as interested in the political scene. The story might focus on Republicans' plans for Medicare.

> Medicare could get more expensive for some Americans.
> Republican lawmakers outlined their ideas for the U-S health care plan for the elderly this morning.
> It calls for seniors to pay higher premiums—up to three times higher for those making more than 100 thousand dollars a year.

Think about the information the news writer left out:

- The House Minority Leader promises that the fight over Medicare may be the biggest and most controversial ever seen in Congress.
- The release ran 59 pages.
- Republicans offered no detailed accounting of their figures, but promise those numbers in a few days.
- There is a provision designed to eliminate fraud in the Medicare system.
- Republicans say their mission is to preserve, protect and strengthen the Medicare system.

Admittedly, a younger, more political audience might find this story uninteresting or disappointing, but the story serves its purpose for an older audience that's concerned about Medicare. The news writer identified the interests and concerns of his or her audience by considering the audience hook, considering what the audience would relate to or find interesting. Then he or she focused the story for the audience.

Now suppose the same story airs on a news station in Chicago. The House Speaker is from Illinois. A Chicago audience might be interested in what Hastert is saying and doing in Washington, D.C., so a news writer in Chicago might have a different focus for the story:

> House Speaker Hastert may be facing one of his biggest political battles since leaving Illinois for Capitol Hill.
> House Republicans this morning released a summary of their Medicare plan.
> Republicans and Democrats would have to agree on the GOP proposals for them to become law.
> And Democrats hint that isn't likely.

Again, the news writer leaves out what might seem an alarming amount of information:

- The House Minority Leader states that the fight over Medicare may be the biggest and most controversial ever seen in Congress. (Although the news writer alludes to this statement in the lead and again in the final sentence.)
- The release ran 59 pages.
- Republicans offered no detailed accounting of their figures but promise those numbers in a few days.
- Details in the summary, including the provision designed to eliminate fraud in the Medicare system, plans to raise premiums for all seniors faster than under current law, and plans to triple premiums for those whose income exceeds 100 thousand dollars.

• Hastert says his party's mission is to preserve, protect and strengthen the health care plan for the elderly.

Again, some audiences might find this story uninteresting or disappointing, but members of a Chicago audience may feel it addresses their interests and serves their needs. Of course, don't recklessly throw out wire copy information, but consider your audience, find a focus for stories and make reasoned decisions about the information you include in your stories.

Back to the Lead

By looking for the news hook, that aspect that will grab your audience, you define a focus. You separate information that should be included in a story from that which shouldn't. You have a general plan for the direction your story will take based on your viewers' interests and concerns. Now, you're ready to pick up a pen or sit at a keyboard.

Types of Leads

Some writers make great effort to classify leads into a broad range of categories: freak event, parody, well-known expression, metaphor, staccato, and the list goes on. In addition, different writers may use the same term to refer to different types of leads or use different terms to refer to the same type. However, let's look at some of the basic lead types with which you should be familiar.

Hard Lead. This is the most basic approach to a lead—just the facts. In general, this type of lead works best for breaking news that needs the story introduced in a factual, straightforward manner.

> The state legislature is considering whether to raise the sales tax by a half cent.

This lead is basic, straightforward and cuts right to the chase.

Soft or Summary Lead. This lead begins with the effect of or potential reaction to the story, drawing the audience in through a softer approach.

> Trips to the grocery store soon may get more expensive. The state legislature is considering whether to raise the sales tax by half a cent.

As you might have noted, you can often write a soft (or summary) lead by adding the statement of what the story is about to the beginning of a hard lead.

About four out of five of your leads will fall into these first two categories. You can rarely go wrong with a clean, well-written hard or soft (summary) lead.

Umbrella or Multiple Lead. This lead can introduce several stories with a common theme or a single story with several parts.

> The state legislature is considering raising the sales tax, cutting education funding, and laying off some state workers.

Your story can then expand on each of these elements in turn.

Throwaway Lead. A throwaway lead is a sentence fragment. We often converse this way, so it's fine to use it from time to time so long as you don't overdo it.

> Bad news for consumers in our state. The legislature is considering raising the sales tax by a half a cent.

Suspense and Delayed Leads. As we will discuss in more detail, in general, the best way to start is with the latest aspect. Then tell the story chronologically. Sometimes, however, it may work well to save the latest or more interesting aspect until the end. What might be considered the lead element is held until the close to create a better story. Saving the punch line for the conclusion can give a story more vitality. This is called a suspense lead, in which you tell the story chronologically from beginning to end. This approach can work well for features.

> Sam Peterson grew up the adopted son of middle-class parents in Dallas. He grew up an only child, and says he lived a full and happy life during childhood. But he always wondered who his birth mother was. He was determined to find her one day, but his adoptive parents had no information on who she was. So Sam began his search.
>
> Sam attended college and eventually earned a master's degree in social work from the University of Texas. Sam began to work as a counselor in Austin, slowly building his clientele. A year after he began, a woman in her mid-40s named Jennifer Sheffield became a client. Over the next few weeks, Jennifer discussed issues she was facing. Among them—the guilt she felt over giving her first child up for adoption. She was 18, it happened during her freshman year in college, and she didn't know what else to do. She wanted to contact her son, but was afraid of how he would react. Sam asked if Jennifer remembered her son's birthday. She did—June 8th, 1974. That was Sam's birthday. She went on to say she learned that the adoptive couple were named Bruce and Maggie Peterson and lived in Dallas. Jennifer had just named Sam's adoptive parents. That's when Sam realized that the birth mother he had searched so long for was sitting in the chair opposite him.

The story has the effect it does because the writer saved the "lead" for the end of the story. The writer could have led with something like,

> A lifelong search for an Austin man's birth mother is over. Austin therapist Sam Peterson, who was adopted, discovered his birth mother was one of his clients.

But it doesn't have quite the effect, does it? This method is good to use from time to time, but never more than once per newscast. Also, a note here on conclusions: A suspense lead necessarily is coupled with what's known as a punch line conclusion.

Another feature approach is to personalize and start the story with background. This extended lead form is called a delayed lead, as shown in the following example.

> Norma Costillo works as a secretary in the state department of transportation. Costillo has worked for the agency for seven years. A single mother of three, she supports her family on the 19-hundred dollars she brings home each month. But yesterday afternoon, Costillo learned she'll be losing her job—a victim of state cutbacks.

Whatever approach you take in looking for your lead, always ask yourself, what is this story about? Why is it newsworthy? What is the main point? What is the focus for my audience?

In searching for a strong lead, don't exaggerate the story. Don't distort it. Don't misrepresent it. Do look for the most compelling way to draw viewers into the story. Your first words may determine whether viewers stay tuned. The lead will introduce your focus, based on your knowledge of your viewers. It will tell viewers what's in it for them.

Which Way to Lead?

Every story potentially has dozens of leads. In searching for a lead, don't get bogged down with the classification scheme discussed above. Just look for a good lead that works. The television news writer's job is to find the best one. To illustrate and expand, let's start with something simple, a story with which most people are familiar—for instance, the story of Cinderella. As a refresher, the events of the story are as follows:

> A young woman in Kingdomville named Cinderella was forbidden by her stepmother to attend a ball at a local palace. A fairy godmother appeared the night of the ball to provide the young woman with a dress and transportation until a midnight curfew. The young woman went to the ball and danced with the host, a prince. Rushing to meet her curfew, the young woman left behind a glass slipper. The prince vowed to find the woman, return her shoe and marry her. The prince conducted a door-to-door search. He found Cinderella scrubbing floors at her stepmother's house. The prince and Cinderella marry.

Now explore leads for a story that will air on the day of Cinderella's wedding.

• In the case of a local story, where it happened or to whom it happened may hook viewers. If they're familiar with the people involved or with the location, they may stay tuned.

> A Kingdomville orphan became a princess today.

• How about a half-sentence that piques the viewers' interest? A lead does not have to be a full sentence, but you must follow quickly with information that tells the story.

> A rags-to-riches story . . .
> The kingdom's prince found his new princess scrubbing floors.

• Would a cleverly worded question work well? Asking viewers a question and then answering it can involve them in the story.

> Do dreams really come true?
> They did today for a Kingdomville woman.

Warning: Leads using questions are easy to write and can easily become a trap for new writers. Keep in mind that your job as a television news writer is to *answer* questions rather than *ask* them. In addition, you may pose a question in which your viewer has absolutely no interest, which can be deadly in this day of remote controls:

> Story lead: "Ever wonder what it's like to work in a carnival?"
> Viewer response: "No." Click.

Use question leads rarely and with restraint.

• Some stories can grab viewers when told chronologically, leading with background information first.

> The prince searched door-to-door for the woman he met at a ball
> last month.
> Today, that woman is at his side at the altar.

• Other stories may be advanced by telling viewers what will happen next, tomorrow, later.

> The kingdom's new princess will move into the palace tomorrow.

• In rare cases, you can lead a story with information from another story with which viewers may be more familiar. But be very certain that the information relates to the story you're writing and that it's information with which your viewers are familiar.

> First it happened to Britain's Princess Di.
> Now it's happened to a local woman named Cinderella.

Try the same exercise with a news story from a wire service.

> (SAN DIEGO)—A bomb scare caused the evacuation of a 10-
> story office building in downtown San Diego Monday afternoon,
> according to authorities.
> The evacuation was ordered after a security guard received an
> anonymous phone call from a man claiming he planted a bomb timed
> to go off at 3 p.m., police said. The caller did not identify himself and
> did not give any reason for the bomb at the Bank of America Towers,

said a police spokesman. The security guard notified the police department.

Police officers went from office to office, evacuating workers while a bomb unit using German shepherd bomb-sniffing dogs searched the building. The bomb-sniffing dog unit was added to the police department two months ago to deal with the threat of terrorism. This was the unit's first assignment. No bomb was found, say police.

The police department declared the building to be safe after the two-hour search, and workers were allowed to return to their offices.

Explore possible leads for the story that will air in Monday night's newscast, several hours after the scare.

- Find a local lead:

A bomb threat forces an evacuation at the Bank of America
Towers.

Presumably, a local San Diego audience is familiar with the building. By identifying the office building by name, the writer grabs local viewers' attention.

- Find a throwaway or half-sentence lead:

A bomb scare today . . .
It happened downtown at the Bank of America Towers.

The dramatic half-sentence lead gets viewers' attention and piques their interest. They stay tuned to hear more.

- Find a lead with a question:

You think you had a rough day at work?

The writer would follow with the story of the rough day office workers at the Bank of America Towers had. The question grabs viewers' attention and invites them to become involved in the story.

- Find a lead using background information:

The police department created its special bomb-sniffing dog unit
two months ago.
Today, the German shepherds were on the job for the first time.

The television news writer sets the stage for the story of the bomb threat, using information from the past about the creation of the bomb-sniffing dog unit.

- Find a lead that advances the story:

Some downtown workers will show up at the office tomorrow
hoping it won't be another day like today.

The writer tells the viewer what will happen. He or she will follow with information about what already happened.

• Find a lead that uses related information:

> Many U-S office workers felt a little less safe after the September
> 11th attack on the World Trade Center in New York.
> Some San Diego workers share that feeling tonight.

The television news writer leads with an event with which most viewers are familiar to create a mood for viewers. Then the writer introduces the information about what happened in San Diego today.

Not every story lends itself to the examples above. Sometimes, you may not have information available to write a background lead, for example. The first step is to be familiar with the many ways to approach a news lead. The goal is to find the most creative, most dramatic and most effective way to interest viewers in the story.

The Latest Lead

Most often, the strongest lead uses the latest information available. Remember that viewers have access to television news around the clock. They watch television expecting to see the latest, most up-to-date, happening-right-now news. A wire service carried the following story early one Sunday morning:

> (POINT LOOKOUT, Md.)—Officials in Maryland say two people
> died after a charter fishing boat took on water and sank in the lower
> Chesapeake Bay late Saturday night.
> Rescue boats and helicopters plucked 23 people from the rough,
> 50-degree water. Officials say survivors had been stranded for two
> hours.
> The charter fishing boat, known as a head boat or party boat, sank
> about four miles from shore. Seas in the area were reported about six
> feet at the time, with gusty 20-mph winds.
> An investigation being conducted into the cause of the sinking is
> focusing on the weather conditions, according to authorities.

This is a dramatic story but, as written, it's a "last-night" story. The wire copy writer relies on the verb *say* to bring present tense writing to a description of past events. The television news writer's job is to find the "today lead" that tells viewers what is happening now. Do you see the lead? Read again the last sentence of the wire copy story. What's happening *today*? The investigation. What's the latest development? The investigation's focus. The television news writer leads with information that the investigation is focusing on the weather. He or she uses the information to construct a lead that offers viewers the latest developments in a conversational way, using present tense and active voice.

> Investigators want to know if bad weather is to blame for a boat
> accident that killed two people.
> It happened last night off the coast of Southern Maryland.

> Officials say a charter fishing boat took on water and sank about four miles from shore.
>
> Crews used boats and helicopters to rescue 23 people.
>
> Survivors battled rough water, gusty winds and cold temperatures for as long as two hours before being rescued.

Viewers get the whole story. The television news writer follows up the lead (the investigation's focus) with details about the accident and rescue. The television news writer offers viewers who are seeing the story for the first time information they need. Viewers who have been following the developments of the story get the latest, most up-to-the-minute information. Everyone is satisfied. (Actually, don't count on it. *Everyone* is one of those red-flag words television news writers avoid because they are so infrequently accurate. Rarely is everyone satisfied with anything.)

Weak Leads

In your search for the latest information, avoid the "continues" trap. Telling viewers that an investigation, fighting in Bosnia or the search for a killer *continues* offers them no new information. If the fishing boat story makes it to a Monday newscast two days after it happened late Saturday night, the television news writer could not rely on an ongoing investigation to grab viewers' attention. The lead below relies on *continues*, propped up by *today*. It uses present tense. It sounds new. But it's lazy. And it won't fool viewers who are looking for the latest information.

> The investigation continues today into a charter fishing boat accident off the coast of southern Maryland.

The warning applies also to using *still* or leading with a countdown.

> Investigators today are *still* looking into the cause of a charter fishing boat accident off the coast of southern Maryland.

or

> Day two of the investigation into a charter fishing boat accident off the coast of southern Maryland.

Both of these leads are lazy. Your job as a news writer is to find the latest newsworthy development. The fact that an investigation *continues* or is in *day two* is not newsworthy. Viewers deserve up-to-the-minute information. If they don't get it from you, they'll change the channel to find it somewhere else.

On the subject of bad leads, consider another. Some news writers lead with words that tell viewers how to react to a story before telling them the story.

> A *horrifying* night for boaters in Maryland . . .
>
> A *sad* story tonight from the city's west side . . .
>
> *Good* news today for homeowners . . .

You want to convey the tone of the story with the facts of the story itself, not with setups in the lead that instruct viewers how to react. The leads above make up the first of a list of weak leads. When you're looking for a lead, pay attention to the following leads to *avoid*:

• Avoid leads that use old information. The advice also applies to leads that try to disguise old information with words such as *continues*, *still*, *another*, *once more* and *again*. And don't forget countdowns (*day four, week 13* . . .). They're bad leads too.

• Avoid leads that use words that tell viewers how to react to a story, such as *sad, happy, good, bad, interesting, disturbing, upsetting,* and so forth.

• Avoid leads that state the obvious, including leads that use the words *in a new development.* You should be able to hook viewers with the development itself. Let your viewers count on you always for the new developments. Also, identifying a *new development* could imply that the rest of the information, which is not specifically identified as new, is old news. Finally, the phrase *new development* is redundant. Developments are always new. That's why they're called developments. You get the idea. Avoid the phrase *new development* in your news stories. The same applies to leads that use *is making news* or *is in the news.* Viewers watching your news realize the subjects of your stories are *in the news* or are *making news.* That's the point of the newscast. Also watch out for *in other news* between stories.

• Avoid leads that use the names of people or places your viewers don't know. If a name in a lead means nothing to viewers, they won't be interested in the story. If viewers lose interest, you lose viewers. If you lose too many viewers, you lose your job. People who are unknown are most likely in the news because of an event or occurrence that involves them. The news is the event or occurrence, not the unknown person. The television news writer even may decide to limit the story to the event, never mentioning the unknown person by name.

> A runaway school bus leaves 30 children shaken, but safe.
> The brakes on the bus failed.
> The bus driver managed to bring the bus to a safe stop.

Another option is to "introduce" the unknown person and define his or her role in the story before telling viewers the person's name. By the time viewers hear the name, it means something to them.

> A *county school bus driver* becomes a hero to the children on her route.
> *Curlin Sullivan* managed to bring her bus to a safe stop after the brakes failed.

This is advice not only about "unknowns," such as the county bus driver who appears in the news because of an event that happened to her. It is advice about "little knowns" too. Do viewers really know the name of the county tax commissioner? The school board representative from the fifth district? Even the U.S. Senator from Idaho? You hope the name means something to Idaho viewers, but can you expect it to mean anything to Massachusetts viewers? Probably not. If the name is not well-known to viewers, set up the story to allow for an introduction first. Don't lead with names viewers don't know.

> A U.S. Senator from Texas announces she'll run for re-election.
> Kay Bailey Hutchison says she'll kick off her re-election
> campaign tomorrow in Houston.

• Avoid leads that assume knowledge. If viewers don't know the name of the school board representative from the fifth district, can they be expected to know or be surprised to learn that he or she is stepping down from the position? Watch for words and phrases such as *in a surprise move, as expected, long-awaited* and *as predicted.* These words and phrases assume knowledge. It's a bad idea to make assumptions about what viewers predict. It's a bad idea to make assumptions about what viewers expect. And it's a bad idea to make assumptions about what viewers will find surprising or have been awaiting. Most viewers come to a newscast with neither expectations nor predictions about the stories they'll see. When a news writer starts with *in a surprising move*, he or she loses viewers for whom the news is not particularly surprising. The implication might be that informed viewers may be surprised. Because the viewer isn't, he or she is not informed. A sure way to lose viewers is to insult them this way.

• Avoid leads that use *no* and *not.* In general, rework negative leads to be positive. Negative leads can cause confusion for viewers. *Not* and *no* are small words that viewers can easily miss if they are doing something else while they watch television. Worse still, news anchors who have not read their stories in advance are at risk of skipping over small words such as *no* and *not*, changing the meaning of sentences dramatically.

> **Negative lead:** Organizers say they will not cancel tomorrow's
> free speech rally outside the offices of the county libraries.
> **Positive lead:** Organizers say tomorrow's free speech rally will
> go ahead as scheduled.

> **Negative lead:** Homeowners admit the passage of the new tax
> comes as no surprise.
> **Positive lead:** Homeowners say they expected the new tax to pass.

• Avoid leads that start with a quotation. Leading with a quotation is a fine idea for print journalists, but it's a lousy idea for broadcast writers. Viewers can't see quotation marks. When faced with a quotation as a lead, viewers make the logical assumption that the words and ideas of the quotation are those of the anchor. The attribution later causes confusion.

> I will not run for president.
> That's the word from Senator Hillary Clinton.

The viewer sees the news anchor announcing he or she will not run for president. Not until the second sentence does the viewer hear that it's not the news anchor, but Senator Hillary Clinton, who's not running for the nation's highest office. Starting stories with a quotation also puts story information before attribution. Remember that placing attribution before information keeps stories conversational, accurate and easy to understand for viewers.

• Avoid leads that start with a dependent clause. Television news writers work to avoid dependent clauses. Television news writers really work to avoid dependent clauses in leads. Television news writers really, really work to avoid dependent clauses at the start of the lead. Stick with subject–verb–object sentence structure and avoid dependent clauses to keep writing conversational and help viewers better understand your stories.

• Avoid leads that back into a story or don't contribute to the telling. For example, don't lead with something like

> The Spring school board gathered for its monthly meeting last
> night.

The fact that they met is not news. Tell the viewer what they did at the meeting that is news.

• Avoid leads that start with a date. If your story involves an upcoming event, the date will not be the most interesting aspect of the story. Plus, those viewers who decide they are interested won't remember when it takes place. Tell about the event, then include when the event occurs at the end of the story.

• Avoid leads that hype or rely on clichés. You want to be accurate and credible, and you don't want to bore the audience with bad writing.

• Avoid leads that use forms of the verb *to be*. I mentioned this earlier about writing in general, and it bears repeating in our discussion on leads. It's not wrong. It's just weak. The verb *to be* is inactive. Look for verbs that express *action* rather than *being*. These verbs will bring your stories to life. These verbs will interest and excite viewers.

> **Less active:** The author's latest book is an exploration of bygone
> days.
> **More active:** The author's latest book explores bygone days.

Remember that passive voice is constructed with the verb *to be*. If you avoid the verb *to be* in your leads, you also protect yourself against using passive voice. And avoiding the verb *to be* helps protect against leads that use *there are* and *there is*. Most often these words can be omitted for cleaner, more quickly paced and more active television news writing.

> **Less active:** There is a new study that says Americans are eating
> less.
> **More active:** A new study says Americans are eating less.

Spend time composing your lead sentences (you can consider the first two sentences part of the same lead) because they're the most important sentences you will write. The time you spend on it will be rewarded by viewers who stay tuned to hear more.

The Middle

A television news writer starts strong with a lead that grabs or hooks viewers. It is the "sell." Then the writer delivers the goods, following the lead with the "tell." Most students of journalism know the five W's—*Who, What, When, Where* and *Why*. Add an H—*How*. These are the six questions journalists traditionally strive to answer in their stories. Your job as a television news writer is to answer questions.

Answering Viewers' Questions

You may not always have an answer to each question. The answers to *how* and *why*, especially, can be hard to come by. Sometimes, it will be a good idea to tell viewers why some of their questions aren't answered.

> Police won't say how the bank robber made his getaway but confirm he escaped with 50-thousand dollars.
> Only the gunman knows what drove him to open fire on the restaurant's lunchtime crowd, and investigators say he isn't talking.

In other cases, the answers are implied so that you don't have to spell them out for viewers.

> Three armed men robbed a convenience store on the south side today

You don't have to add, "They apparently wanted the money." It's implied. Time is always of the essence in television news writing. Brief is better. Each question does not require a full-sentence answer. In the example above, for instance, the television news writer answers all six questions in only 12 words: Who? *Three men.* What? *Robbed a convenience store.* When? *Today.* Where? *On the south side.* Why? (*implied answer*) *Needed or wanted money.* How? *With weapons (the men are armed).*

Obviously, a single sentence is not a complete story. Answering who, what, when, where, why and how is the minimum goal. Remember you may not always have answers to all six questions, and neither should you try to answer them all within the lead, but you should answer those you can in the middle of the story, including details that flesh out the story to make it important, interesting and memorable for viewers.

> Three armed men robbed a convenience store on the south side today.
> Police say it happened in the middle of the day in front of dozens of witnesses.
> No one was hurt.
> But investigators say the store cashier is badly shaken.
> Witnesses say the robbers threatened customers and the cashier with a semiautomatic rifle.
> Investigators say the men got away with more than two thousand dollars.

Can the news writer do better? Probably. The lead is past tense. The word *today* and the phrase *in the middle of the day* are repetitive and waste precious television time. The story uses passive voice to say no one *was hurt*. The television news writer might look for another lead, still making sure to answer all the viewers' questions.

> Police are looking for three armed men who pulled off a midday robbery at a southside convenience store.
> It happened in front of dozens of witnesses.
> The gunmen hurt no one.
> But police say the store's cashier is badly shaken.
> Witnesses say the robbers threatened customers and the cashier with a semiautomatic rifle.
> Police say the men got away with more than two thousand dollars.

One of the worst mistakes a television news writer can make is to raise questions in a story without answering them.

> A local teen is back in school.
> Eric Lawrence says dozens of his classmates at Fairlawn High welcomed him at the school's main entrance when he got off the bus.
> Lawrence thanked classmates for their cards and letters at an early-morning assembly.
> Cheerleaders led students in a deafening round of Three Cheers.
> Lawrence calls the rest of his day business as usual.
> And, like most students, he's already complaining about homework.

The story is filled with colorful details. The writer answers *who* (Eric Lawrence), *what* (is in school), *when* (today), *where* (at Fairlawn High) and *how* (by bus). But what about *why*? The writer's lead raises a big question, "Why is Eric *back* in school? Where was he before returning to school?" The writer raises the question repeatedly, but never answers it.

Review of What's In and What's Out.

All journalists strive to answer the basic questions. As we've already discussed, print and wire copy writers have a luxury television news writers do not—the luxury of time. Print and wire copy stories can fill paragraphs and pages with detailed answers to readers' questions. Television news stories must be short to keep viewers' attention. Think back to the exercise in an earlier chapter in which you read the newspaper story out loud. Remember the amount of detail? Remember how quickly the listeners lost interest? Time constraints on television news stories virtually guarantee writers will be forced to cut some information.

What is acceptable information to leave out of your television news stories? How much is too much to leave out? The answers come with experience. As you become more comfortable writing news stories, you become more confident of the decisions you make about including and omitting information. As you come to know your viewers better, you come to recognize the information that will interest them. As you better educate yourself about the top issues affecting your viewers, you become better able to recognize the information that impacts and relates or adds context to those issues.

Out: Unnecessary Time References.

Viewers, quite rightly, expect stories in a newscast to be stories that happened today or tonight. Therefore, news writers have no reason to tell viewers the story happened today or tonight in every lead of every television story. There is much less reason for them to tell viewers twice and even more often within the same story. And there are reasons for writers not to do it. For one, it is annoying to viewers. When viewers become annoyed, they become distracted. When viewers become distracted, they change the channel. The present tense and words like *now* when used accurately offer time references without reliance on the overused *tonight* and *today*. When you do use or need a time reference, place "when" after "what." Put another way, place the information that dates the story after the verb. If the most exciting thing you can find to write about a news story is that it happened tonight—if the time reference warrants a place before the verb—you might want to reconsider including the story in your newscast.

Out: Unnecessary Words.

As long as you're omitting unnecessary time references, how about examining your writing for other unnecessary words? Start with the word *that*.

> **OK:** City council members say *that* voter turnout was heavy.
> **Better:** City council members say voter turnout was heavy.

> **OK:** A new study shows *that* joggers are less likely to get heart attacks.
> **Better:** A new study shows joggers are less likely to get heart attacks.

Now consider omitting *which*, *of*, *but that*, *the fact that* and *in terms of* from your stories. Read copy aloud. If it sounds wordy, omit words. If the copy makes sense without the extra words, get rid of them. Needless words make stories longer and waste valuable television time. Needless words make viewers work harder to understand the story, and needless words undermine the clarity and force of television news writing. Less is better.

Out: Clichés.

Select words carefully, avoiding clichés. As we've discussed, clichés are expressions that have become trite through overuse. Some phrases sound like good television writing precisely because you're accustomed to hearing them on television. You want to avoid these phrases. The fact that they're familiar is a good indication they are being overused.

Out: Unnecessary Names and Places. Some of the easiest decisions you'll make about omitting information are those about omitting unnecessary names, titles and locations. Print and wire copy writers can be very thorough in their identification of people involved in the stories they cover. They present this identification for readers, not for viewers.

> (WASHINGTON)—Know that theory that women think they
> must suppress anger? Forget it. Women do let off steam, but typically
> at their husbands instead of the person who really angered them. And
> if they cry when angry, that's normal and healthy, a new study con-
> cludes.
> Sandra Thomas, director of nursing research at the University of
> Tennessee, performed what researchers call the first large investigation
> of women's anger, studying 535 women ages 25 to 66.

As you write a television news story, you know you will not write "Sandra Thomas, director of nursing research at the University of Tennessee, says. . . ." It is not conversational, it is too much information to present to viewers at once and the name is unfamiliar to viewers. You can break up the identification.

> A director of nursing research at the University of Tennessee is
> smashing stereotypes about women and anger.
> Sandra Thomas says women do express their anger.
> Her study of 535 women . . .

Or you can omit the name or title or both. Does it affect viewers' understanding of the story that Sandra Thomas is the author? You could argue that it doesn't. You could leave Thomas out of your television news story.

> A new study is smashing stereotypes about women and anger.
> The survey of 535 women shows that many do express their
> anger.

or

> A new study is smashing stereotypes about women and anger.
> The University of Tennessee study shows that women do express
> their anger.

Do you cheat your viewers out of any vital information? Most writers would say no. Do you still effectively tell viewers about the results of the study? Most would say yes.

Whether you include the location of the news event you're writing about depends on your audience, too. Suppose you are writing about a house fire in Lancaster, Pa. If you are writing for a Lancaster audience, it may be important to tell viewers that the fire happened on the city's south side. You may decide to include also the address of the house that went up in flames. Local Lancaster viewers are familiar with the city. They might want to know the exact location of the fire.

But suppose you are writing a television news story for viewers who live in Philadelphia. The interests and concerns of a Philadelphia audience are different from those of a Lancaster audience. You most likely would not include the precise address of the fire. It may be enough to tell Philadelphia viewers that the fire happened in Lancaster.

Now suppose you are writing for a national audience. Some of your viewers live across the country in places such as California and Oregon. Their interests and concerns are different, as is their knowledge of northeastern cities and states. You might need to tell a national audience that the fire happened in Lancaster, Pennsylvania. Or you might decide that saying the fire happened in Pennsylvania is enough for them to know. Certainly, the information that it happened on the city's south side is of little interest to most members of a national audience.

If your audience is worldwide, the information that the fire happened in Pennsylvania may be sufficient. Consider the following wire copy story from Switzerland:

> (DAENIKEN, Switzerland)—Six people died and about 15 were injured, some seriously, today in northern Switzerland in a major railway accident.
>
> A Federal Railways spokesman said a passenger train leaving Daeniken station in northern Switzerland during the early afternoon crashed into the jib of a crane that swung out into its path. The reason for the accident has not been established yet, but human error cannot be ruled out, according to the spokesman.
>
> A goods wagon at the front of the train, which was on its way to Romanshorn on Lake Constance from Biel, was derailed. Three following passenger cars were ripped open at window level.
>
> Rescue helicopters flew the seriously injured casualties to hospitals in Zurich, Berne and Basel, while less gravely hurt people were taken in ambulances to local hospitals. Police and fire services rushed to the scene.
>
> The crane was being used to lay new track on the line between the towns of Olten and Aarau in Solothurn canton. The crane driver was uninjured but is said to be suffering shock.
>
> The line was closed for three hours, forcing other trains to be diverted.

Are most American viewers familiar with Daeniken, Romanshorn, Basle, Olten and Aarau? Probably not. A U.S. audience may need to know only that the accident happened in northern Switzerland. The most idealistic of journalists might argue that it is the television news writer's job to educate his or her audience. But the purpose of this news story is not a lesson in geography. The purpose is to tell viewers about a devastating train wreck. The television news writer who includes city names that confuse viewers impedes their understanding of the news story.

A writer must also ensure that the story has a logical flow. Remember that you must tell the story clearly, answering all questions and filling all holes, the first time through. Once you've found a strong, creative lead, stop and think about where the story must go from there—although you have many options on what lead you'll use, once that lead is written you've set a certain direction for the flow of the story. As mentioned earlier, giving the latest then telling the story chronologically is a good way to go. However, if your story takes another approach, the information you provide must flow logically. The lead you choose will set your story on a given path or set of paths that must be followed. Each statement in the story will pose a question to the viewer, which must be answered, which may pose another question, and so on. If your story fails to flow logically, fails to follow that logical path, you'll simply have a jumbled mass of facts that will confuse your viewer.

> A group of Democratic state lawmakers is hiding out just across the Oklahoma border.
>
> The move comes in response to a Republican bill on the House floor.
>
> The bill would redraw districts to ensure more Republicans and fewer Democrats would be elected to the federal legislature.
>
> However, Texas House rules require at least 100 members be present on the floor to pass a bill.
>
> And being outside Texas means the 51 absent Democrats cannot be brought to Austin by state police.
>
> The lawmakers say they'll return home in a few days when the bill's deadline passes.

This story leads with

> A group of Democratic state lawmakers is hiding out just across the Oklahoma border.

This lead has established a starting point for your story. You can only take it in certain directions. Think about the next logical step. What would the viewer want to know next? You have to answer that question. In your next sentence, you have to begin to explain why they are hiding.

> The move comes in response to a Republican bill on the House floor.

You've begun to explain why, but in doing so have introduced another question. What is the bill? Now you have to explain what that bill is, and how it figures into the action by the Democrats.

> The bill would redraw districts to ensure more Republicans and fewer Democrats would be elected to the federal legislature.

Now your viewer understands the cause, but your viewer will now be wondering why the Democrats responded by fleeing the state.

> However, Texas House rules require at least 100 members be present on the floor to pass a bill.

> And being outside Texas means the 51 absent Democrats cannot
> be brought to Austin by state police.

Now your viewer knows why they left for Oklahoma. Next, you need to move to a conclusion of what the future holds, filling in the last hole.

> The lawmakers say they'll return home in a few days when the
> bill's deadline passes.

You can see a logical progression of this story. It follows a direction that was set by your lead. Your lead starts you at a particular place. You must then go through the important elements of the story, answering the questions that arise with each sentence you write.

Let's look at some other possible leads and what direction each would take your story.

> Texas state troopers are looking for a group of 51 Democratic
> lawmakers.

(The next sentence must say why they are looking.)

> Texas state troopers believe they know where a group of
> Democratic House members is hiding out.

(The next sentence must say where.)

> A group of Democrats has come up with a way to derail
> Republican plans to redistrict the state.

(The next sentence must say how.)

Always think in terms of the questions that will occur to your viewer, given the flow or path of your story. And always answer those questions. If you don't know the answer, state you don't know it, but always make some reference to it.

The End

The conclusion is the second most important part of the story. Many writers, in fact, craft a conclusion immediately after writing the lead and before writing the body of the story. It can be structured in various ways, depending on the goal of the writer. It can summarize the story by restating the key point or points. It can look to see what the future holds, telling where the story will be heading. It can give another, perhaps opposing, perspective on the story. It can be a good place to include additional, related or new facts to the story. And if you have written a suspense or delayed lead—that is, if you have told the story chronologically all the way through to save a punch line for the end—the conclusion will give the punch line of the story.

Whatever path to decide to follow, you must write a solid conclusion. Unlike print stories, the ends of which most readers never reach, television stories are designed to be viewed (and heard) all the way through. The conclusion is what you will leave your audience with. Because it is the last aspect of the story, it colors or frames the way the viewer remembers the story. Because of that, the conclusion is not only important but must be fair and balanced. One danger of the opposing point of view as a conclusion involves giving some group or position an unwarranted level of credibility or notoriety.

Having said all this, however, don't slip into the trap of feeling forced to add unnecessary information or commentary to the conclusion. Avoid ending with such promises as "We'll have more on this story later," or "We'll continue to follow this story and will bring you all the details," or "We'll update you on this story as details become available." These are unnecessary. Viewers should be able to count on you to follow stories that deserve following. They should be able to count on you to report developments as they become available. These are empty promises and a waste of precious television time.

Worse, they can be dangerous promises to make unless the writer happens also to be the producer of a later newscast. The television news writer rarely decides which stories are in a newscast. That is the job of a producer. When a news writer promises "more on this story later," he or she may have no way of making sure there actually will be more later. The television news writer who tacks any one of these lines onto the end of a story is making viewers a promise he or she may not be in a position to keep. In effect, the television news writer may be lying to viewers. Looking for a sure way to lose viewers? Lie to them.

Another ending that finds its way into television news stories is "back to you." What can be said about this? It's awful. It's right up there with "that's all from here." Neither adds anything to the story. Both use valuable television time for no apparent reason. End with a strong, warranted conclusion and move on.

Final Points

Some final points on writing the story. Use transitions. Transition words can show relationships, sequences, comparisons and contrasts. The use of transitions—*however, meanwhile, on the other hand, in contrast to, compared with, as a result* and a host of others—can improve clarity.

Be certain you have not mentally filled in holes that the viewer might be left with. As the writer, you'll tend to assume the audience knows certain basics. Don't. There's a good chance the audience doesn't. Write every story so that it can stand on its own, and make sure you haven't left holes in information or explanations that the viewer might need.

I've said this before, and I'll say it again: Variety is critical to maintaining audience interest. Vary types of leads, sentence length, sentence structure and story type and approach.

Say what you mean and mean what you say.

Finally, read your story aloud. Every story you'll ever write will sound brilliant in your head. The only way to know whether there are problems is to hear it, and the only way to hear it is to read your story aloud. You'll hear how the words sound and how the story overall sounds, you'll better know if it's logical and understandable, and it's the only way to know how long the story actually runs.

Putting It Together

Follow the process of writing a television news story using wire copy as a source and putting together the beginning, middle and end. Remember that rewriting wire copy is a proven method of developing news writing skills.

Step 1: Read the wire copy—Read it all the way through. Read every word. Don't be so eager to start writing that you fail to read all the information. The lead for your television story very well may appear at the end of the wire copy story. Read it all!

Step 2: Understand the wire copy—Reread confusing sentences. Try to understand the facts of the story. It's possible that the wire copy will have information in it that you don't understand. This is the information you will not use in your news story. If you don't understand it, how can you explain it to viewers? The temptation for many writers is to "lift" the information they don't understand, using wire copy word for word in their stories. This is a bad idea. Don't underestimate your intelligence. If the wire copy writing raises questions for you, chances are that it will for viewers too. If you don't understand it, chances are good that viewers won't either. If you lift the wire copy wording, you put yourself in an awkward position. When your producer or anchor asks what your news story means, you're left with one answer: "That's what the wire copy said." It's not a great answer. Television stations don't hire news writers to retype wire copy stories onto television script paper or into computerized scripting programs. They hire news writers to read, understand and use wire copy information to write original stories.

Step 3: Find and mark key facts in the wire copy—Mark them now. It will help you as you start writing. Mark the facts you know you need to include (*who, what, when, where, why* and *how*). Mark the facts for later reference when you check your completed television news story against the wire copy.

Step 4: Think before you write. Are you eager to write? Are you under deadline pressure? Are you tempted to skip Step 4? If you're not now, you will be at some time. Try not to give into the temptation. Step back from the wire copy. Think about the story. Mull over the facts. The minutes—even seconds, depending on your deadline—you spend in thought can save precious time and much frustration later. Some reporters make it a point to get up from the desk, walk from the newsroom to someplace else in the station and then back to the desk in the newsroom before writing the first word. The "distance" from the wire copy allows the writer to organize ideas. Once those ideas are organized, you'll begin. Create a lead. Consider potential story structure or outline. Consider potential conclusions. Write the story, reading it aloud. Rewrite the story, reading it aloud.

Try following Steps 1 through 4, using the wire copy account of the bomb threat in San Diego.

(SAN DIEGO)—A bomb scare caused the evacuation of a 10-story office building in downtown San Diego Monday afternoon, according to authorities.

The evacuation was ordered after a security guard received an anonymous phone call from a man claiming he planted a bomb timed to go off at 3 p.m., police said. The caller did not identify himself and did not give any reason for the bomb at the Bank of America Towers, said a police spokesman. The security guard notified the police department.

Police officers went from office to office, evacuating workers while a bomb unit using German shepherd bomb-sniffing dogs searched the building. The bomb-sniffing dog unit was added to the police department two months ago to deal with the threat of terrorism. This was the unit's first assignment. No bomb was found, say police.

The police department declared the building to be safe after the two-hour search, and workers were allowed to return to their offices.

After you've read the wire copy, understood it and marked it, think about ways your television news story will differ from the wire copy. Think about the four guidelines.

• **Words:** Think small and simple and clear. The wire copy account of the events doesn't have many words that you wouldn't use in conversation. Some writers might feel the word *notify* is overstated: "The security guard *notified* the police department." They might prefer the words *called* or *told*. The phrase *according to* also is removed from television news writing and replaced with *says, complains, blames* or some other more appropriate word.

• **Sentences:** Think short and simple and clear. The wire copy writer uses long sentences with more than one thought; the television news writer cuts sentence length to help viewers better understand the story. The wire copy writer uses dependent clauses; the television news writer eliminates dependent clauses.

• **Tense:** Use present or future when possible, but use them accurately. The wire copy writer uses past tense throughout to describe events that occurred in the past: *caused, ordered, notified, declared* and *allowed*. The television news writer will look for ways to use the present tense accurately.

• **Voice:** Write in active, not passive. The wire copy writer uses passive voice; the television news writer will rewrite for active voice.

Passive Voice versus Active Voice

The evacuation was ordered

versus

Police ordered the evacuation.

The bomb-sniffing dog unit was added.

versus

The police department added its bomb-sniffing dog unit.

No bomb was found.

versus

The bomb squad found no bomb.

The building was declared to be safe.

versus

The bomb squad (police) declared the building safe.

Think about other guidelines we've discussed. When writing the story for television, you will remain true to the facts of the story (accuracy). You will be fair (fairness). You will include all sides of the story, as applicable (balance). You will attribute information that is opinion or belongs to others. You also will attribute descriptions of events you did not witness or know to be true. You will introduce the source of information before the information (attribution).

Finally, think about selecting information you will include in the story, as discussed in this chapter. Find a focus that will interest viewers. Choose carefully the information you will use, with your viewers' interests and concerns in mind.

Step 5: Write—If you've got all that, you're ready to put pen to paper or, more likely, fingertips to keyboard. Start strong with a lead that will grab viewers' attention and introduce your focus. Follow up with information that answers viewers' questions. Omit unnecessary time references. If you use a time reference, place it after the verb. Omit unnecessary words. Select words carefully to avoid clichés. Your television news story might look something like this.

A bomb scare forces hundreds of downtown workers out of their offices.

Police say they ordered the evacuation at the Bank of America Towers after a security guard received a bomb threat.

The guard told police an anonymous caller claimed he planted a bomb set to go off at 3 this afternoon.

Police brought in special bomb-sniffing dogs.

But a two-hour search failed to turn up any bomb.

Step 6: Test the story—Compare the story with the wire copy to make sure it's accurate. Have you included information that will appeal to your viewers? Do you have good reasons for omitting some information? Test the story.

• Does the lead offer viewers the latest information? Yes. The event itself.

• Does the story answer viewers' questions? Yes. Who? *Hundreds of office workers.* What? *Are evacuated.* When? *This afternoon.* Where? *At the Bank of America Towers downtown.* Why? *Because of a bomb threat.* How? *Ordered by police to leave the building.*

• Does the story raise questions it fails to answer? No.

• Is the story accurate? Yes. Facts from the wire copy are the same as those appearing in the story.

• Is the writing conversational? Yes. The story is "written for the ear." The vocabulary is conversational. Sentences are short and direct. Always read stories aloud. If you, as the writer, stumble over words, you can be sure anchors will too. If you, as the writer, get confused, you can be sure viewers will too. Read stories aloud to listen for problem spots. When you find them, rewrite.

• Does the story show immediacy with present tense verbs? Yes. "A bomb scare *forces* hundreds of downtown workers, . . ." "Police *say* . . ."

• Does the story use active voice? Yes.

Summary

Your job as a news writer is to decide which facts to include in a story, based on your viewers' interests and concerns. To help distinguish information that should be included in a story from that which shouldn't, find the audience hook. Finding that hook helps news writers focus their stories to appeal to viewers.

The first and most important sentence of a television news story is called its *lead*. The lead must hook or grab viewers' attention to draw them into the story. In searching for a strong lead, don't exaggerate the story. Don't distort it. Don't misrepresent it. Do look for the most compelling way to interest viewers. Often, the strongest leads use the latest information available. Weak leads use old information, tell viewers how to react to stories, state the obvious, use the names of people or places viewers don't know, assume knowledge, use negatives, start with quotations or dependent clauses and use the verb *to be*.

The middle of a television news story delivers the goods. It answers viewers' questions: *who*, *what*, *when*, *where*, *why* and *how*. It does not raise questions that go unanswered. It does not include unnecessary time references. When time references do appear in sentences, they follow the verb. News writers omit from stories unnecessary words, such as *that, which, of, but that, the fact that* and *in terms of*. They select words carefully to avoid clichés.

A television news story ends when the writer has told the story. Putting the beginning, middle and end of a news story together happens in six steps.

Step 1: Read the wire copy.
Step 2: Understand the wire copy.
Step 3: Find and mark key facts in the wire copy.
Step 4: Think before you write.
Step 5: Write. Read it aloud. Rewrite. Read it aloud.
Step 6: Test the story.

Does the lead offer viewers the latest information? Does the story answer viewers' questions? Does the story raise questions it fails to answer? Is the story accurate? Is the writing conversational? (Read it aloud.) Does the story show immediacy with present and future tense verbs wherever possible? Does the story use active voice?

Exercises

In the exercises that ask you to write stories, follow Steps 1 through 6 outlined in this chapter. Do not skip Step 4. Think before you write. Think about the eight guidelines.

1. **Words:** Think small and simple and clear.
2. **Sentences:** Think short and simple and clear.
3. **Tense:** Use present or future when possible, but use them accurately.
4. **Voice:** Write in active, not passive.
5. **Accuracy**
6. **Fairness**
7. **Balance**
8. **Attribution**

Find the audience hook. Find a focus that will interest viewers. Start strong with a lead that will grab viewers' attention and introduce your focus. Follow with information that answers viewers' questions. Omit unnecessary time references. If you use time references, place them after verbs. Omit unnecessary words. Select words carefully to avoid clichés.

1. Find the unanswered question in the following wire copy story.

> (RICHMOND, Va.)—The state will ask the federal government to lift smog regulations for the Richmond and Tidewater metropolitan areas because of measurable gains in the air quality of the regions.
> Despite a heat wave this summer, ozone levels exceeded a federal health standard just two days in Richmond and none in Tidewater. Ozone is the main component of smog. State officials say the two regions have enjoyed fairly clean air for the past several years. If the EPA agrees to the state's request, industries in Richmond and Tidewater will face relaxed antipollution rules.

2. Rewrite the wire copy story above. Assume the state filed papers this morning requesting that the government lift its ban. You are writing for a noon newscast at a Richmond local affiliate.

3. Rewrite the wire copy story below. Assume the arrest happened this morning. You are writing about it for an evening national newscast in the United States.

> (SAN JACINTO, Calif.)—The mother of three young children who were stabbed to death was arrested early Friday and was to be charged with their murders, police said.
> The bodies of Susana and Vincent Buenrostro, aged 8 and 10, were found in their home Thursday morning, and the body of their 4-year-old sister, Diedra, was found in an abandoned post office several miles away 12 hours later.
> San Jacinto police Sgt. Barry Backlund said the mother, Dora Buenrostro, 34, was arrested early Friday after investigators "discovered several inconsistencies in the mother's statements."

Backlund said Buenrostro went to the San Jacinto police station early Thursday morning and said her estranged husband, Alejandro, 37, had showed up at her apartment and she anticipated a custody dispute.

When police accompanied her back to the apartment, they found the stabbed bodies of the two elder children.

A massive search was launched for Alejandro Buenrostro, who was under a restraining order to stay away from his wife's apartment, and he was apprehended in Los Angeles Thursday afternoon and held for questioning.

He was later released when police established he had turned up for work at his job in a paint factory in Los Angeles that morning and could not have been in San Jacinto, 100 miles to the east, when his wife claimed he was.

4. Rewrite the above story again, this time for a morning newscast the day after the arrest occurred. Assume you are writing for an audience in Los Angeles.

5. Rewrite the following wire copy story. Assume the fire started at 3 a.m. today. Assume you are writing for an 8 a.m. local newscast in Lancaster.

(LANCASTER, Pa.)—Authorities say five people have died in a blaze this morning in Lancaster's south side.

State police fire marshals say the fire began in a row home and spread to the three adjacent houses during the early morning hours.

Five people died after being trapped on the second floor of one of the homes.

Two others have been taken to area hospitals. One of the survivors, a child, was then flown to the children's hospital burn unit in Philadelphia.

Authorities haven't released any identifications yet.

Fire crews remain on the scene, searching for a cause. Authorities say arson has not been ruled out.

One of the homes was completely gutted, and the remaining three homes sustained heavy damage.

The fire was so strong that smoke from the blaze set off smoke detectors in a neighbor's house. That neighbor, Sarah Jones, notified the fire department.

6. Use the story you wrote for Exercise 5. Rewrite the lead to be

(a) a hard local lead
(b) a soft local lead
(c) a throwaway (sentence fragment) lead
(d) a lead using background information
(e) a suspense/delayed lead
(f) a lead that uses related information
(g) a lead that advances the story

You will hand in seven two-sentence leads, as described in (a) through (g) above. You do not need to rewrite the whole story five times.

7. Use the story you wrote for Exercise 5. Read the wire copy below that updates the fire story. Choose elements from the wire copy below to add to or replace information in your original story. Rewrite your story to include new information and delete old information. Be prepared to defend your decisions about the changes you make. Assume the fire started at 3 a.m. today. Assume you are writing for a 9 a.m. local newscast in Lancaster.

(LANCASTER, Pa.)—Authorities say five people died and two were injured in a row house fire this morning in Lancaster's south side. Three other homes were damaged and the cost was estimated at more than $80,000.

Fire Lieutenant Ed Knight says the flames were blowing 15 to 20 feet across the street when firefighters arrived on the scene shortly after 3 a.m.

Knight says the victims were found on the second floor of the first house. He says the dead include two teenagers and three children, and one of the teenagers was pregnant.

Authorities say the only survivors were 36-year-old Carmen Cintron and an infant girl. Angela Guirlando, a spokeswoman at Community Hospital of Lancaster, says Cintron is in serious condition in the intensive care unit with burns, cuts and smoke inhalation. Knight says the infant is in critical condition and is being transferred to St. Christopher's Hospital for Children in Philadelphia.

Identifications of the dead and the infant are not yet released. A cause has not been determined.

Knight says he believes the fire is the worst in Lancaster's history. He says a row house fire in 1969 killed four people.

7

Story Formats:
Some Basics

A newscast consists of a collection of stories, each of which can be classified by the way it is presented and the elements included in that story presentation. This classification scheme is called the story format.

A quick caveat about the word "format": It can refer to just about anything. The way a given script is laid out is called the script format. The producer's run-down on the show (more on that later in the book) is called the show or newscast format. The technology used in shooting and editing the videotape of stories, such as DVC-Pro or Beta, is called the tape format. Keep all those formats straight.

What follows is a list and brief description of the various story formats. Everything presented over the air in television news will consist of one of the following formats or some variation.

The Reader

In a reader, the anchor simply reads a script on camera. Often, the anchor will have a visual graphic relating to the story over his or her shoulder. On occasion, the reader can benefit from additional explanatory visual information through what's called a Full-Screen Graphic (often designated fs/gfx). The fs/gfx is developed in-house and runs full screen during the anchor's story.

The Voice Over and Sound Bite

For a Voice Over, designated VO (spoken "v-o"), the anchor begins reading copy on camera. Then the viewer sees visuals and hears natural sound on an edited videotape as the anchor continues to narrate live from the studio.

If an interview was involved in covering the story, the producer, reporter or writer might decide to include a brief segment of that interview, known as a sound bite. The viewer may go from the anchor reading copy live on camera directly to the sound bite, which is also called an SOT (typically spoken "s-o-t") or a sot (spoken "saht"), which stands for "sound on tape." The sot may be included with the vo, in which case the elements are combined and designated as a VOSOT (typically spoken "v-o-s-o-t"), vo/sot, vosot (typically spoken as VOH-saht), VO-Bite (spoken "v-o-bite"), VOB (spoken "v-o-b"), or Nats to Sound. Different newsrooms will use different terms, but all are correct and all mean the same thing. In addition, you may see these designations capitalized, in lowercase, or in a combination of the two.

The Package and Live Shot

The story's importance or the compelling nature of available visuals and sound might call for a longer and more detailed format called a Package. In a Package, the reporter gathers information as well as pertinent and illustrative sound and visuals including interviews. The reporter then writes a script that combines taped visuals and sounds and the sound bites with his or her narration, all of which is edited into a videotape "package." During air, the anchor reads the introduction live on camera, then the technical crew rolls the preproduced Package, which the audience sees and hears.

The reporter may be called on to do a Live Shot, also called a Remote, during which the anchor will introduce a story, then "toss" to the reporter, who may be live in the field or live in the newsroom. The reporter may do a straight live, have a live interview, or have an abbreviated package, vosot or vo (that the reporter would narrate) that rolls during the Live Shot. A variation of the Live Shot is the Set Piece (or Reporter On-Set), in which the reporter delivers the Live Shot from the anchor set in the studio.

Every story that airs falls into one of the above categories or some variation or combination. Now, let's briefly discuss scripting, then take a closer look at the individual formats and learn how each is scripted.

Scripting—Some Basics

Everything in television news begins with a script. Every element of the show is scripted out in some form, and that includes the ad libbed transitions within the newscast and the show's commercials. If you're putting together a newscast, nothing within your realm of control can be left to chance—you are presenting a live program filled with many complex elements, and you must account for every second. Of course, things will change and people involved in the newscast will have to adjust, often during the show. However, the scripts should reflect those adjustments wherever possible.

In addition, in television news, a script is being written for the benefit of several people who will use those scripts as a guide for building the story or running it on the air. After the writer finishes the script, it may go to the show producer, the executive producer, the editor, the anchors, the show director or the audio technician, and the list can go on. As a result, it's essential for you to write your script in a standardized format or structure so that anyone using the script will know immediately where to look for needed information. Each newsroom will do things somewhat differently, and you have to learn that shop's approach and terminology. However, the basics you learn here can be applied to any TV news operation.

First, all scripts must have certain basic information at the header. The most important information is the slug, which is the two- or three-word descriptor for the story. The slug is determined by a producer or assignment editor when the story is first developed or assigned, and everyone will refer to the story by that slug from that point on. Be certain to use the exact wording. If the story's slug is "Downtown Fatal Fire," that's the slug you use—not "Downtown Fire Fatalities," not "Triple Fatal Fire" and not "Four-Alarm Fatal." A lot of split-second decisions have to be made under intense deadline pressure, and you have to ensure every element of your work is immediately clear and understandable.

A script also needs to include the newscast in which that version is running. Virtually all TV newsrooms have several newscasts scattered through the broadcast day, and you may write one version for the 5 p.m. show, another for the 6, and yet another for the 10 or 11 p.m. show.

Include the date the story runs. A previous version may have been done the night before, or script might be held for air later in the week.

Write the name or initials of the writer. If anyone along the line has a question on the story, they need to know whom to ask.

Most newsrooms want you to write the format of the story, which we'll discuss shortly.

Each script must include the amount of time that story or newscast element will run. An exact time for that story or element is critical. For stories, the time is often figured by the computer. However, this is a rough estimate only, and the best way to figure the time is to time it yourself.

Every element in the newscast is given a page number, which will be included in the header. Page numbers may be assigned you as you are writing, but more often they are filled in later by the producer. Either way, the producer for that show determines the page number that designates exactly where in the newscast—which segment and where in that segment—that element will run. We'll go into more detail in later discussion of the newscast and producing.

All television scripts are written in dual-column format. All copy to be read aloud and any instructions for the person reading are written in the right-hand column. Newsrooms have developed some fairly standard rules for writing copy to make the copy easier to read on the air. First, in writing copy for television news, always indent each paragraph at least five spaces, and write only one sentence per paragraph. When you reach the end of a sentence, hit a hard return and start the next sentence as a new paragraph. Always double space any copy—this makes it both easier to see and allows space in case notes (such as a pronouncer) need to be written on the hard copy of the script. Many newsrooms will also ask you to write anchor copy in all caps, the theory being that it's easier to read and helps distinguish anchor copy from instructions and sound bite transcriptions, which would not be read aloud. In this text, I'll show anchor and reporter copy in upper-

and lowercase. It's much easier to adjust from writing in upper- and lowercase to all caps than the other way around, so you should initially train yourself to upper- and lowercase.

Generally speaking, anything you do not want read aloud that is intended to give information to the anchor should be set off somehow. Many newsrooms use parentheses, others use dashed lines on either side, and some use both. For example, if Sean is reading this story, the right column might start with

- - - - (Sean vo) - - - -

followed by the script that Sean would read—indented, double-spaced and one sentence per paragraph.

You never want to jump from one page to the next midsentence—this can force the anchor to pause at an unnatural place in the copy while he or she tries to find where the copy picks up on the following page. This is generally only a concern when the anchor is reading from hard copy, and most newsroom software will automatically paginate such that you won't have page jumps, but it's a good point to know.

If your story runs two or more pages, you need to write the word "more" at the bottom of each but the last page and to set it off with parentheses:

- - - - (More) - - - -

You also need to designate the end of your story with the word "end" or a series of pound signs:

- - - - (End) - - - -

#####

In the left-hand column will go any visual or technical instructions for the producer, director and technical crew. Those instructions will vary, based on the story format.

Readers and Reader Scripts

A "reader script" is just what it says—a script the news anchor will read on the air. When you write a television news script, your responsibility includes what viewers hear and see. Get used to hearing this: You are responsible for what viewers hear and see.

What Viewers Hear

In a reader, viewers hear the news anchor reading your words. As you learned earlier, your job is to tell viewers the newsworthy elements of a story and to answer their questions without raising new questions that go unanswered. You do so in a conversational way, using short words and sentences. The emphasis here is on short. A reader typically runs 10 to 25 seconds. You'll discover that's not much time to tell a story.

Script Timing

There is no great challenge to script timing. The goal, simply, is to discover how long it takes a news anchor to read the words you write. The amount of time a script lasts is called its total time, total run time, total runs time, or total running time—abbreviated TRT. There is only one way to know how long a reader script runs. Throughout this text, you'll use a stopwatch or the second hand of a clock to time copy. Start the clock. Read the script. Note the time it takes you to read it. That's it.

News writers and reporters in some newsrooms still rely on stopwatches, but most newsrooms have computerized scripting with automatic timing. The reading speeds of news anchors are programmed into the computer and displayed as the writer works on his or her script. As I've mentioned before, however, this is only an estimate. Although you can see there is no great challenge to script timing, there is a challenge to writing scripts to time. Keeping the news script to the required time takes disciplined writing and careful selection of story elements.

Writing the Script

Start by gathering all the information available on the story. Working reporters use interviews, public records, printed reports and other sources for information. Among those sources reporters may use—as you will—is wire copy. They study information available to them to make sure they understand the story. Follow the steps outlined in Chapter 4. Read the following wire copy. Understand it. Find and mark key facts.

> WASHINGTON—A radar-based device that can identify people by the way they walk is being developed by the Pentagon for use in a new antiterrorist surveillance system.
>
> Operating on the theory that an individual's walk is as unique as a signature, the Pentagon has financed a Georgia Institute of Technology research project that has been 80 percent to 95 percent successful in identifying people.
>
> If a prototype is ordered by the Defense Advanced Research Projects Agency, the individual "gait signatures" of people could become part of the data to be linked in a vast surveillance system the Pentagon agency calls Total Information Awareness.
>
> The system could be used by embassy security officers to conclude that a shadowy figure observed a few hundred feet away at night or in heavy clothing at two different times was the same person and should be investigated.
>
> At a restricted facility, the technology could warn security officers that an approaching person was probably not an employee by comparing his gait with those on file.
>
> The system has raised privacy alarms on both ends of the political spectrum.

> In February, Congress barred its use against American citizens without further congressional review.

Think before you write. Think about the eight guidelines. Use short words and simple sentence structure. Look for ways to use present tense. Replace awkwardly phrased passive voice sentence construction with the more conversational active voice. Write a script that is accurate, fair and balanced and that uses attribution. Answer viewers' questions without raising questions that go unanswered. Look for the viewer hook to find a focus that will interest viewers.

If you've read, understood, marked and thought about the wire copy, you are ready to find a lead that will appeal to your viewers. Remember that the best leads often will be the latest development in the story. You follow up with information that fleshes out the story to make it interesting and memorable for viewers. Your script may look something like this:

> The Pentagon is looking into an unusual new weapon in the war on terrorism.
> It's a radar device that can identify people by the way they walk.
> They say the device is 80-percent accurate.
> With so-called gait signatures recorded and stored in a database, the system could help protect high-security buildings.
> However, this is raising privacy concerns.
> Congress has banned its use against Americans until lawmakers can review the system.

Test the script.

• Does the lead offer viewers the latest information? Yes. A new device has raised the Pentagon's interest.

• Does the script answer viewers' questions? Yes. Who? *The Pentagon, researchers, lawmakers.* What? *Want to use this device to identify people.* When? *Now, ongoing.* Where? *Anywhere it's needed.* Why? *To identify potential terrorists.* How? *By analyzing the way people walk.*

• Does the script raise any questions it fails to answer? No.

• Is the script accurate? Yes. Facts from the wire copy are the same as those that appear in the script. The story attributes information about the device to the Pentagon and the scientists who developed the system. The source of the attributed information appears before the information.

• Is the script conversational? Yes. Read it aloud. The news writer rejects wire copy words and wordy clauses and phrases such as *antiterrorist surveillance system* and *used by embassy security officers to conclude that.*

• Does the script show immediacy with present tense verbs? Yes. The Pentagon is looking. They say tests show. The system is raising. But notice that the news writer uses past tense to describe events that happened in the past: Congress has banned.

• Does the script use active voice? Yes.

Active voice:

> • Pentagon is looking into . . .
> . . . system could help protect . . .

Passive voice:

> • Is being developed by the Pentagon . . .
> System could be used by . . .

What Viewers See

Remember that you are responsible for what viewers hear and see. In a reader, viewers see the news anchor on camera. The news anchor appears "full" or with a "box" (left or right):

Full: The anchor (head and shoulders) is centered in the television screen. There are no other visual or audio elements. The anchor reads the news script on the air.

Box: The news anchor (head and shoulders) appears to one side of the screen with a box over the anchor's right or left shoulder (Figure 7.1). Again, from this camera position, the anchor reads the news script on the air.

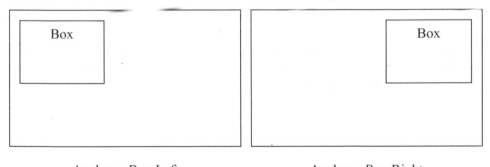

Anchor – Box Left   Anchor – Box Right

FIGURE 7.1

Boxes are computer-generated graphics that can include maps, still photos of people, still frames of video or other artwork created by newsroom graphic artists. When you use a box, you must "write to" the box. You refer to the box early in your script. For example, if you write a script about flooding in the Midwest using a box that shows a map of Missouri, you write first about conditions in Missouri. If you start your Midwest flooding story with information from Ohio, the box confuses viewers. You raise a question without answering it, "Why is there a map of Missouri?"

Boxes are relatively small, taking up less than a quarter of the television screen. They must appear uncluttered. Keep the information in boxes short and simple. As a news writer, you are not responsible for electronically creating the box, but you and the newscast producer will make editorial decisions about the information featured in the box. The anchor centered on camera or with a box over his or her shoulder (right or left) is what viewers see in a reader script.

Format

Until now, you've presented your scripts as you would any other news article—written or typed on a piece of standard 8-by-11-inch paper. But television news writing is different from any other type of writing in style and presentation. The presentation for television news writing involves "script formatting." Script formatting is communicating. Every word in a television news script communicates vital information to news producers, anchors, newscast directors, and countless others in a newsroom. Good script formatting is another way of saying good communication, and good communication ensures a smooth newscast.

In most newsrooms, news writers type their scripts into computers already programmed for a two-column format. The news story appears in the right column, and communication with the newscast director—called director cues—appear in the left column. Figure 7.2 shows the script about the gait signatures properly formatted for television news. The numbers 1 through 12 (in parentheses) identify elements of a properly formatted television news reader script that will be discussed in the following pages. When you write news scripts in format, you will omit the numbers. Remember that the format examples in this book are standardized, even though the television industry offers little standardization among newsrooms. The examples in this book accurately reflect script formats used by some newsrooms, but they admittedly differ from those used by others.

The Top of the Page

Information at the top of the page identifies the script, news writer, newscast and script page number. Look at numbers 1 through 6 (in parentheses) in Figure 7.2 for reference. In computerized newsrooms, some of this information is pre-programmed so that it automatically appears at the top of the page when a news writer logs on to his or her terminal. Without benefit of newsroom computers, you'll be required to include this information in the scripts you write.

(1) **The Page Number.** Script page numbering typically includes a letter and a number. The letter indicates the section, or news block, of the newscast in which the script will appear. News blocks begin with *A* at the top of the newscast and are broken by commercial breaks. After the first commercial break the *B* block follows, after the second commercial break the *C* block follows, and so on. The number shows the order of scripts within the news block. In the scheme used here, the first story within a block is page 10, the second story page 20, and so on.

(1) (A-20) (2) Walk ID (3) Rdr (4) 6 p (5) 5/20 (6) EKG (7) Runs:

(8) anchor - on cam

(9) ---------- (on cam) ----------

(10) The Pentagon is looking into an unusual new weapon in the war on terrorism.

It's a radar device that can identify people by the way they walk.

They say the device is 80-percent accurate.

With so-called gait signatures recorded and stored in a database, the system could help protect high-security buildings.

However, this is raising privacy concerns.

(11) ---------- (more) ----------

FIGURE 7.2 (*continues*)

(1) (A-20a) (2) Walk ID (3) Rdr (4) 6 p (5) 5/20 (6) EKG (7) Runs:

Congress has banned its use

against Americans until lawmakers

can review the system.

(12) #####

FIGURE 7.2 (*continued*)

Numbering generally begins at 10 at the start of each news block and goes up in increments of 10. In a newscast, there will be scripts numbered A-10, A-20, A-30 and so forth; followed by B-10, B-20, B-30 and so on; followed by C-10, C-20, C-30, and continuing that pattern throughout the newscast. In Figure 7.2, the space WALK ID story is page A-20, or the second story the anchor reads in the first block of the newscast. In television news, scripts are identified by their page numbers. The WALK ID story is the "A-20 story." That means that if the story runs more than one page, you do not number the second page of the script A-30. Instead, numbering continues with A-20a, A-20b, A-20c and so forth (see the second page of Figure 7.2).

Some additional discussion about page numbering: In some newsrooms, page numbers appear in increments of 10, in others, increments of 2, and in others, consecutive numbers. There is a particular scheme and reasoning to how page numbers are arranged in a given newsroom. You will find a detailed discussion of page numbering in the chapter on producing. I included it here only as an introduction. However, because the producer numbers the pages, the writer doesn't generally worry about it. For now, we won't either.

(2) **The Slug.** The slug is the story's "title" for the newscast and consists of one or two words that identify the story. The slug is capitalized. In Figure 7.2, the story slug is WALK ID. Newscast producers most often assign slugs. Until you're building your own newscast, you will be assigned slugs for your scripts in the exercises.

(3) **The Format.** You'll need to note the format in which the story is built, such as vo/sot, package, and so on. Our format in this example is reader (rdr).

(4) **The Newscast.** News writers can work on scripts for many newscasts during the day. You need to identify in which newscast the story will air. In Figure 7.2, the WALK ID script airs in the 6 p.m. newscast, marked 6pm.

(5) **The Date.** The news writer identifies the date the story will air. In the example, the WALK ID script will air on May 20, or 5/20.

(6) **The News Writer's Initials.** Scripts are passed from news writers to copy editors to producers to anchors. The news writer's initials tell everyone along the chain where the script originated—and where to go if there are questions about the script. When you write news scripts, you will put your initials in the position shown in Figure 7.2.

(7) **Run Time.** This is a crucial piece of information. A producer must know exactly how much time an element takes. The writer can estimate or whoever is editing the piece can provide an exact time.

The Left Column

The information in the left column speaks to the director of the newscast. Director cues tell the newscast director how the television screen should look to viewers at home. See the number 8 (in parentheses) in Figure 7.2 for reference.

(8) **The Camera Shot.** The director cue "anchor-on cam" tells the newscast director to show the anchor centered on camera. It sometimes appears in lower-case letters and nearly always appears at the top of the left column.

If the news writer had opted to use a box in this script, a cue would appear in the left column, as shown in Figure 7.3. The director cue "box-High-Tech Surveillance" tells the newscast director to use a camera shot that places the anchor off-center with a box appearing over the anchor's shoulder. You do not need to specify in your script whether the box appears over the anchor's right or left shoulder. The newscast producer makes that decision.

The director cues in this example may seem obvious and even unnecessary, but later you'll be using cues to tell the newscast director where full-screen graphics should appear or videotape should roll as well as to communicate dozens of other important instructions. Get in the habit now of always including director cues.

The Right Column

Information in the right column speaks to the news anchor. Here, the news writer lets the anchor know what is happening on the television screen. Most important, this is where the news writer places the script as it will be read by the news anchor on air. Refer to numbers 9 through 12 in Figure 7.2.

(9) **The Anchor Cue.** A broken line tells the anchor the information is not to be read aloud on the air, that it is a cue. In this example, the cue "- - - - on cam - - - -" tells the anchor that he or she is on camera. Anchor cues appear in lowercase letters between dotted lines. Again, the anchor cue in this example may seem unnecessary, but as your scripts become more complicated and you have more information to offer the anchor, the cues become vital. As with director cues, get in the habit now of always including anchor cues.

(10) **The Script Copy.** These are the words the news anchor will read on the air. Script copy is double-spaced, and the first word of each sentence is indented. Remember that paragraphs are one sentence long. It is very important to keep script copy as "clean" and uncluttered as possible to ensure a smooth delivery by the news anchor. Some newsrooms use all uppercase lettering. Often, newsroom computers automatically print uppercase type. Other newsrooms use uppercase and lowercase, as in the example. Throughout this text, you'll use uppercase and lowercase. Many anchors report that it's easier for them to read.

(11) **More.** If your script goes from one page to another, you'll set a page break after the last full line you can fit on the one page. You'll follow the last line on the page with dashed lines and the word *More* set off with parentheses. Remember, use parentheses and dashes to mark anything you want to tell the anchor but don't want the anchor to read aloud. Note that some newsroom computers fill in this step automatically.

(1) (A-20) (2) Walk ID (3) Rdr (4) 6 p (5) 5/20 (6) EKG (7) Runs:

anchor - on cam	---------- (on cam) ----------
box - High-Tech Surveillance	The Pentagon is looking
	into an unusual new weapon in the
	war on terrorism.
	It's a radar device that can
	identify people by the way they
	walk.
	...

FIGURE 7.3

(12) **The End Script.** The pound sign (#) at the end of the script tells the news anchor the script is over. Again, this step often is preprogrammed for writers in computerized newsrooms. However, if you do not have the benefit of newsroom computers, you'll be responsible for including these script markings.

Keeping Script Copy Clean

It's very important to write in a way that makes it easy for the anchor to read. This means returning to all those rules we've already discussed on how to write copy for television scripts.

Readers with Full-Screen Graphics

Some prefer to segregate fs/gfx scripts from Readers. Others include them under the same category because there is no motion video component to either. Follow whatever your newsroom dictates.

Full-screen graphics are like the boxes you used earlier in this chapter, except *full-screen* graphics *fill* the television screen. They add visual elements to reader scripts and help viewers better understand stories. Similar to boxes, full-screen graphics can feature maps, still photos of people, logos, flags and other artwork. Because full-screen graphics are larger than boxes, they can offer viewers more information.

Building and Using Full-Screen Graphics

In its simplest form, a full-screen graphic is made up of two elements: a graphic background and a full-screen text. The graphic background can be plain, such as a solid color or shading. It can include computer-generated artwork, or it can feature a freeze-frame of video. The full-screen text is superimposed over the graphic background.

As an example, suppose you are writing a story about budget cuts that have forced the layoff of county workers. The full-screen text includes a title and information that budget cuts are to blame for layoffs affecting three sheriff's deputies, four county librarians and 23 teachers' aides. The full-screen text, superimposed over a shaded graphic background, becomes a full-screen graphic (Figure 7.4).

Full-screen graphics can be simple, or they can be elaborate works of art. In either case, they are created essentially the same way: by combining graphic backgrounds and full-screen texts (Figure 7.5).

As a television news writer and producer, you are not responsible for using the graphics equipment that electronically generates full-screen graphics, but you do make editorial decisions. You make suggestions about the background the graphic artists will use, and you write the full-screen text.

LAYOFFS

3   Sheriff's Deputies

4   Librarians

23   Teachers' Aides

FIGURE 7.4

Finding Information for Full-Screen Graphics

News writers and reporters find information for full-screen graphics in the same places they find information for scripts. Reporters generating story information through interviews use information from the interviews to create full-screen graphics. Writers using news releases to generate story information get information for full-screen graphics from the news releases. You have been using wire copy to generate your stories, and this is another information source for full-screen graphics. The following wire story provides information for at least five full-screen graphics, as shown in Figure 7.6.

> (WASHINGTON)—Men who eat 10 servings a week of tomato-based foods are up to 45 percent less likely to develop prostate cancer, according to a six-year study of 47,000 males released today.
>
> Tomatoes are rich in lycopene, an antioxidant that may protect against the disease. They appear to be more prophylactic when cooked, as in marinara sauce and catsup and pizza.

When to Use Full-Screen Graphics

Keep in mind a news writer's ultimate goal: to help viewers understand stories. If full-screen graphics make a story clearer for viewers, use one or more. Full-screen graphics are helpful in stories that require numbers. They can illustrate difficult-to-understand concepts. They can provide a frame of reference, as with a map, for viewers hearing about unfamiliar parts of the world or about a specific spot in a familiar city. Sophisticated, animated full-screen graphics have been

Full Screen Graphic

Graphic
Background

LAYOFFS	
3	Sheriff's Deputies
4	Librarians
23	Teachers' Aides

+ Full-
Screen Text

LAYOFFS	
3	Sheriff's Deputies
4	Librarians
23	Teachers' Aides

= Full-
Screen Graphic

FIGURE 7.5

used in newscasts to illustrate events for which no videotape is available. For example, animated full-screen graphics have been used to illustrate the breakup of an airplane after an explosion on board and to retrace the head-on path of colliding trains.

Some people in the television industry believe that full-screen graphics are overused. They believe that viewers tune into television newscasts to see, not read,

<u>Cancer Study</u>
Men who eat
10 servings a week of
tomato-based foods are
45% less likely
to develop prostate cancer.

Tomatoes & Cancer

Marinara Sauce
Catsup
Pizza

Cancer Study

47.000 Men
Six Years

Health News

 10 Servings/Week
= 45% less likely
to develop
prostate cancer

Cancer Study

Tomato-based
foods

Chances of
developing
prostate cancer

(Yours here)

FIGURE 7.6

the news and that full-screen graphics detract from stories by asking viewers to read. Others argue that full-screen graphics are underused. They cite examples of news stories in which the use of full-screen graphics could help viewers better understand stories. How you use full-screen graphics—and how often you use them—will be decided by newsroom policies and procedures at stations at which you work. For now, look for opportunities to use them and learn to use them properly.

Creating a Story with Full-Screen Graphics

What Viewers Hear: Writing the Story

There are countless ways to use full-screen graphics in television news scripts, but there is only one hard-and-fast rule for using them. As with boxes, you must write to full-screen graphics in news scripts. The full-screen graphic and script copy must make sense together. Remember, you are responsible for what viewers hear and see.

Writers most often compose scripts first and then design full-screen graphics that match. For example, the script copy for the LAYOFFS full-screen graphic in Figure 7.4 could read:

> Cuts to the county's budget will force 30 workers off the job.
> County Commissioner Martin Leintz says pink slips are in the
> mail for three sheriff's deputies, four librarians and 23 teachers' aides.

In the full-screen graphic that goes with this story (Figure 7.4), the deputies, librarians and teachers' aides are listed in the order the viewer hears them, but if you write the story differently, you must write the full-screen text differently, too.

> Budget cuts will hit hardest in the county's schools, forcing lay-
> offs of 23 teachers' aides.
> But other county agencies will feel the pinch, too.
> County Commissioner Martin Leintz says pink slips are also in
> the mail for four librarians and three sheriff's deputies.

Figure 7.4 doesn't correspond to this script copy. The viewer first hears about the 23 teachers' aides, but the graphic forces the viewers' eyes to jump across the television screen to keep up. The full-screen graphic should follow the story better, as in Figure 7.7.

You must check and double-check your full-screen text against script copy. Studies show that viewers believe what they see over what they hear. If your script copy tells them four librarians will receive pink slips but an error in the full-screen graphic reads five librarians, most viewers will come away from the newscast

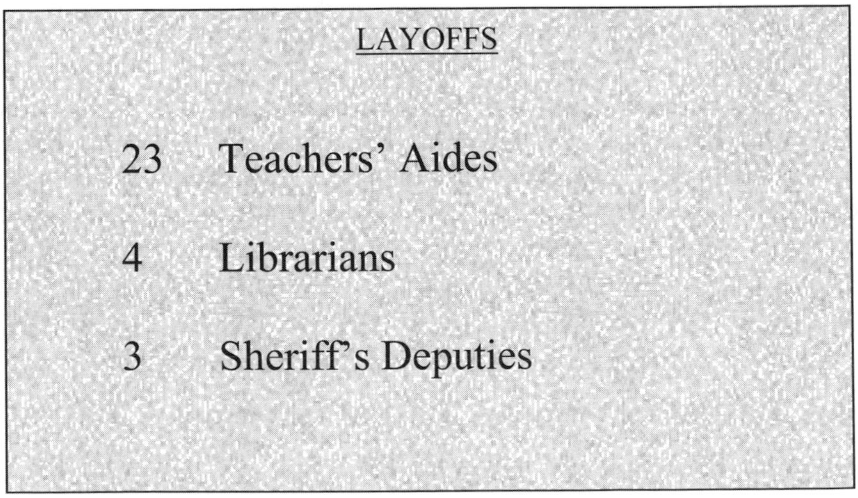

LAYOFFS

23   Teachers' Aides

4   Librarians

3   Sheriff's Deputies

FIGURE 7.7

believing five librarians are losing their jobs. For more astute viewers, you've raised a question you have not answered, "Is it four or five?"

Follow the process of writing a news script with full-screen graphics using wire copy as a source. The first steps should be familiar to you. Read the wire copy. Understand it. Find and mark key facts. Think about the story.

> (AUSTIN, Texas)—Crime in Texas has decreased slightly compared with last year, but most violent crimes were up.
>
> The Texas Uniform Crime Reporting Newsletter, released today, for the first nine months of this year showed the crime index down by 3 percent compared with the first nine months of last year.
>
> All violent crimes except murder increased.
>
> Rape had the largest increase, 6 percent. Robbery was up 4 percent, and aggravated assault, 1 percent. Murder was down by 1 percent, burglary by 5 percent, and larceny and motor theft, 3 percent each.

The information in the wire copy story is overwhelming. The presentation is unclear in places. Someone reading the wire copy can skip ahead or reread confusing sections, taking time to make sense of the information and accompanying statistics, but television viewers get one chance to understand the story. Full-screen graphics can help viewers better understand this story.

First, select information and statistics that will most appeal to viewers to focus the story. Then organize the facts. There are several ways to organize the information. One way might be to separate two sets of statistics: those for violent crimes and those for property crimes. The wire copy jumps between the two. You separate them so that viewers can better understand the story. You might make notes to help you stay on track as you're writing the script (Figure 7.8). The notes will serve as a guide for creating full-screen graphics later.

Will you lead with violent crime or property crime statistics? Both types of crime affect viewers, so you can begin with either set of statistics. Because vio-

---

Notes – Crime Story

Violent Crimes	*Property Crimes*
Rape up 6%	*Burglary down 5%*
Robbery up 4%	*Theft down 3%*
Agg. assault up 1%	*Auto theft down 3%*
Murder down 1%	

Most violent crimes are up
Most property crimes are down
Overall crime rate down 3%

FIGURE 7.8

lent crime is often more newsworthy and as the figures are up, you might decide to start there. Find a lead that hooks viewers. Studies show that viewers repeatedly list crime among their top concerns. Assume you are writing for an audience in Texas.

> A new report shows most violent crime is on the rise.

This lead is simple and straightforward. It is in the present tense. It answers viewers' questions and sets up the news story. It also is accurate. The lead qualifies the statement, saying that figures show that most violent crime rates have increased (remember that the murder rate is down). The lead hooks viewers. Most viewers, concerned about crime, will stay tuned for more information.

Be very careful that your search for a lead that will hook viewers doesn't cause you to overdramatize or draw conclusions you cannot back with fact, such as

> A new report says you're more likely to be a victim of violent
> crime this year.

This lead may be dramatic, but it isn't accurate. The report shows that most violent crime is on the rise, but it doesn't offer any information about the victims of violent crime. The television news writer is drawing a conclusion that is not supported by facts in the wire copy. Let's say a man who was mugged 13 times in the first nine months of last year was mugged 17 times in the first nine months of this year. This means the mugging rate climbs but the number of victims remains the same. It also means that one unlucky guy needs to figure out why he's getting mugged so much. The point here is that the news writer's job is to interpret information. It is not the news writer's job to draw conclusions that aren't there.

Using the simple, straightforward lead, build the rest of the story. Answer questions viewers will ask. Use your notes to present information in an organized way that viewers can understand easily.

> A new report shows that most violent crime is on the rise.
> Figures in today's Texas Uniform Crime Reporting Newsletter
> show an increase in all violent crimes except murder.
> The study covers crimes reported in the first nine months of this
> year compared with the same time last year.
> The biggest jump? Rape is up by six-percent.
> Robbery, four-percent.
> Aggravated assault climbed one-percent.
> And the exception: The state's murder rate is down one-percent.
> The report also shows that property crimes are down.
> Burglary dropped five-percent.
> Theft, three-percent down.
> And car theft specifically, down by the same percentage.
> Overall, Texas' crime rate is down three-percent.

The script answers viewers' questions as they arise. The lead sentence leaves viewers asking, "What report?" The news writer answers the question in the second sentence, and answers when (today) and where (in Texas). The second sentence leaves the viewer with no information about the time period of the study. The question leads to a detailed and cumbersome answer in the third sentence, but it does require an answer. The news writer backs the first three sentences with information, with facts and statistics. The news writer introduces the second set of statistics ("The report also shows . . .") and, again, supports the transition sentence with facts and figures. Test the script for television news writing style.

• Does the lead offer viewers the latest information? Yes. It is a *new* report.

• Does the script answer viewers' questions? Yes. Who? (in this case, the *who* happens to be a thing rather than a person) *Crime*. What? *Is "up" in some areas, "down" in others*. When? *Report released today; figures for first nine months of the year*. Where? *In Texas*. Why? *(implied) People are committing more of some types of crimes, fewer of others*. How? *Various crime rate figures*.

• Does the script raise any questions it fails to answer? No.

• Is the script accurate? Yes. The percentages that appear in the script are those in the wire copy. The news writer draws no conclusions that are not backed by facts in the wire copy. The news writer attributes the information to the study and places the attribution before the information.

• Is the script conversational? Yes. Read it aloud. The script is conversational throughout and written for the ear. Notice that the news writer substituted *theft* for *larceny*. Larceny is not a word most people use in conversation.

• Does the script show immediacy with present-tense verbs? Yes. A new report *shows;* the study *covers;* rape *is up;* aggravated assault *climbs;* murder rate *falls;* property crimes . . . *are;* burglary *drops;* car theft . . . *drops*; and the crime rate *is* down.

• Does the script use active voice? Yes. The doer (subject) of the action consistently appears before the action (verb).

What Viewers See: Full-Screen Graphics

An anchor could present this script on air as a reader. But would viewers understand the story? Probably not. It's too much information. Viewers might become lost in the numbers and give up listening. Full-screen graphics can help viewers understand the story because they will see the information as the anchor reads it. The full-screen graphics will cover the television screen as the news anchor presents the information.

You could list all the figures on one full-screen graphic. But full-screen graphics, like script copy, should be uncluttered and easy to read. The goal is to help viewers understand. A long list of numbers defeats the purpose. So you might decide to split the information between two full-screen graphics. The split should come at a point that makes sense for viewers. Where? How about between the violent crimes and the property crimes? Now you see how helpful your earlier notes can be. The full-screen text will look very similar to those notes.

Start by selecting a graphic background. With so much information, you may decide to use a shaded background or simple Texas state seal. You can offer suggestions for a background to the graphic artists who will create it. Then write the full-screen text. Keep in mind that what viewers hear and see must make sense together. Refer to the script to create full-screen text, including a title and story information, for two full-screen graphics (Figure 7.9).

Format

Review the format for reader scripts, which is the basis for all television news script formatting. As you add new elements, you build on the format. Think first

Texas Crime Report	
Violent Crimes	
Rape	+6%
Robbery	+4%
Aggravated Assault	+1%
Murder	-1%

Texas Crime Report	
Property Crimes	
Burglary	-5%
Theft	-3%
Auto Theft	-3%

FIGURE 7.9

about who needs to know that full-screen graphics appear in the script. You need to tell the newscast director. The director is responsible for putting the full-screen graphics on the television screen at the appropriate times. You need to tell the news anchor, too. The news anchor needs to know that he or she will not be on camera when the full-screen graphics appear. Think about where in your script you communicate with the newscast director and anchor. Assume the script will air in the 6 p.m. newscast on October 9. The slug is CRIME STATS. The format is a RDR/FSGFX, and your target time is :40. You decide when it is appropriate to show the full-screen graphics on the television screen.

The Top of the Page

The top of the page includes cues that identify the page number, the slug, the story format, the time and date of the newscast in which the script will run, the news writer and the run time. Use the numbers 1 through 7 (in parentheses) in Figure 7.10 for reference.

(1) **The page number:** The producer tells you that it likely will run fifth story down in the B-block—B-50. However, she's not sure yet and will assign it later herself, so you leave this space blank.

(2) **The slug:** The slug for this television news script is CRIME STATS. It identifies the script and is capitalized.

(3) **The format:** This story is a reader/full-screen graphics, here designated RDR/FSGFX.

(4) **The newscast:** The script airs in the 6 p.m. newscast, marked 6p.

(5) **The date:** The script airs on October 9, or 10/9.

(6) **The news writer's initials:** When you write news scripts, put your initials here. In the example, the news writer is identified by the initials EKG.

(7) **The run time:** This will be filled in by the computer or by hand, whichever the writer chooses. The computer time can also be overridden by hand. You'll fill this in when you get the story finished, but you're shooting for :40.

The Left Column

The left column speaks to the newscast director with director cues. Use the numbers 8 through 11 (in parentheses) in Figure 7.10 for reference.

(8) **The camera shot:** The news writer begins the script with the anchor on camera, like a reader. The director cue "anchor-on cam" instructs the newscast director to show the anchor on camera. Notice that there is no box. The anchor appears in the center of the television screen.

(9) **Director cue:** The cue "take full screen #1" tells the newscast director to show the first full-screen graphic on the television screen. The full-screen graphic has been created earlier by graphic artists. It is stored electronically and is waiting for the newscast director to punch the button that brings it to the television screen. Place the cue in the left column at the point at which you want the full-

(1) (page) (2) CRIME STATS (3) rdr/fsgfx (4) 6 pm (5) 10/9 (6) EKG (7) Runs:

(8) anchor - on cam

(9) take full screen #1
<u>Texas Crime Report</u>
Violent Crimes
Rape +6%
Robbery +4%
Aggravated Assault +1%
Murder –1%

(10) take full screen #2
<u>Texas Crime Report</u>
Property Crimes
Burglary –5%
Theft –3%
Auto Theft –3%

(11) anchor – on cam

(12) --------------- (on cam) ---------------

(13)A new report shows most violent crime is on the rise.

Figures in today's Texas Uniform Crime Reporting Newsletter show an increase in violent crimes except murder.

The study covers crimes reported in the first nine months of this year compared with the same time last year.

(14) ------------(full screen #1) ------------

The biggest jump? Rape is up by six-percent.

Robbery, four-percent.

Aggravated assault climbs one-percent.

And the exception: The state's murder rate falls one-percent.

(15) ------------(full screen #2)-------------

But the report also shows property crimes are down.

Burglary drops five-percent.

Theft--three-percent.

And car theft specifically, also drops three-percent.

(16) --------------- (on cam) ---------------

Overall, Texas' crime rate is down three-percent.

(17) #####

FIGURE 7.10

screen graphic to appear, alongside the script copy in the right column. In this script, the first full-screen graphic appears after the news anchor reads "compared with the same time last year." It appears on the television screen in time for viewers to follow along as the news anchor reads the figures for rape, robbery, aggravated assault and murder. Notice that the full-screen text is written out in full in the left column. You don't need to include information about the graphic background, but you must include the entire full-screen text. It serves as a guide and record. It helps guide the graphic artists who will create the full-screen graphic before the newscast, and it serves as a record for the news writer. If there is an error in the full-screen graphic when it appears on air, the news writer can refer to the script to discover whether it was an editorial error—the news writer's—or an error made by the graphics department. More important than placing blame (or clearing yourself of blame) is the fact that scripts are passed among many people in the newsroom. Any one of those people might spot an error and correct it before the error goes on air.

(10) **Director cue:** The cue "take full screen #2" tells the newscast director to show the second full-screen graphic on the television screen. In this script, the newscast director punches the button that brings the second full-screen graphic onto the television screen after the news anchor reads "falls one-percent." The full-screen graphic appears in time for viewers to follow along as the news anchor reads the figures for burglary, theft and auto theft. Again, the script does not contain information about the graphic background but does include the complete full-screen text.

(11) **The camera shot:** The director cue "anchor-on cam" instructs the newscast director to return to the anchor on camera. There is no box. The anchor appears in the center of the television screen to end the story.

The Right Column

The right column speaks to the news anchor with anchor cues and includes the script copy the anchor will read on air. Use the numbers 12 through 17 (in parentheses) in Figure 7.10 for reference.

(12) **Anchor cue:** A broken line with the words "on cam" tells the anchor he or she appears on the television screen.

(13) **The script copy:** These are the words, the story, the news anchor will read on the air. The script copy is double-spaced. The first word of each paragraph is indented. Each paragraph is one sentence long. The script copy is clean and uncluttered to ensure a smooth delivery by the news anchor.

(14) **Anchor cue:** The broken line warns the anchor of a change occurring on the television screen. Here, the cue "full screen #1" tells the anchor that he or she no longer appears on the television screen but is covered by a full-screen graphic.

(15) **Anchor cue:** Again, the broken line warns the anchor of a change. Here, the cue "full screen #2" tells the anchor he or she remains off screen while the full-screen graphic changes.

(16) **Anchor cue:** With the anchor cue "- - - - on cam - - - -" the news writer warns the news anchor that he or she is coming back on camera. Anchors may be looking down, reading from the script paper, while off camera, so they need to know when viewers are watching again. The news anchor knows to reestablish eye contact with the camera and, through it, the viewers.

(17) **The end script:** The pound sign (#) tells the news anchor he or she has reached the end of the script.

Variety: The Spice of Life

There are as many ways to write the CRIME STATS story as there are television news writers. In the example script, the news writer used all the figures available in a fairly straightforward account of the newly released report. The news writer created graphics that divided the list of figures by type of crime. On the following pages, three different news writers use different full-screen graphics to tell the same story (Figure 7.11). The script copy changes, too, ensuring that what viewers hear and see make sense together (Figures 7.12–7.14). Read the examples carefully to notice changes in script copy and full-screen graphics.

The CRIME STATS example is a "numbers story," ideal for full-screen graphics. Other stories can benefit from full-screen graphics, too. You can use them to show location (a map), to give information (an address), to create a list or to emphasize a quotation. Figure 7.15 shows good uses of full-screen graphics.

Three Example Scripts by Three Different News Writers		
Example 1 The news writer separates crimes on the rise from those decreasing and writes the script acordingly. The writer also ends the script on a full screen graphic rather than returning to the anchor on camera.	Texas Crime Rates Down ↓ Murder -1% Burglary -5% Theft -3%	Texas Crime Rates Up ↑ Rape +6% Robbery +4%
Example 2 The news writer separates crimes on the rise from those decreasing, reversing order and omitting numbers within the script and in the full-screen graphics.	Texas Crime Report Rape Robbery Aggravated Assault	Texas Crime Report Burglary Theft Auto Theft Murder
Example 3 The news writer uses a single full-screen graphic to summarize the information, writing the news script accordingly.	Crime Trends in Texas * Most property crimes show a decrease * Most violent crimes show an increase	

FIGURE 7.11

(1) (page) (2) CRIME STATS (3) rdr/fsgfx (4) 6 pm (5) 10/9 (6) EKG (7) Runs:

anchor - on cam
box - Crime Report

---------- (on cam) ----------

Texans may not feel any safer, but a new report shows the crime rate is falling.

A study in today's Texas Uniform Crime Reporting Newsletter shows a three-percent drop in crime during the first nine months of this year compared with the same time last year.

Among the crimes on the decline...

take full screen #1
Texas
Crime Rates Down
Murder -1%
Burglary -5%
Theft -3%
Auto Theft -3%

---------- (full screen #1) ----------

The murder rate is down one-percent.

Burglary dropped five-percent.

Theft and car theft specifically each fell three-percent.

take full screen #2
Texas
Crime Rates Up
Rape +6%
Robbery +4%
Aggravated Assault +1%

---------- (full screen #2) ----------

But the report also shows an increase in most violent crimes.

Rape is up six-percent.

Robbery by four-percent.

And aggravated assaults are up one-percent.

FIGURE 7.12

(1) (page) (2) CRIME STATS (3) rdr/fsgfx (4) 6 pm (5) 10/9 (6) EKG (7) Runs:

anchor - on cam
box - Crime Report

---------- (on cam) ----------

Figures released today send a mixed message about the state's crime rate.

A study in the Texas Uniform Crime Reporting Newsletter shows a decrease in most property crimes, but increases in most violent crimes.

The study compares crimes reported during the first nine months of this year with those during the same time last year.

take full screen #1
Texas Crime Report
Rape
Robbery
Aggravated Assault

---------- (full screen #1) ----------

Crimes on the rise ...

Rape, robbery and aggravaged assault are all up.

take full screen #2
Texas Crime Report
Burglary
Theft
Auto Theft
Murder

---------- (full screen #2) ----------

But burglary, theft, and car theft specifically all dropped.

Texas' murder rate, too, fell slightly.

---------- (on cam) ----------

The overall crime rate in Texas is down three-percent.

#####

anchor on cam

FIGURE 7.13

(1) (page) (2) CRIME STATS (3) rdr/fsgfx (4) 6 pm (5) 10/9 (6) EKG (7) Runs:

anchor - on cam
box - Crime Report
	---------- (on cam) ----------
	    Is Texas becoming a safer place to live?
	    A new report suggests it might be.
	    Figures released in today's Texas Uniform Crime Reporting Newsletter show the state's crime rate is down three-percent.

take full screen
Crime Trends in Texas
* Most property crimes show a decrease
* Most violent crimes show an increase
	---------- (full screen) ----------
	    The report says property crimes such as burglary and theft are down.
	    The murder rate also fell.
	    But most violent crimes are up, including rape and aggravated assault.

anchor - on cam
box - Crime Report
	---------- (on cam) ----------
	    The study compares crimes reported during the first nine months this year with those during the same time last year.
	
	    #####

FIGURE 7.14

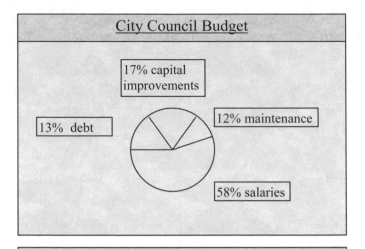

City Council Budget

17% capital improvements

13% debt

12% maintenance

58% salaries

Goodwill

Coats for Kids Drive

P.O. Box 794322
Dallas, TX 75290
or
214-555-1212

"These are the times
that try men's souls."

- Thomas Paine

FIGURE 7.15A

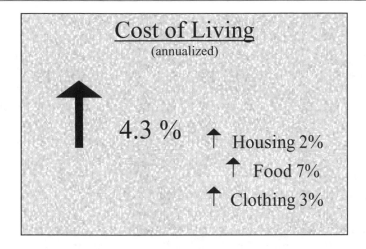

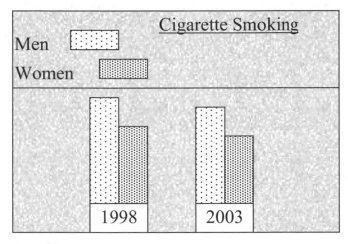

FIGURE 7.15B

Summary

A Reader is a script the news anchor will read on the air. In a Reader, viewers hear the news anchor reading your words. They see the anchor on camera centered on screen or with a box. You are responsible for what viewers hear and see.

Start the process of writing a script by gathering all the information available on the story. Think before you write. Find the Reader hook, the focus for your story. Find a lead that will grab viewers' attention. Remember that the best lead often is the latest development in the story. Follow up with information that makes the story interesting and memorable for viewers. Your script must be well-written, conversational and complete. It also must meet time restraints. To time scripts, use a stopwatch or the second hand of a clock.

Script formatting is communicating. Every word in a television news script communicates vital information to news producers, anchors, newscast directors and countless others in a newsroom. Script pages are divided into two columns. Information at the top of the page identifies the page number (typically filled in later by the producer), script slug, story format, date and time of the newscast, news writer and run time. Information in the left column speaks to the director of the newscast with cues that offer instructions about how the television screen should look to viewers. Information in the right column speaks to the news anchor and includes script copy.

It's important to keep script copy clean and easy to read. Remember the rules on writing and rounding numbers. Remember the rules on abbreviations and acronyms. Remember the rules on writing pronouncers. Keep in mind on hard copy, you don't have to retype or reprint script pages every time you make a mistake. You can strike out minor errors and write the correction above.

In its simplest form, a full-screen graphic is made up of two elements: a graphic background and a full-screen text. Television news writers are not responsible for using the graphics equipment that electronically generates full-screen graphics. But they do write the full-screen text.

Full-screen graphics are helpful in stories that require numbers. They can illustrate difficult-to-understand concepts. They can provide a frame of reference. Sophisticated, animated full-screen graphics have been used in newscasts to illustrate events for which there is no videotape available.

There are many ways to use full-screen graphics in television news scripts. There is only one hard-and-fast rule for using them. You must write to full-screen graphics in news scripts. The full-screen graphic and script copy must make sense together. Studies show viewers believe what they see over what they hear.

News writers and reporters find information for full-screen graphics in the same places they find information for their scripts. They select information and statistics that will most appeal to viewers to focus the story. Then they organize the facts. Making notes can help a writer stay on track while writing the script. The notes can serve as a guide for creating full-screen graphics later.

The format for scripts using full-screen graphics builds on the format for readers. The top of the page includes cues that identify the script, the newscast in which the script will appear, the news writer and the page number. The left column speaks to the newscast director with director cues. The cue "full screen" tells the newscast director to show the full-screen graphic on the television screen. The full-screen text is written out in full in the left column. It serves as a guide and record. The right column speaks to the news anchor with anchor cues and includes the script copy the anchor will read on air. The cue "- - - - full screen - - - -" tells the anchor that he or she no longer appears on the television screen but is covered by a full-screen graphic.

Exercises

As you work on the exercises below, pay attention to writing style and script format. Think before you write. Think about the eight guidelines.

1. **Words:** Think small and simple and clear
2. **Sentences:** Think short and simple and clear
3. **Tense:** Use present or future tense when possible, but use them accurately
4. **Voice:** Write in active, not passive
5. **Accuracy**
6. **Fairness**
7. **Balance**
8. **Attribution**

Find the audience hook for your focus. Remember that you will most likely need to omit some information to meet the time requirements. Carefully choose the information you use with your viewers' interests and concerns in mind. Have a good argument for omitting information you choose to edit out. Read your scripts aloud, timing them with a stopwatch.

For the format, use two columns. Include the page number (if one is assigned), slug, format of the story, time and date of the newscast, your initials and the run time. Write down how long the story actually runs, not how long the producer asked you to keep under. Use director's cues in the left column and anchor cues in the right column. Type your script in the right column. Refer to examples in the chapter.

1. Use the following wire copy to write a reader with box that should run a :30 TRT. Read the script aloud, timing it with a stopwatch, to make sure it runs 30 seconds. The rdr will air on tonight's 11 p.m. newscast in your hometown, with a box, slugged CASINO ROBBERY. You are the writer. Assign the box a title. On a separate sheet of paper, draw the box.

> (ATLANTIC CITY, N.J.)—Five people are expected to be arraigned today on charges stemming from an armed robbery yesterday at an Atlantic City casino. New Jersey State Police say four men and one woman are in custody in connection with the case.
>
> One of those arrested is believed to be the masked gunman who shot a security guard during the robbery at Merv Griffin's Resorts Casino Hotel.
>
> The suspects fled with about $400,000 in cash. Police say all the money has been recovered and at least two casino employees are among those arrested.

2. Use the following wire copy to write a reader with box, TRT :30. Read the script aloud, timing it with a stopwatch. The script will air in tonight's 6 p.m. newscast in your hometown, slugged JAIL CROWDING. Assign the box a title. On a separate sheet of paper, draw the box.

(RICHMOND, VA)—The Virginia Dept. of Corrections has cleared the state's crowded jails of nearly 7,000 inmates sentenced to serve time in prisons.

After a 2-year crackdown by the Virginia Parole Board, the state's prisons and jails were packed with inmates last spring.

More than 2,000 people sentenced to prison were living in jail instead.

Seven Virginia sheriffs filed lawsuits against the state, and judges ordered the Corrections Dept. to take action.

The prison system says that since January, it has removed 6,926 inmates from local jails.

3. Create as many full-screen graphics as you can for the wire copy story below. Draw the full-screen graphics as they would appear on the television screen, including graphic backgrounds and full-screen texts. Be creative. Don't limit full-screen graphics to numbers. Use charts, graphs, text and maps, as appropriate. Make full-screen graphics interesting and informative for viewers.

(WASHINGTON)—Know that theory that women think they must suppress anger? Forget it.

Women do let off steam, but typically at their husbands instead of the person who really angered them. And if they cry when angry, that's normal and healthy, a new study concludes.

Sandra Thomas, director of nursing research at the University of Tennessee, performed what researchers call the first large investigation of women's anger, studying 535 women ages 25 to 66.

Previous studies have been based on women in therapy or in laboratory trials that induce anger.

Thomas asked healthy women to recall their anger at everyday situations—when their teenager was surly, the boss was yelling, the spouse committed a pet peeve, traffic was bad.

What she found challenges stereotypes that women either don't get angry or think it's socially unacceptable to show it—and filled a whole book titled "Women and Anger."

Among the findings:

Women frequently get angry but typically stew for less than one hour.

Family members, followed by coworkers, are the most frequent targets of anger. But only about 13 percent of the women would tell coworkers they're angry. Most expressed anger to their husbands— whether they were angry with them or someone else.

The younger the woman, the more likely she was to get angry and express it. Women over 55 reported the least anger and were most likely to suppress the feeling. Those in their 40s experienced the most physical symptoms from anger.

Crying was the number one physical reaction to fury.

Married women were less likely to hold in anger than unmarried women. Teachers and nurses were more likely to express anger than homemakers or clerks.

4. Create as many full-screen graphics as you can for the wire copy story below. Draw the full-screen graphics as they would appear on the television screen, including graphic background and full-screen text. Make full-screen graphics interesting and informative for viewers.

(SAN FRANCISCO)—A poll of 3,000 Americans finds that most don't know enough about medical concepts to make intelligent choices about their own health care.

Jon Miller, the director of the International Center for the Advancement of Science Literacy, says people think they know how to fight off a head cold. But Miller says most aren't well-prepared for genetic medicine or deciding public policy.

For example, the survey says only one in five Americans knows what role DNA plays in heredity. DNA is that part of a cell that passes down genetic information.

The study also says only one in 10 people can give a scientifically correct definition of bacteria—microscopic organisms that can be useful or harmful to humans.

5. Use the following wire copy story to write a RDR/FSGFX script with full-screen graphic(s) in format. TRT (total running time), :30. The script will air in tonight's 11 p.m. newscast, page B-30, slugged MEDALS. You may use a box. Include the full-screen text or texts on script pages. On a separate sheet of paper, draw your full-screen graphic or graphics, including background and text.

(SALT LAKE CITY, Utah)—The Americans get another chance to take a medal this evening when the Games continue with short-track speed skating events. The short-track events were first introduced to the Olympic agenda in 1992. American phenomenon Apolo Ohno already took the silver medal in the men's 1000 meter individual and the gold in the men's 1500 meter individual. Tonight, Ohno and the American men's team will race in the men's 500 meter individual and the 5000 meter relay. The women will race in the ladies' 1000 meter individual competition.

Thus far, Ohno has been the only medal winner in short-track speed skating for the Americans. China leads the count with four, followed by Korea and Canada with three each. Bulgaria has taken two medals in short-track, and Australia has earned one.

6. Use the following wire copy story to write a script with full-screen graphic or graphics in format, TRT :35. The script will air in the 6 p.m. newscast tonight, slugged CONSUMERS. You may use a box. Include information about full-screen text on script pages. On a separate sheet of paper, draw your full-screen graphic or graphics, including background and text.

(NEW YORK)—Consumer confidence took a hit last month, falling for the first time in three months.

The Conference Board says its Consumer Confidence Index dropped 1.8 percent from two months ago—to 80.8.

The business-supported research group notes that although consumers are increasingly positive in their assessment of the current situation, expectations for the next six months are less positive than two months ago.

The executive director of the Board's Consumer Research Center says it's hard to explain the drop in confidence. He speculates, though, that dreary weather in much of the nation may have played a role.

7. Use the wire copy story in Exercise 3 to write a script with full-screen graphic or graphics in format, TRT :35. The script will air in tonight's 11 p.m. newscast, slugged ANGER.

8. Use the wire copy story in Exercise 4 to write a script with full-screen graphic or graphics in format, TRT :35. The script will air in tonight's 5 p.m. newscast, slugged POLL.

8

The Voice
Over: VO

Your television news scripts so far have included elements audiences can find in other media. Radio uses readers. Newspapers often use graphics. What makes television news different? Videotape. The elements of visuals and sound provided through videotape transport viewers, taking them to foreign countries, to major events, into the offices of the world's most powerful people and into the homes of favorite television stars. Videotape can provide emotion, as viewers witness the events of stories. Visuals and sound on television can tell stories that words can't capture. Videotape can add dimension and meaning to stories.

Videotape can also present a problem. Because television is so dependent on visuals and sound, coming up with compelling video can be a challenge for many stories. Some might not be so obviously visual, forcing the reporter and videographer to become very creative in finding good visuals and sound to illustrate the story. In other cases, access to the scene where those great visuals are happening may be denied to the crew. That situation also requires some creativity by the videographer and reporter.

The basic format incorporating videotape is called a Voice Over, designated "VO" (spoken v-o). This can be designated in upper- or lowercase, depending on the newsroom. As a reminder, this typically is a story read live by an anchor in the studio during which the audience sees visuals and hears natural sound from the scene. There are variations, but let's stay with this description for now. Although the term generally refers to the story format and its accompanying script, it can sometimes refer to shooting videotape intended for a vo (as in, "go shoot some vo of the demonstration") or the tape that holds that video ("can you toss me that vo?").

However, vo does not refer to reporters' narration tracks as would be recorded for a package, as will be discussed later; it refers to someone reading live while the audience is viewing and hearing recorded pictures and sound.

When you use videotape in a news script you write, you are responsible for everything the viewer sees and hears. A critically important aspect to keep in mind is that what the viewer hears in the anchor copy must make sense with what the viewer sees and hears on the videotape.

What Viewers Hear

In a vo, viewers hear both the anchor reading the news script and any sounds recorded on the videotape. Those recorded sounds are called "natural sounds," or nats for short. The term "vo/nats" describes videotape that includes natural sounds. For example, vo/nats of a parade might include pictures of the parade and sounds of marching footsteps, instruments, clapping and any other sounds that one naturally hears at a parade.

When the script airs, the natural sounds typically play at a lower volume, or "under"; this often is designated "nats under." The anchor's voice is louder, or voice over. Viewers hear the anchor's voice telling them the story, and in the background (under), they hear the natural sounds of a parade. It may seem as though it's too much for viewers to take in—pictures, the anchor's voice and sounds from whatever event is taking place in the pictures. But watch a television newscast. Almost all vo is vo/nats. It is natural for viewers to see events and hear the sounds associated with those events. It is not distracting. Remember that your job is to bring the viewer into the scene fully. In fact, an absence of natural sound can itself be distracting. It jars the viewers because they know something is missing.

However, hearing sounds that are not associated with the pictures can be very distracting for viewers. For example, NASA routinely makes videotapes of astronauts in space available to television stations. Almost without fail, the sound on the tape includes a running commentary by NASA officials on Earth. The commentary can be distracting to viewers who are watching astronauts float about in space. The voices of NASA officials are not the natural sounds of space. The television news writer may opt to use what is called "vo/sil" (voice over/silent), which describes pictures without sounds. However, silence itself can be distracting. Use vo/sil only as a last resort. Use it only when the sounds on the videotape are more distracting than the absence of sound.

Be careful about terminology, though. In some shops, vo/nats can refer to bringing the natural sound up full while the anchor pauses to allow the audience to hear what's on the edited video. In this case, typically, the newsroom will refer to natural sound underneath the anchor as "vo/nats under." Your shop may refer to "vo/nats under" (self-explanatory) and "vo/nats" (nats up full), or "vo/nats" (nats sound under) and "vo/nats full" (self-explanatory). Or it may use some other scheme. To avoid confusion, I'll use the terms "vo/nats under" and "vo/nats full." The term "vo/nats" will serve as a generic term for either.

Write to VO

In writing a vo, as in writing any other story form that uses visuals and sound, you must write to your video. This does not mean you write a script and then go through the videotape looking for shots that might go with what you've written.

Recall the steps we used toward building a basic story:

1. **Read:** Read the information carefully.

2. **Comprehend:** Make certain you understand all the information as well as the context—How do various facts relate to each other, how does the information relate to what came before, how does it relate to the people involved?

3. **Sort, arrange and simplify:** Note which facts are essential, important or interesting, and which are relatively unimportant, keeping in mind the audience, the amount of time allotted for the story (more on that later), and what visuals and sound are available (more later on that, as well).

At this point, your next steps were to think, then begin to write. Now we have the added element of visuals with natural sound. You will take the information you have, going through all the visuals and sound you have, and using the information, write the story based on the visuals and sound. So Step 4 is

4. **Consider visuals and natural sound:** You must keep something important in mind early in the story before or during shooting. If there are important elements to the story that need specific visuals, those need to have been considered and shot in the field. You cannot write and edit to videotape that was never shot.

Logging Tape

To know what shots are available, you must first view the tape, even if you shot it yourself. This is called logging the tape. It's also known as doing a shot sheet, or shot-sheeting. Watch the shots as viewers will see them. Make notes on visuals and sound about the shots you have available. Note where they occur in the tape and how long they run (which should be at least 12 seconds). Rate the shots. Decide which are most exciting, dramatic and emotional. More important, decide which visuals and nats best tell your story. Decide which will most effectively capture viewers' attention. These generally are the shots you want viewers to see early, so you will write your story to feature them early. You typically will use the most compelling, scene-setting shot as the opening shot in your story.

In addition, you need to look for what are called sequences—two or more shots that you can edit together in a series. More on that later, but you'll need to note possible sequences on your log sheet. Figure 8.1 shows a typical log sheet.

Avoid using what's called "wallpaper video." This refers to any generic video that remotely goes with the story but tells the viewer little or nothing that's specific, interesting or new. Often, the temptation—especially under deadline—is to use any video available just to cover a section of blank tape, spreading it like bland wallpaper. Pretty boring, pretty lazy, pretty bad. Instead, select shots with sound that work well. Of course, this also means that those great visuals and sound have to be shot in the field in the first place.

In your script copy, you can point out to viewers the specific visual elements you use, called "direct video references." You can use words such as "this" to directly reference video.

Slug _____   Tape _____

Reporter/Writer _____   Photog_____

Shot Location   Description/Notes

_____   _____

_____   _____

_____   _____

_____   _____

_____   _____

_____   _____

_____   _____

_____   _____

_____   _____

_____   _____

_____   _____

_____   _____

_____   _____

_____   _____

_____   _____

_____   _____

_____   _____

_____   _____

_____   _____

_____   _____

_____   _____

_____   _____

_____   _____

Tape Log Sheet

FIGURE 8.1

> Rescue workers used 400-pound cranes *like this one* to reach the child trapped in the well.

Direct video references can guide viewers' eyes to the focus of shots.

> Police say Alfred Hicks, *the man in the plaid shirt*, went on a nine-day killing spree in late June.

And direct video references can be used to include viewers in stories.

> *As you can see*, one-hundred-and-eighty-mile-an-hour winds ripped roofs from buildings and lifted homes from their foundations.

How you reference video in your scripts will depend on newsroom policies and practices. Some television stations encourage direct video references as helpful to viewers. Others discourage it as redundant. Whether your references are direct (as above) or more subtle, it remains your responsibility to make sure pictures and words match. What viewers hear and see must make sense together. Figure 8.2 can serve as a rough guide.

To illustrate the process of writing to vo, we'll use a wire copy story about a new security system that travelers to the U.S. will be facing.

> (WASHINGTON)—Foreign visitors arriving with visas at U.S. airports or seaports next year will have their travel documents scanned, their fingerprints and photos taken, and their identification checked against terrorist watch lists.
>
> Such a tracking system could have stopped two of the Sept. 11 hijackers, Homeland Security Undersecretary Asa Hutchinson said Monday as he gave details of the department's new U.S. Visitor and Immigration Status Indication Technology, or U.S. VISIT.

WRITING TO VIDEO

This is critical. All too often, it's poorly done.
Some things to keep in mind …

Use your best shots.
Reference your shots immediately in your script.
There should be clear reference to at least the first shot in each sequence in the story.
Don't describe what the viewer can obviously see. Instead, explain or add information that isn't obvious from the video.
Identify any noticeable person or activity so the viewer isn't left wondering.

FIGURE 8.2

The system, which takes effect Jan. 1, will check the comings and goings of foreign travelers who arrive in this country carrying visas. Travelers with visas made up about 60 percent, or 23 million, of foreign visitors to the United States last year.

Mr. Hutchinson said such a system would have caught hijackers Mohamed Atta, who had overstayed his visa on a previous occasion, and Hani Hanjour, who hadn't shown up at school as required by his student visa.

Congress has provided about $380 million for the new system, which will replace a paper-based system that has been highly criticized since the Sept. 11 attacks.

Under U.S. VISIT, a visa carrier will be required to provide immigrant and citizenship status, nationality, country of residence and an address where the visitor will be staying.

When the visitor leaves, Mr. Hutchinson said, the system also will verify the traveler's departure and identification.

Americans and travelers not required to have visas to enter the United States will not be subject to the new system.

Immigration advocacy groups have generally supported U.S. VISIT, which eliminates singling out certain groups. It will take the place of the domestic registration of noncitizen males 16 and older from 25 Middle Eastern and other countries.

As before, read the entire wire copy story, understand it and mark key facts. Look for a lead that will hook viewers. Find answers to viewers' questions. Think about present and future tense, active voice and conversational writing. For this story, let's suppose that you want to include some information that helps localize it. Let's also suppose that you're a writer in the Dallas–Fort Worth market. You place a call and learn that the Dallas–Forth Worth airport (DFW) will be implementing the system, and that about a million visa-carrying foreigners entered the U.S. through DFW airport last year. Now, your information is set.

But before you put the first word in your computer or on script paper, you will watch and log the vo/nats available for the story. Remember that in television news writing, available vo/nats decides how you will write the story. The vo/nats for this story includes a list of shots. Figure 8.3 shows how they might appear on your log sheet. Notice the numbers in the left column. These numbers mark where you will find the video in the tape. In this case, your first shot begins at 41 seconds on the tape (00:41) and ends at 59 seconds (00:59). This gives a shot duration of 18 seconds.

Also, notice that each shot's description includes the type of shot it is, such as wide, medium or tight (sometimes designated close up, or CU). This is good to help you remember the shot. Plus, you can build good sequences by going from one focal length, such as a medium shot, to another, such as a tight shot.

Video shots are like information in a story. You lead with the most compelling, scene-setting shots available. The writer decides the most compelling shot

Slug _____   Tape _____

Reporter/Writer _____   Photog_____

Shot Location	Description/Notes
00:41 - 00:59	Wide shot- jet taxis jetway, nats of engines whining
00:59 - 00:17	People walking off jetway into airport
01:17 - 01:34	Wide Shot - line of people waiting at customs
01:34 - 01:53	Medium shot -three people iwaiting, chatting
01:53 - 02:11	Medium Shot - customs agent talking with foreign
	traveler, guy is animated, asking something
02:11 - 02:27	Tight Shot - face of customs guy, shaking his head.
02:27 - 02:41	Tight Shot - passport & visa in visitor's hand
02:41 - 02:58	Tight shot - visitor, listening
02:58 - 03:16	Medium shot - other agent, typing, looking at
	computer screen
03:16 - 03:33	Tight shot - agent writing on form.
03:33 - 03:48	Medium shot -same agent writing on form
03:48 - 04:02	Medium shot - "Welcome to United States" sign
File @17:21	Wide shot - Hutchinson talking at lecturn to
	audience

Tape Log Sheet

FIGURE 8.3

in this example is that of the visitor talking excitedly to the customs agent, and lists out the other shots that work well.

> (shot of animated man with customs agent)
> (shot of passport and visa in visitor's hand)
> (man's face, listening)
> (tight shot of agent writing on a form)
> (medium shot of visitors in line, chatting)
> (shot of agent shaking his head)
> (shot of people leaving the jetway into the airport)
> (shot of jet taxiing up to jetway)

With the vo/nats in mind—always, always writing to the pictures and natural sound—the television news writer produces the following :30 script:

> Foreign visitors to the U-S will face a new computer-based security system beginning next year.
> Anyone trying to enter the country with a visa will first have to go through a background check.
> Agents will scan the traveler's documents, fingerprint and photograph the visitor, and check the traveler's I-D against a list of known terrorists.
> This will also let the government track the visitor while in the U-S.
> The Office of Homeland Security announced the system yesterday.
> It says such a system would have stopped two of the September eleventh hijackers.
> About 23 million visitors with visas came into the U-S last year, a million of them through DFW Airport.

This script was written with the intention of using the following shots:

> *(story begins with anchor on-cam)*
> Foreign visitors to the U-S will face a new computer-based security system beginning next year.
> *(start vo/nats here with shot of man with customs agent)*
> Anyone trying to enter the country with a visa will first have to go through a background check.
> *(shot of passport and visa in visitor's hand)*
> Agents will scan the traveler's documents, fingerprint and
> *(mans' face, listening)*
> photograph the visitor, and check the traveler's I-D against a
> *(tight shot of agent writing on a form)*
> list of known terrorists.
> This will also let the government
> *(medium shot of visitors in line, chatting)*
> track the visitor while in the U-S.
> *(shot of agent shaking his head)*
> The Office of Homeland Security announced the system yesterday.

> It says such a system would have stopped two of the September eleventh hijackers.
> *(shot of people leaving the jetway into the airport)*
> About 23 million visitors with visas came into the U-S last year, a million of them through DFW Airport.

Notice the shots changed at natural points, at the end of a sentence or a phrase. Generally speaking, a shot should stay up for at least two seconds. Unless the shot is extremely compelling, though, you should not leave it up for more than a sentence or so.

As you are selecting your shots and writing your script to them, you must keep one other aspect in mind. The shots selected must be steady and run long enough to cover the copy you have written to accompany that shot. Compare the duration time of the chosen shot to the amount of time it takes to read the phrase or sentence it accompanies. If the shot runs long enough, great. If it doesn't, rewrite the sentence, restructure the story or find another shot that works as well.

For example, the first shot chosen in the vo/nats above was that of the animated man with the customs agent. The writer wants that shot to cover the sentence

> Anyone trying to enter the country with a visa will first have to go through a background check.

Stop. How long will it take the anchor to read that sentence? Let's say it takes her six seconds. Six seconds is the amount of video that needs to be edited. Now, let's suppose that each entire shot on the vo field tape is usable, meaning it is steady, in focus and with good framing from start to finish. The corresponding shot runs 1:53 to 2:07 on the tape, giving it a duration of 14 seconds. The copy the shot is to cover takes just over five seconds to read. We've got it with plenty of time to spare.

The second sentence takes five seconds. Your second shot of the passport and visa in the traveler's hand will have to run five seconds. The shot is steady, in focus and well-framed, and lasts 14 seconds (2:27–2:41). The shot will work.

For this story, each of the shots chosen will cover the copy written for the shot. This will have to be the case for every story you write. If one shot is too short but can be edited next to another shot that works for what you're writing, call for both shots back-to-back.

Also, note that several shots, even one listed as a good possibility, didn't make it into the script. That's okay. You don't have to use every good shot you have. But you do have to use your best video, and every shot you use should be a good shot.

This is as much an issue for the writer as the person editing the videotape. First, you have to know whether the shot you want runs long enough to cover the sentence you're writing to it. Second, as we'll discuss in more detail later, you have to note on your script where the shot can be found on the tape and how many seconds of that shot needs to be edited. The editor must know exactly how long each shot is to run, because each shot is timed with the script. If a shot runs too short or long, the video won't match during the story. You may be asking yourself, How do I know how long each sentence or phrase will take the anchor to read? Many newsroom computer systems can now be set to an individual anchor's read rate, or you might have the anchor read the copy while you're checking a stopwatch and making notes. Failing that, imitate the anchor and read it aloud yourself. It's not exact, but it's pretty close.

Finally, in your shot notations on your script, you will need to indicate how long each shot runs as well as where to find it on the tape. More on that later.

Now, let's check the story itself.

• Does the lead offer viewers the latest information? Yes. The latest information is the announcement that foreign visitors will go through a new, computer-based set of security checks.

• Does the script answer viewers' questions? Yes. Who? *Foreigners traveling with visas, the Office of Homeland Security.* What? *New array of identification and tracking procedures.* When? *Beginning next year.* Where? *At all points of entry into the U.S.* Why? *To track visitors and possible terrorists.* How? *By scanning documents, fingerprints and photos into a database, checking the identity, tracking the person while visiting.*

• Does the script raise any questions it fails to answer? No. Although some information was left out because of the length of the story, the writer included all critical information.

• Is the script accurate? Yes. The facts in the script are those that appear in the wire copy. The new procedures are attributed to the Office of Homeland Security.

• Is the script conversational? Yes. Read it aloud.

• Does the script show immediacy with present- and future-tense verbs? Yes. Foreign visitors *will face*, agents *will scan*, it *says* such a system.

• Does the script use active voice? Yes. The news writer avoids passive writing. The doer of an action consistently precedes the action.

• Did the news writer write to vo? Yes. The vo/nats starts with a shot of a foreign visitor, and the script reads, "Anyone trying to enter the country with a visa will first have to go through a background check." A shot of a passport and visa in the visitor's hand goes with, "Agents will scan the traveler's documents . . ."

What Viewers See

In vo scripts, viewers see whatever news photographers are lucky and talented enough to capture on videotape. Viewers see the best shots first. In editing, remember that shots are arranged onto a vo tape in order and timed to match script copy. The order must make sense to viewers. It begins with the best shots available and follows with a logical sequence. Shot order that is illogical or that shows an unnatural sequence of events can be distracting to viewers. If you use dramatic shots of a burning house at the start of your story, for example, you can follow with shots of firefighters battling the flames and the house reduced to smoldering rubble. But you would not want to follow shots of a burning house with shots of the house before the fire started. The sequence is illogical and detracts from viewers' understanding of the story.

Also remember that not all vo is good vo. Television news writers decide whether vo is worth using by asking the questions, "Does the vo add to the story? Are the pictures compelling? Will the vo help viewers better understand the story? Will it 'take' viewers to the story?" If the answers are no, no, no and no, the television news writer may reject the video. Every second of a television newscast is precious. Just as the television news writer may omit some information from script copy, he or she may omit video that does not measure up. Television newscasts have no time for script copy or video that fails to add information, emotion or a better understanding of the story. The television news writer selects the best shots available—making sure good shots aren't left "in the edit room"—and writes to them.

In general, a vo begins with the anchor on camera. The anchor reads the first sentence of the story, then video rolls in with natural sound under as the anchor continues reading the vo. The viewer continues seeing videotape and hearing natural sound and the anchor's voice until the end of the story. With the next story, the process begins again.

There are occasional exceptions to this structure. Rather than end the story with visuals, the writer might decide to return to the anchor on camera for the last sentence of the story. This would be the exception rather than the rule and would only take place if there were a compelling reason to do so—such as a lack of good video, or a need to reestablish the anchor on camera to transition to another element in the newscast.

If the anchor is reading a series of related vos, such as three stories on the weather or four stories dealing with international news, the producer may decide to "wipe" from one story to the next. That is, the anchor reads the first line of story one on camera, then continues with the vo. At the end of that vo, rather than return to the anchor on camera for the next story, we would see a visual transition—a "wipe"—into the opening shot of the next vo.

Format

The format for a television news script with vo/nats or vo/sil will look familiar to you. The format rules you learned in previous chapters apply. In the example shown in Figure 8.4, use the numbers 1 through 13 (in parentheses) for reference as the script is discussed below.

The Top of the Page

Remember that information at the top of the page identifies (1) page, (2) slug, (3) format, (4) newscast, (5) date, (6) writer, and (7) run time.

(1) **The page number:** That will be assigned later.

(2) **The slug:** The title of the script is VISA SECURITY.

(3) **The format:** This is a vo.

(4) **The newscast:** This script airs in the 6 p.m. newscast, or 6p.

(5) **The date:** This script airs on March 6, or 3/6.

(1) (page) (2) Visa Security (3) VO (4) 6 p (5) 3/6 (6) EKG (7) Runs:

(8) anchor - on cam
(9) box - America's Security

(10) take vo/nats under

(11) (:01) S/ DFW International Airport/
Today

(12) ---------- (on cam) ----------

(13) Foreign visitors to the U-S will face a new computer-based security system beginning next year.

(14) ---------- (vo) ----------

Anyone trying to enter the country with a visa will first have to go through a background check.

Agents will scan the traveler's documents, fingerprint and photograph the visitor, and check the traveler's I-D against a list of known terrorists.

This will also let the government track the visitor while in the U-S.

The Office of Homeland Security announced the system yesterday.

It says such a system would have stopped two of the September 11th hijackers.

About 23 million visitors with visas came into the U-S last year.

(15) #####

FIGURE 8.4

(6) **The news writer's initials:** The script writer is identified by his or her initials.

(7) **The running time:** The allotted time is :30. The exact time will be filled in once the story is finished. As an approximate using these margins, the writer can figure about a second and a half per line of copy.

The Left Column

Director cues in the left column speak to the newscast director. Note that some of the cues for this story will be new to you.

(8) **Camera shot:** The cue "anchor-on cam" tells the newscast director that the story starts with the anchor on the television screen.

(9) **Director cue:** The cue "box–America's Security" tells the newscast director to use a box over the anchor's shoulder and identifies the box with its title, "America's Security."

(10) **Director cue:** The cue "take vo/nats under" tells the newscast director to show vo/nats (pictures with natural sounds under) on the television screen. The cue appears in lowercase letters in the left column at the point at which the news writer wants the newscast director (or the director's assistant or technical director) to punch the button that brings the vo/nat to the television screen.

Be aware that some newsrooms use a different terminology. Because the term SOT technically refers to any "sound on tape," natural sound underneath can be designated "S-O-T under."

(11) **The super:** This is another director cue, designated "S/," telling the director to superimpose the words "DFW International Airport" and "Today" over the vo/nats. In this case, the super, called a "CG" (character generator) by some stations, is a locator. It tells the viewers where (and when) the events they see occurred. Other terminology referring to supers or CGs can include "key," "font," "Chyron" (the brand name of one of the devices that does the superimposing on the screen) and "lower-third" (referring to the fact that supers are laid over the lower third of the screen).

The slash mark (/) after the locator on your script tells the director to drop what follows (the time/day it occurred) down to the next line. Even though the airport tape was shot to illustrate a new policy and did not involve an actual event, I included a time designator with the locator (/Today) to show how it would look.

The super appears on either one or two lines across the bottom of the television screen (Figure 8.5). The best way to understand supers is to watch television news. You rarely will see a vo that does not include a super, telling viewers where and when an event happened. The time cue ":01" tells the director to insert the super one second after the vo/nats under appears on the television screen and to hold it for four seconds. The newscast director (or technical director or assistant director) punches the buttons that bring vo/nats to the television screen. It will take him or her a second to then punch the buttons that superimpose the informa-

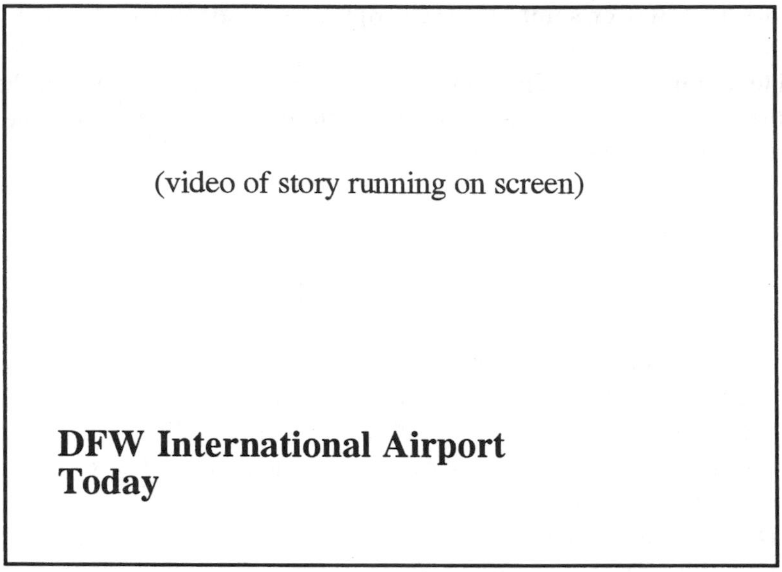

(video of story running on screen)

**DFW International Airport
Today**

FIGURE 8.5

tion "DFW International Airport" and "Today" over the video. Some stations use the time cue :00 to designate a super at the top. Others use :01, allowing the newscast director the second it takes to punch buttons. Throughout this text, you'll use :01 to call for a super at the start of vo. The director will leave the super on the screen for about four seconds, which is long enough for viewers to read it.

The Right Column

Information in the right column speaks to the news anchor.

(12) **Anchor cue:** Directions for the anchor appear between broken dotted lines. The cue "—-(on cam)—-" tells the anchor that he or she is on camera.

(13) **The script copy:** The news story the anchor will read on the air is clean and uncluttered.

(14) **Anchor cue:** The cue "—-(vo)—-" tells the news anchor that videotape is rolling, so he or she is no longer on camera. The vo/nats under is covering the television screen. The anchor does not need to know whether vo is vo/nats under or vo/sil. His or her job (to read the script on air) is not affected by natural sounds on tape or the lack of them.

(15) **The end script:** The pound sign or signs (#) tell the anchor the script is ending..

Shot Notation

You will need to communicate to the editor what shots need to be edited, where they can be found on the vo field tape, and how long each shot needs to run. Some newsrooms have a form that calls for the writer to list out shot location and duration. Most shops have their writers designate editing instructions on a copy of the script that goes to the editor.

Figure 8.6 shows a script with shot designations noted. Notice that the shot descriptions and locations are listed on the right side of the left column, next to the line of script each shot will accompany. The writer has timed each line of the script carefully. He has selected the shots to go with each line. On his script, he has written where each shot can be found and how long each shot should run. If all goes well, the shots should match the script and time out correctly.

Take a special note of the final shot, "people leaving jetway: 1:04–1:18." Those of you astute in arithmetic may have noticed that the writer has called for a 14-second shot to cover four to five seconds of copy. There's a reason for this. You always want to include what's known as pad video at the end of a vo.

Let's say your tape is cut to match the script exactly, with video set to end on the final syllable of the story. If the anchor is reading a bit slowly tonight, or the director starts the video a second or two early, you're in trouble. This means that the visuals will run out before the anchor finishes the script. As a result, viewers will hear the story as they see the final shot, then see the screen go to black before returning to the anchor. Bad situation. It looks unprofessional and sloppy.

The way to fix that problem is to edit pad video at the end of every tape that plays. By extending the final shot an additional ten seconds or so, you ensure that, should anything be off, you won't go to black before returning to the anchor.

Finally, be aware that each shot is not a separate videotape (or, if your station is on a central server, a separate file). One vo can include any number of shots. The various shots are edited in order onto a single tape cassette (or video file) that rolls during your story.

Beginning Scripts with VO, Ending Scripts with Anchor-On Cam

Look again at the list of shots available for the VISA SECURITY story and the script. A close look at the two should suggest another version of the vo/nats under script. You could use more of the pictures available. You have vo/nats to cover more of the script, if you choose. Figures 8.7 and 8.8 show that it is acceptable to end a vo news script with anchor on camera. You don't have to end with vo. If wiping into the vo from a related story, it also is acceptable to start a television news script with vo or to cover the entire script with vo. Look for creative ways to use vo. Look for creative ways to tell and show viewers stories.

(1) (page) (2) Visa Security (3) VO (4) 6 p (5) 3/6 (6) EKG (7) Runs:

(8) anchor - on cam
(9) box - America's Security

(10) take vo/nats under
(11) (:01) S/ DFW International Airport/
Today
(man with customs agent
1:57-2:02)

(passport in guy's hand
2:29-2:33)

(man's face
2:47-2:50)

(agent writing
3:18-3:22)

(people in line, chatting
1:43-1:46)

(agent shaking his head
2:13-2:17)

(people leaving jetway
1:04-1:18)

(12) ---------- (on cam) ----------

(13) Foreign visitors to the U-S will face a new computer-based security system beginning next year.

(14) ---------- (vo) ----------

Anyone trying to enter the country with a visa will first have to go through a background check.

Agents will scan the traveler's documents, fingerprint and photograph the visitor, and check the traveler's I-D against a list of known terrorists.

This will also let the government track the visitor while in the U-S.

The Office of Homeland Security announced the system yesterday.

It says such a system would have stopped two of the September 11th hijackers.

About 23 million visitors with visas came into the U-S last year, a million of them through DFW Airport.

(15) #####

FIGURE 8.6

(1) (page) (2) Visa Security (3) VO (4) 6 p (5) 3/6 (6) EKG (7) Runs:

anchor - on cam
box - America's Security

---------- (on cam) ----------

Foreign visitors to the U-S will face a new computer-based security system beginning next year.

take vo/nats under
(:01) S/ DFW International Airport/
    Today

---------- (vo) ----------

Anyone trying to enter the country with a visa will first have to go through a background check.

(man with customs agent
1:57-2:02)

(passport in guy's hand
2:29-2:33)

Agents will scan the traveler's documents, fingerprint and photograph the visitor, and check the traveler's I-D against a list of known terrorists.

(man's face
2:47-2:50)

This will also let the government track the visitor while in the U-S.

(agent writing
3:18-3:22)

The Office of Homeland Security announced the system yesterday.

(people in line, chatting
1:43-1:46)

It says such a system would have stopped two of the September 11th hijackers.

(agent shaking his head
2:13-2:17)

---------- (on cam) ----------

About 23 million visitors with visas came into the U-S last year, a million of them through DFW Airport.

anchor on-cam

#####

FIGURE 8.7

(1) (page) (2) Visa Security (3) VO (4) 6 p (5) 3/6 (6) EKG (7) Runs:

take vo/nats under
(:01) S/ DFW International Airport/
    Today

                    (people walking off jetway
                           1:02-1:07)

                    (man with customs agent
                           1:57-2:02)

                    (passport in guy's hand
                           2:29-2:33)

                         (man's face
                           2:47-2:50)

                        (agent writing
                         3:18-3:22)

                  (people in line, chatting
                         1:43-1:46)

                  (agent shaking his head
                         2:13-2:17)

                      (people in line
                         1:18-1:32)

---------- (vo) ----------

Foreign visitors to the U-S will face a new computer-based security system beginning next year.

Anyone trying to enter the country with a visa will first have to go through a background check.

Agents will scan the traveler's documents, fingerprint and photograph the visitor, and check the traveler's I-D against a list of known terrorists.

This will also let the government track the visitor while in the U-S.

The Office of Homeland Security announced the system yesterday.

It says such a system would have stopped two of the September 11th hijackers.

About 23 million visitors with visas came into the U-S last year, a million of them through DFW Airport.

                      #####

FIGURE 8.8

Timing the Script

One other important point to bring up here. Once the script is finished, regardless of whether you began with anchor on cam, ended that way, or covered the entire script with vo, you must go back and time the script. If your computer does this for you, you can probably leave the rough estimate the computer will place in the "Runs:" area of the script's header. But make sure it's accurate and within the allotment the producer has given you. The script we just wrote, by my read, runs about :33, which is a tad longer than the producer wanted. If that's the case, make certain it won't be a problem for the producer, and let her or him know the actual running time. This information will likely show up in the producer's rundown once the story is edited, but it's important to give her or him a heads-up. It may be the producer doesn't have the extra seconds to give. If that's the case, you rewrite to get the script down to the allotted time. Period.

Something to Avoid

News writing is a creative process. There are as many ways to tell a story as there are news writers to tell it. Likewise, there are as many ways to use vo/nats and vo/sil in scripts as there are news writers who use them. Previous examples show vo/nats under starting a script, ending it and covering the entire script. As a news writer, you look for the best ways to use the best vo to write the best scripts possible. You are original. You are creative. Your script will look like no other writer's.

Still, you should follow basic guidelines. Figure 8.9 shows an example of script formatting you will want to avoid. It is not a good idea to jump from the anchor on camera, to vo, back to the anchor on camera and so on. Once vo is on the television screen, it's best to leave it there until you are ready to return to the anchor to end the story or to begin the next story in the newscast. Some news writers have tried to hop back and forth between the anchor and vo, and their scripts have suffered for it. That sort of editing is distracting to viewers because they expect the anchor to appear on camera to introduce stories or to end them. They do not expect the anchor to pop up in the middle of stories. Look at Figure 8.9. Picture in your mind the effect on the television screen. It is unexpected, confusing and distracting, and it looks indecisive and disjointed.

One other rule that you must always follow is this: never, never use the same shot twice in the same story. Repeating shots is an absolute sin in writing and editing news video.

Adding VO/Nats Full

In your search for creative uses of vo, you may discover that the natural sounds on the videotape are compelling enough to do some storytelling for you. Remember that viewers hear natural sounds under the news anchor's voice. But

(1) (page) (2) Visa Security (3) VO (4) 6 p (5) 3/6 (6) EKG (7) Runs:

anchor - on cam
box - America's Security

---------- (on cam) ----------

Foreign visitors to the U-S will face a new computer-based security system beginning next year.

take vo/nats under
(:01) S/ DFW International Airport/
    Today
        (man with customs agent
        1:57-2:02)

---------- (vo) ----------

Anyone trying to enter the country with a visa will first have to go through a background check.

        (passport in guy's hand
        2:29-2:33)

Agents will scan the traveler's documents, fingerprint and photograph the visitor, and check the traveler's I-D

        (man's face
        2:47-2:50)

against a list of known terrorists.

anchor - on cam
box - America's Security

---------- (on cam) ----------

This will also let the government track the visitor while in the U-S.

The Office of Homeland Security announced the system yesterday.

take vo/nats under

---------- (vo) ----------

It says such a system would have stopped two of the September 11th hijackers.

        (agent shaking his head
        2:13-2:17)

anchor - on cam

---------- (on cam) ----------

About 23 million visitors with visas came into the U-S last year, a million of them through DFW Airport.

#####

FIGURE 8.9

you might want to bring the natural sounds full, instructing the news anchor to pause while the newscast director increases the volume of the sound. Here's another wire copy example.

> (BEL HARBOUR, Fla.)—The Teamsters union says workers have agreed to go back to work after a dispute was settled with United Parcel Service.
>
> Teamsters members staged a strike against UPS at 9 a.m. today when the company more than doubled the weight limit on packages, to 150 pounds.
>
> The strike was settled when the company agreed at the 5 p.m. close of business not to require workers to handle packages heavier than 70 pounds without a helper or a lifter device.

The vo/nats available for this story includes the following shots. Now that you understand how to log video, I'll dispense with shot locations and just give duration time for each shot.

- Shot of UPS trucks sitting in the company parking lot (:14)
- Shot of boxes piled up in the warehouse (:13)
- Shot of union workers walking on the picket line (:26)
- Shot of a group of union workers chanting strike slogans (:27)
- Shot of a lifting device (:14)
- Shot of union workers standing on the picket line (:21)

Read the wire copy. Understand it. Find and mark key facts. Review available vo/nats. Notice the fourth shot available, a group of union workers chanting strike slogans. The natural sounds of chanting might add to your story. Plan to bring them up full. Write a :30 news script with vo/nats for the 6 p.m. newscast, inserting the natural sound full, or "vo/nats full."

Your script might look something like the one in Figure 8.10. As always, test the script. Does the lead offer viewers the latest information? Does it answer viewers' questions? Does it raise any questions it fails to answer? Is it accurate? Is it conversational? (Read it aloud.) Does it show immediacy with present-tense? Does it use active voice?

Study the script format in Figure 8.10. Pay close attention to numbers 12, 13 and 19. These are the cues that instruct the newscast director and news anchor to include vo/nat full in the script.

The Top of the Page

Numbers 1 through 7 identify the page number (filled in by producer later), the slug (STRIKE), the format (vo/nats), the newscast (6p), the date (3/6), the news writers' initials and the running time.

(1) (page) (2) Strike (3) VO/nats (4) 6 p (5) 3/6 (6) EKG (7) Runs:

(8) anchor on-cam
(9) box - UPS Strike

    (16)---------- (on cam) ----------

    (17) A strike against United Parcel Service is over, eight hours after the workers walked off the job.

(10) take vo/nats under
(11) (:01) S/ Bel Harbour / Today
         (workers walking on picket line)

    (18)---------- (vo) ----------

Teamsters union members formed picket lines this morning outside the U-P-S office in Bel Harbour.

    Workers were protesting a company decision that more than doubled the weight limit on the packages they handle, to 150 pounds.

         (more workers)

    (19)--(pause-nats full :04 & under)--

About an hour ago, the union called off its strike and announced an agreement with U-P-S.

(12) bring nats full :04
         (workers chanting)
(13) cue anchor
        (union officials talking with workers)

    (20)---------- (on cam) ----------

The union says the company agreed to offer workers a helper or lifting machine for packages over 70 pounds.

(14) anchor on-cam
(15) box - UPS Strike

    (21) #####

FIGURE 8.10

The Left Column

Note the new director cues included in the script. Also, note that the news writer has included shots for the vo/nats in the left column.

(8) **Camera shot:** The cue "anchor-on cam" tells the newscast director that the news anchor appears on camera.

(9) **Director cue:** The cue "box–UPS Strike" tells the newscast director that the news anchor should appear off-center with a box identified by its title over the anchor's shoulder.

(10) **Director cue:** The cue "take vo/nats under" tells the newscast director to show vo/nats on the television screen. The natural sounds play under the anchor's voice.

(11) **The super:** The cue "S/" tells the newscast director to superimpose the place and time over vo/nats at the bottom of the television screen (Figure 8.11).

(12) **Director cue:** The cue "bring nats full :04" tells the newscast director to increase the natural sounds of the vo/nats from under to full for four seconds. The cue appears in lowercase letters. The vo/nats full available will determine how many seconds you pause, or use. In the example, four seconds of chanting is enough to give viewers a sense of the event. Three or four seconds is about the minimum amount of vo/nats full you will want to use. But you can use more if it adds to viewers' understanding of the story. If chanters were repeating a slogan that lasted six seconds, for example, you might allow vo/nats full to last :06 so viewers could hear the slogan once in full. Viewers' attention spans probably can't handle more than eight or 10 seconds of vo/nats full, unless there's a very good reason for it. The anchor will pause while the natural sounds are full. Viewers will hear only the sounds on videotape, the sounds of workers chanting (see number 17 below).

(13) **Director cue:** The instruction "cue anchor" tells the newscast director to prompt the news anchor. The newscast director might speak through a line directly to the news anchor's ear, giving the news anchor a cue as simple as "Go." Or the news director might speak over headsets to a studio technician, instructing him or her to give the anchor a hand signal that means "Go." The cue alerts the newscast director when it is appropriate to tell the news anchor to start talking again.

(14) **Director cue:** The cue "anchor-on cam" tells the newscast director to stop showing vo/nats on the television screen and return to the anchor on camera.

(15) **Director cue:** The cue "box–UPS Strike" tells the newscast director that the anchor should appear off-center with a box over the anchor's shoulder.

The Right Column

Information in the right column speaks to the news anchor.

(16) **Anchor cue:** The cue "——(on cam)——" tells the news anchor that he or she is on camera.

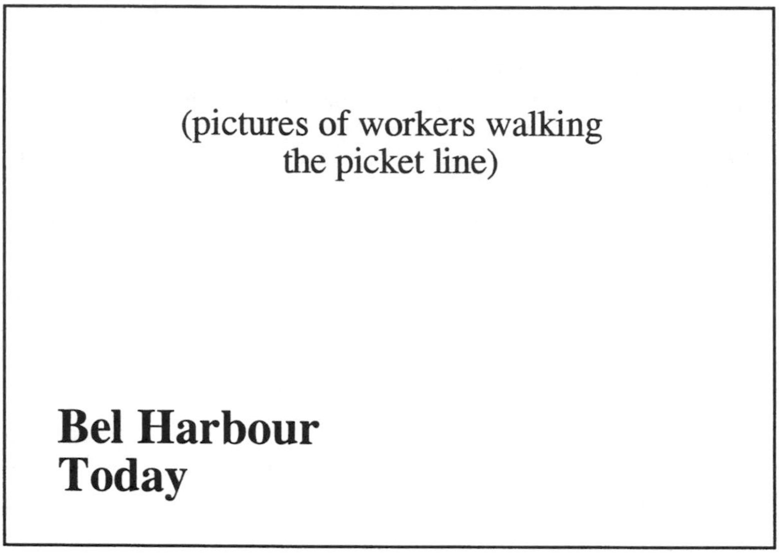

(pictures of workers walking
the picket line)

**Bel Harbour
Today**

FIGURE 8.11

(17) **The script copy:** The story the news anchor will read on the air is clean and uncluttered.

(18) **Anchor cue:** The cue "—-(vo)—-" tells the news anchor that vo is rolling and he or she is no longer on camera.

(19) **Anchor cue:** The cue "—-(pause :04 for nats full)—-" tells the news anchor to stop talking for four seconds. While the news anchor is silent, the newscast director increases the volume of the natural sound on tape from under to full (see number 12 above). The news anchor waits to hear the nat full fade to under and waits to hear the newscast director say "Go" or waits for a hand signal before talking again.

(20) **Anchor cue:** The cue "—-(on cam)—-" tells the news anchor he or she is back on camera.

(21) **Anchor cue:** The pound sign (#) tells the news anchor the story is over.

Script Timing for VO/Nats Full

Adding vo/nats full to a news script adds time to the script. The television news writer needs to account for every second of every news script he or she writes. Suppose the newscast producer assigns you a vo/nats news script with a TRT (total running time) of :30. Now suppose you decide to use :04 nats full in the script. You must account for the :04, so you write :26 worth of script copy (TRT :30 minus :04 nat full equals :26 for copy). Remember that the vo/nats full available will determine how many seconds you use. Three or four seconds is about the minimum amount of vo/nats full you will want to use. But you can use more if it adds to viewers' understanding of the story.

Once you have tallied the script read time with the nats full time, you'll enter that running time total at the appropriate place in the script.

Summary

The abbreviation "vo" stands for Voice Over. Viewers hear the anchor's voice over videotape pictures. When you use videotape in a news script, you are responsible for what viewers hear and see. The two must make sense together.

In a vo, viewers hear the anchor reading the news script along with any sounds recorded on the videotape. Those sounds are called natural sounds. The term "vo/nats" describes videotape that includes natural sounds. When the script airs, the sounds play at a lower volume, or "under." The anchor's voice is louder, or "voice over." Almost all vo is vo/nats. It is natural for viewers to see events and hear the sounds associated with those events. However, hearing sounds that are not associated with the pictures can distract viewers. The term "vo/sil" describes pictures without sounds. Silence itself can be distracting, so use vo/sil only when the sounds on the videotape are more distracting than the absence of sound.

As with boxes and full screen graphics, you must write to videotape. Before you start writing, watch the vo/nats or vo/sil. Lead with the most compelling shots available. Television writers do not write scripts, then fit vo into them. Television writers select shots and then write scripts to feature the best shots early. In editing, shots are arranged onto a vo tape in order and timed to match script copy.

The format for a television news script with vo/nats or vo/sil follows the guidelines you have learned. Information at the top of the page identifies the page number, slug, format, newscast, date, writer and running time. Director cues in the left column speak to the newscast director. The director cues "take vo/nats under" and "take vo/sil" tell the newscast director to show vo/nats under or vo/sil on the television screen. Cues for "supers" (S/) tell the director to superimpose words over the vo/nats. Information in the right column speaks to the news anchor. The cue "vo" tells the news anchor that videotape is rolling.

You can end a vo news script with vo. You can also start a television news script with vo or cover the entire script with vo. Look for creative ways to use vo, but follow basic guidelines. It is not a good idea to jump from the anchor on camera, to vo, back to the anchor on camera and so on.

You may decide that natural sounds are compelling enough to do some storytelling for you. You can bring the natural sounds "full," instructing the news anchor to pause while the newscast director increases the volume of the sound. The director cues "bring nats full" and "cue anchor" appear in the left column of a script that uses vo/nats full. The anchor cue "pause for nats full" appears in the right column of a script that uses vo/nats full.

Three or four seconds is about the minimum amount of vo/nats full you will want to use, but you can use more if it adds to viewers' understanding of the story. Viewers' attention spans probably can't handle more than eight or 10 seconds of vo/nats full, unless there's a very good reason for it. Remember when you are timing your scripts that adding vo/nats full to a news script adds time to the script.

Exercises

1. Use the information in the wire copy story from Switzerland. Write a news script with vo/nats for today's 5 p.m. newscast, slugged SWISS TRAIN WRECK, TRT :30. You may use a box. Choose vo/nats from the shots available. Note your vo/nats shots on your script.

> (SWITZERLAND)—Six people died and about 15 were injured, some seriously, today in northern Switzerland in a major railway accident.
>
> A Federal Railways spokesman said a passenger train leaving a station in northern Switzerland during the early afternoon crashed into the jib of a crane that swung out into its path.
>
> The reason for the accident has not been established yet, but human error cannot be ruled out, according to the spokesman.
>
> A goods wagon at the front of the train was derailed. Three following passenger cars were ripped open at window level.
>
> Rescue helicopters flew the seriously injured casualties to hospitals in Zurich, Berne and Basle, whereas less gravely hurt people were taken in ambulances to local hospitals. Police and fire services rushed to the scene.
>
> The crane was being used to lay new track on the line between the towns of Olten and Aarau in Solothurn canton. The crane driver was uninjured but is said to be suffering from shock.
>
> The line was closed for three hours, forcing other trains to be diverted.

Available VO/nats (super: Northern Switzerland/Today):

(a) Shot of the crash scene (22 seconds)
(b) Shot of the derailed cars (19 seconds)
(c) Shot of the crane (28 seconds)
(d) Shot of ambulances leaving the scene (26 seconds)
(e) Shot of firefighters and police at the scene (24 seconds)
(f) Shot of the damaged passenger cars (16 seconds)
(g) Shot of people crying and hugging (27 seconds).

2. Rewrite the SWISS TRAIN WRECK script to include vo/nats full. Remember that adding a few seconds of vo/nats full changes the TRT of the script. Adjust accordingly to keep your script at TRT :30. Choose the vo/nats full from the following list:

(a) Shot of passengers with sounds of their crying nats full (27 seconds)
(b) Shot of rescue workers loading ambulances with their voices nats full (26 seconds)

(c) Shot of workers trying to right the train with their voices and lifting equipment sounds nats full (28 seconds)

(d) Shot of an ambulance driving from the scene with the sound of sirens nats full (26 seconds).

3. Use the following wire copy to write a news script with vo/nats for today's 5 p.m. newscast, slugged OYSTER BAN LIFTED, TRT :25. You may use a box. Choose vo/nats from the shots available. Note shots on your script.

> (NEWPORT NEWS, Va.)—The Virginia Marine Resources Commission voted today to reopen the oyster harvest on portions of the James River.
>
> The unanimous decision amounts to a victory for watermen and the rejection of the recommendation from the Virginia Institute of Marine Sciences to maintain the oyster ban.
>
> The decision came after a two-hour public hearing in which watermen complained that the current ban made no sense and put them out of work.

Available vo/nats (assume you have adequate video of each shot to cover the copy you have written for it) (super: Newport News/Today):

(a) Various shots of oyster harvesters addressing the commission at the public hearing

(b) Shot of the commission at the public hearing

(c) Shot of the audience at the public hearing

(d) Shot of oyster harvesters cheering and shaking hands after the commission announced its decision

(e) Shot of the James River

4. Rewrite the OYSTER BAN LIFTED script to include vo/nats full. Use the shots listed above, including vo/nats full of oyster harvesters cheering and shaking hands after the commission announced its decision. Be aware that adding a few seconds of vo/nats full changes the TRT of the script. Adjust accordingly to keep your script at TRT :25.

5. Find the best vo script on television tonight. Watch a local or national newscast. As you watch, pay attention to the use of vo/nats, vo/sil and vo/nats full in the newscast. Describe a story that uses vo. Write a short recap of the story in which the vo appears. Describe how the news writer used vo/nats under, vo/sil or vo/nats full effectively. Note the newscast time, station and date.

Sound On Tape: SOT

The term "sot" stands for "sound on tape." It can be pronounced letter-by-letter, s-o-t, or as an acronym, sot. This book will use sot as a word, "a sot," interchangeably with SOT, spoken as letters, "an s-o-t."

A sot can refer to any sound on tape. In fact, a few newsrooms designate natural sound with the cue "SOT under." However, most often, sot means a person recorded on videotape as he or she is speaking. It also is called a sound bite and usually lasts 6 to 18 seconds. Up to now, you have been the storyteller. You have been providing viewers with information about who, what, when, where, why and how. A sot allows viewers to hear directly from people involved in stories. Television news writers use sots primarily to add emotion, reaction and opinion, rather than information, to stories. News anchors can provide information. But fairness and balance prevent them from sharing their emotions about stories. The people involved in stories can provide the emotional elements that help viewers better understand stories.

Finding SOTs

The television news writer is responsible for selecting sots for stories. Usually, a news writer is faced with a four- or five-minute videotaped interview. The news writer must select the :06 to :18 section that best captures the speaker's comments. In choosing that sound bite, the writer must keep some things in mind.

First, the sound bite must carry, meaning it must be interesting and meaningful all the way through. This is true if the sot runs 6 seconds or 26 seconds (although anything over 15 seconds should sound a warning). The sot must be a complete, self-contained statement or response, and the sot should describe how or why rather than saying yes or no. Of course, this means the interviewer needs to have asked how or why questions. We'll talk more about that when we turn to interviewing.

As a rule, avoid bites that wander. The best sots get right to the heart of the matter. Also, don't use bites that recite numbers or statistics or are full of jargon.

They make for truly boring sound bites. If the dry information in the sot is important to the story, you as the writer can lift that information and translate it into more simple, interesting, understandable and meaningful copy.

The best sots are eyewitness accounts, expert evaluations or opinions, or responses to a situation or someone else's claims. The best sots give human effects of something, have a human quality to them, or contain compelling words or delivery.

With practice, sots will jump out at you. As you're reading someone's comments, you'll isolate sots. As you're listening to someone speak in person or on videotape, you'll hear sots automatically. But it takes practice. Consider the recap of the following story.

> A man barricades himself in the restroom of the Montgomery County Hospital. In a note, he tells hospital workers he has a bomb and threatens to blow up the building unless he receives immediate medical attention. Hospital workers call the sheriff's office. Sheriff's deputies evacuate the hospital's first floor and conduct negotiations with the man. The man eventually surrenders. Deputies find no bomb but say the man is armed with a hunting knife. No one is injured.

Now read an interview with Sgt. Joyce Edwards of the Montgomery County Sheriff's Department.

> "The sheriff's department dispatcher received the initial call at or about 1:14 p.m. this afternoon from Montgomery County Hospital advising the sheriff's department that the alleged perpetrator entered the premises at some prior time. At which time, the alleged perpetrator, described as a 34-year-old white male, locked himself in a men's bathroom located in the hospital's main lobby area. The alleged perpetrator, one Rob Moore of 1724 Oak Street in Montgomery County, had apparently made threats of bodily harm to hospital staff. We arrived on the scene at or about 1:20 p.m. and ordered an evacuation of the hospital's first floor. We evacuated the first floor of the hospital building without incident as a precautionary measure. Whenever someone does something like this, we have to take the threat seriously. We didn't know if he had a weapon or not. We had to take the threat seriously. We conducted negotiations with Mr. Moore, eventually convincing him to surrender himself to us at or about 2:24 p.m. Mr. Moore is in custody and will be turned over later for psychiatric evaluation. The incident ended without injury."

We touched on this earlier in the book, but this is really how some law enforcement officers speak. As you should be painfully aware, it is not the way ordinary people speak—stiff, nonconversational, tedious and inappropriate for television news. Still, Sgt. Edwards does provide a usable sot. Do you see it? Look for her comment that would add emotion to the story.

> "Whenever someone does something like this, we have to take the threat seriously. We didn't know if he had a weapon or not. We had to take the threat seriously."

The sot explains why sheriff's deputies proceeded as they did. It adds emotion. It adds to viewers' understanding of the story by answering why.

Rating SOTs

Now suppose you have sound bites available from other people at the hospital. Consider the following sots, all from reliable sources. All of the people speaking about the bomb scare are qualified to speak about it because they witnessed it. Still, some sound bites are better than others. Rate the sots in order of best to worst, rating highest the ones that would add most to the story.

Gene Smith/Hospital administrator:

1. "Nothing like this has ever happened before that I can remember." (Runs :04)

2. "He passed out a note demanding to see a doctor and threatened to hurt members of my staff. He also said he had a bomb." (Runs :07)

3. "I guess he didn't feel like he was receiving the attention he needed. It saddens me that he thought this was the way to get the medical attention he needed." (Runs :10)

Sally Frost/Head Nurse:

4. "Everyone was really calm, if you can believe it. We knew he was in there. We were afraid he might hurt us. It was frightening I think for patients especially, but everyone stayed calm and pretty much in control. I'm glad it ended the way it did but I'm sorry it happened at all." (Runs :15)

Jessica Hollings/Nurse:

5. "He's an idiot. The son of a b— is an idiot. I mean, what kind of an idiot would do something like this? He's an idiot." (Runs :06)

6. "Kind of says something about the current health care crisis, don't it? It's a sad comment." (Runs :05)

Ed Foyles/Patient:

7. "I just couldn't believe it when they told us we'd have to evacuate. I was not really scared at the time, more confused, you know. But now that it's over, I realize it was a pretty scary thing." (Runs :10)

Did you pick number 4 or 7 as best? They are both excellent sots. Both could add to the story. Number 4 is emotional. It captures the feelings shared by the people involved in the incident. Number 7 also adds emotion and captures the feelings of one of the people involved.

How did you rate number 3? It adds emotion but could present a problem. The danger of number 3 is that it allows one person, the hospital administrator, to make assumptions about what was in the mind of another person, Rob Moore. The hospital administrator is making a fairly safe assumption here. But be careful that people speaking about other people's reasons for doing things do not make irresponsible assumptions.

How did you rate numbers 1 and 2? Neither is a particularly good sot. Number 1 does not offer viewers emotion or information. Does it matter whether it has ever happened before? Only if it has. If this is the fourth time in as many months that someone has threatened to blow up the hospital, that is news. Otherwise, you would not have expected it to have happened before so the fact that it hasn't is not news. Number 2 offers too much information without emotion. It's simply a statement about the way events unfolded. It's best to let the news anchor present the facts. Use sots to add emotion, human drama and feelings that the news anchor, who is not involved in the story, can't add.

As for numbers 5 and 6, they should be at the bottom of your list. Number 5 includes profanity. There is no place in a television newscast for profanity. Number 6 does not make sense. It raises questions the nurse fails to answer and the news writer would be challenged to answer. There is no evidence that the events at the hospital are in any way a comment on the current health care crisis. If Moore's note referred to his disillusionment with health care reform, you might be able to make a case that his actions were some form of political protest. But with the information you have, you can make no such argument.

Seeing the sots written out above may have raised some questions. You'll notice that the grammar in number 6 is incorrect: "Kind of says something about the current health care crisis, don't it?" should read " . . . doesn't it?" You use what a person says exactly as the person says it. Newspapers are able to "clean up" a person's grammar. Television, because it's on tape, is not. The same applies for extra words a person may add. In number 7 the extra words "you know" are unnecessary, but it is what patient Ed Foyles says so you include it in the sot.

Trimming SOTs

You do not have to use all of a person's thoughts within a sot. Number 4 offers a good example.

> Sally Frost/Head Nurse: "Everyone was really calm, if you can believe it. We knew he was in there. We were afraid he might hurt us. It was frightening, I think for patients especially, but everyone stayed calm and pretty much in control. I'm glad it ended the way it did but I'm sorry it happened at all." (Runs :15)

You could easily trim this sot to make it shorter. For instance, you could cut the sot to :09 by editing out the last sentence. The sot is still emotional. It is still a complete thought. It is still a good sot. But now it runs :09 instead of :15.

There are other ways to trim sots that allow a tape editor or news writer to delete words from the middle of a sot. Through editing, the original sot from Sally Frost could be shortened by cutting words from the middle.

Sally Frost/Head Nurse: "Everyone was really calm, if you can believe it. We knew he was in there . . . but everyone stayed calm and pretty much in control. I'm glad it ended the way it did but I'm sorry it happened at all." (Runs :09)

The edit is a little more difficult for a tape editor technically. And be aware that when you cut words from the middle of a thought, you might change the meaning of the sot. If you trim sots, do so carefully. Do not make edits that change the meaning of a person's words.

In addition, be aware of the visual effect of editing two sections of a sound bite together as one. When you do this, the edit from the end of the first section to the beginning of the second will be obvious. The person's face will visibly jump on the screen as the edit shows two separate segments have been butted together. This visual jump is known as a jump cut, and it's a problem. All is not lost, however. You can cover the edit by selecting another shot that does not show the person being interviewed. You lay only the video over the edit point, keeping the sound intact. For example, during the first section of the bite, we see Sally Frost. Over the edit point and a few seconds into the second section of the bite, we lay video of calm people. As the second section of the bite continues, we might return to seeing Sally, or continue looking at calm people—that's up to the writer and editor. Problem solved.

Writing to SOTs

Always select a sot first and then write the story around it. It makes for better writing and for better sots on the air. Let's suppose you write the script first. The words and information you choose may eliminate some available sots. You would reject any sots that repeat information you already included in the script. You might reject a strong, emotional sot. You might reject the best sot available. The result could be that a less-than-best sound bite makes it into the newscast. Or you may reject sots that don't fit the focus of the script you've already written. Suppose you approach a story one way, but the best bite available has a different focus. You would lose the opportunity to use that sot.

Selecting sots first can make the job of finding the story's focus easier. Suppose you have a story that you could focus several ways, all of which would be interesting to your audience. Suppose, too, you have a great sot that suggests one focus. And you have several not-so-great sots that suggest other ways to focus the story. Your decision is made. You select the great sot. You focus the story to use the great sot.

Finally, selecting sots first makes writing easier. The words in a sot cannot be altered. They are on tape. The words a television news writer uses in his or her script can be altered easily. A writer can rephrase sentences to select wording that flows smoothly into and out of a sot. It's easier to write around a sot than it is to fit the words of an unchangeable sot into a news script that's already written.

Introducing SOTs

When a newspaper quotes a source involved in a story it is covering, the newspaper writer uses quotation marks to set aside the person's words. By the nature of television, the person's words are set aside already because they are on tape, coming directly from the person's mouth. Newspaper writers identify the speaker by title or role in the story, usually placing identification after the quotation. Television news writers identify a speaker before viewers hear the quotation. You've heard this before: Place attribution before information. By identifying the speaker before viewers hear and see the sot, the television news writer is explaining to viewers in advance why they should listen to or care about the speaker's words. The television news writer also is warning viewers of any bias the speaker may have. Sometimes an identification uses the person's name and title.

> Head Nurse Sally Frost says patients and staffers reacted well to the scare.
>
> "Everyone was really calm, if you can believe it. We knew he was in there. We were afraid he might hurt us. It was frightening I think for patients especially, but everyone stayed calm and pretty much in control. I'm glad it ended the way it did but I'm sorry it happened at all."

But sometimes a generic identification works just as well. Sally Frost's sot could be introduced by, "Hospital officials say patients and staffers reacted well to the scare."

Think about creative, informative and conversational ways to introduce sots. Remember that you want to introduce viewers to Sally Frost before viewers hear her words. How about this introduction?

> According to Sally Frost, who is Head Nurse at Montgomery County Hospital, patients and staffers reacted well to the scare.

Not conversational. How often do you use the phrase "according to" in conversation? The sentence also uses a dependent clause, "who is Head Nurse at Montgomery County Hospital."

What about this one?

> Patients and staffers reacted well to the scare, according to Sally Frost, who is Head Nurse at Montgomery County Hospital.

This introduction incorrectly places information—that the patients and staffers reacted well—before attribution. Again, it uses nonconversational words and a wordy dependent clause.

What about the short, "Head Nurse Sally Frost says . . ."? This incomplete sentence relies on the sot to finish the sentence. The anchor might try to use voice inflection to alert viewers that the sot will finish the thought, but the result is awkward and could confuse viewers. Try reading it aloud to hear how difficult it can be.

Another introduction to avoid is one that offers redundant information.

> Hospital officials say patients and staffers were really calm.
> "Everyone was really calm, if you can believe it. We knew he was
> in there. We were afraid he might hurt us. It was frightening I think
> for patients especially, but everyone stayed calm and pretty much in
> control."

This is called "echoing a bite," stepping on a bite," and various other terms, one of which is simply "bad writing." This is scripting the same words that the viewer hears in the sound bite. Viewers hear the news anchor say the words "really calm," and then the sot echoes them when Sally Frost says, "Everyone was really calm." Do not repeat words within a sound bite to introduce it. Otherwise, you've just created a product of the Department of Redundancy Department.

There are many ways to introduce sots. The introduction does not have to include the person's name and title. In fact, many newsrooms prefer you not use a name and title in a sound bite setup, the theory being that viewers will see that information when the sot is supered. Others believe that there must be some kind of identifier in the sound bite write-in because people may be listening to the story but not watching it. The point is to help prepare viewers for the sot and create a smooth transition from the television news anchor to the person in the sot.

Placing SOTs

Use the information about the incident at the hospital to write a television news script and place a sot into the script. As always, read the information, understand it and underline key facts. Think before you write. Think about the eight guidelines. Find an audience hook or focus. Look for a lead that will grab viewers' attention. Use the first sot you found, the one from Sgt. Joyce Edwards. Make sure to provide a transition to the speaker before viewers hear the sot.

> A bomb scare today at Montgomery County Hospital.
> The Sheriff's Department says a man barricaded in a first-floor
> rest room sent a note to hospital staffers claiming he had a bomb.
> Sheriff's deputies say Rob Moore threatened to blow up the build-
> ing unless he received immediate medical attention.
> Deputies ordered patients and staff to evacuate the hospital's first
> floor.
> "Whenever someone does something like this, we have to take the
> threat seriously. We didn't know if he had a weapon or not. We had to
> take the threat seriously."
> The Sheriff's Department says Moore surrendered after about an
> hour.
> Deputies found no bomb but say Moore did have a hunting knife.
> No one was hurt.

Test the news script.

• Does the lead hook viewers? Yes. Most viewers will stay tuned to hear about something as frightening and serious as a bomb threat. Notice that it is a half-sentence lead that piques viewers' interest.

• Does the script answer viewers' questions? Yes. Who? *Rob Moore.* What? *Allegedly threatened to blow up the hospital.* When? *Today.* Where? *Montgomery County.* Why? *He apparently demanded medical attention.* How? *By claiming to have a bomb.*

• Does the script raise any questions it fails to answer? No.

• Is the script accurate? Yes. All of the information that appears in the script appears in either the summary of events or the interview with the sheriff's deputy. Notice that all of the information naming Moore is attributed to the sheriff's department. There is no libel. The writer does not convict Rob Moore but attributes the accusations against him to the people making the accusations.

• Is the script conversational? Yes. Read it aloud to test it.

• Does the script show immediacy with present-tense verbs? Yes. The Sheriff's Department *says.* Sheriff's deputies *say.* Deputies *say.* Deputies found no bomb, but *say* Moore had . . . But notice that the news writer uses the past tense to describe events that happened in the past, such as *barricaded, threatened* and *found.*

• Does the script use active voice? Yes. One example: "Deputies found no bomb," rather than "No bomb was found by deputies." But notice the passive "No one was hurt." Passive voice works here. The alternative—"the incident hurt no one"—is awkward.

In the example, the sot from Sgt. Joyce Edwards serves as the fifth paragraph in the script. What if the news writer had placed the sot elsewhere?

> A bomb scare today at Montgomery County Hospital.
> "Whenever someone does something like this, we have to take the threat seriously. We didn't know if he had a weapon or not. We had to take the threat seriously."
> The Sheriff's Department says a man barricaded in a first-floor rest room sent a note to hospital staffers claiming he had a bomb . . .

Clearly, the sot makes no sense this early in the story. Viewers don't yet have the information they need about what has happened.

Try placing the sot later in the television news script.

> A bomb scare today at Montgomery County Hospital.
> The Sheriff's Department says a man barricaded in a first-floor rest room sent a note to hospital staffers claiming he had a bomb.
> Sheriff's deputies say Rob Moore threatened to blow up the building unless he received immediate medical attention.
> Deputies ordered patients and staff to evacuate the hospital's first floor.
> The Sheriff's Department says Moore surrendered after about an hour.

Deputies found no bomb but say Moore did have a hunting knife.

"Whenever someone does something like this, we have to take the threat seriously. We didn't know if he had a weapon or not. We had to take the threat seriously."

No one was hurt.

This time, the sot comes too late. Information in the sot addresses the reason deputies evacuated the building but is presented long after the news writer mentions the evacuation. Write script copy to flow around sots. Place sots so they make sense and serve as part of the storytelling.

Writing Out of SOTs

Sometimes it works well to use part of the sound bite to transition into the next sentence or segment of the story. Take the preferred example we just used.

A bomb scare today at Montgomery County Hospital.

The Sheriff's Department says a man barricaded in a first-floor rest room sent a note to hospital staffers claiming he had a bomb.

Sheriff's deputies say Rob Moore threatened to blow up the building unless he received immediate medical attention.

Deputies ordered patients and staff to evacuate the hospital's first floor.

"Whenever someone does something like this, we have to take the threat seriously. We didn't know if he had a weapon or not. We had to take the threat seriously."

The Sheriff's Department says Moore surrendered after about an hour.

Deputies found no bomb but say Moore did have a hunting knife.

No one was hurt.

The writer could have chosen to place the sot a paragraph earlier, then use the sot as a springboard to the next line:

A bomb scare today at Montgomery County Hospital.

The Sheriff's Department says a man barricaded in a first-floor rest room sent a note to hospital staffers claiming he had a bomb.

Sheriff's deputies say Rob Moore threatened to blow up the building unless he received immediate medical attention.

"Whenever someone does something like this, we have to take the threat seriously. We didn't know if he had a weapon or not. We had to take the threat seriously."

So seriously, in fact, that deputies ordered patients and staff to evacuate the hospital's first floor.

The Sheriff's Department says Moore surrendered after about an hour.

Deputies found no bomb but say Moore did have a hunting knife.

No one was hurt.

Tagging SOTs

As you were looking at options for placing the sot, you may have considered placing it at the very end of the script copy. That's usually a bad choice. A sot should rarely if ever have the last word in a television news script, so don't end them that way. Instead, include a tag for the news anchor to read. A tag is simply a continuation of the story that allows the news anchor to have the last word.

This serves two purposes. First, the story needs some form of conclusion, and that will rarely come from a sound bite. The result of going from a sound bite to a completely unrelated story will be jarring the viewer. The story using the sot needs some form of conclusion or tag line that carries the audience from the sot to the end of the story. The second reason relates to the psychological role of the anchor. The anchor serves as a guide for viewers, carrying them through the show. When a news writer uses a sot, he or she releases control of the newscast from the anchor and gives it to the person in the sot. The news writer should return control of the newscast to the anchor before ending the story. This reestablishes the anchor (the guide) to the audience and prepares the viewer for the next story.

On occasion, you'll see a story ending with a sot, which then wipes immediately into a related vo. Here again, though, the related vo is, in a sense, a continuation of the previous story, and the audience returns to the voice of the anchor. The same principle applies.

The tag to a sot should not be a throwaway line. This is the conclusion to the piece. It is as important as the lead and should include information that helps viewers better understand the story. If you wanted to place the sot following information that no one was hurt, you would need to find more information to include in a tag to end the story.

Script Timing for SOTs

Like vo/nats full, sot times count in the TRT of a news script. For example, the sot from Sgt. Joyce Edwards runs :08. If your assignment was to write a TRT :35 reader with a sot, you would write 27 seconds of script copy (TRT :35 minus :08 sot equals :27 script copy). As before, you must write the exact time your script (including the sound bite) runs and communicate that on the script and directly to the producer. You are shooting for a :35 reader/sot, so will try to keep it as close to that as possible without going over.

Another point about editing the sot: The script calls for "anchor on cam" immediately after the out cue of an eight-second sound bite. As a result, you will not simply edit an :08 sot that then goes to black. Recall how we edited ten seconds of pad on the end of the vo in the previous chapter? You'll do the same with the sot for the same reason. For a sot, the best way is to continue the sound bite shot for an additional :10, but at extremely low volume or sil.

Finally, you would designate on the script for the editor on what tape and where on that tape he or she will find the sot.

Format

The script format should look familiar to you by now. In Figure 9.1, only the new elements are numbered 1 through 5 (in parentheses) for reference. However, notice in the heading area of the script that the format is listed as "rdr/sot" (Reader/SOT). Remember that the numbers 1 through 5 appear in the example for reference only. When you write scripts, you won't number script elements.

The Left Column

Director cues in the left column offer instructions to the newscast director.

(1) **Director cue:** The cue "take sot" tells the newscast director to roll the tape or run the computer file that holds the sot. The newscast director (or the assistant director, designated the "AD," or the technical director, designated the "TD") punches the button that replaces the anchor on camera with the speaker, Sgt. Edwards. The cue ":08" is very important, telling the newscast director how long Sgt. Edwards speaks. It is called the "sot runs time." The newscast director knows to return to the anchor on camera :08 after the sot starts. Always include a sot runs time.

(2) **The super:** Again, you need to identify for viewers who is speaking. The cue tells the newscast director to superimpose the name and title "Sgt. Joyce Edwards/Montgomery Co. Sheriff's Dept." :01 after the tape rolls. The slash mark indicates that the super should be shown on two lines, as in Figure 9.2.

(3) **Director cue:** The cue "out:" stands for "out cue." The out cue is the final word or words of the sot. Here, the out cue is "take the threat seriously." The newscast director already knows the sot runs :08, and as those eight seconds are about up, he or she will be listening for the out cue. When the newscast director hears Sgt. Edwards say the words, "take the threat seriously," he or she knows the sot is over and it is time to return to the anchor on camera for the rest of the story. Except that here we have what's known as a "double out." Read the next paragraph carefully.

Caution: Be aware of double out cues, as shown in the example. If the speaker in a sot repeats words or sentences, the out cue can become tricky. Notice that Sgt. Edwards repeats the out cue "take the threat seriously." If the script read only "out: take the threat seriously," the newscast director might break away from the sot and return to the anchor on camera too early—after the first time Sgt. Edwards says "take the threat seriously." You must alert the newscast director to a double out cue. The words "double out" in parentheses warn the newscast director that the sot repeats the out cue.

The Right Column

(4) **Anchor cue:** The cue "- - - - (sot) - - - -" tells the news anchor to stop talking and pause for the sot. It alerts the news anchor to what is happening on the television screen. The anchor is replaced with a sot.

(page) HOSPITAL BOMB SCARE rdr/sot 5p   2/3   EKG   Runs:

anchor - on cam
box - Hospital Scare

----- (on cam) -----

A bomb scare today at Montgomery Count Hospital.

The Sheriff's Department says a man barricaded in a first floor restroom sent a note to hospital staffers claiming he had a bomb.

Sheriff's deputies say Rob Moore threatened to blow up the building unless he received immediate medical attention.

Deputies ordered patients and staff to evacuate the hospital's first floor.

(1) take sot -- runs :08

(4) ----- (sot) -----

(2) (:01) S/Sgt Joyce Edwards/
          Montgomery Co. Sheriff's Dept.

(5)   Sgt. Joyce Edwards/Montgomery Co. Sheriff's Dept:
When someone does something like this, we have to take the threat seriously. We didn't know if he had a weapon or not. We had to take the threat seriously.

(3) Out: take the threat seriously.
         (double out)

----- (on cam) -----

anchor - on cam
box - Hospital Scare

The Sheriff's Department says Moore surrendered after about an hour.

Deputies found no bomb, but say Moore did have a hunting knife.

No one was hurt.

#####

FIGURE 9.1

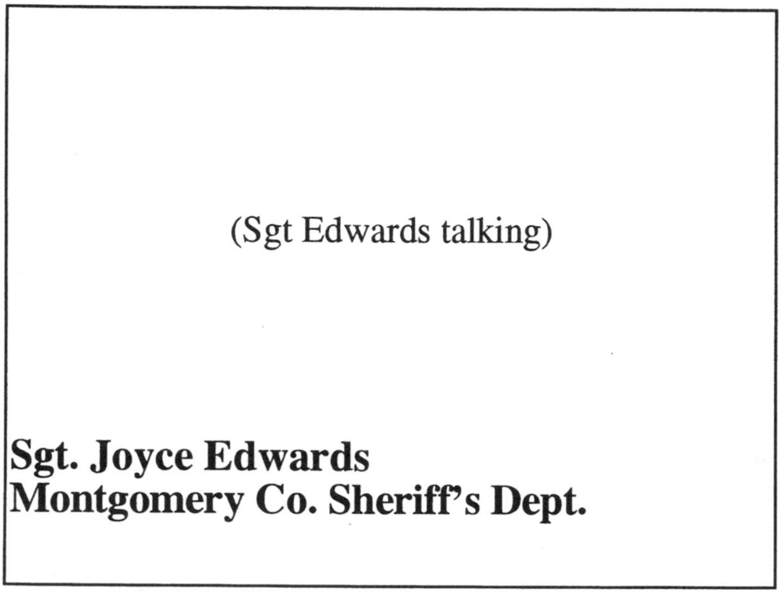

```
(Sgt Edwards talking)




Sgt. Joyce Edwards
Montgomery Co. Sheriff's Dept.
```

FIGURE 9.2

(5) **The sot:** The sot is written out in full, or transcribed. It is single spaced and preceded by the name and title of the person who is talking. By writing out sots, the news anchor can follow along. More important, most newscasts are close-captioned for hearing-impaired audiences. Those viewers deserve captioning not only of the news anchor's words but of the entire newscast. The sot is an important part of the story and of the newscast. Write out the entire transcription of everything that goes over the air.

Adding SOTs

With so many good sots to choose from in this story, you might decide to use another in the television news script. You can add a sot to the story to give viewers more of the story. Suppose you selected a sot from the patient Ed Foyles to add to the script.

> Ed Foyles/Patient: "I just couldn't believe it when they told us we'd have to evacuate. I wasn't really scared at the time, more confused, you know. But now that it's over, I realize it was a pretty scary thing." (Runs :10)

The sot from Ed Foyles could be edited onto the tape with the sot from Sgt. Joyce Edwards for back-to-back sots. The sots from Sgt. Edwards and Ed Foyles share a point of view, in that both speakers are commenting on their experiences during the event—the bomb scare and evacuation. The two sots make sense placed back-to-back because Ed Foyles adds to the thoughts Sgt. Edwards expresses. His sot further describes the experiences shared by those involved in the story.

Introducing Back-to-Back SOTs

The news writer does not need to introduce both Sgt. Edwards and Ed Foyles. The sentence that introduces the sot from Sgt. Edwards (in italics below) serves also to introduce the continuation of her thoughts by Ed Foyles.

> A bomb scare today at Montgomery County Hospital.
>
> The Sheriff's Department says a man barricaded in a first-floor rest room sent a note to hospital staffers claiming he had a bomb.
>
> Sheriff's deputies say Rob Moore threatened to blow up the building unless he received immediate medical attention.
>
> *Deputies ordered patients and staff to evacuate the hospital's first floor.*
>
> Sgt. Joyce Edwards/Montgomery Co. Sheriff's Dept. "Whenever someone does something like this, we have to take the threat seriously. We didn't know if he had a weapon or not. We had to take the threat seriously."
>
> Ed Foyles/Patient. "I just couldn't believe it when they told us we'd have to evacuate. I wasn't really scared at the time, more confused, you know. But now that it's over, I realize it was a pretty scary thing."
>
> The Sheriff's Department says Moore surrendered after about an hour.
>
> Deputies found no bomb but say Moore did have a hunting knife.
>
> No one was hurt.

What would happen if back-to-back sots expressed opposing points of view? This happens all the time. In an effort to be fair and balanced, a news writer may prepare a script with back-to-back sots—one expressing opposition and the other expressing support. The news writer introduces both points of view when he or she introduces the back-to-back sots.

Suppose Democrats and Republicans have opposing views to a proposal to fund the arts. In the sots below, the supers "(D) South Carolina" and "(R) Texas" identify Suzie Jordan as a Democrat from South Carolina and Andrea Mikkola as a Republican from Texas.

> Sen. Suzie Jordan/(D) South Carolina. "Without federal support many artists will not survive. The arts in many small American towns will cease to exist. The government owes it to its citizens to support the arts so that they are available to everyone, not only to the wealthy."
> (Runs :10)

> Sen. Andrea Mikkola/(R) Texas. "The federal government is not
> in the business of supporting starving artists. The government has
> larger responsibilities to its citizens. When we fund the arts, we have
> fewer dollars to provide food, shelter and medicine to the people."
> (Runs :11)

The news writer prepares an introduction that alerts viewers to opposing points of view. The news writer first introduces the second sot and then introduces the first sot.

> - - - - (on cam) - - - -
> Republicans say tax dollars could be better spent.
> But Democrats believe the government has an obligation to sup-
> port the arts.
> - - - - (sot) - - - -
> Sen. Suzie Jordan/(D) South Carolina. Without federal support
> many artists will not survive. The arts in many small American towns
> will cease to exist. The government owes it to its citizens to support
> the arts so that they are available to everyone, not only to the wealthy.
> Sen. Andrea Mikkola/(R) Texas. The federal government is not in
> the business of supporting starving artists. The government has larger
> responsibilities to its citizens. When we fund the arts, we have fewer
> dollars to provide food, shelter and medicine to the people.

The news writer begins the introduction with the Republican point of view and follows by paraphrasing the Democrat's comments. Viewers understand they will hear from both sides. They expect to hear from the Democratic side first. If the sots were reversed, the introduction to them would be reversed, too. To understand why it works to lead the introduction with the second sot, you might want to consider the alternative. Read the example below aloud.

> - - - - (on cam) - - - -
> Democrats believe the government has an obligation to support
> the arts.
> But Republicans say tax dollars could be better spent.
> - - - - (sot) - - - -
> Sen. Suzie Jordan/(D) South Carolina. Without federal support
> many artists will not survive. The arts in many small American towns
> will cease to exist. The government owes it to its citizens to support
> the arts so that they are available to everyone, not only to the wealthy.
> Sen. Andrea Mikkola/(R) Texas. The federal government is not in
> the business of supporting starving artists. The government has larger
> responsibilities to its citizens. When we fund the arts, we have fewer
> dollars to provide food, shelter and medicine to the people.

Viewers hear the Democratic point of view followed by the Republican. Then they have to switch gears to recall the Democratic point of view, followed by switching gears again to listen to the Republican. It is not conversational, and it could cause confusion. Both of which are bad things.

Placing Back-to-Back SOTs

You may already be thinking of another alternative to introducing back-to-back sots with opposing viewpoints. You may be tempted to break up the sots to introduce each point of view separately.

> - - - - on cam - - - -
> Democrats believe the government has an obligation to support the arts.
> - - - - sot - - - -
> Sen. Suzie Jordan/(D) South Carolina. Without federal support many artists will not survive. The arts in many small American towns will cease to exist. The government owes it to its citizens to support the arts so that they are available to everyone, not only to the wealthy.
> - - - - on cam - - - -
> But Republicans say tax dollars could be better spent.
> - - - - sot - - - -
> Sen. Andrea Mikkola/(R) Texas. The federal government is not in the business of supporting starving artists. The government has larger responsibilities to its citizens. When we fund the arts, we have fewer dollars to provide food, shelter and medicine to the people.

However, this is not a good idea. Similar to vo, once a tape containing sots is on the television screen, it's best to leave it there until it's time for the anchor to end the story or begin the next story in the newscast. Remember that viewers expect the anchor to appear on camera to introduce stories or to end them. Viewers do not expect the anchor to pop up in the middle of stories or between sots. Your first choice is to run opposing sots back-to-back. Introduce the second sot first.

There is an alternative, however. At the end of the first bite, the writer can call for an "edit shot" or "setup shot" of the second interviewee to be edited in. In the example above, after Jordon's sound bite, the audience could see a wide shot of Mikkola at her desk (or wherever the interview was shot), perhaps nodding to the interviewer. That video would then cover the anchor's copy, "But Republicans say tax dollars could be better spent." The audience would then immediately see and hear Mikkola's sot. But the first approach is better—and simpler.

And don't forget the tag. The example above can't end on a sot. The news writer should return to the anchor for the last word to conclude the story.

Script Timing for Back-to-Back SOTs

Adding sots changes the TRT of the television news script. Refer to the story from the hospital. The sot from Sgt. Edwards runs :08. The sot from Ed Foyles that you added runs :10. The script copy, as it appears in the earlier example, runs :27. Simple arithmetic shows that you have a TRT of :45 (:27 script copy plus :08 sot plus :10 sot equals TRT :45). If your assignment was to write a :35 television news script with a sot, you haven't done your job. You have several options: cut your script copy to :17, sacrifice the Ed Foyles sot, cut your script copy by :02 and sacrifice the sot from Sgt. Edwards, or ask your newscast producer for more time, making a good argument for why you need :45 to tell the story. Both passionate wailing and bribes can be quite effective in getting the producer to relent and give you more time.

Format: Back-to-Back SOTs

With the addition of a sot, the format requires some changes (see Figure 9.3). Use the numbers 1 through 6 (in parentheses) for reference as the changes are discussed.

The Left Column

(1) **Director cue:** The cue is still "take sot," telling the newscast director to roll the tape or start the server file onto which the back-to-back sots have been edited. But notice the sot runs time has changed. Remember that the earlier sot was :08. Adding Ed Foyles's sot adds :10 to the tape. The sot runs time is the total time on tape—whether it's one sot or 100 of them. You do the arithmetic for the newscast director by adding the sot times together. The two sots add up to :18.

Be aware that some newsrooms use different terminology. Because the term "sot" technically refers to any sound on tape, the sot command may be designated "Take S-O-T up full."

(2) **The first super:** At :01 into the sot tape, you want the newscast director to superimpose the first speaker's name and title over the tape, just as before.

(3) **The second super:** Remember that the Sgt. Edwards sot runs :08. That means from :01 to :08, viewers hear and see Sgt. Edwards speaking. The Edwards sot is followed by patient Ed Foyles speaking. You want the newscast director to superimpose his name and title when he appears on the television screen. Foyles appears on the screen at :08, when Edwards is done talking. Instruct the newscast director to put the second super on screen when Foyles appears.

Recall that with back-to-back sots, a director will typically leave a super up for about four seconds. Suppose the Edwards sot only ran :05 instead of :08. It's unusual because a sound bite generally requires more time, but it's not unheard of. The problem is that the director might be dealing with something else, bring in that super at :02 and leave it until :06 or :07. Now, we have a problem—a super identifying the speaker as Edwards is superimposed over an interview with Foyles. If this is the case, you add the instruction "quick out" to the super, and specify the in- and out-times:

> (:01-:04) <u>Quick Out</u>
> S/ Sgt. Joyce Edwards/
> Montgomery Co. Sheriff's Dept.

Generally, however, you don't want to push it. If you have several back-to-back sound bites of opinions from people on the street, for example, some may run just three to five seconds. It might be a good collection of sots, but there's no (page) HOSPITAL BOMB SCARE rdr/sot 5p   2/3   EKG   Runs:

anchor - on cam
box - Hospital Scare

----- (on cam) -----

A bomb scare today at Montgomery County Hospital.

The Sheriff's Department says a man barricaded in a first floor restroom sent a note to hospital staffers claiming he had a bomb.

Sheriff's deputies say Rob Moore threatened to blow up the building unless he received immediate medical attention.

Deputies ordered patients and staff to evacuate the hospital's first floor.

(1) take sot - runs :18

(2) (:01) S/ Sgt. Joyce Edwards/
        Montgomery Co. Sheriff's Dept.

(5) ----- (sot) -----

(6) Sgt. Joyce Edwards/Montgomery Co. Sheriff's Dept: Whenever someone does something like this, we have to take the threat seriously. We didn't know if he had a weapon or not. We had to take the threat seriously.

(3) (:09) S/ Ed Foyles /
        Patient

(4) Out: ... pretty scary thing.

Ed Foyles/Patient: I just couldn't believe it when they told me we'd have to evacuate. I wasn't really scared at the time, more confused, you know. But now that it's over, I realize it was a pretty scary thing.

----- (on cam) -----

anchor - on cam
box - Hospital Scare

The Sheriff's Department says Moore surrendered after about an hour.

Deputies found no bomb, but say Moore did have a hunting knife.

No one was hurt.

#####

FIGURE 9.3

way that the director can switch supers that quickly or that the audience can absorb the supered information that quickly. The best way to handle that would be to give a generic introduction to whom you talked with and where, then run the sots back-to-back without supers.

(4) **The out cue:** Because you've added a sot and the two are running back-to-back, the out cue for the sot(s) has changed from "threat seriously (double out)" to "pretty scary thing."

The Right Column

(5) **Anchor cue:** Warn the anchor that a sot is coming. The anchor knows to pause while viewers hear and see the sot.

(6) **The sot:** Transcribe the entire back-to-back sot, preceded by each speaker's name and title. Write out every word viewers will hear from Edwards and Foyles.

Summary

A "sot" is "sound on tape." It is most often a person recorded on videotape as he or she is speaking, and it runs about 06 to 18 seconds. A sot allows viewers to hear directly from people involved in stories. Television news writers use sots primarily to add emotion, reaction and opinion rather than information to stories.

It is the television news writer's responsibility to select sots for stories. You reject sots that include profanity and that draw conclusions not backed by the facts of the story. You do not need to reject sots because of grammatical errors or extra words. You can trim sots to make them shorter. If you trim sots, do so carefully. Do not make edits that change the meaning of a person's words. Also, be alert to jump cuts. Good news writers select sots first and then write their stories. By doing so, they get better sots on the air.

There are many ways to introduce sots. The introduction does not have to include the person's name and title. The point is to help prepare viewers for the sot and create a smooth transition from the television news anchor to the person in the sot. Think about creative, informative and conversational ways to introduce sots without "echoing" them through repetition. Do not give a sot the last word in a television news script. You should include a tag for the news anchor to read so that the anchor has the last word and concludes the story.

Sot times count in the TRT of news scripts. The script format for a sot uses the director cue "take sot" in the left column to tell the newscast director to roll the tape that holds the sot. Always include a sot runs time in the left column to tell the newscast director how long the sot runs. You need to identify for viewers who is speaking with a super in the left column. The cue "out:" stands for out cue, or final word or words of the sot. Use the cue "(double out)" when the person in a sot repeats the out cue.

Information in the right column speaks to the news anchor. The cue "- - - - (sot) - - - -" tells the news anchor to pause for a sot. The sot is transcribed, single-spaced and preceded by the name and title of the person who is talking.

You can use multiple sots in scripts. If back-to-back sots express opposing points of view, the news writer generally should first introduce the second sound bite, then the first sot.

Like vo/nats, once a tape containing sots is on the television screen, it's best to leave it there until it's time for the anchor to end the story or begin the next story in the newscast. Adding sots changes the TRT of the television news script and also requires format changes.

Exercises

1. Read the summary of a news story below and the list of available sots. Select the best sot. Defend your selection. List the reasons you reject each of the sots you do not select. Sot runs times follow transcribed sots in parentheses.

> School officials in Columbus, Ohio, are worried that frigid temperatures and ice could keep children out of classes for several more days. Unless temperatures rise substantially, school officials doubt schools can reopen until near the end of the week. Daily highs in the 20s are predicted for the next few days. If schools can't reopen until Friday, officials will have to decide whether it is economical to heat up the buildings for only one day and then close them for the weekend. If schools remain closed through the week, students will lose one day of spring break and their Memorial Day holiday because they will have used the allotted snow days.

Available sots:

(a) Michael Warren/Superintendent: "It doesn't look good for the whole week. I think it will be Thursday at the earliest before we can reopen." (:06)

(b) Matt Hawkins/Asst. Superintendent: "If we can't reopen until Friday, we have to decide whether it's economical to heat up the buildings for only one day and then close them for the weekend." (:12)

(c) James Blackwell/Teacher: "Children may love it now, but they may hate it later. So may teachers. We may be forced to use holidays to make up for these snow days." (:10)

(d) Peggy None/Parent: "If we have to use holidays to make up for these snow days, you can bet both parents and teachers will be p___ about it." (:08)

(e) Ken Flynt/Meteorologist: "Daily highs in the 20s are predicted for the next few days." (:05)

2. Use the story information above and the sot you selected to write a script for tonight's 6 p.m. newscast, slugged CLASSES SNOWED OUT. TRT :35. Add the sot runs time (in parentheses) to script copy length to get the TRT. You may use a box.

3. Use the following wire copy to write a news script with a sot for today's 5 p.m. newscast, slugged POLICE SHOOTING. TRT :45. Add the sot runs time (in parentheses) to script copy length to get the TRT. You may use a box. Choose the sot from the list of those available.

(HOUSTON)—A Houston police officer was in critical condition today after undergoing surgery for wounds he suffered when he was shot in the head.

George Davis, 29, was shot last night while on routine patrol near a shopping center. Authorities had no motive for the shooting.

Police were searching for three teens and a young man placed at the scene by witnesses, said Sgt. Johnnie Johnson, a police spokesman.

Surgeons at Houston General Hospital were unable to remove a bullet lodged in Davis's head, Johnson said. Another bullet went through the officer's left jaw.

Police Chief Patrick Moore called the shooting a cowardly act.

Johnson said Davis was driving down a Houston street about 8:45 p.m. when at least one man approached his patrol car and opened fire.

Neighbors reported hearing anywhere between four and seven gunshots. Police say the gunman fired through the closed window on the driver's side.

Available sots:

(a) Jed Henders/Neighbor: "I came out and I saw the car sitting there. The officer was in the car and he didn't respond. He was trying to get to the button on his car radio. And he was choking on his own blood. I held his head back so I could open up his airway. He never uttered a word." (:14)

(b) Sally Denver/Neighbor: "It was like, 'Plow! Plow! Plow!' Then I heard laughing, and then 'Plow! Plow! Plow!' again. They were laughing like, 'Isn't that funny? Isn't that real funny?'" (:11)

(c) Chief Patrick Moore/Houston Police: "This is nothing more than a cowardly act on the part of the shooters. They will be apprehended. And they will be prosecuted for their cowardice." (:08)

4. Write a second version of the POLICE SHOOTING script using back-to-back sots. The second version also runs :45. Rework script copy to allow a second sot. Add the sot runs times (in parentheses) to script copy length to get the TRT.

5. Use the following wire copy to write a news script with back-to-back sots for today's 10 p.m. newscast, slugged SMALL BIZ. TRT :40. Add the sot runs times (in parentheses) to script copy length to get the TRT. You may use a box. Choose the sots from the list of those available.

(RICHMOND, Va.)—The Senate voted 31-8 today to allow welfare recipients to save money to start up a business. The measure would allow recipients to save up to $5,000 to launch a small business—without losing benefits.

Opponents are concerned about welfare recipients losing money in risky ventures.

Available sots:

(a) Sen. Ed Newfield/(D) Manassas: "This is what America is all about, people raising themselves by their bootstraps. Welfare families, so long out of the mix, can become active members in today's business community." (:11)

(b) Sen. Al Frank/(R) Blacksburg: "There are people out there with dreams of opening their own business, but the law has prevented them from saving and from working toward those dreams. This bill clears the way for people to save money, put it to work and get off the government payrolls." (:12)

(c) Sen. Susan Tierney/(R) Norfolk: "Make no mistake about it, we're not doing Virginia's welfare families any favor here. The money they save can only be used in business ventures. But we're not providing any business training programs for these people. Some of them are going to be taken advantage of and they're going to lose money." (:14)

(d) Sen. Ted Smith/(D) Virginia Beach: "We are taking our welfare families and making them sitting ducks for cons. Many of these people will end up making worthless investments. They'll scrimp and save and lose it all. No one wins." (:12)

6. Find the best sot on television tonight. Watch a local or national newscast. As you watch, pay attention to sots. Write out as closely as possible the sot you decide is the strongest. Write a short recap of the story in which the sot appears. Describe the strengths of the sot. Note the newscast time, station and date.

10

The Voice Over/ Sound Bite: VO/SOT

Sots and back-to-back sots most often are accompanied by vo/nats under or vo/sil in television news scripts. Think about it: If a television news photographer takes the effort to videotape an interview, chances are good the photographer also will shoot visuals of the event in which the interviewee is involved. Watch television newscasts and notice the number of times a vo and sot are used in combination.

Sots on their own are rare, but don't dismiss them entirely. They do have their place in television newscasts. As an example, local news stations often use satellite interviews with Congress members in Washington, D.C., providing an opportunity for viewers at home to hear from their representatives in the nation's capital. Such interviews usually feature the member of Congress speaking from a room set up for interviews or posed outside with the Capitol building in the background. There is often no vo available. The television news writer could use a sot on its own.

At times, a sot on its own may be preferable to using bad video. As we discussed in Chapter 8, not all vo is good vo. The television news writer decides whether vo adds to the story, has compelling pictures, will help viewers better understand the story or "take" them to it. If it doesn't, the news writer may reject the vo and use a sot on its own.

Old Rules

Adding vo to a television news script with a sot does not relieve the television news writer of the responsibility of writing to the sot. The news writer still must introduce viewers to the person who will be speaking. The introduction does not have to include the person's name and title, but it does have to create a smooth transition from the television news anchor to the person in the sot. It should help prepare viewers for the sot. The rule you learned about sot tags also still applies: Do not give a sot the last word in a television news script. You must "write out of the bite," which means you should transition smoothly from the sot to the remainder of the story, whether you continue the story with more vo or return to the anchor on camera. And don't forget the guidelines governing the use of vo. When you add vo to a sot script, you still must write to the visuals you use.

New Format

The format for a vo and sot also is familiar. If you have mastered the formats for a vo and a sot, you should have no problem combining the two. Look at Figure 10.1. Because of your familiarity with television news script formats, you may be tempted to skip the numbered definitions. But take your time. Read it all. Some of it will be review. Other parts will be new to you. Read and understand it now because your understanding of every element of a news script is vital to the work you do in later chapters (and in potential future jobs). Use the numbers 1 through 28 (in parentheses) for reference. (As always, when you write scripts, do not include the numbers.)

The Top of the Page

Numbers 1 through 7 refer to the page number (filled in later by the producer), the slug (CHARITY GOLF), the format (vo/sot) the newscast (5p), the date (1/5), the news writer's initials (EKG in the example, but your initials when you write scripts), and the running time of the story.

The Left Column

(8) **Camera shot:** Tell the newscast director to show the television news anchor on camera.

(9) **Director cue:** Tell the newscast director to show a box over the television news anchor's shoulder. The box is identified as "Chip & Putt."

(10) **Director cue:** Tell the newscast director to roll the tape (or the computer file) that holds the vo with natural sound under.

(11) **The super:** Tell the newscast director to superimpose the words "Birmingham" and "Today" over the vo/nats under on the television screen. The super (designated "S/") tells viewers where and when events in the vo/nats occurred. The slash in the super itself separates the super into two lines (Figure 10.2).

(12) through (16) **Shot notation:** List the shots you want in the order you want them edited onto the tape, along with where they're found on the field tape and how long each shot should stay up (for this example, I've left out where the shots would be found on the field tape, but you would include this information).

(1) (page) (2) CHARITY GOLF (3) vo/sot (4) 5 p (5) 1/5 (6) EKG (7) Runs:

(8) anchor - on cam
(9) box - Chip & Putt

(21) ----- (on cam) -----

(22) People are chipping and putting at Bruno's grocery stores today to help United Cerebral Palsy.

And to get a shot at a one-thousand dollar grocery shopping spree.

(10) take vo/nats under
(11) (:01) S/ Birmingham/Today

(23) ----- (vo) -----

For a one-dollar donation to U-C-P, you can either putt a nine-foot hole or chip a whiffle ball into a shopping cart.

(12) (player putting - :06)

(13) (player chipping - :06)

A successful try puts your name in a drawing to chip and putt at the eighteenth hole at Greystone Golf Club.

And to win the shopping spree.

People of all ages are stepping up to chip and putt.

(14) (more players - :03)

(15) (children chipping - :03)

(16) (Tyler making putt - :03)

(24) This four-year-old, Tyler, sank two putts.

(25) ----- (sot) -----
(26) Rob Murray/Tyler's Father: We just go about every chance we can to go to the driving range and he's been giving me a lot of tips on my swing. Haven't you?
(27) ----- (on cam) -----

(17) take sot - runs :06
(18) (:01) S/   Rob Murray /
Tyler's Father
(19) Out: ... Haven't you?

If you missed the Chip and Putt today, you can try next Saturday at the Eastwood and Hoover Bruno's stores.

(28) #####

(20) anchor - on cam

FIGURE 10.1

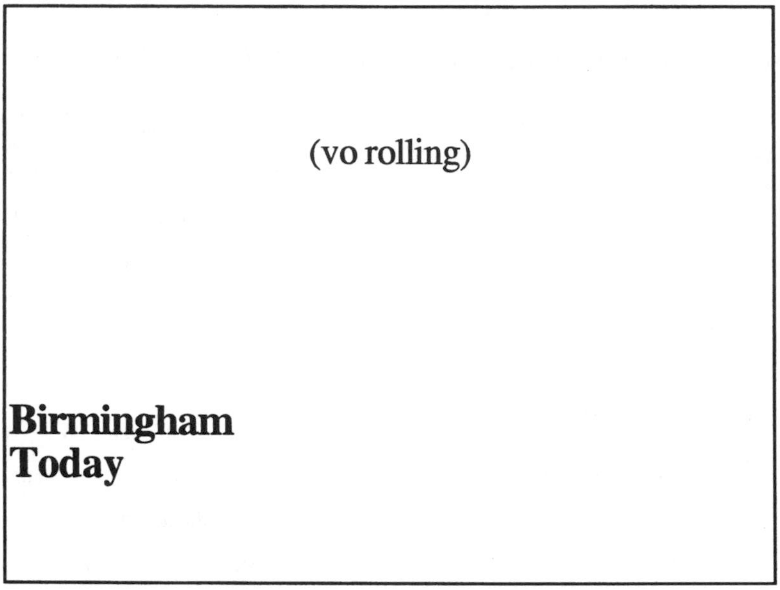

(vo rolling)

**Birmingham
Today**

FIGURE 10.2

The shots correspond with the news script copy so that what viewers hear and see make sense together. The shots appear in parentheses in the left column alongside the point in script copy at which you want shots to appear. Notice that the news writer uses a direct video reference in the right column to call viewers' attention to Tyler specifically: "*This* four-year-old, Tyler, sank two putts."

(17) **Director cue:** Tell the newscast director to remove the vo/nats from the television screen and replace it with the sot. At this point, it might be good to discuss some technical aspects of vo/sots. As you know, a story that begins with vo has a certain amount of copy the anchor must read and a certain amount of corresponding video on the tape that accompanies the copy. The shots are timed to match the script. In an ideal world, when the anchor gets to the point of the sound bite, the sound bite will play. However, if it's all edited on the same tape (or same server file), problems can arise. If the vo begins playing late or if the anchor is reading quickly, the anchor will finish the copy before the sot comes up on the tape or in the file. This results in a gap during which the viewer hears neither the anchor nor the sot. This gap is known as dead air, and it's not good. The other problem that can arise is even worse. In this case, the anchor is reading too slowly or the tape starts a few seconds early. The anchor is still reading the vo when the sound bite hits, meaning you're hearing both voices at the same time. This is called "stepping on a bite," and it's even worse than the dreaded dead air.

The answer to this problem is to put the sound bite on another tape or server file. The vo tape that begins the story is cued and ready to play, as is the second tape (or server file) that has the sot or sots and any additional vo on it. The anchor begins the vo, the first tape plays. When the anchor gives the cue line for the sot, the second tape begins, and the director cuts or dissolves from the vo tape to the sot tape, replacing the visuals on the screen with the sound bite. The timing works out.

Take a look at Figure 10.3 and visualize the tapes. The vo/nats under and the sot are on two separate tapes, both cued. The first tape rolls during the vo, with the second (sot) tape still cued and ready. At the end of the vo portion, tape 2 with the sot rolls.

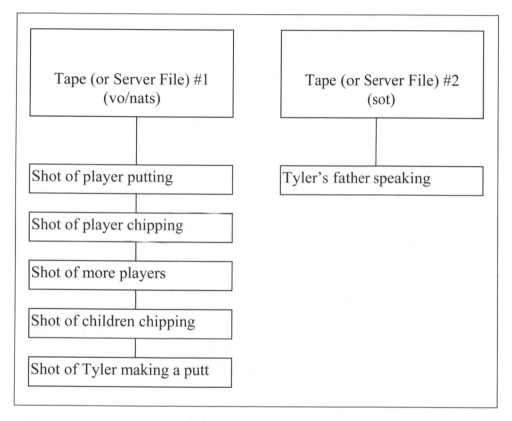

FIGURE 10.3

This same approach can be used with multiple sots and vo within the same story. Let's say you've written a vo-sot-vo-sot-sot-vo (which would still be called a vo/sot). Let's think about how to lay the video on the tapes. You'll begin with the vo. For the reasons we just stated, we'll put the first sot on a second tape and continue editing. Following the first sot, we have more vo, which we edit on tape two after the first sot. But wait—we hit another sot, then another sot, then more vo. That series (sot-sot-vo) will be edited on a third tape. Think about why. After the first bite, the anchor reads more vo. That has to time out perfectly to hit the next sot, right? So that next sot, and everything after it, goes on yet another tape, which will be cued and waiting to play.

Back to the script (Figure 10.1). A sot is always accompanied by its runs time. The cue ":06" tells the newscast director that Rob Murray talks for six seconds. The newscast director will return to the news anchor on camera six seconds after Murray begins speaking.

(18) **The super:** Identify for viewers the person who is talking. The newscast director superimposes the speaker's name and title over the sot (Figure 10.4).

(19) **The out cue:** Alert the newscast director to the final words of the sot. Here they are, "Haven't you?" The newscast director listens for the words and uses them as a cue to return to the news anchor on camera.

(20) **Director cue:** Tell the newscast director to return to the news anchor on camera for a tag. Here, the news anchor is centered on camera without a box.

The Right Column

(21) **Anchor cue:** Tell the news anchor he or she will appear on camera.

(22) **The script copy:** Write out the script copy as the news anchor will read it on the air. Keep copy clean—uncluttered and easy to read. As in all script copy, the news writer answers viewers' questions, raises no unanswered questions, offers the latest information, is accurate, uses conversational wording, shows immediacy with present- and future-tense verbs and uses the active voice.

(23) **Anchor cue:** Tell the news anchor that vo/nats under is coming. The news anchor no longer appears on the television screen but is replaced by vo/nats. From this point, script copy should correspond with the shots you select. Words and pictures need to make sense together.

(24) **More script copy:** This paragraph is marked for reference to remind you to write a smooth transition into the sot. Alert viewers that a sot is coming. Here, the transition into the sot is, "This four-year-old, Tyler, sank two putts." It sets up the sot with Tyler's father. The introduction doesn't identify Tyler's father by name or title, but it still provides a smooth transition. Viewers expect to hear more about Tyler's accomplishment, and they're not disappointed.

(25) **Anchor cue:** Tell the news anchor to stop reading so that viewers can hear the sot with Tyler's father. The cue "- - - - (sot) - - - -" lets the anchor know of the change taking place on the television screen as vo/nats is replaced by the sot. The anchor knows to stop talking so that viewers can hear the sot.

(26) **The sot:** Transcribe the sot exactly as the speaker says it, beginning with the speaker's name and title. The sot transcription is single-spaced.

(27) **Anchor cue:** Tell the newscast anchor he or she is returning on camera.

(28) **The end script:** The pound sign (#) tells the news anchor the script is over.

As a final thought, be aware that you can (and typically should) write out of the sound bite as well as write in to it. Take our sot from Rob Murray. He uses the phrase, "and he's been giving me a lot of tips on my swing." The writer could have used that phrase as a springboard into the remainder of the story:

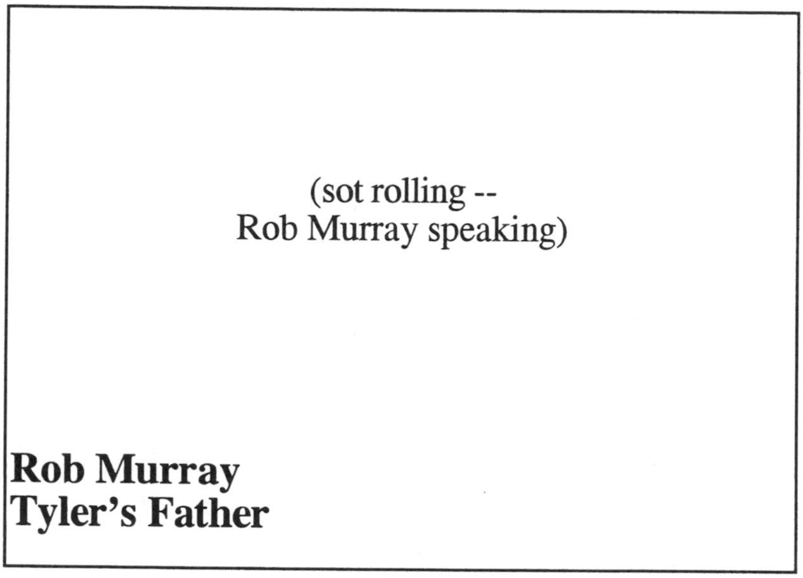

```
                    (sot rolling --
                 Rob Murray speaking)




Rob Murray
Tyler's Father
```

FIGURE 10.4

> If you feel like your swing is up to par but missed the Chip and
> Putt today, you can try next Saturday . . .

It makes for a good transition out of the sound bite.

Read through the example below that shows the process of writing a television script with vo/nats under and a sot, using wire copy as a source. Although there are no new script elements for you to learn, you will be using old script elements in new ways. As always, start with wire copy. Read it. Understand it. Find and mark key facts.

First, some background for this story. In July of 2002, American millionaire Steve Fossett became the first person to circumnavigate the globe alone in a balloon just before he landed in Australia. However, his first five attempts failed. The story that follows recounts how the first attempt ended.

> (NEW BRUNSWICK, Canada)—Tired, cold, off-course and out
> of power, an American millionaire made a rough landing in a field
> today after aborting his bid to become the first person to circle the
> Earth nonstop in a balloon.
>
> Steve Fossett had lifted off from South Dakota's Black Hills two
> days ago and rapidly encountered extreme cold, a dead heater and
> trouble with his autopilot system.
>
> By this morning, after covering more than 1,800 miles but getting
> just three hours of sleep in two nights, he was jettisoning equipment
> into the water off New Brunswick in a desperate struggle to stay aloft.

Fossett, 51, bounced around inside his all-weather capsule as it dragged 100 yards across a field and stopped just shy of woods about 65 miles from the Maine border.

Fossett said his electrical system failed before dawn, knocking out his equipment. Fearing a landing in the frigid waters of the Bay of Fundy and being pushed north by a storm, he changed plans and headed for the Canadian coast. The failed trip cost him $300,000.

Make some notes about the information in the story, answering *Who? What? When? Where? How?* and *Why?* (see Figure 10.5).

Before writing, consider the vo/nats and sots available for you to use in the script.

Available vo/nats (super: New Brunswick, Canada/Today):
1. Shots of Fossett's balloon landing in the field (including shots of it touching down, dragging across the field and coming to a stop by the woods).
2. Shot of Fossett climbing out of his all-weather capsule.
3. Various shots inside the capsule, showing failed equipment.
4. Various shots of Fossett walking around outside the balloon.

Ask yourself which vo/nats shots are most compelling. The shots of the balloon landing provide the most action and might be of most interest to viewers. These are the shots you want to place early in the vo/nats.

Now select a sot. Sot runs times appear in parentheses.

Available sots:
1. Steve Fossett/Balloonist: "I'm rather disappointed and embarrassed that I didn't do better on this." (:05)
2. Steve Fossett/Balloonist. "I had to throw equipment into the water to stay aloft." (:04)
3. Steve Fossett/Balloonist. "I was afraid if I didn't come down here now, I might be forced down later in the bay. I had to change course to land on ground instead of in the water. It's disappointing but it's something I felt I needed to do." (:11)

Ask yourself which sot is most compelling. The first sot offers emotion as the balloonist reacts to the aborted mission. It's a good sot. The second sot is a description of an event, offering little emotion. The news writer may decide to paraphrase this sot in script copy rather than show it on the air. The third sot offers emotion (disappointment) and information (further reasons for the balloonist's decision). It may be the strongest sot available. Use it.

Now think about the best way to write the script to answer viewers' questions, use vo/nats, set up the sot and tag it. Use your notes and the wire copy for reference. Find the viewer hook, the audience appeal to find a focus for the story. Find a present-tense lead that will hook viewers. Use active voice. Your script may look something like the one shown in Figure 10.6. Test the script. Ask yourself, Does the lead offer viewers the latest information? Does the script answer viewers' questions? Does it raise any questions it fails to answer? Is it accurate? Is it con-

---

Story Notes - Balloon Trip Fails
Who: American millionaire Steve Fossett
What: aborts his round-the-world balloon trip
When: Today
Where: New Brunswick (Canadian province near the Maine border)
How: Landing his balloon
Why: He was cold and tired. Off-course. Some equipment had failed.

Other Interesting Information: The trip cost $300 K. Fossett lasted only about three days and 1800 miles. If he had succeeded, he would have been the first person to circle the earth nonstop in a balloon.

FIGURE 10.5

versational? (Read it aloud.) Does it use present tense and active voice? If you answer "no" to any of these questions, revise the script to pass the test.

Notice the format of the script in Figure 10.6. It should be familiar to you. The story will air in the 6 p.m. newscast on January 31, slugged BALLOON TRIP FAILS. Notice that in the script, the writer writes to vo/nats under, placing the most compelling shot first and following with a logical sequence of shots.

Adding a SOT

You'll be asked in the exercises to write scripts with vo/nats and back-to-back sots. As an example, add a sot in the balloon story from someone who watched the balloon come down in the field in Canada. Suppose the witness is a woman named Nancy Turner.

> Nancy Turner/Watched Landing: "I'm sorry he had to give up, but it was beautiful to see the balloon land. A little scary at first when it skidded across the field. But then he got out OK. It's a shame but it surely was something to see." (:09)

Insert the sot into the script. If you decide to play Turner's sot before Fossett's, you need to rewrite the script copy to prepare viewers for Turner's comments. Otherwise, you can add Turner's sot to the back of Fossett's without script copy changes. Figure 10.7 shows the script with back-to-back sots. The changes

(page) BALLOON TRIP FAILS vo/sot 6 p 1/31 EKG Runs:

anchor - on cam

----- (on cam) -----

An American balloonist blames bad weather and bad luck for grounding his attempt at a world record.

Steve Fossett wanted to be the first person to circle the Earth nonstop in a balloon.

----- (vo) -----

But this is how his trip ended, less than two-thousand miles from where it started.

Fossett brought his balloon down today in a field in New Brunswick, Canada.

He says cold weather, a dead heater and trouble with his autopilot system forced him to cut short his trip.

Fossett spent two sleepless nights in the balloon before deciding to give up.

He says he had to throw over equipment just to stay in the air until he could find a place to land.

----- (sot) -----

Steve Fossett/Balloonist: I was afraid if I didn't come down here now, I might be forced down later in the bay. I had to change course to land on ground instead of in the water. It's disappointing but it's something I felt I needed to do.

----- (MORE) -----

take vo/nats under
(:01) S/ New Brunswick, Canada / today
(balloon touching down)

(balloon dragging across the field, coming to stop)

(Fossett getting out of capsule)

(inside of capsule)

(Fossett walking around the balloon)

take sot - runs :11
S/ :01
Steve Fossett / Balloonist

Out: needed to do

FIGURE 10.6 (*continues*)

(page) BALLOON TRIP FAILS vo/sot 6 p 1/31 EKG Runs:

anchor - on cam   ----- (on cam) -----

                                             The three-day trip cost 300-
                                     thousand dollars.

                                                      #####

FIGURE 10.6   (*continued*)

(page) BALLOON TRIP FAILS vo/sot 6 p 1/31 EKG Runs:

anchor - on cam	----- (on cam) -----
	An American balloonist blames bad weather and bad luck for grounding his attempt at a world record.
	Steve Fossett wanted to be the first person to circle the Earth nonstop in a balloon.
take vo/nats under	----- (vo) -----
(:01) S/ New Brunswick, Canada / today (balloon touching down)	But this is how his trip ended, less than two-thousand miles from where it started.
(balloon dragging across the field, coming to stop)	Fossett brought his balloon down today in a field in New Brunswick, Canada.
(Fossett getting out of capsule)	He says cold weather, a dead heater and trouble with his autopilot system forced him to cut short his trip.
(inside of capsule)	Fossett spent two sleepless nights in the balloon before deciding to give up.
(Fossett walking around the balloon)	He says he had to throw over equipment just to stay in the air until he could find a place to land.
	----- (MORE) -----

FIGURE 10.7 (*continues*)

(page) BALLOON TRIP FAILS vo/sot 6 p 1/31 EKG Runs:

* take sot - runs :20	----- (sot) -----
(:01) S/ Steve Fossett /	Steve Fossett/Balloonist: I was afraid if I
Balloonist	didn't come down here now, I might
	be forced down later in the bay. I had to
	change course to land on ground instead
	of in the water. It's disappointing but
	it's something I felt I needed to do.
(:11) S/ Nancy Turner /	* Nancy Turner/Watched Landing: I'm
Watched Landing	sorry he had to give up, but it was
	beautiful to see the balloon land. A little
	scary at first when it skidded across
	the field. But then he got out OK. It's a
* Out: ... was something to see.	shame but it surely was something to
	see.
anchor - on cam	----- (on cam) -----

     The three-day trip cost 300-

thousand dollars.

#####

FIGURE 10.7 (*continued*)

caused by the addition of a second sot are marked on the script. Remember that the script now runs nine seconds longer than it did with just the one sot. If a newscast producer had given the news writer a total run time (TRT) for the script, he or she would have had to make changes to the script copy to accommodate the second sot. In the example, the news writer uses two tapes for vo/nats and sots (Figure 10.8).

Keeping SOTs Back-to-Back

In the example, the sot from Nancy Turner is edited onto the sot from Steve Fossett to create one tape that holds back-to-back sots (Figure 10.8). Remember that it is not a good idea to jump from the anchor on camera, to vo, back to the anchor on camera, to a sot, back to the anchor on camera, to a sot and so on. Let vo lead into sots. Let sots lead into other sots or vo. Remember that viewers expect the anchor to appear on camera to introduce stories or to end them, not to pop up in the middle of stories.

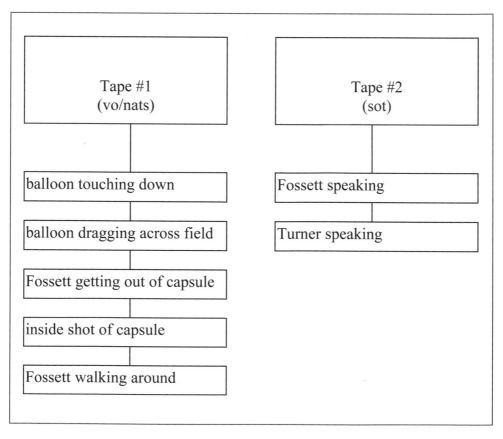

FIGURE 10.8

For instance, imagine how it would look to viewers if the two sots are separated by the reappearance of the news anchor on camera:

- - - - (vo) - - - -

[anchor speaking script copy] He says he had to throw over equipment just to stay in the air until he could find a place to land.

- - - - (sot) - - - -

Steve Fossett/Balloonist. I was afraid if I didn't come down here now, I might be forced down later in the bay. I had to change course to land on ground instead of in the water. It's disappointing but it's something I felt I needed to do.

- - - - (on cam) - - - -

A woman watched the balloon come down.
Nancy Turner says it was a sight worth seeing.

- - - - (sot) - - - -

Nancy Turner/Watched landing. I'm sorry he had to give up, but it was beautiful to see the balloon land. A little scary at first when it skidded across the field. But then he got out OK. It's a shame but it surely was something to see.

- - - - (on cam) - - - -

The three-day trip cost 300-thousand dollars.
#####

Another thing to avoid doing, generally speaking, is separating multiple sots with vo/nats. If not done well, the result can be distracting to viewers, so be careful in the way you do it. It can use extra time, making the script longer. Also, if done poorly, it fails to make for the conversational, smooth, "tight" writing that television writers strive to achieve. The following example shows how not to do it. See if you don't agree that placing sots back-to-back, rather than breaking them up the way it's been done here, makes for better storytelling.

- - - - (vo) - - - -

[anchor speaking script copy] He says he had to throw over equipment just to stay in the air until he could find a place to land.

- - - - (sot) - - - -

Steve Fossett/Balloonist. I was afraid if I didn't come down here now, I might be forced down later in the bay. I had to change course to land on ground instead of in the water. It's disappointing but it's something I felt I needed to do.

- - - - (vo) - - - -

[the vo/nats here is Turner looking at the balloon while the anchor reads over]

A woman watched the balloon come down.
Nancy Turner says it was a sight worth seeing.

- - - - (sot) - - - -

Nancy Turner/Watched landing. I'm sorry he had to give up, but it was beautiful to see the balloon land. A little scary at first when it skidded across the field. But then he got out OK. It's a shame but it surely was something to see.

- - - - (on cam) - - - -
      The three-day trip cost 300-thousand dollars.
      #####

However, there will be times that you want to include a second sound bite that doesn't connect well with the first. This especially would be true if using visuals with bites from different locations, or if each of two bites gave perspectives on separate but related issues. On occasion, there's too much needed information required to set up both sound bites before running the first. It could junk up your copy and get confusing.

For example, let's say that another balloonist, Jerad Fackley, is preparing to make the same attempt. You have visuals of Fackley's people working on his balloon in a hangar in Houston, and a sound bite from Fackley after hearing of Fossett's failure:

> "I've got a good machine and a good crew. If the weather cooperates, I'm feeling very confident. Now's the time."

You decide that you'd rather have the Fackley bite than the woman who witnessed Fossett's crash. If you were to opt for one vo/sot with back-to-back sots, your copy to set up the second bite simply might not work. You would have too much to explain, setting up the second bite before setting up the first. By the time you set up the first bite, run the first bite, then get to the second bite, your audience might be confused. You decide (advisedly) that you need additional vo between the bites to tell the story adequately.

So you can write a single story incorporating vo/sot/vo/sot, or write two separate but related stories. In addition, given the fact that you're changing locations in the story, some sort of visual transition, such as a wipe, will help establish the new location. At minimum, you'd need a super indicating the change. The first way, you'll be using four tapes. Using the second approach, you could get away with three.

Approach 1:

[tape 1, already playing]
- - - - (vo) - - - -
      [anchor speaking script copy] He says he had to throw over equipment just to stay in the air until he could find a place to land.
      [take sot-tape 2]
- - - - (sot) - - - -
      Steve Fossett/Balloonist. I was afraid if I didn't come down here now, I might be forced down later in the bay. I had to change course to land on ground instead of in the water. It's disappointing but it's something I felt I needed to do.
      [wipe to vo-tape 3, with new locator super]
- - - - (vo) - - - -
      [the vo/nats here is Fackley's team working on his balloon]
      Meanwhile, another balloonist is getting ready to attempt the

same record. Jerad Fackley heard of Fossett's fate. Although he feels bad for Fossett, he says it's quite a motivator.

[take sot-tape 4]

- - - - (sot) - - - -

Jerad Fackley/Balloonist: I've got a good machine and a good crew. If the weather cooperates, I'm feeling very confident. Now's the time.

- - - - (on cam) - - - -

Fackley will try to lift off in less than two weeks.

Approach 2:

[tape 1, already playing]

- - - - (vo) - - - -

[anchor speaking script copy] He says he had to throw over equipment just to stay in the air until he could find a place to land.

[take sot-tape 2]

- - - - (sot) - - - -

Steve Fossett/Balloonist. I was afraid if I didn't come down here now, I might be forced down later in the bay. I had to change course to land on ground instead of in the water. It's disappointing but it's something I felt I needed to do.

[continue vo-tape 2, with new locator super]

- - - - (vo) - - - -

[the vo/nats here is Fackley's team working on his balloon]

Meanwhile, another balloonist is getting ready to attempt the same record. Jerad Fackley heard of Fossett's fate. Although he feels bad for Fossett, he says it's quite a motivator.

[take sot-tape 3]

- - - - (sot) - - - -

Jerad Fackley/Balloonist: I've got a good machine and a good crew. If the weather cooperates, I'm feeling very confident. Now's the time.

- - - - (on cam) - - - -

Fackley will try to lift off in less than two weeks.

However you decide to do it, as you can see, it gets complicated. It's always best to simplify as much as possible.

Tagging SOTs with VO

You can combine vo and sots in yet another way. You can cover tags with vo. Suppose you want to run back-to-back sots with Fossett and Turner in the BALLOON script but you want to end (tag) the script with vo rather than returning to the news anchor on camera. The vo/nats to cover the tag is edited onto tape 2 following the back-to-back sots (Figure 10.9).

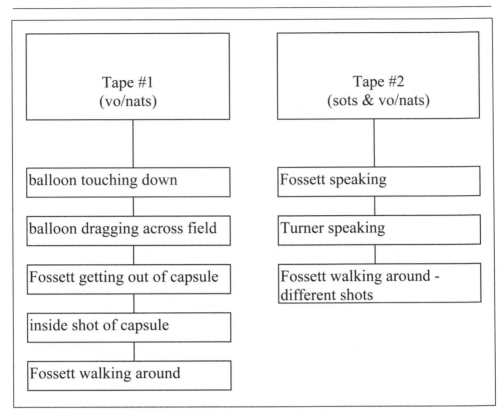

FIGURE 10.9

The format changes are minimal but necessary. Remember that formatting is communicating. You must communicate your decision to tag with vo/nats to the people it affects—the newscast producer and news anchor. In the left column of the formatted script (see Figure 10.10), use the cue "vo/nats continues" to tell the newscast director to keep tape 2 on the television screen after the sots end. As the tape continues to roll, viewers see more shots of Fossett. They hear natural sounds of him walking. And they hear the news anchor's voice as he or she delivers the tag. The anchor will not appear on camera again until the next story. There is no need to super the vo/nats tag again, unless the events of the vo/nats happened elsewhere. The vo/nats tag in this example continues with more (different) shots of Fossett walking around his balloon. Viewers can assume the earlier super still applies. In the right column, tell the news anchor that he or she is covered on the television screen by vo. Note in Figure 10.10 how the format changes are designated in the script.

(page) BALLOON TRIP FAILS vo/sot 6 p 1/31 EKG Runs:

anchor - on cam

----- (on cam) -----

An American balloonist blames bad weather and bad luck for grounding his attempt at a world record.

Steve Fossett wanted to be the first person to circle the Earth nonstop in a balloon.

----- (vo) -----

take vo/nats under
(:01) S/ New Brunswick, Canada / today
(balloon touching down)

But this is how his trip ended, less than two-thousand miles from where it started.

Fossett brought his balloon down today in a field in New Brunswick, Canada.

(balloon dragging across the field, coming to stop)

He says cold weather, a dead heater and trouble with his autopilot system forced him to cut short his trip.

(Fossett getting out of capsule)

Fossett spent two sleepless nights in the balloon before deciding to give up.

(inside of capsule)

He says he had to throw over equipment just to stay in the air until he could find a place to land.

(Fossett walking around the balloon)

----- (MORE) -----

FIGURE 10.10 (*continues*)

(page) BALLOON TRIP FAILS vo/sot 6 p 1/31 EKG Runs:

take sot - runs :20	----- (sot) -----
(:01) S/ Steve Fossett /	Steve Fossett/Balloonist: I was afraid if I
Balloonist	didn't come down here now, I might
	be forced down later in the bay. I had to
	change course to land on ground instead
	of in the water. It's disappointing but
	it's something I felt I needed to do.
(:11) S/ Nancy Turner /	Nancy Turner/Watched Landing: I'm
Watched Landing	sorry he had to give up, but it was
	beautiful to see the balloon land. A little
	scary at first when it skidded across
	the field. But then he got out OK. It's a
Out: ... was something to see.	shame but it surely was something to
	see.
* continue vo/nats under	* ----- (vo) -----
(other shot of	The three-day trip cost 300-
Fossett walking around)	thousand dollars.
	#####

FIGURE 10.10 *(continued)*

Summary

Most often, sots and back-to-back sots are accompanied by vo/nats or vo/sil in television news scripts. Adding vo to a television news script with a sot does not relieve the television news writer of the responsibilities of writing to the sot and writing to vo. The television news writer still must introduce viewers to the person who will be speaking. The introduction does not have to include the person's name and title, but it does have to create a smooth transition from the television news anchor to the person in the sot.

The format for using a vo and sot in a script is familiar. The vo/nats and sots can be on separate tapes, although not all television stations do this. Some stations edit sots onto vo tapes, following the last shot. But separate tapes guard against imprecise timing and make for a smoother newscast. A sot is always accompanied by its runs time.

The process of writing a script with vo/nats and a sot is reviewed, with guidelines introduced for adding additional sots. The sots should appear back-to-back rather than separated by an anchor on camera or (generally) vo/nats. Tags at the ends of scripts can be covered with vo.

Exercises

1. Use the following wire copy to write a script with vo/nats and back-to-back sots for today's 6 p.m. newscast, slugged WEST BANK. TRT (total runs time) :50. Add sot runs times to script copy length to get the TRT. You may use a box. Choose vo/nats from the shots available. Note the shots on your script. Choose the sot or sots from those available.

> (ATERET, West Bank)—Shots were fired at an Israeli bus traveling to a West Bank settlement north of Jerusalem today, wounding at least two people seriously and one lightly, an army spokesman said.
>
> The identity of the gunmen was unknown, but Moslem groups have vowed to avenge last month's massacre of some 30 worshipers in a West Bank mosque by a Jewish settler.
>
> Near the village of Bir-Zeit, shots were fired from an ambush on the left side of the road toward the front of the bus, according to an Israeli spokesman, Yehiel Hamdi, secretary of the Jewish settlement of Ateret, where the bus was headed.
>
> He said one woman from the settlement was shot in the lung and was in serious condition. The driver was also badly wounded, and the two were evacuated by ambulance to a Jerusalem hospital.
>
> A young girl from a nearby settlement was lightly wounded, an army spokesman said. Others who were on the bus told officials they were fine but badly shaken.

Available vo/nats (super: West Bank/Today):

(a) Shot of the scene (road and bus)
(b) Shot of the bus with bullet holes

(c) Shot of the side of the road

(d) Shot of people looking at the bus

(e) Shot of people crying and hugging

(f) Shot of ambulance leaving the scene

(g) Shot of the Jewish settlement of Ateret.

Available sots:

(a) Yehiel Hamdi/Jewish settler: "Near the village of Bir-Zeit shots were fired from an ambush on the left side of the road toward the front of the bus." (:06)

(b) Saul Goldman/Bus passenger: "Nobody saw anything. The firing came from nowhere. Bullets hit the front of the bus but nobody could tell where the firing was coming from." (:05)

(c) Golda Bloom/Bus passenger: "I was in the back of the bus. I didn't know what was happening. But I heard the shots and I saw the driver slump over the steering wheel. I didn't know what was happening but I fell to the floor." (:08)

(d) Joseph Hamdi/Jewish settler: "This is another vicious attack upon the Jewish people. The shooting at the mosque last month seems to have opened a new age of violence for the West Bank. I don't know if the peace process stands a chance now." (:10).

2. Rewrite the script from Exercise 1 to run :30. You may omit some vo/nats and one sot.

3. Use the following wire copy to write a news script with vo/nats and one sot or back-to-back sots. TRT :50. The script will air in tonight's 11 p.m. newscast, slugged BOMBING SUSPECT ARRESTED. You may use a box. Choose vo/nats from the shots available. Choose the sot or sots from those available.

ASHEVILLE, N.C.—Olympic park bombing suspect Eric Rudolph appeared before a federal judge Monday for the first time since his capture, acknowledging his identity but not entering a plea.

Attorney General John Ashcroft said Rudolph will face trial first in Birmingham, Ala., where an abortion clinic was bombed in 1998, and then in Atlanta, site of the 1996 Olympic bombing and other blasts linked to Rudolph.

Rudolph, wearing a blue bulletproof vest over an orange prison jumpsuit, spoke only briefly at the 30-minute hearing before U.S. District Judge Lacy Thornburg.

He sat straight-faced next to attorney Sean Devereux, appointed because Rudolph says he does not have the money to pay a lawyer, as Assistant U.S. Attorney Jill Westmoreland Rose read the charges against him.

Rudolph faces six charges of using an explosive against a facility in interstate commerce and could face the death penalty. Besides the Olympic and Birmingham bombings, he is accused of 1997 bombings in Atlanta outside a gay nightclub and an office building that housed an abortion clinic. In all, two people were killed and about 150 injured in the four attacks.

There was no immediate indication when Rudolph would be moved to Alabama.

Earlier Monday, Rudolph was brought to Asheville in western North Carolina under heavy guard from Murphy, some 90 miles away, aboard a National Guard helicopter. He was captured Saturday near Murphy after five years on the run.

Rudolph stared defiantly at reporters during his transfer from the jail in Murphy.

Before the 36-year-old former soldier and survivalist was arrested, he had last been seen publicly in July 1998, when he took supplies from a health food store owner in Andrews, near Murphy.

Available vo/nats (Super: Asheville, NC/Today):

(a) Rudolph, leaving a National Guard helicopter, under heavy guard, wearing a blue bulletproof vest over an orange prison jumpsuit; nats of helicopter winding down.

(b) Rudolph, being led to a police car, glaring at reporters; nats of reporters calling out questions.

(c) Rudolph, under heavy guard, being led into the courtroom.

(d) Others going into the courtroom.

(e) Shots of faces of those in the courtroom, listening.

(f) Shot of the judge, listening.

(g) Shot of the prosecutors, talking together.

(h) Shot of Rudolph, being led out of courtroom, nats of reporters questions.

Available sots:

(a) Rudolph, responding in a strong voice when Thornburg asked if he was Eric Robert Rudolph: "Yes, your honor." (runs :02)

(b) U.S. Attorney Robert Conrad, after the hearing: "The defendant is waiving his right to enter a plea of guilty here and instead will face charges where those charges are pending." (runs :07)

(c) U.S. Attorney General John Ashcroft, in Washington, on having Rudolph tried first in Alabama and then in Georgia: "This will provide the best opportunity to bring justice to all of the victims of the bombings and to each community that experienced these attacks." (runs :09)

4. Identify scripts with vo and sot or sots in a national newscast. Count the number that appear in the newscast. Create a work sheet (see Figure 10.11) on which you list the stories that use vo with sot(s) and where those stories appeared.

Newscast: Network: <u>ABC</u>
                                 Title: <u>World News Tonight</u>
                                 Time: <u>5:30 p.m.</u>
                                 Date: <u>Thursday, March 23</u>
                                 Anchor(s): <u>Peter Jennings</u>

First Block:

A-10 <u>Bush-Tax Cut</u>   <u>vo/sot</u>
A-20 <u>Weinberg-Iraq rebuilding problems</u>   <u>vo/sots (2)</u>
A-30 _____
A-40 _____
A-50 _____
A-60 _____
A-70 _____

Second Block:

B-10 _____
B-20 <u>Middle East peace talks</u>   <u>vo/sots (2)</u>
B-30 <u>North Korea nukes</u>   <u>vo/sot</u>

(etc)

Putting the Formats Together

11

Review the elements you have used to write television news scripts.

- On cam (and on cam with a box)
- Full-screen graphics
- VO (vo/nats under, vo/sil and vo/nats full)
- Sots (and back-to-back sots).

Television news scripts can combine two, three or all of these elements to help viewers better understand news stories. You can use on camera, full-screen graphics, vo and sots in an endless number of combinations. You've already learned to combine vo and sots. Consider the possibilities when you start combining other elements.

Combination 1: VO/Nats Under and Full Screen Graphic (FS/GFX)

Use the following wire copy story to write a television news script using vo/nats under and a full-screen graphic. Available vo/nats might include various shots of University of Michigan seniors in a classroom and elsewhere on campus, an on-campus job placement office, and the career counseling office with counselors at work talking with students and on the phone. When you see the statistics (numbers) in the story, you should be thinking about full-screen graphics you can create.

> (LANSING, Mich.)—For the first time in three years, there is a little good news for prospective college graduates. The Collegiate Employment Research Institute says employers expect to hire 1.1 percent more college graduates this year than a year ago.
>
> The news follows declines in hiring ranging from just over 2 percent last year to more than 13 percent the year before. The three-year downturn was the longest recorded in the 23 years the survey has been taken.

> The Institute's director says the latest survey should send a bit of optimism to students who have believed there was no point in job hunting because there weren't any jobs.
>
> The director says the small increase indicates employers realize they need to bring in new blood but remain cautious about the economy.

Write a television news script with a TRT (total running time) of :30. Use information from the wire story to write notes that can help you design a full-screen graphic. As always, read the wire copy, understand it and underline key facts. Look for an audience hook to find a focus. Think before you write. Think about the eight guidelines. Start strong with a lead that will grab viewers' attention. Follow with information that answers viewers' questions. Omit unnecessary time references. Omit unnecessary words. Select words carefully to avoid clichés. Your script may look something like the one shown in Figure 11.1.

The full-screen graphic complements the script copy (Figure 11.2). What viewers hear and see make sense together.

As you can see from the way the script is formatted in Figure 11.1, COLLEGE-GRADS is a vo/nats/fs/gfx that airs on the 11 p.m. newscast on June 6. The television news writer begins the script with vo/nats under of students, which is followed by the full-screen graphic. The script ends on the full-screen graphic. The news anchor does not appear on camera at all in this story. The cues in the script should be familiar to you.

Combination 2: On Cam, VO/Nats Under, VO/Nats Full and SOT

The basic elements of a television news script offer endless opportunities for variety. To explore another combination of news script elements, look at a story you encountered in Chapter 8 about a UPS strike in Florida. Review the wire copy and the available vo/nats.

> (BEL HARBOUR, Fla.)—The Teamsters union says workers have agreed to go back to work after a dispute was settled with United Parcel Service.
>
> Teamsters members staged a strike against UPS at 9 a.m. today when the company more than doubled the weight limit on packages, to 150 pounds.
>
> The strike was settled when the company agreed at the 5 p.m. close of business not to require workers to handle packages heavier than 70 pounds without a helper or a lifter device.

The vo/nats available for this story includes the following shots:

• Shot of UPS trucks sitting in the company parking lot
• Shot of boxes piled up in the warehouse

A-30   COLLEGE GRADS   11 pm   6/3   EKG   Time:

vo/nats
S/ :01   University of Michigan/Today

(students in classroom)

(students walking on campus)

full screen
Employment
New College Grads
2004   +1.1%
2003   -6%
2002   -2%

----- (VO) -----

A new study may offer hope for this year's college graduates.

The Collegiate Employment Research Institute says employers will open their doors this year to more new graduates.

----- (full screen) -----

The study forecasts a one-point-one percent hiring increase over last year.

It would mark the first increase in three years.

Hiring of new college graduates dropped two-percent two years ago and another six percent last year.

#####

FIGURE 11.1

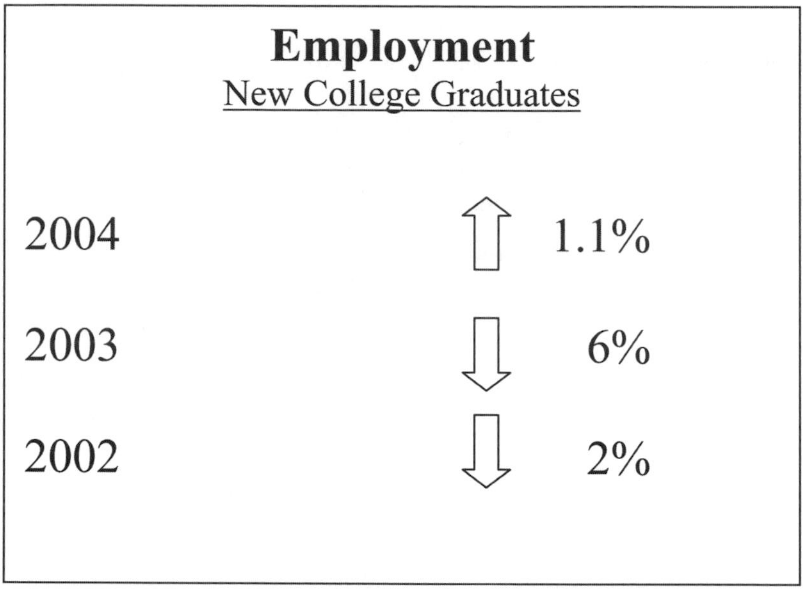

Employment
<u>New College Graduates</u>

2004   ⇧   1.1%

2003   ⇩   6%

2002   ⇩   2%

FIGURE 11.2

- Shot of union workers walking on the picket line
- Shot of a group of union workers chanting strike slogans
- Shot of a lifting device
- Shot of union workers standing on the picket line.

Earlier, you wrote this script using on cam, vo/nats under and vo/nats full. Now add a sot and vo/nats tag. Look at the script in format in Figure 11.3 to see one way this can be done.

Combination 3: On Cam, SOT and Full-Screen Graphic

You have already combined vo/nats and a sot. Now use a sot with another element, a full-screen graphic. Use a script you've already written, slugged WEST BANK in the exercise section of Chapter 10. Here's the wire copy.

> (ATERET, West Bank)—Shots were fired at an Israeli bus traveling to a West Bank settlement north of Jerusalem today, wounding at least two people seriously and one lightly, an army spokesman said.
>
> The identity of the gunmen was unknown, but Moslem groups have vowed to avenge last month's massacre of some 30 worshipers in a West Bank mosque by a Jewish settler.
>
> Near the village of Bir-Zeit shots were fired from an ambush on the left side of the road toward the front of the bus, according to an Israeli spokesman, Yehiel Hamdi, secretary of the Jewish settlement of Ateret, where the bus was headed.

A-30   STRIKE   6 pm   3/6   EKG   Time:

anchor - on cam box - UPS Strike	---------- (on cam) ---------- A strike against United Parcel Service is over eight hours after the workers walked off the job.

vo/nats
S/ :01 Bel Harbour / Today
      (workers walking on picket line)
 	
      (more workers)
	---------- (vo) ----------
	Teamsters union members formed picket lines this morning outside the U-P-S office in Bel Harbour.
	Workers were protesting a company decision that more than doubled the weight limit on the packages they handle, to 150 pounds.

bring nats full :04
      (workers chanting)
cue anchor
    (union officials talking with workers)
	----(pause-nats full :04 & under)----
	About an hour ago, the union called off its strike and announced an agreement with U-P-S.

sot – runs : 11 S/ :01 Bob Johnson / Teamsters Local President Out: … settlement so quickly.	---------- (sot) ---------- Bob Johnson/Teamsters Local President: I am so glad it's over. We all are. we didn't want to strike. We have families to feed. But the new policy was unfair. We're happy we could reach a settlement so quickly.
vo/nats continues (lifting machines)	---------- (vo) ---------- The union says the company agreed to offer workers a helper or lifting machine for packages over 70 pounds. #####

FIGURE 11.3

He said one woman from the settlement was shot in the lung and was in serious condition. The driver was also badly wounded, and the two were evacuated by ambulance to a Jerusalem hospital.

A young girl from a nearby settlement was lightly wounded, an army spokesman said. Others who were on the bus told officials they were fine but badly shaken.

The available sot is from Golda Bloom, a bus passenger: "I was in the back of the bus. I didn't know what was happening. But I heard the shots and I saw the driver slump over the steering wheel. I didn't know what was happening but I fell to the floor." (:08)

Write a news script with a sot and a full-screen graphic showing a map of the West Bank with the bus route, the site of the attack, the village and Jerusalem all highlighted. Assume the script airs in the 6 p.m. newscast on March 6, with a box, slugged WEST BANK AMBUSH.

Your script might look something like the one in Figure 11.4. The television news writer begins the script with the news anchor on camera with a box. The writer uses the full-screen graphic (map) to show viewers where the ambush happened. The full-screen graphic is replaced on the screen by the sot. Finally, the anchor appears on camera to tag the sot and end the story.

Combination 4: On Cam, VO/Nats Under, VO/Nats Full, SOT and Full-Screen Graphic

Because the possibilities for combining script elements are endless, this chapter could be endless too. But look at one more combination. Look at the script in Figure 11.5, which uses all four script elements in one script. Pay attention to newscast director cues in the left column. They should be familiar to you, as should the cues for the news anchor in the right column. If the way the news writer uses cues in the example is not familiar, this is the time to review. Make sure you know how to use script elements in combination. Make sure you know how to let the newscast director and news anchor know that your scripts contain many elements.

Summary

The four basic elements of news scripts are on cam (and on cam with a box), full-screen graphics, vo (vo/nats under, vo/sil and vo/nats full) and sots. These elements can be used in many combinations in news scripts.

A-30   WEST BANK AMBUSH   6 pm   3/6   EKG   Time:

anchor - on cam
box - BUS ATTACK

---------- (on cam) ----------

The Israeli Army is looking into an

attack today on Jewish settlers in the

occupied West Bank.

---------- (full screen) ----------

full screen
(Map of West Bank showing
bus route, village and Jerusalem)

An Israeli spokesman says gunmen

opened fire on a bus carrying the settlers.

The ambush occurred along a road

north of Jerusalem near the village of

Bir-Zeit (beer-ZEET).

The army confirms at least three

people are hurt, including the driver, and

other passengers are badly shaken.

---------- (sot) ----------

sot runs .08
S/ :01 Golda Bloom/
    Bus Passenger

Golda Bloom/Bus Passenger: I was in
the back of the bus. I didn't know what
was happening. But I heard the shots and
I saw the driver slump over the steering
wheel. I didn't know what was
happening but I fell to the floor.

Out: ... fell to the floor.

---------- (on cam) ----------

anchor on cam

Officials say they're unsure

who's behind today's ambush.

But it comes less than a month

after a Jewish settler attacked a West

Bank mosque, killing 30 people.

#####

FIGURE 11.4

A-50   SALVATION ARMY   12 noon   12/3   EKG   Time:

anchor - on cam
box - Salvation Army

---------- (on cam) ----------

Shoppers in Dallas this morning spotted one of the first signs of the holiday season.

vo/nat
S/ :01 Dallas/Today

(kettle)

---------- (vo) ----------

The Salvation Army's familiar red kettle.

This one is larger than usual for a good reason.

(parking lot, kettle & people)

The Salvation Army brought its big Christmas kettle to the civic center parking lot to kick off this year's fundraising campaign.

bring nats full :06, then under

(band playing)

----pause :06 for nats full, then under----

cue anchor

(Salvation Army band)

The Salvation Army wants to raise 90-thousand dollars this holiday season.

The money will help buy food for needy families and toys for children on Christmas morning.

(people att ceremony)

---------- (more) ----------

FIGURE 11.5   (*continues*)

A-50   SALVATION ARMY   12 noon   12/3   EKG   Time:

(Chaffin making donation)

This year's Campaign Chairman Ron Chaffin made the season's first donation.

---------- (sot) ----------

sot - runs :21
S/ :01 Ron Chaffin/
   Campaign Chair

Ron Chaffin/Campaign Chair: Too many children in our area wake up on Christmas morning to find no presents under the tree. For too many children, Christmas is just another day they'll go hungry. Donating to the Salvation Army helps make a child's Christmas special.

S/ :13 Jenny Albert /
   Made Donation

Jenny Albert/Made Donation: I work really hard to make sure Christmas is a special day for my children. It should be for all children. That's why I'm here and that's why I put money in the kettle.

Out: ... money in the kettle.
Full screen

---------- (full screen) ----------

If you want to give to the Salvation Army, you can seend a donation to post office box two-two-nine in Dallas, zip code 75206.

Salvation Army
P.O. Box 229
Dallas, TX 75206

Or you can drop a donation into a kettle.

---------- (on cam) ----------

anchor - on cam

The Salvation Army says its kettles will be out at other shopping centers later this week.

FIGURE 11.5   (*continued*)

Exercises

1. Use the wire copy story below and available script elements to write a television news script using on cam with a box, vo/nats, vo/nats full, the sot and a full-screen graphic in any order. TRT :40. The script will air in tonight's 10 p.m. newscast, slugged PENTAGON MASKS.

> (WASHINGTON)—The Pentagon has handed out 25,000 emergency gas masks to prepare defense employees for possible chemical or biological terror attacks.
>
> That completes about one-third of the effort started in late February, when officials began training an average of several hundred people a day in the use of "emergency escape hoods." On Monday, they gave the masks to a few dozen members of the news media corps who work daily in the Defense Department headquarters.
>
> The masks are designed to give wearers up to about an hour of protection to flee chemical or biological contamination, officials said.
>
> Some 80,000 masks are to be made available for department employees and other workers as well as visitors at the Pentagon and its annexes in other office buildings throughout the Washington area.
>
> Workers normally keep their masks at their desks, but if a high-threat period is declared, they are to carry them at all times in a case that hooks onto their belts.
>
> The Defense Department had been working to protect the Pentagon from biological or chemical attacks since the 1995 sarin gas attacks by a doomsday cult on the Tokyo subway system, officials have said. But it decided to issue the masks after a number of additional precautions were instituted following the Sept. 11, 2001 terrorists attacks on the Pentagon and World Trade Center.

Available vo/nats (super: Pentagon/Today):

> Various shots of the masks being handed out to workers in offices, masks laid across a desk, mask in its case hooked onto a belt, worker walking down corridor with mask case on belt, nat sot of velcro ripping with visuals of mask being pulled out of a case, people looking over masks, people trying masks on; shots of exterior of the Pentagon.

Available sot:

> Gerald Krantz, Deputy Public Information Officer, Department of Defense: "Given the world we live in and the threats we face, we felt this move was necessary. This is just part of a much larger strategy we're using to protect our people." (runs :10)

2. Rewrite the PENTAGON MASKS script for tomorrow morning's 7 a.m. newscast. Change the lead to offer viewers the latest information. Change the super to "Pentagon/Yesterday." The new script runs TRT :25.

3. Use the wire copy story below and the available script elements of your choice to write a television news script for today's 6 p.m. newscast, slugged LONDON KILLER. TRT :50.

>(LONDON)—Police said today a 10-year-old boy found raped, strangled and buried near London could be a new victim of the so-called Station Strangler, Britain's worst serial killer.
>
>Police spokesman Raymond Dowd told reporters the boy, who had been dead about two weeks, was found about 30 km (18 miles) from the township of Mitchell's Plain, outside London, where most of the Strangler's 21 known victims were found in February buried in shallow graves.
>
>The killer became known as the Station Strangler because he lured some of his earliest victims, all boys aged between 9 and 15, from railway platforms.
>
>The child, identified as Elroy Rooyen, was found face-down in the sand with his hands tied behind his back. Dowd said he had been sodomized and strangled.
>
>More than 300 men have been questioned by a team of 80 detectives, and psychiatrists have issued a profile in the search for the killer. No arrests have been made.
>
>Self-appointed strangler hunters from the terror-stricken Mitchell's Plain community have harassed innocent men in their attempt to find the killer.

Available sots:

(a) Raymond Dowd/Police spokesman: "We can't say for sure it is the Strangler, it could be a copycat, but the killing matched his modus operandi." (:08)

(b) Basil Scott/London police: "We're working on the assumption it's he. I can't believe there can be more people of this nature out there. The Strangler killings are the worst I've ever come across." (:11)

Available vo/nat and vo/nat full (super: Near London/Today):

>Various shots of the crime scene, as police discover the boy's body and people from the community look on. Some shots offer vo/nat full sounds of police investigators as they do their jobs.

(a) Create your own full screen graphic or graphics.
(b) Create your own box.

4. Rewrite the script you wrote in Exercise 3 trimming :15 for TRT :30. Trim script copy and omit elements, as necessary. The script airs in tonight's 10 p.m. newscast, slugged LONDON KILLER.

12

Interviewing: Conversation with a Goal

We've discussed how to write into and out of good sots, but for the reporter in the field, much of the work comes in conducting the interviews designed to get those good sots in the first place. Getting good bites is part of the writing process, and good reporting and good interviewing make for good sound bites. You must do the research ahead of time to gather whatever background you can on the story. The more you know about the story going in, the better your questions will be. Better questions give you better sound bites.

To review, a bite needs to be a complete thought, a self-contained response or statement. It tells how and why rather than yes or no—meaning the reporter must ask how or why questions. Although an entire book could be devoted to interviewing, it's important to spend some additional time here talking about the interview process, with a brief discussion on the reporting that goes with the interview.

Sources

Good sources can supply you with good story ideas as well as good interviews. You should develop good sources by establishing a relationship with those in various agencies and offices who might be helpful. Those potential sources include public relations specialists with the governmental offices, firms and organizations—just because they have the best interests of their companies and agencies in mind does not mean they can't serve as good sources. When you have a spare minute in the newsroom, work the phones to make contact, reestablish contact or just fish for stories. I've gotten countless stories this way.

It's also a good idea to talk with people you meet—people in the neighborhood, on the bus, in the store, at church, at parties, at the local pubs and hangouts, and so on. Talk to people, get to know what they do and what they think and why and how they live their lives. You will wind up not only with good story ideas but with good sources (or contacts for good sources) as well.

As a reporter, you'll often need sources at the scene of an event. As you talk with these sources, make sure you get their names and contact information, whether they are fire captains, police sergeants, business managers or eyewitnesses. You might need to get in touch with them again to check status, with a follow-up question, whatever.

Interview Types

There are basically three types of interviews. The first is the research and background interview. With a backgrounder, you're looking to gather information relating to an issue or event—you're not necessarily going after a sound bite. These can come after reading a newspaper article that inspires a related story, or reading a press kit from a local not-for-profit organization, or a discussion with your garbage collector or neighbor. Using the Internet (and its host of resources) or clip files also can be useful in getting ideas, which would then lead to making some phone calls to gather more information. A warning: Be careful about information on the Internet. Anyone can put anything up on a Web page, so carefully check the credibility of the source.

You may also conduct an interview for an interview segment of a longer program. This is more of a discussion to flesh out an issue and can include more than one interviewee. Because it's a longer format, you're not so much looking for a sound bite as insight into the issue or event being discussed, or presentation of various points of view. You need to go into this type well-researched and with a large list of potential questions, arranged by topic. The key here is to keep the discussion moving and to keep it on track, which takes an enormous amount of concentration. In live situations especially, your subjects may take off in a different direction. If it works for the purpose of the interview, fine—but it typically doesn't. Keep your interviewees on a short leash, and don't be afraid to jump in to direct the discussion back to the topic at hand. It will take great mental focus, creativity, diplomacy and assertiveness—all at the same time.

I was anchoring a half-hour public affairs program in Reno a few years ago when one of my guests—who was blessed with neither succinctness of language nor clarity of thought—began reading word for word from the first of a stack of legislation with which he had issues. To my horror (and that of my guests, judging by their faces), he planned on reading it all. I asked him to summarize his issue with the first piece of legislation, which he was unable to do after 30 seconds. I was witnessing a train wreck, and what was worse, I was driving the train. With my three other guests waiting patiently, I literally had to step in, summarize the man's point for him, and move to the other guests, being careful from that point on to ask him only yes and no questions and jumping in immediately after his response. That sort of thing happens. Often.

A third interview type is the focus of our discussion—going for sound bites. These generally occur in two forms: the prearranged interview and the interview that occurs at the scene of a story, especially a breaking news story. There are other categories, but let's focus on these.

Strategy

In either type of interview (prearranged or spot news), you want to make the person being interviewed as comfortable as possible. Put him or her at ease both with your presence and the presence of the camera, microphone and lights. Engage him or her in some light conversation if time is needed to set up equipment, which is typically the case.

In a prearranged interview, you generally should begin with the easy questions first, then move up to the more difficult ones. In any situation, have a list of potential questions handy. Don't go for basic information while you're rolling tape—you won't use the sots, and it's that much more to slog through once you're back at the station reviewing tape. In fact, under most circumstances, you already should have gotten that basic information over the phone or during your research. Doing the homework ahead of time will save you a lot of time later, not to mention give you a better sense of the story, a better sense of what questions to ask and better sound bites (and a better story) as a result. Plus, you'll earn a lot more respect from the person you're interviewing because you just might give the impression you know what you're doing.

For spot news interviews, things may be happening quickly and you may have little time for the interview. If that's the case, go for the sound bites immediately. Get the best questions out there trying for the best sots right off the bat.

The best sound bites come from asking for emotional reactions, eyewitness accounts, opinions and their unique, colorful or usual perspectives. Phrase questions to get the responses you'll need on tape. Remember that yes-or-no questions get yes-or-no responses—you want to know how or why, not yes or no.

If you are digging for information, pose a pithy question and be quiet. Watch giving the natural response of saying, "Uh-huh," or frantically bobbing your head. Although you may feel as if this may bring out responses easier, keeping yourself from doing it will accomplish two things. First, you avoid sounding like an exuberant cheerleader by punctuating the conversation with an incessant, insipid "Uh-huh!?" (which will be heard clearly in the audio—trust me), and if you're framed in the video, you'll keep from looking like one of those bobble heads that some people put in the back of their cars. Second, when you pose a tough question followed by silence, that silence will subconsciously pressure your interviewee to fill in the dead space. You may wind up with a great sot that you otherwise would not have gotten.

You may have occasion to interview someone who might not be thrilled by the prospect of talking to a television reporter. You do not need to supply a list of questions you'll be asking. They'll sometimes demand it. Don't do it. However, it would be helpful (and courteous) to let them know the general topic and perhaps a few specific points you'll need information on. The interview will go better because the interviewee will be better prepared. However, only give them the informational topics. Do not let them know the specific questions. You're looking for spontaneous responses on their thoughts and feelings. You don't want something that's rehearsed.

Sometimes, in the course of the interview, you will hit a question or topic that the interviewee doesn't want to answer. If the interviewee becomes antagonistic, stay calm. Do not get emotional. Simply ask your questions politely and give him or her the chance to respond. The interviewee may also be evasive in responding. You should continue to phrase the question in different ways until you get a good response.

Listening

This leads to the next point. During the interview, you'll be consulting your list of questions. It's essential that you also listen to the responses. This seems obvious, but even seasoned reporters can be focused on phrasing the next question and fail to hear the answer to the question currently on the table. Listening to the answer will serve several purposes.

First, you'll know whether the person is answering the question. He or she may want to evade giving the answer, or may misunderstand the question you've posed. Either way, you need to follow up.

Second, you'll know if you understand what the person is saying and can hear the way he or she is saying it. If you don't understand, you can ask for clarification or an explanation. Also, if they are speaking in arcane terms you know your audience won't understand, you can ask them to rephrase in conversational language.

Next, you may hear some point you hadn't thought of. Make a quick note and pursue it. It may even change the direction of your story. Be open to taking a detour if you think it might prove useful, then return to your other questions later. However, maintain the focus of the story—you need to make the most efficient use of your time as well as that of the person interviewed. Also, the interview itself may wander through several of your questions in a different order than what you've sketched out. Check off each question as it's answered so that you don't repeat yourself.

Finally, listening to the answers will let you know when you've got a good sound bite. Make a quick note on the potential sot so that you can look for it in the tape later. And because you're listening, you can avoid bites that are long and wandering. If you're getting that sort of response from your interviewee, jump in and reset the focus. Listen for potential bites during the interview.

A Few Other Points

In coming up with questions, don't be afraid to ask obvious questions. Don't be afraid to ask not-so-obvious questions. Unusual questions can get great responses from people, especially if they're unexpected.

If you are using a stick microphone, always maintain control of the mic. Although this is usually not a major concern when doing a prearranged interview with a lavalier (a lapel mic), in covering breaking news, your time and your control of the situation are critical. When you allow someone to take the mic out of your hand, you've given them control of the interview. During a live shot especially, this can be a train wreck waiting to happen. Hang onto the mic.

If the focus of your story is on some activity in which the interviewee is involved, one great technique is to clip a lavalier on the person and let him or her go. Have them demonstrate something, or walk the viewer through a process, all the while explaining or commenting on what they're doing.

Technical Considerations

Your interviews must sound good. Make certain you have good sound by listening through a headset and watching the audio meter on the camera (if you have one). Ensure the mic cord has no shorts, which can create static or cut out sound altogether. When you are shooting the interview, be aware of unwanted background sound, such as a radio playing or a loud air conditioner. Ambient sound, on the other hand, is fine. For example, if you're talking with a highway repair crew chief alongside the highway, traffic sounds in the background are not only acceptable, your interview would sound strange without them.

Interviews also must look good. The chief point to keep in mind is the framing of the shot (see Figure 12.1). Shoot the interview at the eye level of the subject. If she's tall, crank up the tripod. If he's short, lower the legs of the tripod. If the interviewee is seated, the reporter should be seated as well, and the tripod adjusted accordingly. Also, have the interviewee looking at the reporter, who should be right beside the camera. Do not have the interviewee look into the camera lens. It's jarring to the viewer and can be intimidating to the person giving the interview.

You want to leave a touch of space between the top of the interviewee's head and the top of the screen, so as not to crowd the look of the shot. This is known as "head space." You also want to show both eyes of the person talking. Do not shoot the person from the side, showing him or her in profile. This is known as the notorious "talking ear" shot, typically found in very small markets where beginning videographers have not learned better. Show both eyes.

The back/side of the person's head should be close to one edge of the screen. Give a slightly larger amount of room between the front/side of the face and the

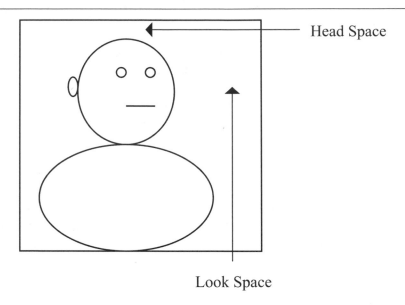

Head Space

Look Space

FIGURE 12.1

edge. This is called "look space" or "nose room," and you place it for psycholog-ical effect. It looks cramped to have someone's eyes right at the edge of the screen, especially if there's too much room behind the head.

Be aware of the background. It's good to put the person in their natural envi-ronment, or an environment that makes sense to the story. At the same time, make certain you avoid problem backgrounds, such as a sign or tree growing out of the interviewee's head, or the drunk guy across the street waving his arms for the camera.

Also, be aware of backlighting, a major problem for interviews. For example, never let an interview subject sit with his or her back to an open window during the day. The amount of sunlight flooding in from behind (even on a cloudy day) will be enormously brighter than the light on the subject's face. This means one of two things will have to happen. If the camera's exposure is set for the light from the window, the interviewee will be cast into silhouette, which is fine is he's in the witness protection program and doesn't want to recognized. Otherwise, you have a talking shadow. Not the best visual. In contrast, if the camera is exposed for the subject's face, the background will be completely washed out and give an unearth-ly glow around the subject. Unless the effect you're looking for is heavenly lights surrounding the interviewee, go for another lighting situation. The answer is to close the blinds, move the subject or move the camera to get rid of the backlight. It's just that simple.

One other concept worth discussing here is called the "axis" (and we're not talking the Axis of Evil). This is also called the "180," the "180 axis" and the "line," among other terms. The concept works as follows.

John is interviewing Mary (Figure 12.2). The camera is set up by John's right shoulder and is getting a shot of Mary. This means that Mary, who is looking at

Overhead View: Camera over John's right shoulder

John   Mary

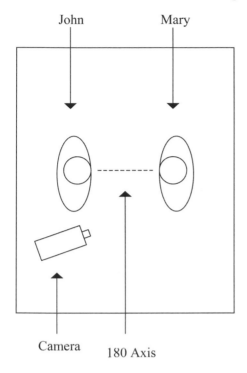

Resulting shot of Mary,
looking screen left

Camera   180 Axis

FIGURE 12.2

an off-camera John, is looking slightly screen-left. Screen direction of the "action" is to the left. Now suppose you need a reversal shot. This is a shot of the reporter, listening intently to what Mary is saying. Recall that Mary is looking screen left. For the reversal shot to make sense, John has to be looking screen right so they appear to the viewer to be looking at each other. To accomplish this, the camera has to be at Mary's left side, so that John, looking at Mary, is looking screen right (Figure 12.3). Now, when you edit Mary talking (looking screen left) followed by a shot of John listening (looking screen right), the two shots make sense. They appear to be looking at each other (Figure 12.4).

The way to keep it making visual sense is to shoot on the same side of the 180 axis. Look again at Figures 12.2 and 12.3. The action is occurring between the interviewer and the interviewee. Draw an imaginary line between the two of them. That's your axis line. If you stay on the same side of that line to shoot, the relationship between the two of them will make visual sense. Shots of them edited one after the other (Mary talking, then John listening) will make them appear to be looking at each other, because they will be looking at opposite sides of the television screen.

However, if you "cross the axis," you put them both looking in the same screen direction. Look at Figure 12.5. The videographer has taken the first shot

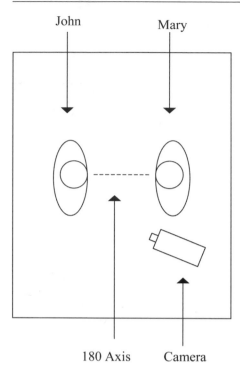

Resulting shot of John, looking screen right

FIGURE 12.3

Edited result: Mary and John appear to be looking at each other.

FIGURE 12.4

over John's right shoulder, putting Mary facing screen left. For the second shot, however, the photog "crossed the axis," shooting over Mary's right shoulder as well. As a result, John is also looking screen left. When the two shots are edited back-to-back, John and Mary will appear to the audience to be looking the same

Overhead View:
1st shot: Camera over John's right shoulder
2nd shot: Camera over Mary's right shoulder

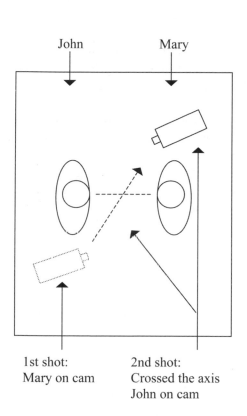

John   Mary

1st shot: 2nd shot:
Mary on cam   Crossed the axis
                  John on cam

Resulting 1st shot:
Mary looking screen left

Resulting 2nd shot:
John also looking screen left

FIGURE 12.5

direction rather than at each other. It just doesn't work visually. It's confusing to the audience and breaks one of the basic rules of visual grammar.

The same principle is true of any relative action shown in a news story. Although it's beyond the scope of this book to get much deeper, understand the concept as it applies to interviews, and you'll be able to apply it to all of your news stories.

Keep in mind also that you might want to combine one short sot early in the interview with a later sot, editing them together as a single bite. This is easily done with an edit shot (often called a "cutaway") to hide any jump cut. One such edit shot is that reversal shot of the reporter we just talked about. However, the same rule applies here as applies to any use of sots and the way you write into and out of those sots: Whatever you present must be an accurate and fair representation of the story.

Another aspect beyond the scope of this book is lighting. However, you should learn good two- and three-point lighting techniques. Also, be certain to white balance the camera every time you move it.

And, unless it's breaking news and you risk losing the shot, always, always use a tripod. Nothing looks more unprofessional than shaky video. You don't want your stories looking like Uncle Walter's birthday videos, shot with his new camcorder. Use a tripod.

You must keep in mind that coming up with questions, conducting the interview and listening for sots are all part of the writing process. The sots you come back with will play a major role in your story and how you write it.

Finally, one way to become good at interviewing is by listening to those who do it well. Two of the best in the business are Ted Koppel of ABC's Nightline and Terry Gross of NPR's Fresh Air. Listen to the questions they pose, the way they pose them, and the general manner in which they conduct their interviews. You will develop your skills much more quickly.

Summary

Be curious about people and talk with them. Learn how to get people to talk with you. Develop sources and story ideas, and pursue them. Story ideas can come from anyone.

Make the interviewee comfortable. In a prearranged interview, get background information ahead of time. If you're doing an interview for sound bites, don't ask informational questions while the camera is rolling. Go for sot-eliciting questions instead. Begin with easy questions, then move to the hard ones. In spot news, go straight for the key questions that will give you the best sots. In all cases, phrase questions so that you get the responses you need.

Remember that good sots

Are compelling,
Give a human quality,
Are self-contained,
Find ways to capture the moment or the idea,
Carry well throughout, and
Are conversational.

Pose a question and be quiet. Don't supply questions ahead of time, but do give a general topic so they can be prepared with information. Always stay calm, polite and professional during an interview.

Listen to the responses: (1) to know whether the person is answering the question, (2) to make sure you understand the response, (3) to follow up and include points you might not have thought of, and (4) to listen for good sound bites.

Don't be afraid to ask questions. Control the interview. Look for creative ways to do the interview, such as putting a mic on someone while she demonstrates and explains something.

Get good-quality sound. Be aware of sounds around you. Make sure the equipment works properly. Frame the shots well. Be aware of visual background, and avoid backlighting. Stay on one side of the axis and shoot cutaway (edit) shots. Use a tripod.

Exercises

1. Based on the scenario below, list 10 questions you will ask the source, Fred Dawson.

> Scenario: You are a reporter for the ABC affiliate in Macon, Ga. A source at the Humane Society, Fred Dawson, informs you he is going this morning to investigate reports of illegal pit bull fighting at an abandoned farm in a nearby county. He invites you along. You accompany him to the farm where you see evidence of an illegal dog fight (trash, betting stubs, a ring, footprints, etc.). As you're leaving, the two of you spot an obviously injured pit bull tied to a tree. The Humane Society worker, using proper safety procedures, cages the dog for transportation to a veterinarian.

2. Assume in the above scenario that Fred Dawson calls in the County Sheriff's office to investigate. You watch as investigators cordon off the scene and begin collecting evidence. List five questions you will ask Sheriff's Deputy John Jacobsen.

3. Using the scenario in Exercise 1, list five questions you will ask the owner of the farm.

4. Using the scenario in Exercise 1, list vo/nats you alone or you and a photographer would shoot.

5. Watch and videotape a television newscast. Go back through and listen to the sound bites. List the questions that might elicit those sots.

6. Watch and videotape a long-format interview program, such as ABC's Nightline. Pull three good sound bites from the show. Then go back and write out the questions that prompted those sound bites.

7. Watch a television newscast. Watch carefully to evaluate sots. For one story, list the sots. Describe them with words and diagrams. Evaluate framing and composition.

8. Find somebody you think has a story to tell. Arrange for an interview with the person. Conduct and record the interview with a tape recorder. Use your recording to write a script with a sot, taken from your interview. Be certain to know how long that sot runs.

9. Using the above interview, do additional research and develop (in your mind) what visuals would tell the story well. Write a vo/sot with visuals noted.

The Package

Thus far, we've discussed how to incorporate scripted words with graphics, visuals, natural sound, and sots in the form of sound bites. We've learned the various formats that use one or more of those elements, and how to script them out. We've also made the point that good stories depend on more than good writing. They depend on good reporting, good visuals, good sound and an ability to weave all those elements together in an effective and compelling way.

All the formats we've covered so far—readers, vos, sots and various combinations—are structured for the anchor to read live from the studio. However, while watching television news you will have noticed that the anchor often introduces a taped story narrated by a reporter. This type of story is called a package and includes the story itself, an anchor introduction, and sometimes an anchor tag.

Anchor Introduction

Start at the beginning. Start with an introduction. Most often the news anchor reads the introduction on camera. The introduction answers viewers' questions and offers them information. But it also teases viewers. It gives them some facts to understand the story but leaves them wanting to hear more about it.

Reporter Tosses

The introduction also introduces viewers to the reporter who will narrate the story. The introduction includes the news reporter's name in a "toss" to the package. In the toss, the anchor releases control of the newscast to the reporter. Look at a story with which you are familiar: the kickoff in Charlotte of the Salvation Army's fund-raising campaign from Chapter 11 (Figure 11.5). An introduction to this story would set up the story, offer some information and introduce, or toss to, the reporter.

> Is it too early to start thinking about the holidays?
> Not for the Salvation Army.
> The group kicked off its annual Christmas campaign this morning in Charlotte.
> Jennifer Lyle shows us one of the first signs that the holiday season is here.

The news writer answers viewers' questions. Who? *The Salvation Army.* What? *Kicked off its fund-raising drive.* When? *This morning.* Where? *In Charlotte.* Why? *To raise money during the Christmas season.* How? *No answer.* Viewers understand the story. Many of their questions are answered. Yet, they want to stay tuned to learn more. The writer introduces the reporter with a toss: "Jennifer Lyle shows us . . ." When the package tape rolls, viewers will hear Jennifer Lyle's narration. They will know it is her voice because the anchor has prepared them for it.

The toss is not a throwaway line. Always look for creative ways to include information about stories in tosses. The example does that. It is a strong toss. Throwaway lines would include "Jennifer Lyle reports"; "Jennifer Lyle has the story"; and "Jennifer Lyle shows us how it happened." These weak tosses could be used for almost any package by Jennifer Lyle. They are a waste of precision television time because they offer little information. Other than the reporter's name, these tosses add nothing to viewers' understanding of the story. They are boring and do not encourage viewers to stay tuned to hear more. When you write package scripts in the exercise section, toss to yourself. You will be both the news writer and the reporter.

Package

A package is made up of the news reporter's narration, called a "voice track" or "trax," along with any combination of what we have, until now, called vo, vo/nats under, vo/nats full (natural sound held up high for a few seconds, then under), full-screen graphics and sots. The package—voice track and all other elements—is edited onto a single videotape. Viewers watching a package might see the equivalent of vo. Over the pictures and natural sounds, they hear the news reporter's voice track. Or they might see a full-screen graphic accompanied by the reporter's voice track. When the reporter is not speaking, viewers hear and see people in sound bites, or sots.

Because these elements are all edited into a different sort of presentation, however, some of the terminology changes. The term vo would not be used in a package. Recall that vo refers to an anchor reading copy live over recorded visuals and natural sound. Instead, the visuals with nats under or nats full are called video, visuals or B-roll. The term "B-roll" harkens back to the old days, when television news was shot on film. A camera was set up into which the news film was projected. The editors would edit two reels of film: one with the interview/sound bites (the "A-roll"), and the other with the visuals and natural sound from the scene (the "B-roll"). The terms have stuck. When a TV journalist refers to B-roll, he or she is talking about the supporting visuals and natural sound shot for the story. Also, any pictures gathered in the field should have natural sound. The writer would exclude natural sound from field video only if the natural sound somehow interfered with the telling of the story.

The news writer or videotape editor combines reporter voice track, B-roll with nats, full-screen graphics and sots onto a single tape. Look at the diagram of a package tape in Figure 13.1. Viewers hear and see the reporter's voice trax and B-roll with nat sound, a sound bite, the reporter's voice trax again and more B-roll with nat sound, another sot, the reporter's voice trax accompanied by a full-screen graphic, another sot, and finally, the reporter closing the story by speaking on camera, known as a "standup." The result is a single tape that combines all these elements—a package.

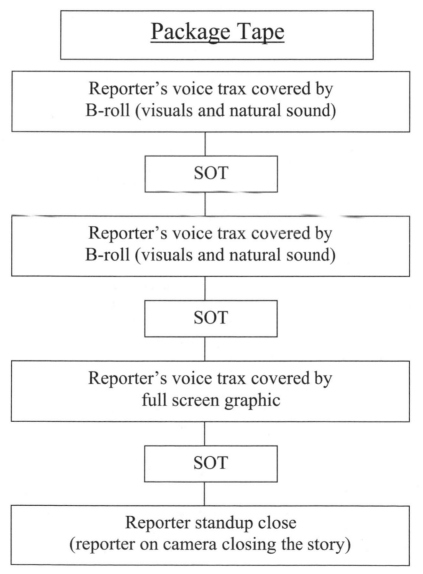

FIGURE 13.1

Look again at the Salvation Army example. In the reporter toss the writer promised viewers that Jennifer Lyle will show them one of the first signs that the holiday season is here. The writer might decide to start the package with B-roll/nats under of the Salvation Army kettle and build from there, writing to B-roll/nats and introducing sots. Assume that Jennifer Lyle put together her package and look step-by-step at how she decided to tell the story.

1. This is it.
The Salvation Army's red kettle.
When you see this, you know the holiday season is here.
You're not ready to believe it?
Well, listen to this.
2. *B-roll/nats full of the band playing (:04)*
3. The Salvation Army brought out its band and its biggest kettle to mark the start of its Christmas fund-raising campaign.
4. *Ron Chaffin/Campaign Chair. "Too many children in our area wake up on Christmas morning and find no presents under the tree. For too many children, Christmas is just another day they'll go hungry."*
5. Ron Chaffin is this year's campaign chairman.
He announced Charlotte's 90-thousand-dollar campaign goal.
Then he made the season's first contribution.
6. *B-roll/nats full of Chaffin making a contribution and crowd applauding. (:03)*
7. The Salvation Army uses kettle donations to buy food and toys for needy families on Christmas Day.
8. *Jenny Albert/Made Donation. "I work really hard to make sure Christmas is a special day for my children. It should be for all children. That's why I'm here and that's why I put money in the kettle."*
9. Like Jenny Albert, all these people have reasons for giving.
Salvation Army Captain Ron Miller says there's one reason that matters most.
10. *Capt. Ron Miller/Salvation Army. "The light in a child's eyes on Christmas morning is the best reason to give."*
11. The Salvation Army asked shoppers here to fill this large kettle by the end of the day. Look for smaller kettles outside area shopping centers later this week. Jennifer Lyle. W-N-F-T News. Charlotte.

Use the numbers alongside the package as reference to imagine the package as it will appear on air.

1. The reporter starts the package with various shots of the kettle accompanied by her voice track.
2. Here, she inserts B-roll with nats full of the band playing holiday music for four seconds.
3. After the B-roll/nats full, viewers see more shots of the kettle, the celebration and people at the event. They hear Jennifer Lyle's voice track as she continues the story.

4. Now she's ready to use a sound bite. She has introduced the sot so that viewers expect to hear someone speaking about the unhappy holidays some people face—and with Ron Chaffin's sot she doesn't disappoint them.

5. She returns to B-roll/nats under showing Ron Chaffin at the podium announcing the goal. Shots of Chaffin making a contribution follow. Throughout it all, viewers hear Jennifer Lyle's voice track over the natural sounds of the events on tape. In her voice track, she identifies Chaffin's role in the story and calls viewers' attention to his actions.

6. Here, the script pauses for three seconds of B-roll/nats full. Viewers see Chaffin making his contribution and hear sounds of the crowd applauding.

7. The package continues with B-roll/nats under showing the kettle and more people making donations. The voice track continues the story.

8. A sot follows featuring someone who has made a donation.

9. More B-roll/nats under follows featuring shots of Jenny Albert and Ron Miller. Jennifer Lyle's voice track continues, too.

10. The reporter has prepared viewers to hear and see a sot from Ron Miller, and here it is.

Reporter Standups

11. Finally, Jennifer Lyle ends the package with a "standup close." A "standup" is the reporter's chance to be on air. The photographer shoots video of the reporter at the site of the story. The taped standup offers information and allows viewers to see the reporter. We'll discuss standups in more detail later.

Reporter Tag, Out, Sig Out or Sign Off

In the example, the final words of the standup are called the "reporter tag," "out" or "sig out" (signal out) or "sign off." Before ending the package, Jennifer Lyle identifies herself, the station for which she works and her location: "Jennifer Lyle. W-N-F-T News. Charlotte." Even if the package ended with reporter's trax and B-roll/nats under, the story would still end in a reporter's tag. The reporter tag or out is standardized for a given newsroom, and the reporter has to speak it exactly that way. The vast majority of packages will end with a standard out. On occasion, a reporter will want to end a piece with a so-called nonstandard out. If this is the case, the reporter will note the words "nonstandard out" in the script, describe what the outcue of the package is, and communicate that to the editor, the producer, and the writer (if someone else is writing the package). The producer will then communicate that information to the newscast director so that everyone knows exactly how and when the package ends.

Anchor Tag

What's left to say? For some stories, there may be an additional bit of information the writer or reporter wants to include after the package. In that case, the writer scripts an anchor tag to follow the story. This can also be a good device to re-establish the anchor prior to moving to the next story. Not all packages warrant an anchor tag, however, so if one doesn't occur naturally, don't force it. The anchor already gets enough face time.

For this story, however, you might decide to expand on other ways the Salvation Army raises money during the holiday season, with the anchor adding,

> The Salvation Army also raises money through an annual mail campaign.

Whether your packages include anchor tags will depend on the newsroom in which you work. Some newsrooms require anchor tags for all packages, and others do not. In the exercises, you will be asked to include tags in package assignments.

Script Timing

Each part of a package script—introduction, package and anchor tag—counts in the TRT (total running time). When you are assigned a TRT, you add to the time of the package the time it takes to read the introduction and anchor tag, if there is one. A story with TRT 1:45, for example, may include 12 seconds (:12) for the introduction, one minute and 28 seconds (1:28) for the package and five seconds (:05) for the tag. Adding together the time of each part of the package results in a package that is one minute and 45 seconds (1:45) long.

Determining runs times for introductions and anchor tags is easy. As before, read the anchor intro and tag script copy and time it with a stopwatch. Determining a runs time for a package offers more of a challenge. One way is simply to wait until the piece is edited. That way, there's no question—you have an exact running time of the package. However, if you're trying to time out the package before editing, you need to keep several things in mind. In addition to timing script copy (reporter's track) with a stopwatch, which can be inaccurate if you're not the reporter filing the story and don't read at the same rate, you must account for sots, standups and pauses for nats full. Figure 13.2 shows our Salvation Army example with the runs times of each element in the left column. (Remember, when you are adding up runs times listed as seconds, that there are 60 seconds in a minute. In Figure 12.2, the total seconds add up to :88. Sixty seconds equals one minute, with 28 seconds left over: 1:28.)

Packages without introductions and tags can run anywhere from :50 (rarely shorter) to 2:30 (sometimes even longer), depending on the television station at which you work. About 1:15 to 1:30 is average. It's not much time to tell a story, but it's certainly more time than is allowed in most other types of scripts.

Script Format

When the script for a package is formatted, each part gets its own page. The introduction and tag pages will look familiar to you (Figures 13.3 and 13.4). They

:08 (reporter trax)	This is it. The Salvation Army's red kettle. When you see this, you know the holiday season is here. You're not ready to believe it? Well, listen to this.
+ :04 (pause - nats full)	B-roll/nats full of the band playing (:04)
+ :11 (trax)	The Salvation Army brought out its band and its biggest kettle to mark the start of its Christmas fund-raising campaign.
+ :13 (Chaffin sot)	SOT: Ron Chaffin/Campaign Chair. "Too many children in our area wake up on Christmas morning and find no presents under the tree. For too many children, Christmas is just another day they'll go hungry."
+ :08 (trax)	Ron Chaffin is this year's campaign chairman. He announced Charlotte's 90-thousand-dollar campaign goal. Then he made the season's first contribution.
+ :03 (pause - nats full	B-roll/nats full of Chaffin making a contribution and crowd applauding. (:03)
+ :06 (trax)	The Salvation Army uses kettle donations to buy food and toys for needy families on Christmas Day.
+ :08 (Albert sot)	SOT: Jenny Albert/Made Donation. "I work really hard to make sure Christmas is a special day for my children. It should be for all children. That's why I'm here and that's why I put money in the kettle."
+ :09 (trax)	Like Jenny Albert, all these people have reasons for giving. Salvation Army Captain Ron Miller says there's one reason that matters most.
+ :05 (Miller sot)	SOT: Capt. Ron Miller/Salvation Army. "The light in a child's eyes on Christmas morning is the best reason to give."
+ :13 (standup)	STANDUP: The Salvation Army asked shoppers here to fill this large kettle by the end of the day. Look for smaller kettles outside area shopping centers later this week. Jennifer Lyle. W-N-F-T News. Charlotte.

= :88 = 1:28
Pkg Runs Time = 1:28

FIGURE 13.2

(page) / Salvation Army / Pkg-Intro / Noon / 12/3 / JML / Total Run Time:

anchor on-cam
box - Salvation Army

---------- on cam ----------
    Is it too early to start thinking about the holidays?

    Not for the Salvation Army.

    The group kicked off its annual Christmas campaign this morning in Charlotte.

    Jennifer Lyle shows us one of the first signs that the holiday season is here.

(1) Take Pkg / Runs 1:28

(8) ---------- pkg ----------

(2) (:01) S/ Charlotte/Today
(3) (:24) S/ Ron Chaffin /
Campaign Chair
(4) (:58) S/ Jenny Albert /
Made Donation
(5) (1:13) S/ Capt. Ron Miller /
Salvation Army
(6) (1:18) S/ Jennifer Lyle /
Reporting

(9) out: standard

(7) Out: Standard

FIGURE 13.3

are scripts the news anchor will read on camera. In the figures, cues that are new to you are numbered for reference only.

The Formatted Introduction

In the package introduction (Figure 13.3), there are some new cues at the top of the page. Just as in the scripts you've been writing, the information at the top of the page identifies the slug, format, newscast, date, and writer. The page number (which the anchor will determine) may have a special designation showing this is the anchor intro for a package. In other newsrooms, the "Intro" designation is attached to the format, as you see here ("Pkg-Intro"). Another aspect to keep in mind is the "Runs" designation for time. Typically, the writer will show the time for the entire story (intro, package and tag) in the header information: the total run time.

In the left column, familiar cues tell the newscast director to begin with the news anchor on camera with a box. The numbers 1 through 7 identify cues that are new to you.

(1) **Director cue:** The cue "take pkg" tells the newscast director to roll the tape that holds the package—the voice track and other elements. The newscast director punches the button that brings the package tape onto the television screen. Some newsrooms will designate "SOT Full" as well. In essence, the package is a giant sot—everything is prerecorded with audio levels set, and it runs just as a sot would run. However, most newsrooms simply designate "Pkg," because the "sound on tape full" aspect is understood.

The cue is accompanied by the package runs time, 1:28. To get a package runs time, the news writer can add the time it takes to read the voice track to the length of sots, standups and pauses for nats full. When you write package scripts, use a stopwatch to time voice track and standups. Use information provided in the exercise sections to add sot times. And don't forget to add the seconds you set aside for nats full. Add the times of all elements to get a package runs time. Of course, this will give a very good estimate. The final edited package will give you an exact time.

Numbers 2 through 6 are *supers:* Begin at the start of the package. Start a stopwatch there at :00.

(2) **Director cue:** One second (:01) after the package begins, tell the newscast director to superimpose the words "Charlotte/Today" over the package. The super appears over B-roll of the kettle. This super is a locator, telling viewers where and when events of the story took place.

(3) **Director cue:** Keep timing from the start of the package to the appearance of the first sot. In the example, the Ron Chaffin sot appears :24 from the start (:00) of the package. The cue "(:24) S/ Ron Chaffin/Campaign Chair" tells the newscast director to superimpose Chaffin's name and title 24 seconds after the package begins. The super appears over the sot from Chaffin. It appears on two lines at the bottom of the television screen.

(4) **Director cue:** Keep listing supers, still timing from the start of the package (:00). In the example, the next super, "Jenny Albert/Made Donation," appears :58 from the top of the package. All the elements before Albert's appearance count in the time. In other words, Albert appears on the television screen following :07 nats full (:04 music and :03 clapping), plus :09 of Ron Chaffin speaking, plus :42 of script copy (the news reporter's voice track), for a total of :58.

(5) **Director cue:** Time the appearance of the sot from the start of the package again. Tell the newscast director to super "Capt. Ron Miller/Salvation Army" one minute and 13 seconds (1:13) from the start of the package.

(6) **Director cue:** Super the news reporter. Identify for viewers the person who is telling them the story. Here, the news reporter is identified by name and function. The cue "Jennifer Lyle/Reporting" appears on two lines at the bottom of the television screen. Different stations identify their reporters differently. Some use the reporter's name on the first line and the station name on the second. When you write packages, use the reporter's name and function, as in the example.

Note that sots get supers on their first appearance only. Suppose the writer had used a second sot with Ron Chaffin later in the package. The newscast director would super Chaffin only once, on his first appearance.

(7) **Director cue:** As with a sot, the newscast director needs a package out cue. In the example, the last words of the package are "Jennifer Lyle. W-N-F-T News. Charlotte." Many newsrooms use the cue "out: standard" to describe a package out cue that is a standard sig out. Most packages end with standard outs, and virtually all newsrooms use standard outs. When you write package scripts in the exercises, use the cue "out: standard" when the final words of the package are a standard reporter tag, or sig out. It is easier than writing out the station's call letters and location. It saves time and space on the television news script. The newscast director listens for the sig out and uses it as a cue to return to the news anchor on camera.

Now look back at the right column of Figure 13.3. Familiar cues tell the news anchor that he or she is on camera. The numbers 8 and 9 identify cues that are new to you.

(8) **Anchor cue:** The cue "—-(pkg)—-" tells the news anchor he or she is no longer on camera. The news anchor is replaced on the television screen by the package. The cue tells the anchor to stop speaking. The voice viewers hear next will be the reporter's.

(9) **Anchor cue:** Alert the news anchor to the final words of the package script. The news anchor listens for the out cue and uses it as a cue to resume speaking. As with the director cue, use "out: standard" when you write package scripts.

The Formatted Tag

Now look at Figure 13.4—a properly formatted package tag. Most everything in the tag should be familiar to you: the top of the page identifies the format, slug, (page) / Salvation Army / Pkg-Tag / Noon / 12/3 / JML

anchor on-cam
box - Salvation Army

---------- on cam ----------

    The Salvation Army also raises money through an annual mail campaign.

#####

FIGURE 13.4

newscast, date and news writer. As with the intro, the tag may be designated in the page number. For example, if this were the second story in the second block, the page numbering for this story might revolve around the designation "B-20." The tag for the package might be designated "B-20T," the "T" standing for "tag." In our example here, we're designating the "tag" with format ("Pkg-Tag"). Also, note that no time is listed. The total time of the package (intro, package and tag) has already been designated. However, a quick glance at the tag tells the producer it runs about five seconds. As will be discussed in the chapter on producing, the producer might need to drop the tag to save those five seconds so long as the information is not critical to the story.

The format in both columns is the same as for the reader. Remember that the script for a package tag is a separate page.

The Formatted Package

Figure 13.5 shows the formatted package script. Note the differences in the header. The page numbers will be associated with the story page, but with a different designation. If our story is B-20, for example, some shops will designate the script pages B20a, B20b, and so on. Other newsrooms will use other designations, and still others don't worry about giving page numbers to packages at all. Package scripts, often called "interior scripts" or "verbatims," are for the reporter's and editor's use only. Package script pages don't make it to the anchor desk or to the newscast director, and there's little reason they should. The introduction and tag pages include all the information the newscast director and news anchor need to know.

The package script is divided into two columns. The left column includes video shot notations and other notes that offer direction to the reporter or videotape editor who is putting the package together. Typically, the reporter would also designate on what tape and where on that tape these shots can be found. The right column is the script the reporter will read to record his or her voice track. The sots, standup and pauses for nats full appear in the right column, too.

In some newsrooms, script copy in the right column is capitalized and double-spaced. The sots would appear in uppercase and lowercase letters and are single-spaced. The standup, like the script copy, would be capitalized, but it is single-spaced. In short, in some shops, all words that are the reporter's are capitalized, and all words that belong to anyone else appear in uppercase and lowercase. In many others, however, the format follows upper- and lowercase, as you see here.

The Reporter's Approach to Writing the Package

Until now, we have discussed a basic approach on how a writer would build a package using information and tape, even if gathered by someone else. However, with rare exception, the person writing the package is the reporter who (page) / Salvation Army / Pkg / Noon / 12/3 / JML / Pkg Run Time:

(close-ups / kettle)	This is it.
	The Salvation Army's red kettle.
	When you see this, you know the holiday season is here.
(people listening to band)	You're not ready to believe it?
	Well, listen to this.
(band playing)	(Nats full - band playing :04)
(child singing	The Salvation Army brought out its band and its biggest kettle to mark the start of its Christmas fund-raising campaign.
(crowd)	
(Chaffin sot)	SOT: Ron Chaffin/Campaign Chair. "Too many children in our area wake up on Christmas morning and find no presents under the tree. For too many children, Christmas is just another day they'll go hungry."
(Chaffin at podium)	Ron Chaffin is this year's campaign chairman.
	He announced Charlotte's 90-thousand-dollar campaign goal.
(Chaffin making contribution)	Then he made the season's first contribution.
(nats full - applause)	(nats full - applause :03)
	----- (more) -----

FIGURE 13.5 (*continues*)

(page) / Salvation Army / Pkg / Noon / 12/3 / JML / Pkg Run Time:

(people making donations)	The Salvation Army uses kettle donations to buy food and toys for needy families on Christmas Day.
(Albert sot)	SOT: Jenny Albert/Made Donation. "I work really hard to make sure Christmas is a special day for my children. It should be for all children. That's why I'm here and that's why I put money in the kettle."
(At "these people," people making donations)	Like Jenny Albert, all these people have reasons for giving.
(Miller)	Salvation Army Captain Ron Miller says there's one reason that matters most.
(Miller sot)	SOT: Capt. Ron Miller/Salvation Army. "The light in a child's eyes on Christmas morning is the best reason to give."
(standup close)	STANDUP: The Salvation Army asked shoppers here to fill this large kettle by the end of the day. Look for smaller kettles outside area shopping centers later this week. Jennifer Lyle. W-N-F-T News. Charlotte.

FIGURE 13.5   **(continued)**

is covering the story. This creates another layer of consideration and emphasizes an important point. For a television reporter, every step in covering the story, from the initial story idea to laying the final edit on tape just before air, involves writing and is part of the writing process.

Put another way, writing is an integral part of every aspect and element of the story—the research and reporting, the shooting, the interviewing, the editing and, of course, the scripting of the reporter's voice tracks. Remember that television news writing is story telling—you are telling a story, and the words you write and the information you use are only a part of how you tell that story. Visuals, natural sound and sound bites are all part of that, as are the order and manner in which you as the reporter would present all of these elements. You have to ask yourself at the beginning, what is the best way to tell this story that will carry the greatest meaning and impact to the viewer? Although this is not a textbook on reporting, shooting or editing, we must bring those aspects into our discussion.

For the reporter building the story, then, the writing process begins at the beginning. Let's break the process down into the following:

- Concept/research
- Visualization/visuals and natural sound
- Interviews
- Standup
- Scripting
- Voicing
- Editing.

Concept/Story Idea and Research

Try to go with stories that are newsworthy and rich in both visuals and natural sound. Know the news value of the story. Know why the story is important.

As soon as you first generate the idea for the story, or are first handed the story by the assignments editor or producer, ask yourself, "What background do I have here?" "What additional information do I need?" "What are the who, what, where, when, why and how aspects of the story?" Do the research first. This may include original documents, newspaper clips, interview sources for preliminary interviews, the Internet—whatever may give you the background information you need.

Be certain you understand the story. Be able to explain the story conversationally to a friend: What is this story about, what does it mean, how does it work? Talk the story through.

Remember also that context can be critical. Make certain you understand enough background on the story to give adequate context.

These rules all figure into the writing process. You must ask yourself what information to include and exclude, and how to contextualize it. Keep in mind, however, that you can't get locked into one way of telling the story at this point.

The story will grow and change as other elements develop or as new information is discovered, so it's important to stay flexible.

Visualization

After deciding what additional information you need, the next step is thinking in terms of how to visualize the story. Visuals help tell the story, and the nature of the visuals will be a key element in how that story is structured. While thinking of potential visuals, you will likely come up with phrases to go with them. Write them down. Again, don't get locked into either those potential visuals or the phrases that might accompany them—you may get to the story and find visuals you hadn't considered, or find that the visuals you had thought would be there are not.

Find a way to tell the story that makes it interesting. Humanize the story. We are telling stories primarily about people. Find a way to tell the story through the eyes of one or a few of those affected. Find a way to show tangible, understandable examples in daily life, examples to which we can all relate.

One of the biggest challenges is coming up with interesting, creative and telling visuals for a story that, on its face, is not extremely visual story. If the story is based on a governmental action, do not give us a story on the meeting in which that action was taken—the meeting is simply the news peg. To expand on a point made earlier in the book, the most boring stories on the air are those that show nothing but meeting video with a few sound bites. Instead, tell and show a story on the human effects of that action. Get creative.

Interviews

Who are you going to interview for sound bites? Develop ideas for specific people or certain roles you might need, such as neighbors of the victim, coworkers of the man accused or owners of affected businesses. As you begin to report the story, some of those possibilities will fall through, and others you hadn't considered may appear. Again, be flexible. Also, be resourceful. Learn how to get people to talk with you on camera.

Do not stop at one sound bite—you should have at least three short interviews to use for a package. And don't just interview the officials involved in a story. Sometimes they're a necessary evil, but most of your sound bites should come from the people affected by the story.

As you continue to build the story, you will see pieces or segments start to develop. You know you will have to address certain aspects of a given story, but the way you do that will continue to shift until you're nearly complete. While in the field, look for good, telling, scene-setting visuals and natural sound that will help tell the story. Listen for compelling sound bites as you're interviewing people. Think about ways to write into and out of those sots, and jot them down. You are gathering segments of your story that you will later arrange into a coherent story. Keep in mind, too, that one compelling sequence of shots or a dramatic sound bite can change the way you structure the story. It's all part of the writing process.

Shooting the Story

While in the field shooting the story, listen for sound, especially scene-setting natural sound that can be used to open or close the story or to bridge from one segment of the story to another.

Look for visuals, especially opening- and closing-shot possibilities. Look for telling, interesting visuals. Look for two-, three- and four-shot sequences in your visuals. Look for variety in your visuals. This includes shooting a variety of focal lengths (wide, medium and tight shots). It also means physically moving between every shot to get a good variety of angles and frames.

Get close. Shoot faces. Shoot a lot of tight shots. Shoot cutaways and edit shots. These are shots that show many different angles and focal lengths of the action, or shots showing something away from the action. You'll need these shots for greater visual variety, to create sequences, and to cover jump cuts. Be flexible, be innovative, but cover the basics.

Another point to keep in mind is to shoot efficiently: When you have just more than enough video to cover, go to something else. You should generally have about 12 to 15 minutes of video (not including interviews and standups), and rarely if ever more than 30 minutes of B-roll for a story (there are exceptions). Shoot quality visuals, and make each shot count. However, it is always best to have too much video than too little. You can always leave shots out. You can't go back and create them later.

Another important point is to shoot as circumstances dictate. If you're in danger of losing certain shots, shoot them first. You can always resequence shots later during the editing process.

Shooting the Interviews

Remember to ask short questions that require elaboration rather than yes-or-no answers.

Try not to roll tape on questions and answers you won't use.

Search for opinions, thoughts and beliefs, perspectives, and so on—not a litany of facts. Remember that you, as the writer, can summarize those much more effectively that the person being interviewed.

Do not allow the person to ramble. Bring the interviewee back in. Keep the person focused.

You should generally have about five minutes of tape on any single interview. On occasion, you may have to go longer. However, sometimes one to two minutes will suffice perfectly well.

As you are building the story in the field, you are writing. Sketch out the story, the various elements, how they might interplay, where they might be placed in the story script. Write down specific phrases that occur, and what visuals might support.

Never lose sight of the fact that the writing process is always taking place, from conceptualization until the final edited version is handed in.

Standups

The standup is an important part of most stories and warrants some additional discussion here.

As I've already mentioned, a standup shows the reporter speaking on camera. This is not to be confused with a live shot, which we'll discuss in a later chapter. A standup is shot on videotape and edited into the package.

There are various reasons to shoot a standup and edit it into your story. The audience gets a chance to see your face with your voice, which helps sell the story to the viewer. A standup can lend credibility to the story. The standup also can show that you were actually at the scene covering the story. A standup is the reporter's way of visually putting his or her signature on the story. One final reason to do a standup is a very simple reality—you may have something you need to say, but don't have any video to show it. If that's the case, you have some built-in video in the form of your face. Write out what you need to say, roll tape and say it, and voila—you now have your video.

A standup is typically classified by where it appears in the story, using the terms open, bridge or close. An open begins the piece with a standup, and a close ends the story. A bridge means the standup occurs during the piece and, typically, "bridges" one part of the story to another. Let's look at the reasons for each type and how to approach it.

Standup Bridge

I believe a bridge generally is the best way to do a standup, because it's incorporated into the flow of the story. A standup bridge can be used to show a transition of some kind, moving from one element of the story to another, or even to move the viewer from one physical location to another. Bridges are good to demonstrate something. For example, you might reach up and peel off pieces of paint and drywall to show what bad shape the dilapidated apartment complex is in. I once did a story on a manhunt in central Missouri. Law enforcement was having a hard time finding an escaped prisoner because the trees and brush were so thick. To demonstrate, I stood in the brush about 15 feet from the camera and, invisible to the audience, began my standup. Midway through, I took three steps toward the camera and came into clear view, showing how difficult it was to see me despite being so close. Think creatively.

A bridge can also show relationships, perspective, or a contrast. If you wanted to show the size of a gigantic tree trunk, for example, you could start off with a tight shot of you, then zoom back to show you—as a reference—standing next to this huge tree. Or, if you wanted to show how the car left the road before a fatal crash, you might walk the viewer along the tire tracks describing what happened. If you're talking about the demolition of an old landmark, pick up a piece of smashed brick as you're talking about it.

Bridges are also among the most difficult standups to do, because they must be written in the field—and done so with a sense of how the entire story is going to be structured or, at the very least, where that standup might fit with the story structured a few different ways. This is one of many reasons it's important to constantly be thinking about how best to tell the story, mentally juggling the information, visuals and sound, sound bites and standup. Throughout this process, phrases will occur to you that might either match video you've already shot or that might call for you to shoot certain visuals to match the phrase or phrases you've written. In addition, it's during this process that a good standup might occur to you.

Standup Close

A standup close can work quite well and may be the best type of standup for a given story. A close simply concludes the story and can be used to express a final point or thought. The close can summarize the story, or it can give a sense of where the story goes from here. The most commonly used standup by network reporters covering a major beat, in fact, is the close.

Standup Open

A brief word about the standup open. You always want to use compelling, scene-setting visuals and sound to open your story. You may debate what the best opening shot might be, given the way you want to tell your story, but I think I'm safe in making the following statement. Although you may be a very pleasant-looking person, chances are high that the best visuals to open your story will not be your face. So this is when you use a standup open: Never. During a 10-year career, I may have shot 10 standup opens. I think one of them may have worked. Don't do it. It's almost always the worst choice.

Doing the Standup

There is no hard and fast rule on how long the standup should be, but you generally should go for two to three sentences, running 8 to 16 seconds in length. A one-sentence standup is generally too abrupt, running only five or six seconds, and usually won't flow well. Especially if you're doing a static standup—standing in one place with no camera movement—more than three sentences is likely too long. Plus, it means more to memorize.

As you're considering your standup, think about what you want your viewers to see. Do you want to move in the standup? Do you want to begin with a tight shot of your hand doing something, followed by a zoom out to include you in frame as you're talking? Do you want to begin the standup on some other object, then have the camera zoom back and pan to include you? Keep in mind, though, that whatever you decide has to be motivated. The standup has advance the story, to add to the telling of the story. Remember that you are not the story. The story is the story. You are simply telling it. The idea is not to make you part of the story but to bring the story home to viewers. You don't want to be a wall separating viewers from the story. You want to take viewers with you into the story.

The way you want to tell that part of the story will give you ideas about how to shoot the standup, and the way you want to shoot the standup and what you want to say will help you decide how to write it. If someone else is shooting for you, discuss your ideas with the videographer. And always, always script out your standup. Run through it several times aloud to memorize it. Reading it aloud will also let you know whether you have a phrase that's tough to say and needs to be rewritten. Once you have it down, walk through it a few times with the videographer so he or she knows how best to shoot it. Then roll tape. First, say what take it is, then give a 3-2-1 countdown (this is known as an audio slate). Then do it. Don't worry if you bust a few takes. Everybody does. Just reset and begin again with a new take number and a countdown. And always do two good takes of the standup.

A few other things to keep in mind. Be aware of facial expressions and gestures—they are magnified on the screen. Be aware of your on-camera presence, and deliver the standup with confidence and energy directly into the lens.

Do be innovative with your standups. Interesting standups help sell the story. However, do not try to be cute: Stay away from anything even remotely cliché and—to repeat—do not use the standup as a way to star in your story. Watch a lot of stories done by others to see how they do their standups. This will also tell you what works well and what works poorly.

So, throughout the process, search for a standup—one that advances the story, one that shows or tells something pertinent to the story. Look especially for potential standup bridges, falling back on a standup close, if necessary. Do not do a standup open. Write out the standup, rehearse it, and do several takes.

Putting It All Together

As you've been gathering visuals, sound (both natural sound and sots) and information for your story, you've been sketching out ideas on how to structure it. The package typically will have certain segments to it, each of which introduces and then elaborates on an important aspect of the story. By the time you're heading back to the station to put the story together, you've jotted down some phrases you think might work, and you have a rough idea of what to include and in what order.

Now you're back at the station. Your next step is *not* to sit down at the computer to start scripting. Your next step is to sit down at the edit bay, rewind your tape, load it if your station uses a computerized video server, and log it. Make a note of every shot and the natural sound that goes with it, including where it appears on the tape. At the same time, give the shot a grade based on how good you think it is. Given how you think you might tell the story, would this make for a good opening shot? A good closing shot? Which shots can be sequenced together nicely? Where is the really good natural sound? Which shots tell this part of the story well?

Do the same with your sots. Transcribe the potentially good ones. Which sound bites are the most compelling? Which are the most interesting? Which do the best job of telling certain aspects of the story? Only after you've logged the entire tape are you ready to begin to script the story.

Before sitting down to script your package, remember that you should be using the visuals and sound (including bites) that tell the story in an accurate, balanced and fair manner. You should be using visuals and sound that will show the human elements, tell the human side of the story. Tell the story of the people affected by the issue, the circumstances or the policy, and find visuals and sound to allow you to do that. Consider different ways to tell the story, given the visuals and sound you're able to develop. Is it best to tell the story chronologically? Might it be better to start with the current situation, then give background as the story progresses? Should the viewer get to know the person first, then learn about her involvement in some organization or activity? Or should you hit the newsworthy activity first, then fill in with background on who she is and why she's involved?

Remember that the visuals and sound you choose to shoot, and the visuals and sound you choose to include in your edited package, make a difference in how you tell the story. Put another way, once again, the visuals and sound are a critical part of the writing.

Writing to the Shots and Bites

Now that you know what your visuals are, you begin the scripting process that I described earlier. You write to the video and sound that you have, explaining (not describing) what the audience is seeing and hearing, and how it relates to the larger story. You note which shot and nat sound goes with each sentence or even phrase you are writing. I have often scripted a shot change on a specific syllable of a word. Write effectively into and out of the sound bites, ensuring that you segue (pronounced "sehg-way," meaning transition) into the bite without repeating with bite with your setup line, and use some aspect of the bite in scripting the transition into the next segment of the story. Note on your script exactly what shots and sound will be used, how they will be used and where on the field tape (or server file) they can be found. It is during this scripting process that you are weaving together the visuals, the sounds and your narration into one coherent presentation.

Voicing

Even voicing the narration tracks is part of the writing process. You are writing words to be performed by you and heard by the viewer. The flow and sounds of the words are important. Equally important is that your vocal delivery must carry the sense and meaning you are trying to convey in your story. This is your chance to tell the story, and good delivery depends on good writing. It's easy to do a poor job reading a good script. It's harder to do a good job reading a lousy one.

Reporting and Writing a Package: An Exercise

It's one thing to identify package elements and put them in format. It's another to write a package from scratch. The following example takes you through the process of creating a package. It may seem overwhelming at first, but the process is similar to writing any other type of script.

Step 1: Gather Story Information

The information for packages most often comes from interviews that reporters conduct in the field and over the phone. In the example that follows and in the exercises of this chapter, you'll be given reporters' notes from which to write introductions, packages and tags.

Step 2: Understand the Story

A reporter's notes often are scrawled across many pages in a notebook, sometimes in shorthand only the reporter understands. In our example, the notes are collected into a recap of the story. Read carefully through the reporter's notes to make sure you understand the story so you can intelligently and creatively retell it for viewers.

> A day care center at a northern Virginia high school is helping teenage mothers become better parents and providing them with support they need to graduate. The day care facility at Stonewall Jackson High School is inside the school building, making it unique. The day care is the only one of its kind in northern Virginia, according to educators. Lynn Robinson is an assistant principal who helps oversee the program, which started this school year. Four boys and two girls who are children of Stonewall Jackson students are cared for in the day care center. The facility also serves as a vocational education lab where students can earn credit by gaining experience in child care. Young mothers enrolled in the program must pay $100 a month, enroll in a special parenting class and supply food and diapers for their babies. The school pays a nanny an annual salary of $12,000. One young mother enrolled in the program is Vanessa Adams, a senior

at Stonewall Jackson. Vanessa takes seven classes. She's enrolled in cosmetology classes to get her professional certificate. Vanessa and another girl, Missy, are scheduled to graduate this spring. Gretchen Almstead, the day care center's director, and the girls' teachers believe the girls will get their diplomas. School officials said they hope more girls become aware of the program. Last year, 565 teenage girls became pregnant in Prince William County, where Stonewall Jackson is located. Educators say the inability of young mothers to obtain affordable day care is one of the biggest obstacles they face when trying to continue their education. The program at Stonewall Jackson was opposed by some members of the community on moral grounds. School systems across Virginia are trying to help teenage mothers, but generally they set up separate programs or facilities, rather than a day care center within the school. Norfolk public schools do not have on-site day care, but more than 100 teenage mothers attend the Coronado Alternative School. The school's principal, Vandelyn S. Whitehurst, said she supports the program at Stonewall Jackson. Roanoke, which does not have a day care center at a high school, tries to provide flexible scheduling and options for young mothers such as night classes, according to school spokeswoman Lissy Runyon.

Step 3: Note Key Facts

Use the recap above to underline, circle or make notes about the information you want to include in your introduction, package and tag.

Step 4: Catalog Story Elements

Log the B-roll, nat sound, sots and full-screen graphics you might use. We'll separate out and begin with the sound bites. Keep in mind that, in an actual log sheet, you'd note the time in and the time out of the sot, which would give you the duration time of each bite. You'd also note on what tape you'd find the sot.

Available sots:

1. Gretchen Almstead/Program Director: "All of our young ladies are passing and their attendance is above average." (:04)

2. Vanessa Adams/Teen mother: "It'd be really hard. I don't have anyone to take care of my baby. If we couldn't come here, I don't know where we'd go." (:07)

3. Lynn Robinson/Assistant Principal: "The purpose of the program is to help the teenage parents graduate and break the cycle of no jobs, welfare and being at home." (:08)

4. Lynn Robinson/Assistant Principal: "There were people opposed to the program on moral grounds. But we have not heard any complaints since the initial debate over the day care center." (:08)

5. Lynn Robinson/Assistant Principal: "The students have been very accepting of this program. The young ladies are the first ones to tell their fellow students this is a hard life." (:07)

6. Gretchen Almstead/Program Director: "They're coming to school. They're trying to keep up with their grades. They spend a lot of time here. We're kind of their home within the school." (:08)

You've also logged your available B-roll. All of the shots listed carry natural sound that might be used as nats under or nats full. Once again, in an actual log sheet, you'd note the time in and the time out of the shot, and you'd give it a grade or other notation ("good shot—use," "possible opener," "great nat sot at 3:47," "sequence with shots at 6:51," etc.).

Available B-roll with nat sound:

1. Various shots of children in the school's day care (playing, napping, etc.)

2. Various shots of teenage mothers, including Vanessa

3. Various shots of teenage mothers, including Vanessa, in class

4. Shots of teenage mothers, including Vanessa, with their children in the school's day care

5. Shots of Assistant Principal Lynn Robinson walking the school halls

6. Shots of the nanny playing with the children

7. Shots of the teenage mothers talking and joking with other students.

Create any full-screen graphics you might use in the package script. Use information from the reporter's notes to create full-screen graphics.

Step 5: Think Before You Write

This is simply the final step of the thought process you've been using throughout covering any story. You've been asking, what information will be interesting to viewers? What is the audience hook for the story? You might start with basic information about the program—where it is, whom it serves and what its goals are. This is all good information for the introduction, but continue thinking about what brings the story alive for you. Keep thinking about information in your notes that really hits home. Keep thinking about information that stays in your mind. By this point, you should be well along the road to finding a focus for your story, to finding that audience hook. Once you're in front of the computer, you're finalizing, seeing what might work and what won't, deciding whether that first bite or the third one best goes with the visuals you now believe best tell the story. It's now that you're committing that story—the one you've been writing all day—to a script.

Something else to keep in mind while you're writing is why people watch television. They watch to get information. They watch to be entertained. They watch to see people. At the risk of being redundant, people want to hear and see about other people. People respond to people. People bring the story alive for people. People want to hear and see the spy who sold secrets to China, the lottery winner who donated winnings to an orphanage, the athlete who overcame a disability to win a race, and the teenage mother who's working toward her high school degree. Personalize. Personalize. Personalize. This is so important. The best news packages are people stories. A package about a new highway becomes interesting to viewers when the news writer focuses on the woman who will lose her house to make room for the road or on the man whose commute will be cut by an hour because of the road. A package about a plant closing becomes interesting to viewers when the news writer focuses on a worker who will lose his job or on the plant owner who is losing the company that's been in her family for five generations. A package about the Internet becomes interesting to viewers when the news writer focuses on a computer user who's making the most of new technology or on a computer novice who's just discovering the system. A package about a school for teenage mothers becomes interesting to viewers when the news writer focuses on a young mother who is making her way through the program.

To restate, packages about things or issues can be dry. They can bore viewers. Packages about people are exciting. They hold viewers' attention. Look for the people in stories you're assigned. It's not always easy. At times you'll have to stretch your imagination to personalize a story. Other times, you'll be forced to select one person's story over those of many other equally interesting people. But personalizing news stories serves viewers' needs. It makes stories interesting.

Personalizing also often helps viewers better understand stories. Viewers can't be expected to understand the emotions of 500 men and women losing their jobs when a plant closes. Viewers better understand those emotions when they are illustrated through one person's or one group's story about the disappointment and hardships ahead. Personalizing a news story can allow for more depth. A television news writer doesn't have time to describe in detail the shared emotions of 500 people. A television news writer does have time to focus on one person's or one family's feelings and circumstances.

As you tackle the teen pregnancy story, you may choose to focus on one young mother. The package script will include many voices. It will include information about the program. But it will do so with its focus—the young mother—in mind. Read the reporter's notes again to find the young mother on whom you might focus the story—the one about whom you know most. Vanessa. What do you know about her? You know she is in the program. She is a senior. She is taking seven classes and working toward a professional certificate in cosmetology. And you know that teachers predict she will graduate on schedule. What's even better, you have an available sot that expresses her concerns about a lack of day care. You also have B-roll of Vanessa. She will be the focus of the story.

Look back at available B-roll. Remember that you want to start the package with the most compelling shots. You might decide they are shots of the children in the high school day care center. It's unusual to see infants in high school. And people love to see people, especially if those people are babies. Also review the sound bites for the best available. Select the sots that will add to the story. You know you want to use the sot from Vanessa because you will focus the story on her. Select other sots that fit the focus. You might include these in the package. Keep full-screen graphics in mind, too.

You have read back through your reporter's notes. You understand the story. You have made notes about information you want to include. You have shot good visuals and sound. You have logged your available elements. You have decided on a focus. You are ready to write your script.

Step 6: Write the Script

You have set aside information you might want to include in the introduction—where the program is, whom it's for and what its goals are. Start there. Toss to the package. Start the package with B-roll of babies. Focus the package on Vanessa. Use the tag for information that adds to the story but perhaps doesn't fit in the package. Write an introduction, package and tag. Assume the story will air in the 6 p.m. newscast on March 6, slugged DAY CARE, with a box. Your producer has generously given you 2:00 for the total time. You wind up using every second of it.

At the risk of repetition, there are as many ways to write this story as there are news writers. An example of one way is shown in Figures 13.6(a–c). Look carefully at the format. Notice specifically that you may opt to use back-to-back sots in packages. Notice supers on the introduction page. Assistant Principal Lynn Robinson appears two times in the package, but she is supered only on her first appearance. Notice the reporter's standup. It's a standup bridge appearing in the middle of the package. But notice the package script still ends with the reporter's standard out.

Step 7: Test the Script

Test the introduction, package and tag as you would any other script. Make sure you inform viewers as well as entertain them and touch their emotions.

• Do you offer viewers the latest information? Yes. A *new* program is helping teen mothers stay in school.

• Do you answer viewers' questions? Yes. Who? *Stonewall Jackson High School.* What? *Provides day care for teen mothers.* When? *At present. The school is in session. Students are attending classes.* Where? *At the school.* Why? *To help young mothers stay in school.* How? *By providing day care.*

• Do you raise any questions you fail to answer? No. Notice that in the introduction the script mentions the school is tackling teen pregnancy in a *new* way.

(page) / DAY CARE / PKG/Intro / 6p / 3/6 / MNW / Total runs 2:00

anchor - on cam
box - School Day Care

---------- on cam ----------

    A northern Virgina high school is tackling the challenges of teen pregnancy in a new way.

    Young mothers are bringing their children to school.

    A nanny cares for the children while their mothers attend class.

    Melissa Wittmeier shows us the new program is helping teen mothers to stay in school.

Take Pkg – Runs 1:32

---------- (pkg) ----------

(:01) S/ Stonewall Jackson High School / today
(:31) S/ Vanessa Adams /
Teen Mother
(:38) S/ Lynn Robinson /
Assistant Principal
(:57) S/ Gretchen Almstead /
Program Director
(1:01) S/ Melissa Wittmeier /
Reporting

Runs: 1:32
Out: standard

Out: standard

FIGURE 13.6A

(page) / DAY CARE / PKG / 6p / 3/6 / MNW / pkg runs 1:34

(children in day care)	This is Stonewall Jackson High School?
(nats full :04)	(nats full of kids playing)
(kids playing)	These children don't look like high school students.
	And they aren't.
(medium shots-teen moms)	They're the children of students here – of students such as Vanessa Adams.
(tight shot-Vanessa)	She's a high school senior – and a
(medium shot-Vanessa w/ baby)	teenaged mother.
	Adams is part of the new program that offers in-school day care.
(wide shot-class)	She's taking seven classes and
(tight shot-Vanessa listening)	working toward a professional certificate in cosmetology.
	But without the day care, she might
(tight shot-Vanessa's hand, writing)	not be here at all.
(Vanessa sot)	Vanessa Adams/Teen Mother: It'd be really hard. I don't have anyone to take care of my baby. If we couldn't come here, I don't know where we'd go.
(Robinson sot)	Lynn Robinson/Asst Principal: The purpose of the program is to help the teenage parents graduate and break the cycle of no jobs, welfare, and being at home.
	----- (more) -----

FIGURE 13.6B (*continues*)

(page) / DAY CARE / PKG / 6p / 3/6 / MNW / pkg runs 1:34

(Robinson walks in)	Assistant Principal Lynn Robinson oversees the program that cares, right now, for four boys and two girls.
(kids)	The school pays a nanny 12-thousand-dollars a year to watch the children.
(nanny with kids)	
FSGfx (1st 2 lines to start - reveal, starting line 3): In-School Day Care Teen Mothers - Pay $100/month - Provide food - Provide diapers - Attend parenting classes	Adams and the other mothers pay 100-dollars a month. They supply the children's food and diapers. And they take special parenting classes.
(Almstead sot)	Gretchen Almstead/Director: All of our young ladies are passing and their attendance is above average.
(Standup bridge)	Standup: Teachers here admit the in-school day care has had its critics. Some are opposed the plan, citing moral reasons. But teachers say opposition has quieted. And they're quick to add that the program doesn't encourage teenage pregnancy.
(Robinson sot)	Lynn Robinson / Asst Prin: The young ladies are the first ones to tell their fellow students this is a hard life.
	----- (more) -----

FIGURE 13.6B   (*continued*)

(page) / DAY CARE / PKG / 6p / 3/6 / MNW / pkg runs 1:34

(shots of Vanessa
playing with kid
in day care ctr)

Adams says this in-school day care center is helping her beat the odds stacked against teenage mothers.

She's scheduled to graduate this spring and her teachers predict she'll get her diploma on time.

(classroom)

(Vanessa in class)

In Prince William County, Melissa Wittmeier, W-N-F-T News.

#####

FIGURE 13.6B (*continued*)

(page) / DAY CARE / PKG/Tag / 6p / 3/6 / MNW / Total runs

anchor - on cam
box - School Day Care

---------- on cam ----------

Other school systems in Virgina

offer programs for teen parents.

But none other offers in-school day

care.

In Norfolk, more than 100 young

mothers attend an alternative school.

And in Roanoke, teenage mothers

can choose flexible class schedules that

include night classes.

#####

FIGURE 13.6C

The news writer follows immediately with a description of the program. In the tag, the news writer emphasizes that it is *new* by comparing it with other teen pregnancy programs.

- Are you accurate? Yes.
- Are you conversational? Yes. Read the introduction, package and tag aloud.
- Do you show immediacy with present-tense verbs? Yes.
- Does it time out properly? Yes. The intro runs :14, the package itself runs 1:32, and the anchor tag runs :14, for a total of 2:00—exactly what the producer allowed.

Summary

A package includes at least two parts: the introduction and the package. It can also include a tag. The news anchor reads the introduction on camera. It offers viewers information but leaves them wanting to hear more about it. The introduction also introduces viewers to the reporter who will narrate the story. It includes the news reporter's name in a "toss." In the toss, the anchor releases control of the newscast to the reporter. The toss is not a throwaway line. It should include information about the story.

The package is made up of the news reporter's narration, called a "voice track," along with any combination of B-roll with nats under, B-roll with nats full, full-screen graphics and sots. The package—voice track and all other elements—is edited onto a single videotape.

Packages include standups. A standup is the reporter's chance to be on air. The photographer shoots video of the reporter at the site of the story, and the taped standup is inserted in the package script. The standup offers information and allows viewers to see the reporter. It is not a throwaway line. It should include information that adds to the story. The standup appearing at the end of the package is called a close. A standup appearing in the middle of a package is called a bridge, and it can be useful in making a transition between place, time or mood within the package. It can serve to demonstrate something or show relationships or contrasts.

The final words of a package are a reporter's tag, out, sig out (signal out) or sign off. Before ending a package, the reporter identifies himself or herself, the station and location. An out may be part of a standup close, but if you use a standup bridge, you still need to sign off. The last line of the package still ends with your name, station and location. You don't need to reappear on camera to give this information.

If it's needed, the anchor tag can give the news anchor the last word and return control of the newscast to him or her. Whether your package scripts include tags will depend on your newsroom, the producer and whether the reporter believes a tag is warranted.

Each part of a package—introduction, package and (if there is one) tag—counts in the TRT. When you are assigned a TRT, you add the time it takes to read the introduction and tag to the runs time of the package. Determining runs times for introductions and tags is easy: Time them with a stopwatch as you read them. Determining a runs time for a package requires waiting until the piece is edited, or timing out and adding up all of the package's elements. In addition to timing script copy (reporter's track), you must account for sots, standups and pauses for nats full. Packages without introductions and tags can run anywhere from 1:00 to 2:30 or even longer, depending on the television station at which you work. About 1:15 to 1:30 is average.

Each part of a formatted package script gets its own page. The introduction and tag pages are scripts the news anchor will read on camera. Many of the cues are the same as those for reader scripts. Also, like readers, a package script—also called an interior script or a verbatim—is divided into two columns. The left column includes video shot notations, which working journalists often include in their package scripts, and other notes that give reminders to the reporter or directions to the editor who is putting the package together. Unlike the examples in this chapter, the shot notations will include where the shots can be found on the tape. The right column is the script the reporter will read to record the voice track on tape. The sots, standup and pauses for nats full appear in the right column, too. Script copy in the right column is double-spaced. The sots are single-spaced. The standup is single-spaced.

You as a reporter will constantly write throughout the story, thinking of good visuals, sound, bite possibilities and standup possibilities. You'll sketch out possible structures to the story, and jot down phrases or ideas that might work. Before scripting the story, you'll log video and sound, then write to that video and sound. You find good transitions to use to write into and out of sound bites. You'll look for words that carry good sounds and express verbally what you're trying to say in the story.

Finally, as a reporter, stay flexible and creative. Always look for ways to advance the story, to bring the audience into the story. And tell stories about people. Personalizing a story is almost always the best way to tell it. People respond to other people. Personalizing news stories serves viewers' needs. It makes stories interesting and often helps viewers better understand stories. Personalizing news stories can allow for more depth. When you write packages in the exercises, consider ways to personalize them.

Writing an introduction, package and tag happens in seven steps: 1) Gather story information, 2) understand the story, 3) find and mark key facts, 4) log and catalog story elements, 5) think before you write, 6) write, and 7) test the package script. Test the package as you would any other script. Make sure you inform viewers as well as entertain them and touch their emotions.

Exercises

As you work on the exercises below, pay attention to writing style and script formatting.

1. Rewrite the story below to create a package. Use the following recap of a reporter's notes. Create any full-screen graphics you want to use. Create a log of available B-roll/nats under and nats full by imagining the shots you and your photographer would have on tape after the interviews/events. Use the list of available sots. Keep the TRT (introduction, package and tag) at 1:50. Assume the baby was found just before 3 a.m. today. Also assume you were the reporter who covered the story throughout the night and early morning. Your package is for the 8 a.m. newscast today on KXYZ, slugged BABY-FOUND. Write and format an introduction, package and tag.

Rebecca Bruchey is less than 3 weeks old. Police say she apparently was snatched from her mother's car Thursday night about 9 p.m. and held for more than five hours in a bizarre robbery that sparked a manhunt through miles of wooded mountains in northern Frederick County. The infant was found unharmed and bundled in a blanket early Friday morning when the search team combing the tall brush heard her cries. But sheriffs' deputies say they have few clues as to who took her or why. Frederick County Sheriff's Sgt. Scott Hopkins found the infant about 2:40 a.m. Friday. The abduction occurred as Karen Sue Bruchey was driving her daughter home along Highland School Road, near Myersville. She says she came to a sudden stop when two men, dressed in black and wearing hunting paint on their faces, stepped into the road in front of her Chevrolet Blazer. Bruchey apparently struck one of the men with her car, though not hard enough to seriously injure him. She told police one of the men walked around to her door, grabbed her by the hair and pulled her from the car, putting a knife or other sharp instrument to her neck. As one man held Bruchey, the other grabbed the infant from the car seat. A short time later, Chris Holcomb, a Frederick County schoolteacher, was driving home and was flagged down by Bruchey. Holcomb drove Bruchey to Holcomb's home and called 9-1-1. Sheriffs' deputies turned Holcomb's home into a command post, sending teams of deputies, search dogs, helicopters and volunteers on the trail. Among the searchers was Rebecca's father, Robert Bruchey, a 27-year-old construction worker. At 2:45 a.m., Hopkins and his search party heard a faint cry coming from a patch of tall grass off Fisher's Hollow Road, about a mile from the abduction site. They found Rebecca still warm in her blanket with nothing more than a couple of scratches on her head. Two miles away, Robert Bruchey heard the call over a deputy's radio. The baby was taken to Frederick Memorial Hospital and released. Residents have flooded the sheriff's office with tips and sightings, said one deputy. None has panned out.

Available sots:

(1) Sgt. Scott Hopkins/Frederick County Sheriff's Dept.: "Maybe it was ransom. Maybe they just grabbed her and didn't know what to do with her after that." (:05)

(2) Sgt. Scott Hopkins/Frederick County Sheriff's Dept.: "She's just lucky to be alive. A baby that young wouldn't have survived very long." (:05)

(3) Sgt. Scott Hopkins/Frederick County Sheriff's Dept.: "They took her jewelry, wedding ring and money and cut her several times on the face." (:04)

(4) Sgt. Scott Hopkins/Frederick County Sheriff's Dept.: "It's possible they were trying to use the child to force her to give them more money, but she didn't have any more. They threw the keys in the field so she couldn't come after them, then they ran with the baby." (:12)

(5) Sgt. Scott Hopkins/Frederick County Sheriff's Dept.: "We were concerned it was getting too cold for her." (:03)

(6) Sgt. Scott Hopkins/Frederick County Sheriff's Dept.: "They must have just set her on the ground, because she couldn't have been warm if she'd been left alone for any length of time." (:06)

(7) Chris Holcomb/Neighbor: "She was running up the road, crying hysterically. She was bleeding, and she said, 'Please help, they took my baby!'" (:07)

(8) Robert Bruchey/Baby's father: "I was pretty optimistic for the first four hours, but it was dark and getting colder. You try not to think the worst, but I was getting scared." (:08)

(9) Robert Bruchey/Baby's father: "When I heard they'd found her, I just turned and started running back to the command post as hard as I could." (:06)

(10) Mike Bruchey/Baby's uncle: "Karen's been very traumatized by this. Right now the family is trying to stay close together." (:05)

(11) Doris Bidle/Neighbor: "It's a real shock for everyone in the community to think something like that could happen here." (:04)

2. Rewrite a story that appears in your local newspaper to create a package. (Remember, as a news writer or reporter, you would not use a copyrighted newspaper story as a source for a script.) Use quotes that appear in the newspaper story as sots. Create any full-screen graphics you want to use. Create a list of available B-roll/nats under and B-roll/nats full by imagining the shots you and your photographer would have on tape after the interviews/events. Assign a slug and page number to the story. Your package is for the 6 p.m. newscast today on KXYZ. TRT (introduction, package and tag) is 1:45. Write and format an introduction and package.

3. After studying the example below, read the descriptions (stories A through C) of news stories and events. Suggest ways to personalize each story.

> EXAMPLE: A rare gem is about to be cut. It is one of the world's largest and most perfect diamonds. It is a difficult procedure. A single slip of the cutting instrument could damage the stone, rendering it worthless. The stone will be cut in three pieces. The stone's owner

> plans to give one section to each of his three daughters as wedding presents. Suggest four ways to personalize the story.

(1) Focus on the stone cutter. Include information about his or her qualifications, fears, hopes and preparations for the difficult task ahead.

(2) Focus on the daughters. Include information about their excitement, their plans for their sections of the stone and their fears that one mistake could make their wedding gifts worthless.

(3) Focus on the stone's owner. Include information about his reasons for cutting the stone, his hopes that it will be done properly and his fears that it won't.

(4) Focus on the insurance agent who issued the policy for the stone. The agent and the agent's company stand to lose a lot of money if there is a mistake. Include information about the agent's fears and hopes.

> Story A. A new project is aimed at immunizing small children. Research shows poor children do not receive the immunization shots they need. A local hospital bought a van. Doctors will staff the van, and it will drive into the area's poorer neighborhoods. They will offer free immunization shots to families who can't (or don't) otherwise make it to the hospital for the shots. Suggest three ways to personalize the story.

> Story B. A local PTA is protesting plans to close down a neighborhood school. It is being closed because the school board says it serves too few students and costs too much. Suggest four ways to personalize the story.

> Story C. A blizzard hits New Jersey, closing schools and all but a few businesses. Roads are impassable. Area airports are closed. Most events are canceled, and much of the state is snowbound. Suggest 10 ways to personalize the story.

4. Find, describe and critique one local and one national package on television tonight. Note the newscast time, station and date for each. Write short recaps of the stories, including the writing, sots, visuals and use of nat sound. Describe the strengths of the packages. Describe their weaknesses. Use information in this chapter for reference.

5. Find, describe and compare two packages from two news outlets that cover the same story. If you have a VCR, watch a local or network newscast on one while you tape a competitor on the other. If not and if your local news offers multiple early evening newscasts, watch the 5 p.m. coverage of a story on one station and the 6 p.m. coverage of the same story on another station. Once you find and describe the coverage offered in the two packages, compare the writing. How are the packages alike? Did the outlets use the same sots, B-roll or natural sound? Did they focus the story similarly? How do the packages differ? Is one package missing information the other offers? Which outlet do you believe did a more effective job covering the story? Why?

An Interview
with Deborah Potter

Deborah Potter is executive director of the Radio-Television News Directors Foundation, part of the Radio-Television News Directors Association. The organization examines issues important to electronic journalism, facilitates training and promotes quality in electronic news. Potter is executive director of Newslab, a nonprofit resource for television newsrooms that focuses on research and training. Potter spent 16 years as a correspondent for CBS and CNN, covering the White House, the State Department and Congress. She has hosted programs for PBS, and is a featured columnist for American Journalism Review. In her current role with Newslab, Potter provides workshops and resources to help broadcast journalists become more effective storytellers and communicators.

Deborah spoke with me about television news writing. Her comments follow.

On Her General Philosophy of Writing News

Among many things, organization really matters. I see an awful lot of stories that have the end at the beginning, and the middle is fuzzy, and they don't actually have an end, so I think part of that is directly traceable to the fact that reporters write in a hurry and don't plan. So as one overarching guidepost, I would say that planning is one step that they shouldn't skip.

The other is revising. I don't see enough stories that I think show much effort at revision. The draft goes on the air. And unfortunately that means that often the best work is not getting on the air.

Potter's Approach to Writing and What to Look For

It's important to collect all your elements and then figure out what works best for this particular story.

I think sometimes TV writers are enthralled by the "great picture," whether or not it tells what the story is. So a story can be distorted in part because the great picture seizes control and the story itself becomes almost secondary.

It requires a great deal of discipline to resist going with the flow when there's a great picture, resist making that the very first thing you give to your viewer, when in fact a great picture might have much more impact if the story leads up to it in such a way that it has meaning for the viewer.

I think if you have a plan and you decide the order, it's best to give the viewer the information he or she needs. You can maximize the impact of great picture and still convey the importance, the significance and the meaning of the story.

On the Interplay between Reporting and Writing

I think you write at the same time you report, if you're really focused on producing the best possible outcome. Writing is not a process that only occurs when your fingers touch the keyboard. It something that occurs in your head as you're thinking through a story early in the day, as even the story idea comes your way, and it's something great writers do all throughout the reporting process. They are thinking of phrases, they are putting elements together, and writing this in their notebooks all day long. It's no good to have this great idea, and when you get back and actually start to produce a script, it's gone. Great writing requires a lot of prewriting. A lot of that is conceptual. A lot of it takes place when you're on the scene. The better organized you are, the faster it goes at the end of the day.

On Challenges to Good Writing

Particularly for beginning writers, one great challenge is recognizing that what someone says is not necessarily the best way to say it. I think too many writers feel obliged to use exactly the language that an official or a politician or a police officer might use, when there are clearly better and more comprehensible ways to say things. I think it takes a certain amount of confidence to become a translator when you're writing—to recognize that not all phrases deserve to be used in your final copy, however accurate they might be. They may not work for your viewer, so I think writers need to spend a little more time figuring out what things mean. Sure, it's important to get the quotes accurately, but if they're meaningless to the audience, it's time to find a different way of saying something.

Another challenge is that whole interplay between pictures and words. Pictures show and tell, words can help the viewer decide what to pay attention to. But too often, television news is full of pictures that are then described in words, which one hopes aren't necessary for the viewer and wind up being a lost opportunity. When you have pictures that you can put on the air, you are providing your viewer only a slice of the whole story. So the function of the words in many cases is to add meaning to the pictures—not to tell me that I'm looking at a dog, but perhaps tell me how old the dog is, or how long the owner has had the dog. Give me something that the picture doesn't convey. As opposed to, "Daisy is a yellow lab." Well, I can see that. Tell me something I can't see. The best writers write, as some say, to the corners—they tell you what's outside the frame in order to give meaning to what's inside the frame.

Annoyances in Television News Writing

False present, or worse, no verbs at all.

In an effort to make newscasts appear current and important, too many writers tend to resort to the "false present"—telling me that something happens, when in fact it happened. "A plane crashes into a golf course" is not something that you want to tell me four hours later. It just makes no sense. What I find about that kind of language is it's distancing, it pushes the audience back, it's essentially a way of saying, "We don't speak your language." No one would call home and say, "Guess what, a plane crashes this afternoon." It just doesn't make any sense. It's that kind of false conversational writing that really irritates me.

And taking a step beyond that, it's the exclusion of verbs altogether in an effort, once again, to write punchy copy. There's a good reason that for half a century, since television news came into being, the mantra has been conversational writing. That means that we ought to write in such a way that it's easy for the viewer to process what we're telling them, not more difficult. And I think the kind of language we've just been discussing, then add in jargon and such—"newscaster-ese"—all of those things get in the way of understanding, they make it more difficult for viewers. And watching television news is not easy in the first place. We're asking viewers to process information—visual information and information coming in through the ear at the same time. This is hard for the brain to do, and anything we do that makes that more difficult is an additional hurdle. I think there are lots of good reasons in terms of good writing to make it easier, but there are additional reasons in terms of good processing to help viewers make sense of what they're watching without interposing these additional levels of difficulty.

On What Makes for Great Writing

I think really great writing is almost like poetry. It's spare, it conveys enormous meaning, it allows viewers to take away what they want to from a story, it doesn't preach at them.

It provides detail that adds levels of understanding, but doesn't include a lot of language that suggests to viewers that this is how they ought to understand that story. I'm particularly speaking of what I like to call worthless adjectives—"senseless," "tragic," "gruesome"—often associated with crimes and accidents—that are essentially designed to tell viewers what they ought to feel. Great writing gives you the details that allow you to feel something. It's not full of loaded, preachy language.

Final Thoughts

Writing remains somewhat undervalued. For all the attention that some of us pay to it, you still run into people in the newsroom who'll say, "I'm just a writer." What do you mean, just a writer? You write the words that those anchors are going to say. This is important stuff. In fact, there's probably nothing more important than what the writers do in newsrooms, and yet they're so undervalued.

My great mentor Ed Bliss used to say, "seeing is believing, but it isn't understanding." Without the words, there isn't understanding. That's the missing link in too many newscasts.

The Live Shot

15

Thus far, we've been talking about writing and scripting for anchors reading live and for reporters building packages. In addition, reporters often have to go live from a scene. This can be one of the most frightening tasks of a beginning reporter, but also one of the most exciting. It's the reporter's chance to take an audience live to a scene and explain the story there.

The technology now has become so affordable and simple that virtually every station, large and small, has the ability to go live from the field. And these days, every television reporter must know how to do a live shot. We'll talk about some of the forms live shots take, then cover some of the basics of writing and preparing for a live shot.

1. **Straight-up live:** This is something like an extended standup, also called a "thumb-sucker." The anchor introduces the story, then tosses to the reporter live at the scene. The reporter picks up the story, references the location, then describes the story using the visuals and natural sound behind him or her. The reporter then wraps up the story and tosses back to the anchor.

2. **Live with interview:** Here, the reporter takes the anchor toss, references the location, discusses certain points of the story and sets up the interview, then does a quick interview (two or three questions, typically) with some newsmaker at the scene. The reporter then wraps and tosses back to the anchor. Time is a major concern in a live interview. The reporter is responsible for controlling the interview to keep it within the allotted time. If responses go longer or shorter than expected, the reporter will have to adjust accordingly. Not keeping within time on a live shot can create problems for the rest of the newscast.

3. **Live with sot:** In this case, the interview has already been done on tape. It may be better to have the taped SOT if the interviewee isn't available when the reporter goes live, or if the reporter wants to ensure the bite only runs a specific amount of time. The reporter will edit a specific sound bite or set of sound bites, which are ready to roll either at the station or from the live truck. The anchor tosses to the reporter; the reporter references the location, begins the story and sets up the sound bite just as a writer would do for a SOT read by an anchor. The reporter gives a specific "roll cue" in his or her delivery, which tells everyone when the tape needs to roll. At the end of the bite, the audience returns to the reporter live, who wraps up the story and tosses back to the anchor.

4. **Live with vo:** Often, live shots go on the air after the activity the reporter wants to show has ended. If this is the case, the reporter and photographer may decide to shoot visuals and natural sound on tape, then edit the tape down and roll it in during the live shot.

A live with vo works much the same way as a vo read by the anchor. The anchor tosses to the reporter, who references the scene and continues the story. When the reporter gives a prearranged roll cue, the vo is rolled in, and the reporter explains what the viewers are seeing. The viewers then return to the reporter, who wraps and tosses back to the anchor. Graphics can also make for good visuals in this format.

5. **Live with vosot:** Again, this works the same way as the vo/sot read by the anchor, with the vo and sot elements already edited. After the toss, with the reporter established on camera, the reporter will continue the story, set up the visuals the audience is about to see, then give a roll cue calling for the vo to roll. The reporter continues to narrate live over the visuals and natural sound, then sets up the sound bite and gives a roll cue. Following the bites, we return to the reporter live, who wraps and tosses to the anchor.

6. **Live with package:** This is often referred to as a "live package," an "insert package," a "live insert," or a "donut." The reporter and videographer will do a short package in advance of the live shot, which is edited and waiting to roll. This is often a good technique if the crew finds telling and compelling visuals and sound at the scene that will not be there when the live shot goes on the air. In this format, the anchor tosses to the reporter, who picks up the story, references the scene, and sets up the package. When the reporter delivers the prearranged roll cue, the package runs and the audience leaves the live scene to see and hear the preedited package. At the end of the package, the viewer returns to the reporter live, who wraps and tosses back to the anchor.

The live-shot format you decide to use will be a function of what visuals and sound are available and when, and how you want to tell the story.

Writing and Scripting

Writing for a live shot is somewhat different than for other types of stories, with the exception of the insert package. Typically, the reporter will not be working from a locked-in script, for several reasons. There will be dramatically less time to prepare your live shot if the event you're covering is breaking news. Because of the immediacy of the live shot, the best delivery is often ad libbed, working from key bullet points you've arranged in the order you think best suits the telling of the story. In the case of a vo or vo/sot, those bullet points will need to match the edited video.

Because you are going live, you have to expect things to change. And they often do, just before or even during your live shot. Focus and be flexible. And develop a good sense for timing, which is even more critical during a live shot because it's not committed to tape, which can be timed precisely to the second. Know how long the various elements are going to run, and know how long you're running during the shot. A producer periodically will tell you through your earpiece how much time is left, and you must be able to adjust what you have to say accordingly.

Steps in gathering elements—relevant information, sound bites, visuals and natural sound—are much the same as putting together any other story, keeping in mind that you first must tell the viewers why you are at that location at airtime when you go on the air. And all the while, you are thinking in terms of structure.

Which Format to Use?

Determine the best way to tell the story, based on what visuals and sound are happening at the time and what will still be going on when your live shot hits. Another factor to consider is the time available for the shot, which will normally be 1:15 to a 1:45. Discuss the story with the show's producer, who will work with you to decide the best format to use. Once you've locked in the format of the live shot, go back to your essential elements—the information as well as the visuals and sound—and structure the live shot. Of course, as is the case with the package, you will be considering what structure the live shot will take as soon as you're assigned the story, and will continue to reshape that structure up until—and sometimes during—the live shot itself.

Line up what you'll need during the live shot itself, such as access to a particular shot or an interview you might want to do live. If you have just arrived and will be going live soon, you probably won't have time to shoot tape. Plan on a straight-up live, build on what you what information you have, and aggressively seek out those who can tell you what you need to know. Line up an interview if need be, then keep that person on a short leash as airtime approaches. Get their full name and title ahead of time, and get that information to the producer for the super. Jot down two or three quick questions, tell them what you'll be asking, and explain you need the answers to be short and to the point. Look for available visuals that you can show live, and work to position your camera so you can show them. These will be part of the storytelling, and you'll need to reference them in your delivery. As always, structure the story as you go, noting what information should be at the top and what information should be further down and where.

Once that's laid out, your "scripting" for your portion of the live shot will consist of bullet points of the major elements you need to discuss. Write these in your notepad. When the live shot hits, you'll be wearing a lavalier microphone and an earpiece, holding your notes at waist level, and looking directly into the camera. You'll need to pick up where the anchor left off, reference the scene, and explain to the audience what they're seeing and hearing in the scene behind you. You'll be ad libbing into the camera, based on the bullet points on your notepad. As you're finishing one point, glance down to see the next and then deliver the next point in the camera. Having said that, it's all right to look at some part of the scene you might be referencing. Nearly all of your delivery, however, should be directly into the camera.

Move quickly from one element to the next, telling just enough to explain but without verbally wandering around to fill time or search for the perfect phrase to make a point. You might want the videographer to pan off of you to show something of interest happening at the scene. If you have an interview, you'll note where you want that to come (letting the producer know as well), then briefly introduce the interview and ask your questions. Don't be afraid to jump in to ask for clarification, or to get them to the point, or to move them to the next question. The clock is ticking, and you're on live television. Move to the wrap-up, which can be much like any other conclusion—a summary, what the future may hold, where the story stands now.

If you're going with tape in your live shot, use your sketched-out structure to lay out any editing that needs to be done. If there's a sot, you likely will need to supply the producer a complete transcription. However, your notes for the live shot "script" in your note pad should include only the in- and outcues of the sound bites and how long they run. Note what shots you want for a vo, in which order, and how long each shot should run. You'll communicate this to the editor and give any super information to the producer. Sketch out what you want to say to introduce the story, reference the location and why you're there when you hit air, sketch what you'll want to say before your tape rolling, then write into the tape. Keep in mind that calling for tape requires you to write a specific roll cue of a phrase—four to five words that must be spoken word for word on the air as you have written them. The producer, director, tape operator and a few others will be listening for that specific roll cue to roll the video. This is the one place you absolutely cannot ad lib. All this information is then passed on to the producer.

You'll sketch the main points you want to make during the vo, keeping in mind the visuals you'll be referencing. Finally, you'll sketch out the wrap-up and toss back to the anchor. Once that's laid out, write down the bullet points that will cue you on the elements you need to include in your live shot. Include your roll cues, word for word.

As your vo is rolling, you'll see the vo in your field monitor and hear the natural sound through your earpiece. Gauge delivery of your bullet points to the shots you're referencing as they come up by glancing between your notes and the monitor. With a sound bite, as you approach the sot, set up the bite and read the roll cue word for word. The director will then roll you sot, which you'll be able to hear in your earpiece and see on the monitor. At this point, you're listening for the sot's outcue. As soon as you hear it, you'll pick up with your next bullet point and continue. If more vo follows, you'll continue through the rest of the story with one eye on the monitor. However, you should always return live on camera to wrap up and toss back to the anchor.

Whether you're back on camera immediately after the bite or after more vo, when the camera takes you live, the audience should see you either moving eye contact from the monitor to the camera or, better still, looking directly into the camera. You do not want to be looking down at your notes when the camera takes you live. Once you've made that initial eye contact with the camera, then you can check your notes quickly.

If you're doing an insert package, take much the same approach as you would with a standard package. Using your sketch of the story and the visuals, natural sound and sound bites you want, script the package, lay your narration tracks and edit the story to tape. You might edit back at the station, you might feed the raw video back with editing instructions for someone else at the station to build, or you might be editing in the live truck. Make certain you write a good transition introduction to your package, one that does not echo the intro the anchor will give before tossing to you live. Also, you'll need to write a good wrap coming out of the package that you'll use to toss back to the anchor.

There are a couple of key differences between a standard package and an insert, though. First, you will not use a standup in the package—you're already live on camera to set up and close out the story. Second, you will use a nonstandard out on the package, because you'll be delivering the outcue live, following the package, when you toss back to the anchor. As with anything else, all element times and super information should go to the producer as early as possible.

Ending the Live Shot

Your live tag/sig out/toss line back to the anchor may be a matter of station policy. However, the best way to handle the toss is to wrap up your conclusion, then simply say the anchor's name and be quiet. Do not come up with filler such as, "so that's the situation here," or "that's all for now," or "we'll let you know if anything develops here." These are meaningless and waste time. The viewers will know "that's all for now" when the story ends, and it's the journalist's job the let the viewers know "if anything develops." Likewise, producers need to avoid scripting the anchor to say, "Eric, you'll stay there and let us know if anything develops, all right?" Again, an utter waste of time. Plus, it sounds staged. And finally, chances are high that it's not the anchor who decides whether Eric will stay to continue covering the story—that's someone else's job. Enough said.

At the end of the live shot, the anchor may want—or, more likely, the producer may want the anchor—to ask the reporter a question for additional information. This is called an "ask-back," a "Q/A," a "debrief," a "toss question," or simply a "question." You may have wondered whether the reporter knows the question ahead of time. The answer almost invariably is yes. The reporter knows exactly what's coming so he or she can make the most efficient use of time and better inform the viewers. In fact, the reporter is nearly always the one supplying the question.

If the producer wants an ask-back, she and the reporter will discuss it. The reporter will hold back a bit of information from the story and supply a set-up question from the anchor to elicit that information. The producer will then script out the question on the page for the toss back from the reporter so the anchor will know to ask a question and know what to ask. The reporter and producer should look for a question that elicits a response that lends meaning and context to the story. Don't waste the Q/A reciting another fact. This is the chance to show that the reporter and anchor can carry on a conversation and show some expertise, while at the same time giving viewers meaningful information.

Although scripting out a question ahead of time is the preferred approach, it doesn't always happen that way. On occasion, a legitimate question will occur to the anchor that wasn't covered in the story, especially if it's a breaking news story. If that's the case, and the reporter doesn't yet know the answer, it's all right to say, "we don't yet know, we're trying to find out now."

But if there is ample time, script the question and hope the anchor asks it. I once worked with an anchor who had a terrible habit of ignoring the question I'd supplied and instead asking something I wasn't expecting, didn't know, had specifically given instructions not to ask or—worst of all—was something I had just explained in detail not 30 seconds previously. Bad situation. In the last situation, I then had the task of restating the information without making the anchor (and, as a result, the station) look idiotic. It happens. Should it happen to you, you must resist the temptation to say, "Well, sushi brains, if you'd been listening to my story, you'd know that . . ." Instead, just be prepared. Handle it professionally and diplomatically. You don't want anything to reflect badly on you or the station. Sushi brains, on the other hand, is on his own.

Now let's turn to a script of a live shot with an interior package (Figures 15.1 and 15.2).

Note the similarities and differences here from other formats (Figure 15.1). The anchor gives a set-up introduction, then mentions the reporter. At that point, we will go to shots of both the reporter and the anchor (probably in a double box on the screen). The anchor, in essence, hands the baton to the reporter, who picks it up and continues with the introduction, explaining why she's at the location this evening. Note that the reporter is supered at this point. She has preproduced a package that will roll into the live shot. At the end of her introduction, the reporter speaks the roll cue word for word—in this case, ". . . and tonight, Vanessa finally realizes her dream"—and the director rolls and cuts to the package. Notice the super times, which come in at those points in the package. The package carries no standup. Also, notice the nonstandard out, which everyone is listening for. When the director hears those words (which should come at 1:01), he or she will cut or dissolve back to the reporter live, who has been watching and listening to the package over the air.

We now move to Figure 15.2. The reporter picks up at the cue, ad libs her wrap, and tosses back to the anchor. The two of them are again both on screen. Now, the anchor gives an ask-back. The question is generally scripted out this way. During the reporter's response, the director may take the reporter full screen, then return to the split screen or double box with both anchor and reporter.

Finally

Writing and scripting of a live shot is obviously much looser than other formats because of the nature of the live shot. But it also forces the reporter to think (page) / DAY CARE / LIVE/Intro / 6p / 3/6 / MNW / Total runs 2:00

anchor - on cam
box - School Day Care

--------- (on cam) ---------

    For the past two semesters, a northern Virgina high school has been tackling the challenges of teen pregnancy in a new way.

anchor/reporter - on cam

    Melissa Wittmeier tells us the new program not only is helping teen mothers to stay in school, but tonight marks the school's first success.

    Melissa?

take reporter / live remote
(·01) S/ Melissa Wittmeier /
Reporting

----- (reporter live) -----

    [Melissa talks about the location, the high school auditorium, where Vanessa Adams attended school.

    The first girl in the program to graduate.

    Tonight is graduation ceremony.]

roll cue: " ...and tonight, Vanessa finally realizes her dream."
Take Pkg – Runs 1:01

---------- (pkg) ----------

 (:01) S/ Vanessa Adams' Home /
Today
(:31) S/ Vanessa Adams /
Teen Mother
(:38) S/ Lynn Robinson /
Assistant Principal
(:52) S/ Gretchen Almstead /
Program Director

Nonstandard out: "... her life is ahead of her."

    Runs: 1:01

    Nonstandard out: "... her life is ahead of her."

FIGURE 15.1

(page) / DAY CARE / LIVE/Tag / 6p / 3/6 / MNW / Total runs

take reporter / live remote   ----- (reporter live) -----

                                                 (wraps—talks about other in the
                                                 program there)

                                                        (toss)

                                                 ---------- (on cam / live) ----------

                                                     Melissa, any sign of whether

                                                 support is growing for programs such as

                                                 this one that helped Vanessa?

take reporter / live remote   ----- (reporter live) -----

                                                     (Melissa answer, toss back)

                                                     --------- on cam/live ---------

take anchor/reporter/   All right, Melissa.
          double box
                                                 Thank you.

FIGURE 15.2

clearly under pressure, say exactly what he or she intends to say and be acutely aware of the clock throughout the story. As I mentioned at the beginning of the chapter, it can be intimidating. But it can also be the most exciting form of writing and performance of that writing that you will find in television news. If reporting is your goal, you absolutely must learn to write and perform a live shot.

Summary

Any reporter needs to learn to do a live shot competently. A live shot can come in various subformats: straight-up live, live with interview, live with vo, live with sot, live with vosot, and live with a package. Which format the reporter uses will depend on such factors as what visuals and sound are available when the crew arrives and when the live shot hits air. In each form, the anchor will read an introduction to the story on camera, then "toss" to the reporter at the scene, who picks up the story, references the location, explains why he or she is there and continues. At the end of the live shot, the reporter concludes on camera and tosses back to the anchor, who might then ask a follow-up question.

Scripts for the anchor will look like any other format, with minor changes. The reporter, however, will arrange the story elements, then work from bullet points in his or her notepad. If the story calls for a vo, sot, vosot or package, the reporter must supply the director and producer a specifically worded roll cue, then give that roll cue on the air to call for the visuals and sound. A good sense for timing is essential, as are focus and flexibility.

Exercises

1. Watch (and, preferably, videotape) three local newscasts, looking specifically for the live shots. Watch and listen for how the anchor copy and camera shots and any additional visuals set up and transition to the live shot. Note the format of the live shot. Note how the reporter delivers the live shot, and listen for phrasing. Note any roll cues and how the next element comes in. Note how the reporter writes, delivers and generally handles each element. Note how the reporter picks up after each element, then wraps the story and tosses back to the anchor. At the end of the shot, consider the overall approach to and structure of the live. How effective was it? Could anything have been done differently or better? Finally, pull out a notepad and go back through the live shots once again, jotting down how you would script each element of the live.

2. Develop "mock live shots" from earlier exercises in the book. If possible, videotape the live shots for review later.

    a. Use the wire copy or story notes for the straight-up lives. Decide what the scene is behind you, and work with that. An "anchor" will read the intro and toss to you. You will pick up there, "live on camera," and give the live shot. You will have a "producer" watch the time and give time cues that count down to the end (30 seconds, 15 seconds, and wrap). When you are no longer on camera, the "producer" will call, "clear." Make sure you maintain your on-camera presence until the "clear" signal, remembering that you treat any camera as a hot camera until you're certain you're no longer on. Total time 1:00.

b. Use wire copy and story notes plus one or two sots for the live with sot. As above, decide the scene and work with it. An "anchor" and a "producer" will give you cues. You will decide a roll cue for the sot, and hit it exactly. A third person will deliver the sot, and you'll listen for the out cue. At the out cue, the "producer" will call "cue" or "go," and you'll finish the live tag and toss back to the anchor. As before, maintain presence until you're told, "clear." Total time 1:15.

c. Use the same information and approach as above, but this time you'll be doing a live with interview. Your "interviewee" can rely on background information or listed sots for his or her responses. You'll set the scene, then set up the interview, then bring the person on and ask one or two questions. Be aware of the time. Wrap and toss back. Total time 1:15.

d. Using the same type of information and approach, plus notes on available visuals (vo), you'll do a live with vo. You will list out the visuals and exactly how long each shot runs. Remember your roll cue for the vo. With each "change of visuals," the "producer," who is watching the time, will call, "change." This will cue you that the next shot is now running on the screen. At the last shot, as you come back live on camera, the producer will call, "on cam." You'll wrap and toss back to the anchor, as before. Total time 1:15

e. Set up a live with vosot, following the same approach. Remember your roll cue for the vo and the sot. Total time 1:30.

16

An Interview with Beverly White

Beverly White is a general assignment reporter for KNBC in the Los Angeles market, which she jokingly refers to as the land of Hollywood and Botox. White specializes in live TV reporting and has covered such stories as the Malibu floods, the Laguna fires and the Northridge earthquake. Before joining KNBC in 1992, White worked as a reporter and anchor in such markets as Miami, Cincinnati, San Antonio and Waco, Texas, where she started her career in 1981. White was part of a team that earned a Peabody Award, and she has covered a range of local, regional and national stories.

She has worked as an adjunct professor of broadcast journalism and has served as president of the Black Journalists Association of Southern California, an affiliate chapter of the National Association of Black Journalists.

Beverly spoke with me about writing and performing live shots. Her comments follow.

On White's Philosophy of Writing

It really comes down to fundamental storytelling—a beginning, a middle and an end, which often, I fear, we don't do enough of. We assume people come in with the frame of reference we do, when we receive the assignment. And that's simply unfair. Maybe the viewers didn't watch the five o'clock news before the eleven o'clock news, so we have to start from scratch and assume it's a clean slate for everyone in our viewing audience. That may be redundant to some folks, but I also think it's most effective. Otherwise, you've got a well-told story that's only the second part of the well-told story because you assume they come from the same place you do. And that, to some folks is simplistic, but this is the most effective approach for me.

I think you have to treat viewers [with respect by] not talking down to them, not insulting their intelligence, but not leaving them out either. Not assuming they've got a wealth of knowledge on that particular topic. Because it's simply unfair. You have to help them understand the importance of the topic by giving it to them in one tidy package. And that includes the anchor lead-in, the reporter lead-in if you're on a live report, before you toss to the tape. The tape in your mind may be self-contained, but to the viewer, it's all a part of a product that starts the moment the anchor opens his or her mouth introducing that story. Here comes the reporter to say a little more about the story, and now the reporter tosses to tape, and perhaps tags the tape live. Those three or four pieces need to be seamless. Otherwise I think you lose people's interest, and you haven't delivered on the product, you haven't completed what you came to do, which is inform them—and not insult them—and give them pictures that match the concept, and not something from left field. Not sound bites that don't match the copy that came before, or standups that have no value other than to show the reporter's face.

When viewers compliment my work, it's often because they think I didn't leave them hanging, I didn't assume they knew a great deal and I didn't leave any questions unanswered, which is a challenge in a minute-fifteen or a minute-thirty, but you have to at least skim the surface as best you can in a comprehensive fashion and make sure your words match your pictures.

Writing as It Relates to the Reporting Process

We often open our pieces—in fact it's often underscored—natural sound is the driving force of a lot of our stories. That's a concept I have no problem with. I've worked for those who never paid attention to natural sound, or it was laid in the control room or disregarded, so it would still appear as if you have a reporter talking over silent pictures. And that, too, is a disservice. You have all these elements that you can fold into your package, and it makes it more interesting. If you're covering a war protest, and you hear people chanting, "USA, USA" in the beginning, it pins the viewer to their seats, and they're excited and interested about what comes next, whether or not they agree with the point of view contained in your report.

These days, a lot of our stories have been woefully lopsided because the protest, or whatever, will only feature one point of view. And if you're doing a day-of, here's the event, these are the people who showed up, it may be only the folks who are supporting the war [in Iraq]. We've had a lot of that lately in southern California. Yet, outside the Oscars, we had both points of view, and both sides were contained in the reports. My preview report included a lot of people who were on the other side of the fence who were absolutely against the war. They were the only ones on scene, they were the only ones we included. The natural sound was profound, the ranting, the chanting, the pushing and shoving with the police. Subsequently, the many arrests that we witnessed all made it into our piece. You have to write to those, frankly, so people don't assume they're being arrested only for freedom of speech. That's not against the law. What is against the law is failure to disperse when you sit in the middle of a busy street. That's what people were busted for, and that's what we had to explain in our copy. It's a matter of making sure your words match your visuals.

And that to me is such a basic of television news gathering, and yet I see a lot of folks miss the point, or think it's beneath them to write to their pictures or scratch around until they have all the pictures they need to make the story work. But I think it's a tremendous disconnect if you don't have the words married to your visuals.

And if you don't have the visuals to sustain the theme, it behooves you to know how to work the library, the archives, internal and external resources that aren't at your fingertips. It may take more time to find all your elements than it takes to write the story. I'll spend five hours on research and 20 minutes writing the story. That doesn't mean the story is shallow or incomplete. It simply means I put a lot preparation into it before I hunker down before my keyboard—or some days I still do it in longhand—but the writing will flow if you know exactly what to work with.

Differences in Writing between Package and Live Shot

I think the delivery is often contained in the field. We edit in our news vans. Sometimes I'll do a package at headquarters, but my days are typically in a live truck, almost always presenting live packages. I'm live for 15 seconds, I have a minute-fifteen tape piece, come back and tag it in another 15, for a whopping minute-forty five, which is rare (for length of most story formats), but if we're live, we tend to give stories more time than if they're straight packages.

And again, I need to make sure it's a stand-alone piece. In my newsroom, reporters do not write the anchor lead-in; we often don't hear the anchor lead-in until the story is running on the newscast in real time. I'll hear what the anchors are saying to introduce my piece. It's written by someone who's familiar with my assignment who may have talked with me along the way to confirm that I got the elements I was assigned to find, but ultimately, I have no ownership of the anchor lead-in. I am singularly responsible, however, for the package, the top-to-bottom, self-contained story that bears my name and my voice. So I try to make that a hundred percent of my story. If it's a package, it's all my elements, my beginning, my middle and my end.

In my live shots, however, I try to save a juicy nugget for the beginning (live intro after the toss) to validate the location of my live presentation. If I'm covering a war protest, and that's what's in my taped piece, which may be a minute or a minute-fifteen, my lead-in, 15 seconds worth, is absolutely going to reference where I'm standing and why. "We're on the corner of Hollywood and Highland where there's still some debris from last night's protest," or "Bike racks and barricades are up in anticipation of the protesters who are coming tomorrow for the Oscars." I will tell you, first and foremost, why I'm there. Otherwise, there's a disconnect between my words and my backdrop. People don't just see me in my live introduction, they see my backdrop, my location, and there needs to be some relevance.

Often, frankly, we will be talking heads in space at a dark scene where everything's gone away. The house burned this morning and the reporter's still there at 11 p.m. It's hard to justify why you're still there, other than we have the technology and the boss made you do it. But the viewers don't care. I still have to find a way to separate my personal disdain for this irrelevant live shot and make the location count. So, "It's here, it's dark, the firefighters are just driving away, fire was put out three hours ago, it's smoky and you can still smell it." If I'm adequately lit, I won't just be a talking head in space, my photographer will accommodate me with a quick scan of the scene behind me to the debris at my feet where once someone's home stood. "Over here in the distance you can see the chimney, that's all that's left of the burned out house, and now let's go to the tape to hear what the victims, the displaced home owners have to say." Something about my introduction has to tie my setting with what's coming next, and of course the piece that will follow will explain more about the war protest, more about the house fire, more about the crime scene where people perished and just moments ago the coroner drove away with the body.

We're often late, live, because I work the night shift. I'm on at 11 p.m. at plenty of places where there's no longer any meaningful newsworthy activity, but I've got to stay there as assigned, and make it happen, and not let my emotions translate into my copy. It can be a challenge because you're often offended, you'll fight and you'll lose—Why am I here, there's nothing left, city council meeting was over two hours ago, they've already voted on our topic, we should come home and make this a straight up package. And the producer will say, "No, no, we need a live shot for pacing at the bottom of the first block. You stay where you are, and do your story from the field." And there's the rub. We all work for somebody. If it were Beverly's TV station, the live shots would all be important and relevant and show some activity, but that's not always the case. And a good reporter will shake off all the personal angst of doing an unnecessary live shot and try to find a way, creative without being melodramatic, to make that live location count.

Scripting and Organizing Live Shots

Bullet points are helpful. To me, there's no point in scripting it, that's the joy of live. Things behind you can change in an instant, and if you've written it down verbatim, you're bound to be distracted, derailed or just upstaged by something better. Last week I was at the airport for one of those homeland security airport stories. We'd been shooting pictures of police, and stressed-out passengers, the whole nine yards, one of those stories you could write in your sleep, but we had to go back it up with a location. So there we are, standing by the international terminal at LAX. Luckily I hadn't scripted my live shot. The most I will write down verbatim is the few words of my roll cue. That's my marker for the folks in the control room to roll my tape, whether it's a package or a voice over, during which I'll continue talking from the live location. The roll cue is vital for everybody in the pipeline. I try not to deviate from that so I don't confuse my colleagues. The team is counting on me to hit those words so they know to play, at that instant, and everybody comes out on time. They will roll the tapes on my cue. The cue is critical, but what precedes the cue can ebb and flow with time.

So at the airport, talking about security, having fed back everything else we needed for two tapes—one was a voice over, the other was three soundbites edited back-to-back. So we're good to go. As we're on, I witness, 10 feet away from me, as the anchor is reading my lead-in, a couple of cops getting out of the car with the canine unit. And the dog was chomping at the bit. I don't know if he smelled something or had to go to the bathroom, but it was a very anxious dog at the end of the leash, and it made for a good shot. So I gestured to my photographer, let's use this, and we did. I said, we're here to talk about security, and over there you can see what we mean, canine units and cops at the ready, running into the terminal—which is what they did next, as if I had scripted this. But it made for an interesting transition to my story, which was all about security anyway. I couldn't have anticipated that, but you don't want to fail to use a good visual if one happens on your watch.

So, a live story should leave lots of room for flexibility, and keeping your peripheral vision open the entire time you're on the air. Of course, you address the camera, but you and your photographer have to be in lock step. If my photographer sees something I don't, I will trust him to pan around and find it, and I will follow his lead, and reference whatever it is he aiming for. That's not terribly difficult, but there is an element of trust, that he won't pan off to something idiotic, and when I see him make that move, I will adjust my information accordingly and still hit my roll cue to everybody's satisfaction.

Live Formats: Insert Package versus Voice Over

I like the fluidity, the fact that you have more wiggle room with a live vo. If I'm in a voice over, and something at my location changes, and again, I like to believe the location is dynamic, that it justifies going live. So again, if I'm at the house fire, and my tape includes the distressed home owner, and the fire rekindles during my vo, I can cut my voice over short and come right back to the live location. You're often boxed in when you do an insert package as compared to when you voice over some tape or a straight up live shot, where it's all about the scene behind me as it unfolds.

If we're at a bank robbery, and it's still underway, and the FBI is staging and pushing people back, and screaming and shouting, live as we're standing there, to me, there's little reason to go to the tape that explains what happened five hours ago. I'd rather paraphrase that over the current picture. The live picture sustains the day.

We cover so much live … this is a live-driven community. We have a fleet of live vans, and we've got the chopper overhead, to back us up. If I'm at a scene that's really interesting and the chopper's there at my disposal, I'll reference our news chopper overhead, let's check the aerials, you can get a big picture of what we're seeing here on the ground. "Thirteen hundred protesters have shut down Westwood, near our Federal Building, where most of the protests against the war have taken place, and from the chopper, you can see better than I can here on the ground how some of them are being pushed back by police in riot gear, and a lot of the people are not accepting those terms and are now being arrested and herded off on a police bus." You can often see that better from the chopper than I can on the ground, although I can hear it, and my natural sound sustains what I'm telling you. But the viewers tend to respond favorably to live television as opposed to packages in the live shot. Packages imply it's over with. Live presence, the excitement in the reporter's voice … you can't not be excited watching dozens of your neighbors being arrested and police in riot gear wielding billy clubs.

High speed chases … this is the market that invented the high-speed chases, and I've been a party to that. And it breaks my heart because you blow up real television and stay with knuckleheads who've stolen cars, for hours on end. But you'd be amazed at how our ratings spike when those things happen. Because I'm a live specialist, I've been involved in a lot of that coverage, in the vans doing phoners over chopper video, I've been on the ground at the conclusion, I've been on the journey watching them circle their neighborhoods trying to find a place to park in a stolen car with 20 cop cars behind them. It's amazing to watch, corny, almost irrelevant in the scheme of things, but it's one of those news stories that has a lot of "gee whiz" attached, and there's no better place to do gee-whiz journalism than live TV.

Importance of Mastering the Live Shot

A student coming out needs to do everything in their power to not only respect the live format, but master it. I've seen it happen on my watch. I've been doing this 23 years, and I remember in my third year, working in Waco, the live technology became as portable as it can be. For the longest it was cumbersome, required a lot of engineering and electronics—now it is simplified, not just in setting it up but doing it.

Live television can carry your career. It has helped me relocate—I'd say that my last three jobs were probably built, almost exclusively, on my ability to do live television. I'm a big proponent of live, and not just because we have the technology. If you can do live, you can be a viable part of the station's best coverage. I mean, investigative has its place, enterprise and beat all have their place, but at my shop and many others, a specialty beat is not enough. They still want utility players who can go from covering the courthouse one day to covering the crime scene live the next. It's just another arrow in your quill. Maybe it's not your bread and butter, not everybody wants to do it or enjoys doing it, but if you at least have some proficiency with live television, I think you'll be better off than those who don't.

I have seen people lose jobs because their live skills were wobbly. And that's jarring when you realize that these same people were very good writers, were very good at smoking out interesting, innovative features and telling them in compelling ways, but they couldn't go live. And in the end, that stood out like a sore thumb, because it is expected of almost everybody to one day, when you least expect it, gather your stuff, step in front of a live camera, and stay there for hours. Be it a brush fire or a standoff with an armed suspect. Whoever is closest to the incident when it breaks out needs to be ready to step in front of a live camera, or at least contribute live updates by phone that are coherent—with a minimum of stammering, indecision or confusion—and the willingness to filter out the information and only go with what you know. If you're going to scintillate, misrepresent or fabricate, if you stumble and fall—those are shortcomings that will be in stark relief on live television.

It's in everybody's best interest, if you want to be good at live, that you go someplace where you can get as much practice under your belt as possible. Make those live mistakes in smaller markets—because that's what small markets are for—to spread your wings and improve the muscle that is live story telling. It can be a key point on a resume, that this is what I can do—"I can enterprise, I can investigate, but most importantly, I can go live at the drop of a hat." And, if you have the tape to prove it and the skills to prove it, that will endear you to most managers in this day and age. Because virtually all stations, large and small, have the technology. It's become affordable, it's preferred, it's a pretty slick way to fill your newscast with something that may not be the biggest story of the week, but will compel the viewers to stick around and wait for the important stories contained in your show.

Live isn't all we do, but we do live every day. At my station, every day, there's a live story in a newscast, often five or six of them. And for those of us who work the second shift, which at my shop is the most important shift—we have more viewers, and frankly we make more money at eleven p.m., than all the other newscasts combined. Coming out of premier programs in prime time, they are especially concerned to have people with the live skills, ready to roll. There are four of us who work the night shift at my station, and we have mastered the live shot. We wouldn't have lasted on this shift if we hadn't. I've been on this shift for nine years, one of my colleagues has been on it for 15. It's a good shift if you're comfortable not seeing your family at dinner, but see them mornings, and I don't work weekends.

Live is vital. Some people have bright, shining, rewarding, promising careers without being good at live television. But those people are rare, and are becoming more rare every day. Network correspondents, we're used to seeing them stand, ramrod straight and delivering a quick introduction to a package, are no longer being allowed to do just that. Some of the icons of good writing at the network level are also expected to go live if the story is big enough. During nine-eleven [the September 11th attacks] you saw a lot of people who weren't ready step in front of the camera and try to go live.

The Craft of Good Writing, of Tight Writing

Big proponent of the active voice. They don't necessarily have to be all short declarative sentences, because I think you should write the way you talk. We talk with ellipses, we talk with phrases, we'll speed up something that's important, and we'll slow down to drive home a point of something we want people really to hear the first time. I think that's the thrill of television news—they only get it the first time. We're not the newspaper. People can't come back and reread my glittering yet confusing prose. I've got to nail it the first time. And if it means pausing for punctuation, or really picking up the pace because I know people listen like that, I have to accommodate it in my copy, and mark it up [make notations on vocal delivery] if that helps me remember to nail it on the microphone the same way I would nail it on a phone call in a conversation with a dear friend. That to me is the hallmark of television storytelling—that we treat it like a story we are telling to somebody we care about, and we know we'll only have a short time to tell it.

And there is a place in journalism for understanding grammar and parts of speech. A conversation may not be perfect grammar, but we need to aspire to that place. If it's clunky, unappealing to the ear, if your words are badly chosen, if they are out in left field without the laser-guided sensitivity to the point you're trying to make—if your words aren't exactly what you want to say, make it right. If you're trying to make a point and make it plain and make it cogent in the first hearing, read it out loud, and read it to your photographer before you put it on the microphone and commit it to tape. Don't be afraid to ask for help—there's nothing wrong with that. I think often we get in our little box and say, "I'm the reporter, nobody else can weigh in on what I'm about to do but me." And that's blind arrogance—I don't think anyone is served by that. Everybody works with somebody in TV—this is not an independent operation. From the folks in the control room to the guy who ordered the videotape that you restock your truck with on your way out the door, everyone is in it for the same purpose—to get an interesting, truthful newscast on the air. And your two minutes or minute-fifteen isn't the only thing they're going to remember, but you want it to be memorable, and memorable for the right reasons. You should want the water cooler story, the one everyone is talking about the next day: "Hey, did you see that story that Bev White did last night? Man, that was something." That's what you want.

17

Producing the Newscast

A newscast producer holds perhaps the single most important role in the newsroom. Put concisely, the producer has to apply solid news judgment, a good sense of aesthetics and ample technical knowledge toward the goal of filling a newscast with content. The producer also is responsible for the on-air look of the newscast. Ultimately, it's the producer who gets the show on the air, and it's the producer's responsibility if anything goes wrong.

In addition to running the newscast (with the newscast director), the producer is the key gatekeeper. He or she decides what stories to run, how to present them, and what context in which to set them. The producer must give the audience a meaningful sense of the day's issues and events and do so in a way that's relevant and interesting to the viewer. The producer needs to understand the role of the newscast for the community and the advertisers who buy time.

He or she is also a baseline manager. A producer has to work well with others and coordinate a host of people, tasks and elements to bring them all together in one professional-looking presentation. During the day, a producer will sort through stories, choose the stories that he or she will run, decide in what order they should run, and write a good portion of those stories. The producer works closely with the assignment desk, the reporters filing stories, perhaps other writers, the executive producer and other supervising managers, and the newscast director. The producer will determine the visuals and order graphics for the show, make critical decisions about the content as the day progresses, and time out the show so that it ends at the precise second it's scheduled to end. It's a lot to do. But a good producer can pull it off and do so without suffering a nervous breakdown. At least, most days. Breathing exercises and a bottle of aspirin nearby can be most helpful.

A Basic Newscast

No doubt you've noticed a certain standardized structure to the many (hopefully, by this time) newscasts you've watched. What follows is a basic format for a "typical" newscast (Figure 17.1).

Preshow Teases - :30
Preshow Break - 2:00

A-Block
Open - :15
Lead story
Other stories
Teases - :15

Break 1 - 2:00

B-Block
Lead story for B-block
Other stories
Teases - :10

Break 2 - 2:00

C-Block: Weather -- 3:30 for the block
Toss to weather
Weather
Toss back to anchors

Break 3 - 1:30

D-Block: Sports -- 3:30 for the block
Toss to sports
Sports
Toss back to anchors

Break 4 - 1:00

E-Block: Kicker
Feature stories
Goodbye
Close - :20
Pad - :30

Terminal Break - 3:00

FIGURE 17.1

This is a fairly typical-looking newscast. Before the show, the anchors "tease" upcoming stories—they tell the viewers some interesting aspect about each of two or three of the stories the show will air, always including the lead story. The show then moves to a commercial break of two minutes, then comes back out the first segment or block of the newscast. Each block typically is designated with a letter: the first is the A block, the second the B block, and so on. The lead story begins the A block, followed by other stories. Toward the end of the block, the anchors will tease some stories coming up later in the show. The newscast then goes to the first break, comes back to another block of news, more teases, then the second break. The third (or C) block is devoted entirely to weather, the D-block is set for sports, and often newscasts have a final short block—the kicker segment—set aside for a few short lighter stories. The newscast begins with a preproduced open and ends with a preproduced close. Increasingly, newscasts also will have a cross-promotional tease (a tease for an upcoming newscast) that might run after weather or on either side of the kicker.

Notice that there are times filled in next to some of the items. These are elements that, for the most part, are set. Although there is some wiggle room in several of these, the times for the commercial breaks for a given newscast are set in stone, and the commercials themselves are sacrosanct—you don't ever jump out of a commercial or shorten a commercial break. At least, not if you want to stay employed. The producer's job now is to fill in the rest of the newscast with news. Let's take a look at how that's done.

The Mechanics of Producing

During the morning meeting, reporters, producers, the assignment editor and others will decide what stories the newsroom will be covering that day. Producers will also know what stories the network and other feed sources are planning to cover and feed down. During the day, the producer will also scan wires to look for interesting stories that might fit in the newscast, and breaking news may shift what stories the producer will include. But the morning meeting provides a basic "budget" of stories from which to choose. Either alone or in consultation with a manager, the producer will pick from the pool of available stories to get a basic story list—that show's story budget. With that list of stories and their likely formats (package, vosot, etc.), the producer gets to work. After determining the stories the producer will use, he or she will write many of them, decide the order in which the stories will appear and in what format, stay apprised of the status of stories filed by others, decide on all additional visuals (such as graphics), then put them all together and run the show.

Determine the News Hole

First things first. The initial question the producer must answer is, "How much time for stories do I have?" That available story time is called the "news hole," an old newspaper term that carried over to television.

The producer will consult the program log for that day to find out how much commercial time has been sold for that newscast. The commercial breaks come at approximately the same times in each show, and certain commercial spots may already be slotted into certain breaks.

One additional consideration involves something called continuity. The producer might work with someone in the sales or traffic department (traffic refers to the department in charge of scheduling programming and commercials) to ensure there are no conflicts between the stories to air and the content of the commercials set to run in the newscast. As an example, suppose there's a story the newsroom is covering on the crash of a passenger jet. Also suppose that a commercial for that same airline is slated to run during the newscast. Not good. As another example, let's say you're planning on running a story on the car with the best safety record, and, as fates would have it, you're scheduled to run a commercial for the same car company. That's a problem, as well. The best thing to do in either case is hold that commercial to run at another time. The producer is one of several people who may be assigned to check for just such problems.

Back to the newscast. There are several ways to determine the news hole. One common approach is to set the "out time" for the program, subtract the "in time," then subtract all the other elements for which the times are preset. Let's say our intrepid producer is running the 6 p.m. show. The preshow hits at 5:57:30, and the show is out at exactly 6:29:30. Let's use the times shown in the basic format we just looked at (Figure 17.2).

FINDING THE NEWS HOLE

Out	**6:29:30**
In	**- 5:57:30**
Pgm time	**32:00**
Breaks (6)	**- 12:00**
Weather	**- 3:30**
Sports	**-3:30**
Teases	**- :55**
Open/Bye/Close	**- :55**
Pad	**:30**
News hole	**10:40**

FIGURE 17.2

Notice that there are 30 seconds extra added into the breaks. The transition of going into and out of each break will eat up about 5 seconds. As a result, six breaks will take up an additional 30 seconds.

Each of the weather and sports blocks has 3:30 for the entire block. What the weathercaster and the sportscaster and producer do with that time is up to them. They simply have to make it fit. On some days, either sports or weather may need more time, depending on the amount of sports or weather to talk about. Other days may require less. On occasion, if it's a light day for either block, the weather or sports anchor might be willing to "donate time" from their blocks to the news hole, but most newscast producers don't push it too often.

The last two lines designate "open/bye/close" and "pad." The open is pre-produced on tape, you need time for the anchors to say goodnight to the audience, and the close is typically a music bed with credits rolling over the screen. The producer can abbreviate the close if necessary. Many producers will "pad" the show by 30 seconds or so in case some elements run longer than anticipated.

After figuring all of this up, our producer has 10:40 available for all the news stories he or she wants to include. Not a lot.

Another approach is to take the so-called "skeleton time" and subtract it from the program time. It's just a different way of looking at the same process. Newsroom computer systems have template rundowns of each newscast. The set elements already have many of the times filled in, and the producer can adjust the break times if necessary. The computer will show the total skeleton time on the screen, the producer can add a pad element at some location in the rundown, and the computer subtracts this subtotal from the program time. Voila, the news hole. Incidentally, most good producers will do a double check of times in their heads or on a scratch pad, just to make sure. Take a look at the skeleton rundown in Figure 17.3. It shows all the elements that are there before the producer filling in his or her show. You'll notice that the times already filled in reflect exactly what we listed already.

The Skeleton Rundown

Perhaps now would be a good time to mention the column headings. "Page," the first heading, stands for page number. A quick review of page numbering: Script page numbering typically includes a letter and a number. The letter indicates the section, or news block, of the newscast in which the script will appear. News blocks begin with "A" at the top of the newscast and are broken by commercial breaks. After the first commercial break the "B" block follows, after the second commercial break the "C" block follows, and so on. The number shows the order of scripts within the news block. The first story within a block is page 10, the second story page 20, and so on. Numbering begins at 10 at the start of each news block. In a newscast, there will be scripts numbered A-10, A-20, A-30 and so forth, followed by B-10, B-20, B-30 and so on, followed by C-10, C-20, C-30, and on. If a story numbered A-30 ran more than one page, you do not num-

Page	Slug	Wrt	Anc	Shot	Video	Bdgt	Time	Back
Pre	Pre tz		h/b	2s	vo/oc		:30	
	--- Pre-Break ---				sot		2:05	
A00	Open				sot		:15	
A-last	1Tz				vo		:15	
	--- Break 1 ---				sot		2:05	
B-last	2Tz				vo		:10	
	--- Break 2 ---				sot		2:05	
C10	Toss weather		h/b/w	3s				
	Weather		w	1s	ck/gfx			
C90	Toss back		h/b/w	3s			3:30	
Clast	Sports tz		h/b	2s	oc			
	--- Break 3 ---				sot		1:35	
D10	Toss sports		h/b/s	3s				
	Sports		s	1s	oc/vo/sot		3:30	
D90t	Toss back		h/b/s	3s				
	--- Break 4 ---				sot		1:05	
E10								
Elast	Goodbye/Close		h/b	2s	oc/sot		:30	
PAD							:30	
	---Terminal Break ---				sot		3:05	
			TOTAL				21:10	
			PROGRAM				32:00	
			OVER/UNDER				-10:50	

FIGURE 17.3

ber the second page of the script A-30. Instead, generally, the numbering continues with A-20a, A-20b, A-20c and so forth.

Many but not all newsrooms number in increments of 10. There's a good reason for this. The producer may need to insert a story into the newscast once the lineup is set and the pages are numbered. Let's say there are seven stories already set in the A-block, A-10 through A-70. The producer wants the new story to go just after the second story in the A-block. Rather than renumber all the stories that will follow the new one, the producer simply numbers the new story A-25 and slots it after the second story. The number for A-30, now the fourth story, still makes sense because it follows A-10, A-20 and A-25. Problem solved.

However, other newsrooms do it differently. In some, the page numbers go up in increments of two. In still others, they go up in increments of one, the idea being that the story order (and, therefore, the page numbers) won't be set until just before the newscast. If breaking news comes in at the last minute, a producer can use the prefix "pre-" and still insert it. Let's say for tonight's Five (the five p.m. newscast), your lineup is set: A-1, A-2, A-3, A-4 and so on. A breaking story comes down 16 minutes before air, it's big enough to lead your newscast, and you'll have a reporter there in five minutes who'll get a live shot for the top of the show. With the order already set, you'll insert the story before A-1 and call it "Pre-A-1." In still other newsrooms, the blocks are numbered rather than lettered. Every newsroom does it slightly differently.

Back to the rundown skeleton. The next column, "Slug," refers to the story slug. Because there are set places for the teases, that slug, designated "tz," already appears along with associated times. "Wrt" designates the writer, "Anc" designates which anchor will read the story (most of these will be filled in later), and "Shot" refers to the type of camera shot used from the studio. "1s" stands for "one-shot," meaning the camera will center on a single anchor; "2s" refers to two anchors on camera, and "3s" stands for three anchors in frame. Some shows end with a wide shot of the studio, designated "wide." In some newsrooms, this column would also designate whether the anchor has an over-the-shoulder box in frame (designated "box"). This is important because the camera has to pan right or left to give room for the box. If the camera stayed centered, most of the anchor's face would be covered by an on-screen graphic. Although it's true that some producers would love to obliterate the faces of certain difficult anchors from time to time, it doesn't make for the best camera shot.

The next column, "Video," refers to what visuals and sound that element will require. "OC" stands for on camera. While some newsrooms place "box" in the "Shot" column, others place it here. You already know what vo, sot, vonats (natural sound up full), fs/gfx (full-screen graphics), live (designated "lv") and pkg stand for. Some newsrooms will designate a vosot as a "vo/bite" or a "vob." Also, some newsrooms will designate a package as "sot," the reasoning being that the entire package is the equivalent of a sot—a very long sot.

The next three columns deal with timing the show. "Bdgt" stands for budget time, the approximate time the producer has allotted for that element. "Time" stands for the actual time that element winds up running. Recall the average run times for various story formats and elements, and remember, these are average times—they can vary:

Reader:15
Vo:20
Sot:10
Vosot:40
Toss:05
Pkg intro:15
Pkg1:30
Pkg tag:10

The final column, "Back," designates "backtime," which we'll get to shortly.

Now, the producer turns to setting the story order. Like everything else in this business, there are many ways to approach this, some clearly laid out, some dependent on the instincts of the producer. But three key factors should guide the producer in this decision (which actually is not one major decision but a series of decisions and adjustments throughout the day). Also, these factors are influenced by the structure of the newscast. Remember, there are two news blocks at the top of the show, and a "kicker" segment at the end. Often, a producer will use the first block for the hard news, holding the second block for softer news and news features, and saving the lightest feature or two for the end of the program.

Newsworthiness and Prioritizing

In determining the story order, perhaps the most critical aspect depends on the newsworthiness of each story. The producer has to be cognizant of how to prioritize the stories according to their newsworthiness. This is especially true of deciding which story will lead the newscast. This can set the tone for the entire show, and if the producer fails to hook the audience with the lead story, credibility suffers and viewers go elsewhere. Not a good thing.

However, a good producer does not simply list the stories in order of perceived importance and then slide them into the newscast. Which brings us to the next factor.

Story Flow and Clustering

Rather than place the most newsworthy story at the lead and simply assign each remaining story in descending order of newsworthiness, the producer has to find a way to make the stories flow together. Once the lead is set, the producer might look for other stories that relate to that lead story. This is known as clustering, or setting a story pod. A producer will also be thinking about what story would be appropriate to lead the second block. Just as each story must have a logical flow within it, so must the segments of the newscast, as well as the newscast itself. The story order must make sense to the viewer and have some sense of how the stories are related. The producer can cluster two related stories with the lead, then cluster another three related stories immediately after. A good producer will also write transitions and segues to connect related stories, or script a verbal shift to move from one cluster or pod to another. Something else to avoid is putting two stories together that would emotionally jar the viewer: a story about a child with cancer followed by a story on a clown who performs at elementary schools, or a story on the fatal crash of a small plane followed by one on a local recreational flying club.

Before we move on to the third guiding factor, let's look at Figure 17.4 to see an example story budget for today's show.

Let's say you're producing the six o'clock newscast for a Dallas network affiliate. Typically, you'll focus more on local, state and regional news, but you'll include national and international stories if there's a good local tie in. You scan through the stories and think about what will most appeal to your audience.

Cop Murder Trial is big news locally, and a reporter is covering the story— likely a package. You'll want to slate it (include it) in your show. There's a natural tie in with Cop Murder/Rape, but little or no video, so you'll probably write a reader or a vo for it.

Plano Utility Poles is a somewhat interesting story you may want to run if you have time. Probably not worth much more than a reader, but that could become a vosot if the reporter gets sound and if other things fall through.

Hillsboro Church Burns is a good potential story, related to the intense thunderstorms that blew through last night. A reporter is working on a package with possible live intro. You'll slate it, more than likely.

Gaming Crackdown is also a good potential package with possible live. The reporter covering the story will keep you apprised, but you place it in your line-up.

Muslim Criticizes Violence is a possibility; reporter is getting sot with the cleric and some cover video of the mosque.

Murder/Kidnapping Arrest is another good local story. The problem is you don't have any video or sound. Likely reader.

StreetSense is a new program, worth a mention, being shot today. The Five producer is running it, but you might opt for a vosot.

DFW Shutdown you're unsure of. The Ten (ten p.m. show) producer ran it on her show the night before, it's run twice on the morning show, and the Noon producer has it slated for her show as well. By the Six, it'll be old news. Kill it.

More Shuttle Woes has a definite local and statewide connection—NASA's in Houston, and parts of the Columbia were scattered across northern Texas (including the DFW area), so you want the story. The network is feeding a vo/sot, so you're leaning toward placing it in your show.

Diabetics Stroke Drugs is a good medical story, which plays well with your show's audience. The network is feeding a package, so you write it in.

Hammas Attack is an important international story, especially on the heels of

STORY BUDGET

In House:

Cop Murder Trial: A man accused of killing a Dallas police officer while escaped from prison goes to trial—jury selection completed today.

Cop Murder/Rape: Prosecutors say the same man accused of murdering the cop is linked to a rape two days earlier through DNA evidence.

Plano Utility Poles: The city of Plano (a Dallas suburb) is erecting utility poles in a new housing development; residents don't like it, but Plano city manager says it's the only way to keep up with growth.

Hillsboro Church Burns: A lightning strike burned Hillsboro (just outside DFW area) Church of the Nazarene church to the ground last night.

Gaming Crackdown: Several gambling establishments in Ft. Worth claim they're legal because they donate some proceeds to charity; Dist Atty says wrong, shutting them down.

Muslim Criticizes Violence: Local muslim cleric (Richardson, Dallas suburb) speaks out against violence in mid-east by both Isreal and Hammas.

Murder/Kidnapping Arrest: Man accused of killing Irving (DFW area suburb) woman and kidnapping eight-year-old daughter arrested overnight during traffic stop; kid and others in car.

StreetSense: New local program to identify kids and teach them street-smarts; response to kidnapping concerns.

DFW Shutdown: DFW airport terminal C shut down for three hours last nite after man charges through security.

Wires/Feeds/Austin:

More Shuttle Woes: The nets designed to catch bolts that explode to allow booster separation are failing, raising the potential of doing severe damage to the heat-resistant tiles on the shuttle. VO/SOT – feed.

Diabetics Stroke Drugs: New research shows statin drugs can help diabetics avoid strokes.

Hammas Attack: Hammas has attacked again, this time with a suicide bomber on a bus in Jerusalem; 14 dead, 36 injured.

Bush Medicare Plan: Prez says this plan will help seniors; Dems disagree.

Medicare Rx Probs: Dems say new prescription benefits for Medicare proposal have hidden costs that Reps aren't talking about.

Gov/Senior Health: Governor announces new health care program for seniors; saves money, cuts benefits

State/Education Cuts: State legislature tightens budget by cutting education, after school programs.

Gov/Biz Incentives: Governor pushes through funding for business incentives, cattle breeding.

Congress/Welfare Cuts: Fed gov cuts funds for nursing homes, welfare mothers.

Dems Criticize Cuts: Fallout from not including working poor in several tax cuts and rebates.

OK Tornadoes: Tornadoes in Norman, OK (south of Oklahoma City) overnite, damage to 14 homes, 5 buildings, no deaths.

FIGURE 17.4

the Roadmap to Peace being touted by the president. Plus, there's a good local tie-in with the Muslim cleric story, and religion and politics both make for good viewer interest. The network is feeding a package, with additional video and sound. You'll place it and have the editors build a vosot.

Bush Medicare Plan and Medicare Rx Probs are important stories, and the network is feeding visuals and sound on both. They tie in well with the Gov/Senior Health story, a package coming in from the Austin bureau, and that ties in with State/Education Cuts and Gov/Biz Incentives, both vosots being fed from Austin. Congress/Welfare Cuts and Dems Criticize Cuts also deal with government spending/benefits cutbacks, and they all might make for a nice pod (collection of related stories) somewhere in the show. However, the lineup is starting to feel a bit full.

Finally, the OK Tornadoes story is important, and might be a good segue to weather. In fact, you think, the Hillsboro church fire story (caused by weather) might be a good story to precede that. The story came across the wires, but a quick check of the regional feeds tells you a package, video and sound will all be fed from the Oklahoma City affiliate. You'll go with a vosot, for now.

So now, let's draft out the preliminary lineup, with stories, potential formats and potential times, and see what it looks like. First, we'll decide on the lead story. Then, we'll try to cluster according to priority and story flow. At the same time, we'll begin to consider the third factor in determining the choice and placement of stories: pacing and variety.

Pacing and Variety

Recall that variety is important to break up the sameness in a story. You want to strive for variety in sentence length and structure. You want variety of visuals and of sound bites in your stories. Variety is also important in the newscast. You'll maintain the audience interest much more effectively if you vary the formats of stories and vary the anchors reading them. You would not want to run four packages in a row, for example. One or two packages should be followed by a vosot or two, perhaps a reader, then another package, then a couple of vosots. Keeping variety and pacing in the show keeps the audience interested, which means they will keep watching. That is a good thing. At the same time, we'll be keeping an eye to the amount of time we have available.

A note of caution, however: In an ideal newscast, each story flows and connects into the next. Unfortunately, the ideal newscast has never aired. Your job is to cover the news, not determine it, and often, stories that need to go next to each other simply don't relate. If that's the case, write an appropriate transition and move on. Don't stretch trying to connect stories that have nothing to do with each other.

One other consideration that could fall under this heading concerns whether you're including enough of your market from a geographic perspective, known as "reach." Over a period of time, you need to relate news of interest to your entire market. If you start ignoring certain areas, they'll begin to ignore your newscast.

You block the newscast on a scratch pad, as shown in Figure 17.5.

You decide the Cop Murder Trial is definitely your lead story. The murder of the police officer two years earlier was a huge story, and the trial story has the greatest newsworthiness value for your audience. The Rape story is a natural tie-in. The Murder/Kidnap story is another crime story, so you place it third. The StreetSense story tries to keep kids safe from crime, so it follows nicely.

The Hammas Attack story: You're not sure where that should be placed. It's an international story, deals with violence; you're just not sure. Wherever it goes, though, the Muslim Criticizes story has to follow it.

SCRATCH BLOCKING

A-BLOCK:

Cop Murder Trial	pkg	1:30
Cop Murder/Rape	vo	:20
Murder/Kidnap Arrest	rdr	:15
StreetSense	vosot. :45	
Gaming Crackdown	lv/pkg/lv	1:40
Hammas Attack	vonats/sot	:45
Muslim Criticizes Violence	vosot. :45	
More Shuttle Woes	vosot	:45

B-BLOCK

Diabetics Stroke Drugs	pkg	1:30
Bush Medicare Plan	vosot	:45
Medicare Rx Probs	vosot	:45
Gov/Senior Health story	pkg	1:30
State/Education Cuts	vosot	:45
Gov/Biz Incentives	vosot	:45
Plano Utility Poles	rdr or vosot	:30
Hillsboro Church Burns	pkg/live	1:40
OK Tornadoes	vosot	:40

FIGURE 17.5

Shuttle Woes doesn't really fit nicely anywhere. It's a science-related story, so perhaps near the Diabetics Stroke Drugs story. We'll see. Now, you're wondering what should lead the second block. You were thinking of the Diabetics story, followed by Bush Medicare, because that's medicine related. Then the Medicare Rx story, there's a natural tie-in there, as well as the Gov/Seniors Health story. State Ed Cuts deals with state finance and programs, as does the Gov Biz Incentives. But you're getting an uneasy sense that these stories are going to push you over your time allotment.

Plano Utility Poles doesn't really fit anywhere. The Hillsboro story is good, and that with the OK Tornadoes story should get you to weather. But, no story for the kicker segment so far. That's okay, you can just write teases for the Ten (ten p.m. newscast) and give them a goodbye for that block. In spite of that, you're feeling reasonably good about the show's lineup, but you're certain you're over on time.

Timing the Show

You add the times together and come up with 15:35. Yep. Your news hole is 10:40, which means you're a whopping 4:55 over. Yikes. Now to cut some stories and reshuffle the lineup.

You scan back through. The Plano Utility Poles story is gone. That saves :30. Cop Murder trial will likely need all of that 1:30 for the anchor intro and the package. You call the reporter quickly to find out. He says he can keep the package to 1:15, and write a :10 intro. You ask him to write a :10 tag, which you'll run with a box, talking about the rape connection. He says he will and you hang up. You've saved another :15. Still a long way to go.

The Murder/Kidnap Arrest will already be fairly tight at :15. Even though you hate to do it, the StreetSense story might be trimmed down to :30. We've now saved 1:00 total. Hammas Attack can be trimmed to a :25 vo, and you can run a :10 bite from the cleric. Time saved is up to 1:55.

You contact the reporter doing the gaming crackdown story. He says he'll need every bit of the 1:40—:10 for the intro, :10 for the toss to the live shot and the reporter's intro, 1:10 for the package, and another :10 for the live tag. You suggest the story run as an anchor intro/pkg/live reporter tag, with no Q&A at the end. He begrudgingly agrees. You've just saved another :10 for a total of 2:05.

More Shuttle Woes is a story you don't want to drop or cut back too much, but you figure you can get :05 from it. You're also thinking that perhaps Shuttle Woes could lead your B-block and move to the Diabetics story. You drop Shuttle Woes to B10 and cut the time to :40. You consult the feed log and learn that the network has a time for the Diabetics Stroke Drugs story—the package will run 1:37, meaning 1:47 including the anchor intro. You just lost :17, which means your total saved is 1:53. You turn to the two Medicare stories. They've just come in through the feed, so you check the visuals and listen to both sots. The one from the president is okay, the one from Senator Ted Kennedy criticizing it is pretty good. You check with the Five producer, who's running another version of both stories. She's going with a single sot from Bush, so you opt for one sot from Kennedy. You also decide to combine the two into one vo/sot and make it around :45 total, reslugging it Bush Kennedy Medicare. Time saved, 2:38.

You scan the wire copy and the feeds list and decide you can combine all of the stories on the state decisions on spending cuts and priorities into one vo/sot, with perhaps two bites. That will run 1:00 at most. You reslug it State Spending. You've now saved 4:38.

You look at the OK tornadoes story and decide that it can get by with a :20 vo, and if there's great sound, you'll make it a :30 vo/bite. You plan on the latter. Time saved, 4:48. You contact the reporter doing the Hillsboro Church story, and she says she'll need the 1:40. There's apparently great video and nats from the night before, plus a good bite from one of the church members, and she thinks she'll get good sound from the minister. Plus, she wants a live intro and tag. You acquiesce. You've trimmed a total of 4:48, leaving you with 10:47 of news, just seven seconds over. You're within tolerance now, and remember you've got a pad of :30. In actuality, at this point, you're :23 under.

Finally, you look at the mix of formats and how each block times out individually. The format mix is good, so you're pleased with how the show will pace. However, you have a problem with the block times. You want the A-block to run at least six minutes, so you mentally rearrange. You're not married to the idea of the Shuttle story being next to Diabetics Drugs. Also, you've got the OK Tornadoes story to get into weather, so the Hillsboro church burning could possibly be moved around. It might follow the Muslim cleric story fairly well. Either Shuttle or Diabetics would be a good lead for the second block, with the Medicare story after Diabetics. Medicare would lead into State Spending nicely. This doesn't quite give you six minutes in the first block, but you're close. After some more thought, you decide that Shuttle Woes might be a solid story to end the first block. Finally, you decide to move the StreetSense story to the kicker block. You make the changes, and now your lineup looks like Figure 17.6.

One last scan and you decide this will work pretty well. Nice mix of times, nice mix of formats, you're leading the show with the right story, you like your choice of second block lead, and the story flow is good. The general mix of stories for the first block feels right, as does the second block. Good mix of geographic appeal. And the blocks time out about where you want them—the A-block runs about 6:15 and the B-block should run just over 4:00. The StreetSense story is about keeping kids safe, so it's somewhat uplifting, making it a good choice for the last story in the show. Most of life is not about crime and tragedy, so some good news stories, especially an uplifting (or humorous) story at the end or the show, can help make for a more balanced (and accurate) representation.

LINEUP

A-BLOCK:

Cop Murder Trial	pkg/lv	1:35
Murder/Kidnap Arrest	rdr	:15
Gaming Crackdown	pkg/lv	1:30
Hammas Attack	vo	:25
Muslim Criticizes Violence	sot.	:10
Hillsboro Church Burns	pkg/live	1:40
More Shuttle Woes	vosot	:40

B-BLOCK

Diabetics Stroke Drugs	pkg	1:47
Bush Kennedy Medicare	vosot	:45
State Spending	vo/sot/sot	1:00
OK Tornadoes	vosot	:30

E-BLOCK

| StreetSense | vosot. | :40 |

FIGURE 17.6

Filling the Rundown

Now you fill the rundown with the lineup. Some producers actually skip scratching out the lineup as we just did, and go straight to filling in the skeleton. You place the stories in the rundown, but without assigning page numbers or anchors yet to most of the stories. Those might change as the day progresses. The approximate time for each story goes in the "Bdgt" column. Your filled rundown, then, looks like Figure 17.7.

Note that this matches the scratched-out show blocking you completed earlier. Also, take a look at the "Total" and the "Over/Under" cells. With all the times filled in (approximate as they may be), the computer has totaled the times and recalculated. As stories come in, more information on each will be filled in, including the exact time, and information in some cells will change. Notice also another column heading marked status. This lets the producer know whether the story is finished and allows her or the executive producer approve the script. All known times and formats are put in their respective columns. All commercial breaks, for example, are prerecorded and will play, in their entireties, as sots. All the teases (in this newscast at this shop, at least) are vos or on camera.

Page	Slug	Wrt	Anc	Shot	Video	Status	Bdgt	Time	Back
Pre1	Pre tz		h/b		vo			:30	
Pre2	Pre tz		h/b		vo				
Pre3	Pre tz		h/b	2s	vo/oc				
	--- Pre-Break ---				sot			2:05	
A00	Open				sot		:15		
	Cop Murder Trial				pkg/lv		1:35		
	Murder/Kidnap Arrest				rdr		:15		
	Gaming Crackdown				pkg/lv		1:30		
	Hammas Attack				vo		:25		
	Muslim Criticizes Violence					sot.		:10	
	Hillsboro Church Burns				pkg/live		1:40		
	More Shuttle Woes				vosot		:40		
A-last	1Tz				vo		:15		
	--- Break 1 ---				sot			2:05	
	Diabetics Stroke Drugs				pkg		1:47		
	Bush Kennedy Medicare				vosot		:45		
	State Spending				vo/sot/sot		1:00		
	OK Tornadoes				vosot		:30		
B-last	2Tz				vo		:10		
	--- Break 2 ---				sot		2:05		
C10	Toss weather		h/b/w	3s					
	Weather		w	1s	ck/gfx				
C90	Toss back		h/b/w	3s				3:30	
Clast	Sports tz		h/b	2s	oc				
	--- Break 3 ---				sot			1:35	
D10	Toss sports		h/b/s	3s					
	Sports		s	1s	oc/vo/sot			3:30	
D90	Toss back		h/b/s	3s/2s					
	--- Break 4 ---				sot			1:05	
E10	StreetSense				vosot.		:40		
Elast	Goodbye/Close		h/b	2s	oc/sot			:30	
PAD								:30	
	---Terminal Break ---				sot			3:05	
	TOTAL							31:57	
	PROGRAM							32:00	
	OVER/UNDER							-:03	

FIGURE 17.7

Front Timing

The executive producer checks your rundown and agrees it's solid. Next you run what's called "front time" for the rundown. To front time (also called "forward time"), you begin with the time on the clock that the first element of the show should hit, then continue adding time to the clock for every successive element. The final clock time should be close to the actual time your show is supposed to be out. If it's off, you'll know what to do to fix it. In addition, front timing is a good way to know at what time each element should hit. This is important, for example, if you have to hit a certain story or commercial break within a certain window. Let's look at the filled rundown in Figure 17.8, substituting "Front Time" for "Back Time."

In the far-right column, the front time will show what the time on the clock should be for each element to begin. The ending time shows at what time you will actually get out should every element run as planned. Your out time shows 6:29:37, seven seconds beyond when you're supposed to get out, which is also reflected in the "+:07" in the "Over/Under" line. This is what you figured before, again keeping in mind you have a :30 pad.

Front-timing the show will also show you at approximately what time an element should hit. This would be extremely important if you were taking a satellite report, for example, and only had the satellite for a set window of time. Let's say Hillsboro Church Burns is an extremely long distance out of town, beyond the range of your microwave live trucks. You send a satellite truck out to cover the story. You learn your satellite transponder window is 6:03:00 to 6:09:00. A quick check of the front time shows you should hit the Hillsboro story at 6:04:15. You should be okay. You'll double-check later when you have more exact times in.

Your next step will be to create script pages for every element in the show. Even the break has a script page with the break designation printed across it. There must be a page there for the director and others (including possibly you) who need pages with instructions for each element. One point about script pages and the rundown that warrants discussion here: As you know, all packages and live shots have an anchor intro, and many will have an anchor tag. Each of these will have a separate page, of course. In some newsrooms, the producer will list the intro, story and tag on their own individual lines on the rundown with their own page numbers. In other newsrooms, the entire story will be listed on the rundown as one story and page set. Once your dummy pages are set up, you will turn to writing stories and teases.

You decide that for your three teases in the preshow, you'll run Cop Murder Trial (naturally—it's the lead), the gaming crackdown, and the story on diabetics and strokes. These are appealing stories, and it's not a bad idea to pull one of the three teases from the second block or later. At the end of the first block before the first break, you'll retease the diabetics story and tease the Medicare spending debate.

Page	Slug	Wrt	Anc	Shot	Video	Status	Bdgt	Time	Front
Pre1	Pre tz		h/b		vo			:30	5:57:30
Pre2	Pre tz		h/b		vo				
Pre3	Pre tz		h/b	2s	vo/oc				
	--- Pre-Break ---				sot			2:05	5:58:00
A00	Open				sot			:15	6:00:05
	Cop Murder Trial				pkg/lv		1:35		6:00:20
	Murder/Kidnap Arrest				rdr		:15		6:01:55
	Gaming Crackdown				pkg/lv		1:30		6:02:10
	Hammas Attack				vo		:25		6:03:40
	Muslim Criticizes Violence					sot.	:10		6:04:05
	Hillsboro Church Burns				pkg/live		1:40		6:04:15
	More Shuttle Woes				vosot		:40		6:05:55
A-last	1Tz				vo			:15	6:06:35
	--- Break 1 ---				sot		2:05		6:06:50
	Diabetics Stroke Drugs				pkg		1:47		6:08:55
	Bush Kennedy Medicare				vosot		:45		6:10:42
	State Spending				vo/sot/sot		1:00		6:11:27
	OK Tornadoes				vosot		:30		6:12:27
B-last	2Tz				vo			:10	6:12:57
	--- Break 2 ---				sot		2:05		6:13:07
C10	Toss weather		h/b/w	3s					6:15:12
	Weather		w	1s	ck/gfx				
C90	Toss back		h/b/w	3s				3:30	
Clast	Sports tz		h/b	2s	oc				
	--- Break 3 ---				sot			1:35	6:18:42
D10	Toss sports		h/b/s	3s					
	Sports		s	1s	oc/vo/sot			3:30	6:20:17
D90	Toss back		h/b/s	3s/2s					
	--- Break 4 ---				sot			1:05	6:23:47
E10	StreetSense				vosot.		:40		6:24:52
Elast	Goodbye/Close		h/b	2s	oc/sot			:30	6:25:32
PAD								:30	6:26:02
	---Terminal Break ---				sot			3:05	6:27:32
									6:29:37

OUT AT	
TOTAL	32:07
PROGRAM	32:00
OVER/UNDER	+ :07

FIGURE 17.8

Teases

A quick detour to discuss teases. Teases are a critical part of the producer's writing day because they're a critical part of the newscast. Viewers stay tuned, in very large part, because they're interested in seeing the stories that have been teased. Your job is to identify the most compelling, interesting and important stories, those that will carry the most appeal and relevancy for your audience.

Different newsrooms have different philosophies on how to approach teases, but the key is understanding that a tease is not a news story but an enticement. Teases must lure the viewers into staying with your newscast to see the stories.

The key to writing a good tease is understanding what about this story will appeal to the viewer. Personalize the tease: Make it relevant and interesting to the individual viewer. How will this story affect a given viewer? Do not write generic information. That rarely inspires someone to stick around. Instead, take it from the viewer's perspective, and use just enough detail of the story to bring it alive. Get that viewer intrigued. At the same time, you don't want to reveal too much. You have to offer a benefit to the viewer for staying around and watching the story. And, like all other television news writing, you must write conversationally.

This means having a good understanding of the story—all of the story. You must know what the audience hook is, and what the payoff of watching the story will be. This also necessitates getting into the story to use the most compelling visuals and natural sound. And as you're crafting your tease, avoid telegraphing the upcoming break with phrases such as, "when we return," or "later in our newscast." This signals the viewer a commercial is coming up, and they may already be headed to the bathroom or refrigerator before your brilliantly written teases hit the air. Just get into the tease and hook that audience to continue watching.

At the same time, deliver on what you promise. Nothing is more annoying or angering to the viewer than to have been subjected to :45 of teases about some story, only the find the story is a :17 vo that doesn't deliver on what it promises. You've no doubt experienced something like this: At the top of the show, shots of some black, gooey substance on the pavement, with the high-volume anchor excitedly spouting out, "Mysterious black substance appears on a residential south Dallas street. What is it, and does it pose a health hazard to the neighborhood? We'll have that story." Then, during the newscast, you watch two more versions of the tease, all implying this is a critically important story about a potentially toxic substance that somehow got onto south Dallas streets. And you're downright hacked off when the story finally appears, as a kicker, and you learn that this "mysterious substance" is wax that melted from candles stacked in the back of a delivery truck parked in the sun. Don't do that.

Take a look at these examples:

Not great: Later in our newscast, disclosure laws on inspections of homes for sale allow some problems to go unreported. What those laws state and how home buyers can respond, coming up.

Much better: An inspection on the home you're buying is supposed to turn up any serious problems with the house, right? Not necessarily. Reporter Larry Listentothis shows how you can make sure your home inspection tells you everything you need to know, right after this.

Not great: Coming up after the break, Congress has just passed legislation regarding identity theft. As part of that legislation, consumers can now request information on identity theft prevention. We have the story.

Much better: Identity theft is getting worse in this country. The problem is, someone may have stolen your identity and you might not even know. We'll tell you how to find out, the new laws to protect you, and steps you can take to prevent it, coming up next.

The Visual Look of the Newscast

Part of the producer's day is determining and setting visuals for the stories and order graphics. The station has a store of stills that can be used for graphic backgrounds. The station will also generally have an artist who can build graphics from scratch, and visuals for a story can often be lifted from video shot for that story. Each newsroom has a slightly different procedure, but in each procedure, the producer must decide whether he or she needs an anchor box and what should fill it, or whether a full-screen graphic is needed for any given story. Once that decision is made, the producer makes certain it's created, assigns it a file number so the producer and director can find it, and then assembles all the graphics and the supers in the order they'll be needed in the show.

Using a box graphic is typically the right move. The better you can illustrate the story visually, the more interesting and understandable it will be to your viewer. However, you don't want to assign a box to every story. There's a need to provide some variety in the camera shots, and the most powerful shot in television is the headshot or bust shot, with the anchor centered. With this shot, the anchor is providing the viewer solid eye contact with no distractions, so it's a good idea to mix this shot in from time to time.

The producer has to consider other aspects of the visual look and pacing of the show, as well. What camera shots and effects to use are big parts of that planning.

A brief word on terms: A one-shot refers to one person being on camera. In the case of a studio anchor, the shot shows the anchor either centered or with a box. A two-shot refers to two people on camera (typically the coanchor team), a three-shot shows three people, and so on. Some newscasts use a studio wide-shot to establish the studio (and its anchors and, by proxy, the entire news team). These are best used at the very top and bottom of the show, and perhaps when coming back from a break. Three-shots (showing the two news anchors with either the sports or weather anchor) should be used when transitioning to or from the sports or weather block. A two-shot of the news anchors should be used at the top of the show and when transitioning into teases or the break. These shots reestablish both anchors, but are not necessary, for example, when coming into the second block of news stories. The most commonly used shot should be the one-shot, which you'll assign to nearly every news story either anchor reads. This is the most powerful shot in your arsenal, so use it.

Two other terms to know: If your anchor is reading a reader with a box, and you want that same anchor to read the following vo that doesn't have a box, you can instruct the shot to "push" into the anchor, which typically means panning slightly and zooming in slightly to center the anchor. The opposite terms also apply. If one anchor is reading an on-camera tag, and your next shot is a two-shot going into prebreak teases, you might instruct to "pull" from the one-shot to the two-shot.

Also, be aware of some of the common visual effects used and when you should use them. A straight cut from one camera shot to another is almost always the best bet. A wipe is one of many effects in which the screen seems to "wipe" from one video scene to another. Reserve this for related stories. For example, if you are running two vos on policy protests in different parts of the country, you might wipe from one to the other. This signals to the audience the story is different but related. Finally, a dissolve shows passage from one point in time or one physical place to another. The director will likely dissolve from the teases visuals or anchor shot to black before hitting a break, for example. Once the break is done and the screen dissolves to black, the director will dissolve the anchors back in to begin the next block.

Continuing to Build the Show

Back to building our newscast. As the day moves on, more stories are completed and more times are finalized. Some producers will automatically round any story time up the next :05 increment. This is to account for the fact that each story needs a second or two of transition time. At the end of one story, an anchor will pause for a beat before starting the next story to let the audience know we've moved on. Every story element, in fact, will take an extra one to two seconds, which, by the end of the newscast, can expand the estimated time by 15 seconds or more. Others account for that time in the "pad." It's generally up to the individual producer.

As your stories keep rolling in, you nter the information into your rundown (Figure 17.9). By this time, your rundown is set, barring any breaking news that might change things. You go ahead and number pages. A-10 is running 1:17, including intro. That gives :18 for a live tag, which may run less, and you let the reporter know there's no time for a Q&A afterward. You've written A-20, and it runs :14, which you'll leave as :15 to pad. So far, so good. A-30's package, with intro, is running 1:27. You give the reporter :10 for a live tag (which will likely run slightly more), meaning your actual time is 1:40, :10 more than budgeted. You're not happy, and hope that nothing else runs long.

Page	Slug	Wrt	Anc	Shot	Video	Status	Bdgt	Time	Back
Pre1	Pre tz		h/b		vo			:30	5:57:31
Pre2	Pre tz		h/b		vo				
Pre3	Pre tz		h/b	2s	vo/oc				
	--- Pre-Break ---				sot			2:05	5:58:01
A00	Open				sot			:15	6:00:06
A10	Cop Murder Trial		b/h	2s/1s	boxpkg/live		1:35	1:35	6:00:21
A20	Murder/Kidnap Arrest		h	1s	box/rdr		:15	:15	6:01:56
A30	Gaming Crackdown		h	1s	box/pkg/lv		1:30	1:40	6:02:11
A40	Hammas Attack		b	1s	vo		:25	:27	6:03:51
A50	Muslim Criticizes Violence 6:04:18		b	1s	sot/oc			:10	:14
A60	Hillsboro Church Burns		b	1s	pkg/live		1:40	1:30	6:04:32
A70	More Shuttle Woes		h	1s	vo/sot		:40	:33	6:06:02
A-last	1Tz		h/b	2s	oc/vo			:15	6:06:35
	--- Break 1 ---				sot			2:05	6:06:50
B10	Diabetics Stroke Drugs		b	1s	box/pkg		1:47	1:48	6:08:55
B20	Bush Kennedy Medicare		b	1s	oc/vo/sot		:45	:42	6:10:43
B30	State Spending		h	1s	oc/vo/sot/sot		1:00	1:04	6:11:25
B40	OK Tornadoes		h	1s	oc/vosot		:30	:37	6:12:29
B-last	2Tz		h/b	2s	oc/vo			:10	6:13:06
	--- Break 2 ---				sot			2:05	6:13:16
C10	Toss weather		h/b/w	3s					
	Weather		w	1s	ck/gfx				
C90	Toss back		h/b/w	3s				3:30	6:15:21
Clast	Sports tz		h/b	2s	oc				
	--- Break 3 ---				sot			1:35	6:18:51
D10	Toss sports		h/b/s	3s					
	Sports		s	1s	oc/vo/sot			3:30	6:20:26
D90	Toss back		h/b/s	3s/2s					
	--- Break 4 ---				sot			1:05	6:23:56
E10	StreetSense		h	1s	oc/vosot.		:40	:34	6:25:01
Elast	Goodbye/Close		h/b	2s	oc/sot			:30	6:25:35
PAD								:20	6:26:05
	---Terminal Break ---				sot			3:05	6:26:25
	OUT AT								6:29:30
	TOTAL							31:59	
	PROGRAM							32:00	
	OVER/UNDER							-:01	

FIGURE 17.9

A-40 runs :27 and the A-50 sot runs :13, both of which you pad by a second. The package/live for A-60 (Hillsboro Church Fire) turns out to be 1:19, including intro. The reporter can keep the live tag to :10 and doesn't need a Q&A, so you adjust the time to 1:30. The A-70 vosot on the shuttle turns out to be :32, so you fill in :33 under "Time."

B-10 was already done, and you pad it by a second. As a side note, it's rarely a good idea to slate a package or long story during the kicker segment. If you're running :20 long coming into the last block, and the only material left to work with is 1:15 package, you'd better pray you've padded enough time into the good-bye and close to let you pick up that :20 by abbreviating both. Otherwise, you have two choices: run the package and dump out with :20 left (really bad) or don't run the package. This leaves you :55 seconds to fill. Hopefully you've supplied your anchors with some wire copy they can read cold, and they can fill the rest by ad libbing a recap of the day's news. Either way, your show looks bad and so do you. The way around that is slating one or two short pieces for the kicker segment. If you're running long, it's easy to drop a :20 feature and come out on time. The news doesn't suffer, and neither does the newscast or your reputation. Back to the rundown.

B-20 winds up running :41, so you adjust the actual time to :42. B-30 comes in at 1:03, which you enter as 1:04, and some great video and sound on the Oklahoma tornado story (B-40) pushes the time to :36, which you enter as :37. However, the kicker story (E-10) turns out at :33, which goes in as :34. You tally up the times and check them against the computer. You're now :09 over (versus :07 by your estimate), but you still have that :30 of pad, which you adjust to :20. This now makes you :01 under with :20 of pad. You can always stretch time if necessary. Anchors can chat a bit about the day's events, transitions to weather and sports can be filled with a bit more conversation, and you can always have a short piece of wire copy available as fill. Coming in heavy, however, is a recipe for disaster. You'll be looking for stories and teases to drop as soon as you start the show. You're uneasy, but with that :23 to play with, you think it will run okay. You let all your live reporters know once again that they cannot go over their allotted time in their live tags.

You're also filling in which anchors (Harry Handsome and Barbara Beautiful with news, Sam Sportsguy with sports, and Walter Weatherdude with weather) will read what stories. Most producers want a given anchor to read an entire story pod. Simply going back and forth from anchor to anchor gives a kind of ping-pong effect that can be a turn-off. The end of a story pod can also be a good place for an anchor tag. That anchor is seen one last time on camera, followed by a shot of the coanchor beginning the next cluster.

Okay, so you've filled in the anchors and associated video instructions. All your element times are in. Now, you turn to back timing the show.

Back Timing

Back timing is basically the reverse of front timing. Rather than begin at the top with the "program in" time and working down, you'll start at the bottom with the "program out" time and work up. You'll subtract each element in turn from the clock time, working your way backward to the first element of the show. This way, you'll know the latest each element must begin to get out on time. Take a look at our final rundown in Figure 17.9. You fill in our program out time ("Out At"), which is 6:29:30, subtract the run time of the previous element (terminal break that runs 2:05) and fill in that time (6:27:25) on the line above "program out" and beside the element time. This means you must hit the terminal break at 6:27:25 to get out on time.

Continuing the process up, your pad is :20, which you must "hit" (which is theoretical—it's only there to add time) at 6:27:05. Your anchors will need to begin the goodbye at 6:26:35 and must begin E-10 (StreetSense) at 6:26:01 to stay on time. With the back timing filled in completely, a quick glance during the newscast at the back time for any element tells the producer if the show is early (light), late (heavy), or right on time. Say, for example, Barbara Beautiful began reading Hammas Attack (A-40) at 6:03:45. The back time shows you should be starting that story at 6:03:51, six seconds later. This means that you're slightly ahead of schedule, or running light at that moment. On the other hand, let's say you're coming out of the first break and starting the B-block. Barbara starts the intro to B-10, but the clock shows 6:10:10. You know you're :15 over, or heavy. If you've timed out the rest of the show properly, you'd better start looking for places to trim and things to drop.

Live Shots and Other Matters

One other consideration (or set of considerations) involves the live shot. The producer is ultimately in charge of making sure that live shot comes off well. In a live shot, a truck (equipped with video editing gear) becomes a miniature television station. The live truck uses a microwave transmitter to send a signal to the TV station or one of the relay towers. The signal must be line of sight, meaning the sending dish must be able to "see" the receiver. The live truck engineer extends the sending dish, mounted on a collapsible mast, above the truck, then points the dish toward the receiver. Once the signal is "tuned in," the engineer will send video (from the camera, already in place and cabled to the truck) and audio (from the microphone the reporter will use) to ensure both signals are clear. As the live shot approaches, the producer (or an associate producer or live shot coordinator) will check the IFB (interruptible feedback) system to ensure the producer (or whoever) can communicate directly with the reporter (and videographer). IFB systems are now often handled through assigned telephone lines and accessed through cell phones, but various stations use various approaches, depending on available money and technology.

Once the technical elements are in place, the live shot can go off. The producer must know the status of all of those elements. As the live shot approaches, the producer ensures the photographer and reporter are in place, and all video elements and supers for the shot are ready to go. Communication is critical, so newsrooms go to great lengths to make sure all the key players can communicate effectively, clearly and immediately.

That's the basic process. Other details are involved, of course. You'll have to make certain stories get edited (and perhaps edit a few yourself), work constantly with the desk, other producers and writers, reporters, the director, other staff and management. You'll have scores of tasks the come up during the day. You'll have to pay enormous attention to detail. And you'll need to be able to make quick (and correct) decisions under deadline pressure, especially during the newscast. However, if you do your job well in the preparation stage and develop enough experience and news sense, you can handle any snags during the show. And there's nothing quite like the feeling of walking away from producing a newscast that really cooks.

So What's the Appeal?

So why would you want to go into producing? It's an exciting, fast-paced job that deals with the larger picture rather than one narrow task. It carries some power and weight in the newsroom and is a good entry-level management job. In addition, news directors are desperate for good producers. For every 10 or more reporters who apply for an open position, one producer does. You can get in easier, move up faster and make a very comfortable living. Speaking of comfort, there are other advantages. A reporter may be sent out in muggy 104-degree heat while talking about highway repairs. Or in 12-degree cold with a windchill of 20 below zero and sleet coming down while talking about bad weather and road conditions. Meanwhile, the producers partly responsible for sending the reporters out on those stories will sit in 72-degree comfort with a cup of coffee at their sides. If you love television news, can write well, can work well under pressure, have good news judgment, can get along well with people and like to manage and coordinate, producing is the job for you.

Summary

The producer has to apply solid news judgment, a good sense of aesthetics and ample technical knowledge toward the goal of filling a newscast with content. The producer also is responsible for the on-air look of the newscast. Ultimately, it's the producer who gets the show on the air, and it's the producer's responsibility if anything goes wrong.

The producer works from a story budget, always looking for any unexpected developments or breaking news. The producer must determine the news hole, then work to fill that available news hole with stories. The producer will decide on the lead story and set the story order, typically waiting until later in the day to lock in that story order and number the pages of the show. That order is set according to newsworthiness and prioritizing, story flow and clustering, and pacing and variety. The producer decides how to transition from one story or story pod to the next. The producer works with the reporters and news managers to decide the format of the story. The producer will decide what stories to tease and will write the teases as well as many of the stories that will run in the newscast.

Another responsibility is timing out the newscast to the second. The producer needs to front time and back time the newscast. The producer must stay in communication with all other major players, including the reporters, the assignment desk, the editors, the live coordinator (if there is one) and the executive producer. The producer decides which anchors will deliver what stories, what the camera shots are, and whether and where to use graphics; orders all graphics and supers; and makes certain the live shots are ready to go.

Exercises

1. Watch a local newscast as you videotape another. In each, jot down all the elements of the newscast, including times. For each story, note the major points and the formats. For anchor pieces, note all visuals (camera shots, use of boxes, visual transitions) as well as scripted transitions within and between story pods.

Consider each newscast individually, looking for story placement, flow, formats, writing (including the teases) and visuals. What seemed to work well, and what didn't? Did you agree with the choice of lead story and the story order? Why or why not? Did the transitions and teases work well?

Then, compare the newscasts. Which was the better show, and why?

2. Watch and record an evening newscast and a late newscast from the same station. Compare the two using the same criteria as in Exercise 1. What differences do you note?

3. Take a copy of your local newspaper. Jot down each story with a one- or two-line description. Use this as your story budget. Pretend you're producing the late local newscast, which should contain a mix of national and international as well as local and regional news. Pretend you have any visuals and sound you want. Build a newscast, using the skeleton rundown found in the chapter.

18

The Station and the Newsroom

How newsrooms organize their personnel varies from station to station, depending on the market size, the financial status of the station, the number of employees in the newsroom and the newsroom's culture. Figure 18.1 shows a typical newsroom organizational chart.

The smaller the newsroom, the more roles each member of the team has to fill. The larger the newsroom, the more specialized the roles become. However, we can get a sense for basic newsroom organization by discussing some of the positions you'd commonly see in a medium-sized television newsroom.

Newsroom Positions

The list of newsroom positions that follows begins somewhere near the top of the hierarchy and ends somewhere near the bottom. The job descriptions will apply to some stations but not to others.

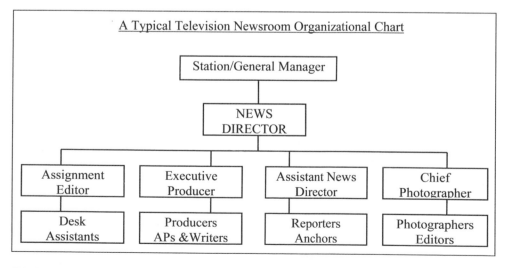

FIGURE 18.1

Management Positions

The station manager oversees all operations of the television station: news production, sales, promotions, engineering, traffic (organizing the programming and commercials), accounting, programming, engineering and any other departments operating within the station.

The news director is responsible for the operations of the news department. He or she oversees all news programming. The news director is often the person who makes decisions about resources the station will commit to newscasts and to specific news stories. His or her responsibilities can include setting the news budget, hiring and firing newsroom employees, scheduling employees' working hours and vacation time and approving rundowns and scripts. In larger stations, shift scheduling and script approval are handled by others. In all stations, the news director sets the tone and philosophy for the on-air product—what kinds of stories are covered and how.

The assistant news director is the news director's right-hand man or woman. He or she assumes duties as assigned by the news director. Responsibilities can include hiring and firing, scheduling, setting budgets and overseeing special news projects or series. Typically, the assistant news director supervises reporters and will often approve their scripts. However, most small and many medium-sized newsrooms don't have an assistant news director, leaving those responsibilities to the news director and the executive producer.

The executive producer is responsible for nearly every aspect of newscasts during his or her shift. The executive producer often makes decisions about which stories news reporters will cover and which stories will be included in newscasts, especially if there is no assistant news director in that newsroom. He or she is most often responsible for script and rundown approval. In all shops, the executive producer is responsible for the content and look of the newscast. The executive producer assumes other duties as assigned by the news director, which can include responsibility for news specials or series, hiring and firing and scheduling. Some small-market newsrooms don't have an executive producer on staff, leaving those responsibilities to the news director and newscast producers.

The assignment editor tracks news stories and helps decide which stories reporters and photographers will cover. The assignment editor keeps a daily file of events happening or planned within the viewing area. He or she pairs news reporters with photographers (unless reporters shoot their own stories), helps to set up the stories they cover, and provides locations of stories assigned. The assignment editor monitors police scanners for breaking news stories and assigns reporters and photographers to cover them as needed. The assignment editor in a smaller market might also schedule satellite and microwave feeds. He or she knows at all times where all newsroom employees are and what they're covering and where to find answers about the day's news events. Larger stations will employ desk assistants to carry out the basic tasks of running the desk, enabling the assignment editor to spend more time in story and logistical planning.

The chief photographer is responsible for photography equipment and, often, news vehicles. It is the chief photographer's job to make sure equipment is operating properly. He or she assigns equipment to news photographers and makes recommendations about equipment the newsroom should purchase. The chief photographer assumes other duties that can include setting photographers' work schedules and screening job applicants for photography positions. He or she also critiques the work on the other videographers to maintain technical and aesthetic quality in the on-air produce.

In larger markets, there are many more management positions, with each manager in charge of a more specialized area. The smaller the market, the broader the area of responsibilities and necessary skills.

Content Positions

The producer is responsible for a newscast's content, flow, video, graphics, camera shots, timing and much more. In short, he or she is responsible for the newscast. The newscast producer builds the rundown. He or she decides what format stories will take (readers, vo/nat, sots, packages, etc.). The newscast producer sets the camera shots and makes decisions about full-screen graphics and over-the-shoulder boxes. Often, the producer is responsible for script approval of stories that appear in the newscast. Equally often, the producer writes scripts that are not assigned to news reporters, news writers or anchors.

In larger markets, producers can take on a range of other roles as well. For a morning show with two hours to fill, for example, a producer might be in charge of just one segment in the show. Special projects might have one producer assigned exclusively. Again, the larger the market, the more specialized the roles. The smaller the market, the broader the roles.

The news anchor is the person who appears nightly in viewers' homes to tell them the latest events of the day. Often, viewers can't identify the station or network they watch, but they can recall instantly the names of the people they watch and "know." The news anchor's job responsibilities include being friendly, professional, knowledgeable and credible. Appearance is also part of the job. News anchors are clean, neat, well-dressed and physically fit. Performance, too, is part of the job. News anchors speak well. They use good grammar. They don't mispronounce names of people and places in the news. When they're not on the air, especially in smaller markets, news anchors help prepare the newscast. They often write scripts. They usually read, edit and, in some markets, approve scripts before air. In the smallest markets, anchors may also produce newscasts. Anchors assume other responsibilities that can include hosting special reports, station-sponsored town meetings and debates. They also can assume managerial responsibilities. Some anchors hold titles such as managing editor and executive producer.

The general assignment reporter is responsible for generating and covering news stories. The reporter finds stories, interviews and video. He or she writes scripts and works with photographers or tape editors (or alone at some smaller stations) to edit the stories. The reporter is permitted—even encouraged—to make decisions about stories. Reporters in the field often call the newsroom to alert the assignment editor and producer that a story is not panning out or is bigger than originally thought. The reporter limits his or her reports to the time allotted them in the rundown. The reporter, like the anchor, is a "guest" in viewers' homes and must appear friendly and knowledgeable on air. In some smaller stations, reporters are photographers too. They are solo crews—forgive the contradiction in terms—who do it all: shoot video, conduct interviews and write and edit the stories.

Some larger stations employ field producers, who set up the logistics of the stories reporters will cover, conduct the research and accompany reporters in the field. The field producer arranges interviews and may conduct them. Field producers also can approve reporters' scripts. The field producer reports to the assistant news director, in general.

The associate producer, or AP, is the producer's right-hand man or woman. The associate producer writes stories and makes certain all the technical elements for a given newscast are prepared and ready to go on the air. You will typically find associate producers in the larger markets. He or she will report to the producer or the executive producer.

Larger stations also may employ news writers, who are responsible for scripts not assigned to producers, anchors or reporters. News writers often use wire copy or phone interviews for their information. They get video for their scripts from network satellite feeds. News writers submit properly formatted scripts that run no longer than the time allotted them in the rundown. News writers can make suggestions about visual elements that would add to scripts.

Production Positions

The news photographer, sometimes called a videographer, is responsible for getting sound and pictures. The photographer knows his or her equipment—how to use it and how to do emergency repairs. He or she makes decisions about how to set up lighting, which microphones to use, how to frame shots and what to shoot. Photographers work closely with reporters. At times, photographers may cover stories without reporters. They shoot video, record sots and gather information for the producer or writer who will prepare the script. The photographer often is responsible for editing videotape.

The tape editor, at the risk of being redundant, edits videotape to accompany scripts that appear in the newscast. A tape editor could edit vo/nat, sots and packages—or, more likely, all of the above.

In some ways, the associate producer job can be considered a production position. The AP is often in charge of seeing that stories are edited and live shots are set.

Specialty Reporting

Sports. The sports department is separate from but part of the newsroom. As in the newsroom, there is a sports director who makes decisions about which events the sports department will cover and which elements will appear in the sportscast. A sports producer builds the sportscast and often gathers and edits video that will appear. Sports reporters, like news reporters, cover stories. Sports photographers shoot the stories. Sports anchors deliver sportscasts. Sports department employees often are required to produce special reports in addition to the nightly sportscast within the newscast. Many stations have Friday night high school football shows, coaches' shows and other special sports programming. As on-air personalities, sports anchors and reporters are responsible for being professional and credible. In many sports departments, especially in mid- and small-sized markets, reporters and anchors may double as producers.

Weather. The weather department is also separate from but part of the newsroom. Weather anchors (who are often meteorologists) follow weather-related news and events. They gather information from many sources and use the technology available to best present the weather to viewers. Weather anchors often are called on to do public relations for the station by addressing school and civic groups. As on-air personalities, weather anchors are responsible for being professional and credible.

Other Specialty Positions. Specialty reporting is not limited to sports and weather. Some large-market newsrooms hire specialty health, business and science reporters and producers who work exclusively on reports in their fields of expertise. Many major-market newsrooms also have an investigative unit of reporters and producers who spend time developing depth stories. Typically, however, even in those stations with assigned beats, all reporters also act as general assignment reporters. If a news story comes up that's outside of a reporter's beat area, the reporter will still need to be able to cover it.

Other Positions

Many more people are vital to the production of every newscast. Many of them hold technical positions and are hired through the engineering department. Some of these positions include the newscast director, technical director, audio operator, studio camera operator, playback operator and graphic artist. These jobs most often are not newsroom positions but, again, are vital to getting the news on the air.

Again, keep in mind that the descriptions above can serve as a useful guide, but every newsroom is different. One of your tasks in joining a new newsroom is learning how the hierarchy is arranged, who is responsible for what, and above all, what your responsibilities are.

A Typical Day in a Typical Newsroom

Are there such things as typical days and typical newsrooms? Every newsroom operates differently. And every day is different, defined by the news the station is covering. Still, the typical newsroom schedule that follows might give you an idea of the excitement and action that occurs in newsrooms across the country. It is an example of a midsize station that airs half-hour newscasts at 6:30 a.m., noon, and 5, 6 and 10 p.m.

8:30 a.m.: Newsroom employees begin showing up for the workday. They've read the morning paper. They've watched morning national newscasts. They've listened to morning radio newscasts on their way to work. Once at work, they scan wire copy to catch up on what happened overnight. They compile lists of story ideas. The assignment editor prints out or pulls the assignment file for the day. Photographers load equipment in news vehicles.

9 a.m.: Morning meeting. The news director, assignment editor, executive producer, producers, anchors and reporters plan the day's news coverage. They discuss story ideas and rundowns for the early evening newscasts. Reporters get their assignments.

9:45 a.m.: The morning meeting breaks up and newsroom employees get to work. Producers begin building rundowns. The assignment editor coordinates the day's activities while monitoring police scanners. Reporters set up interviews. As interviews are confirmed, reporters team up with photographers to go into the field. Throughout the morning, the assignment editor is in contact with reporters who are covering assignments in the field. He or she is ready to respond as news happens or stories fall flat.

11 a.m.: The producer of the noon newscast prints scripts. Reporters are still filing late scripts to the newscast. The executive producer, producers and anchors are reading, editing and approving scripts as they come in. The edit bays (usually a series of rooms large enough to accommodate only editing equipment and one or two people) are full, as reporters, photographers and tape editors prepare the video for the newscast.

11:30 a.m.: Reporters with live shots scheduled in the newscast are in place in the field. With photographers, they establish microwave and satellite shots for on-location reports. They may be "feeding" back video to the newsroom for the associate producer to edit. The assignment editor makes sure all the live shots are acceptable for air.

11:45 a.m.: The producer reports to the control room to contact any live shots in the newscast. The anchors report to the studio. The associate producer delivers the videotapes to the control room or to an area known as "playback," where videotape operators load tapes into playback machines so they can appear on air.

Noon: The newscast airs. As news happens, the assignment editor sends out reporters and photographers to cover it. He or she keeps the producer notified of unfolding events. The producer may drop or add stories as required by time or by news events. In the newsroom, employees working on the 5 and 6 p.m. newscasts are still working on their stories.

12:30 p.m.: The noon newscast crew goes home (they have been at work since about 4 or 5 a.m.). Meanwhile, the 5 and 6 p.m. newscast crews are hard at work. Reporters are in the field with photographers working on stories. Producers are building the rundowns.

1:30 p.m.: The crew for the late newscast (executive producer, producer, anchors, reporters and photographers) arrives at work. They go through the same preparations as the morning crew. They read wire copy and catch up on news events of the morning. Photographers load equipment in news vehicles.

2 p.m.: Afternoon meeting. Again, the news director, assignment editor, executive producers, producers, anchors and reporters (those who are not in the field covering stories) discuss the early evening and late newscast rundowns. Early-evening producers make changes to their rundowns based on events of the day. The late newscast rundown begins taking shape. Reporters for the late newscast get their assignments. By 2:45 the meeting breaks up and the employees get back to work.

3 p.m.: Reporters who have been in the field begin returning to the newsroom to write and edit their stories. They have been in contact throughout the day with the newsroom, keeping the assignment editor and producers updated on the progress of their stories. The associate producer has started organizing tapes for the early newscasts. The executive producer, producers and anchors are reading, editing and approving scripts as they become available.

By 4 p.m., events are similar to those that occurred as everyone prepared for the morning newscast. The producer of the 5 p.m. newscast prints scripts; reporters are filing late scripts; the executive producer, producers and anchors are reading, editing and approving scripts as they come in. Again, the edit bays are full.

4:30 to 4:45 p.m.: As in the morning, reporters with live shots are in place in the field, establishing microwave and satellite shots for on-location reports. The associate producer edits any video they may be "feeding" back to the newsroom. The assignment editor makes sure all the live shots are acceptable for air. The newscast producer contacts any live shots in the newscast. The anchors report to the studio. The associate producer delivers the videotapes to the control room or to playback.

5 p.m.: The newscast airs, with all the action of the noon newscast. In the newsroom, employees working on the 6 p.m. newscast are still writing and editing, and the associate producer begins organizing videotapes for that newscast.

5:15 p.m.: The 6 p.m. newscast producer prints scripts for the newscast. The executive producer, producers and anchors are reading, editing and approving late scripts as they come in. The edit bays still are full, as reporters, photographers and tape editors prepare the video for the 6 p.m. newscast.

5:30 to 5:45 p.m.: Yet again, reporters with live shots are in the field preparing for their reports. The associate producer edits their video, and the assignment editor reviews all the live shots. The 6 p.m. newscast producer contacts any live shots in the newscast. The anchors report to the studio. The associate producer delivers the videotapes to the control room or to playback.

6 p.m.: The newscast airs. As with the other two newscasts of the day, the assignment editor sends out reporters and photographers to cover news as it happens and keeps the producer notified of unfolding events. The producer may drop or add stories as required by time or by news events.

6:30 to 10 p.m.: At 6:30, the early newscast crews go home. But the 10 p.m. newscast crew is hard at work. From this time until the final newscast of the day, the newsroom flurry repeats itself again: reporters and photographers are in the field; the producer builds the rundown; scripts are written, edited, reviewed and approved; videotapes are organized and edited.

By 9 p.m., the producer prints the scripts, even though reporters may still be filing late scripts to the newscast. The executive producer, producer and anchors are reading, editing and approving scripts as they come in. Reporters, photographers and tape editors continue to edit for the newscast.

10 p.m.: The newscast airs. In the newsroom, overnight employees are coming to work.

10:30 p.m.: The employees of the 10 p.m. newscast go home. But the newsroom is still active. A smaller crew for the early-morning newscast is at work. At 4 a.m., the crew for the noon newscast arrives. The cycle repeats itself as the early morning and noon newscasts air, by which time the crews of the early evening newscast are already working on the next evening's news.

As you can see, the newsroom is a place of constant coming and going. Employees for various newscasts arrive for and leave work, some overlapping for a few hours, others never seeing one another. Reporters and photographers come and go between covering news in the field and preparing scripts and tapes at the station. Most newsrooms operate 24 hours a day. Don't be surprised to land the graveyard shift on your first job. Remember that news doesn't stop at the end of the standard workday. If you're going into the television business, expect to work weekends, holidays, odd shifts and long hours.

Summary

Different newsrooms require different duties of their employees. The number of positions and job descriptions differs from station to station, too. And different newsrooms have different "personalities."

Management positions in the newsroom include the station manager, news director, assistant news director, executive producer, assignment editor and chief photographer. Content positions include producers, associate producers, anchors, reporters, field producers, news writers and researchers. Production positions include photographers (videographers), associate producers and tape editors.

Sports and weather are specialty reporting areas. Sports and weather staffers are newsroom employees but often work independently. Many newsrooms also hire specialty health, business and agriculture reporters and producers. Lines are often blurred between specialty reports and stories the newsroom staff covers. Many more people are vital to the production of every newscast, including, at some stations, the newscast director, technical director, audio operator, studio camera operator, playback operator and graphic artist.

Every newsroom operates differently, and every day is different, defined by the news the station is covering. Still, a typical newsroom schedule shows the excitement and action that occurs in many newsrooms across the country. Newsrooms are places of constant coming and going. Most newsrooms operate 24 hours a day. If you're going into the television business, expect to work weekends, holidays, odd shifts and long hours.

This chapter thus far has provided a very general sense of how the day runs in an "average midmarket station." Now we turn to a detailed look at a top-rated major market station, WFAA-TV in Dallas.

Exercises

1. Consider the job descriptions outlined in this chapter. Choose the newsroom position that appeals most to you. Contact someone working in local television who holds that position. Conduct an interview over the phone or face-to-face with the person you contact. Prepare your questions in advance about the difficulties of breaking into the position, the joys and pitfalls of the position, the requirements, the needed qualities and the duties. Write a paper about what you learned in the interview. Then, consider the areas in which you believe you need more experience and education to become a qualified applicant.

19

A Look Inside: WFAA-TV, Dallas

The News Operation

On the southwestern edge of downtown Dallas stands an imposing, glass-fronted building bearing the letters WFAA-TV. WFAA is the ABC affiliate in Dallas–Fort Worth, the seventh-largest television market in the country at the time of this writing. The television station, owned by the Belo Corporation, sits in the center of a massive complex of four buildings that take up several city blocks. To the west of WFAA stands the Dallas Morning News, and behind it, TXCN, the Texas Cable News network. Across the street from WFAA towers the national headquarters for Belo, the company that owns all three entities as well as 18 more television stations, four newspapers, nine regional or local cable news channels, and 34 Web sites, with plans to continue growing. Within the WFAA building, a team of nearly a hundred people fills a wide range of roles with the daily goal of gathering and presenting the news to the Dallas–Fort Worth viewing audience.

The newsroom itself is enormous, measuring about 25 paces by 50 paces. About 50 work cubicles grouped in clusters of four or six spread across the room. Reporters, producers and writers script their stories and build their newscasts here. Each desk has a computer, at least one small television set, a telephone, a collection of reference books and filing cabinets. Lining the newsroom on either side and across the front are the glassed-in offices where the newsroom's managers and anchors work. A large conference table with computer screens and office chairs sits in a recess along the front. The table is flanked by white boards and maps. Large studio lights are positioned around the newsroom, and in the far corner is a studio camera with a TelePrompTer to shoot newsroom live shots. Slightly elevated along the base of the room stretches the assignments desk, home to five work stations, each equipped with a computer. The desk is punctuated with radios and telephones, and behind the desk sit filing cabinets, a large assignment board and several maps.

Arcing out into the newsroom above the assignments desk are mounted 20 TV monitors tuned to 10 different channels, one full complement viewable from any position in the newsroom. To one side of the assignments desk are tucked two small rooms, both glassed-in, with an array of video monitors and racks of other video equipment. One of these rooms is designated to take satellite feeds, sent from ABC network, CNN, other Belo stations and various other sources. The other room is devoted to tuning in live shots from WFAA's reporters and videographers in the field. At any given time, WFAA could go live from nine locations around the area.

A short hallway on either side of the assignments desk leads to 16 video edit bays, each one a glassed-in booth, as well as two soundproofed audio booths, where reporters will lay their package audio tracks. A few paces to the east takes one into the archives, a room of moveable shelves on which are stacked labeled videotapes. A few more steps down the hallway, one finds a dimly lit room appointed with computers, monitors and sophisticated-looking controls at each of several work stations. Here, graphics artists will develop the graphics that will give visual support to the stories.

This is the control center of WFAA-TV's news operation, a workplace where the lights burn 24 hours a day. We're going to enter this realm to give you a sense of what life is like for a producer, a reporter and some of the news managers who supervise them.

Wednesday: The Day Begins

Jack Beavers arrives at WFAA's newsroom at 8:19 and immediately goes to the assignments desk to double-check potential stories for that day. The overnight crew, which reported at 10:30 the night before, has just left for the day, and the morning crew has been in since 3:00 a.m. All have been involved in gathering and assembling news for the morning and noon newscasts.

As managing editor, Jack is in charge of coverage, overseeing stories being worked that day, communicating with partnered news organizations about current and upcoming stories, and planning for WFAA's stories for the days ahead. Jack must ensure no stories are missed and that the people and equipment needed to cover those stories are available. Jack's day usually ends about 7:30 in the evening, which is when he's finished setting the next day's lineup. Three assignments editors, half a dozen desk assistants, and a few others report to Jack. These are the people charged with assigning crews to cover stories in the field, checking status on stories and working the phones and radios to stay on top of what's happening around the area. In the seventh-largest market, there's a lot to keep up with.

By 8:55, Jack has scanned the day's lineup and checked to see which reporters and photographers are working. He moves to the large conference table at the north end of the newsroom and begins to set up the storyboard for the morning meeting at 9:00. The morning meeting involves a brief discussion of the previous night's newscasts if it's warranted, and discussion of potential stories for that day's shows. The stories will be assigned to reporters during the meeting, with news director David Duitch making the final determination. As people begin to wander over, Jack is writing down the names of reporters working that day and consulting his list of potential stories each reporter has pitched. He'll fill in the stories once they've been decided in the meeting.

Within five minutes, people are assembled: the news director, assistant news director Connie Howard, all of the newsroom's dayside executive producers, the promotions director, photographers, reporters and the video coordinator. Typically, the Five (5 p.m. newscast) and Six (6 p.m. newscast) producers would be at this meeting, but the station is being careful with overtime following an enormous investment into covering the Iraqi war. The producers will be in by 9:30 and will go over the discussion with the assistant news director.

On one side of the table, two computer flat screens with keyboards stand ready. This enables anyone to access files and rundowns on today's stories as well as any other information pertinent to the meeting. In the center of the table lies a speakerphone bridge through which they'll include WFAA's bureaus in Fort Worth/Tarrant County, Collin County (a heavily populated suburban area north of Dallas), and Austin (the state's capital). All the bureaus link in by speakerphone, and the meeting begins.

What follows is a round-robin discussion of stories that reporters, photographers (yes, photographers develop story ideas, too), assignment editors and managers (and, typically, producers) think are worth covering or need to be followed. They begin by discussing a shooting that occurred the day before at a Fort Worth shopping mall. If it was a domestic shooting, news director David Duitch is shying away from assigning a package. Fort Worth will check. David then expresses concern over how the story was handled on the previous night's Ten, specifically the shots showing the victim's body bag and the dead woman's crying mother. In David's opinion, it was invasive. It showed the body bag too long, and he was uncomfortable with the long nats shot of the mother weeping just after she learned of her daughter's death. All acknowledge the concern.

Several other stories are discussed, including a story on a layoff at DFW airport while they're going ahead with construction on a new terminal.

A story held from last night to cover the mall shooting is available.

Collin County's reporter discusses an upscale mall trying to appeal more to middle- and upper-middle-class shoppers by a marketing campaign designed to change its image.

In-house, a reporter discusses another breaking story from the day before on daycare workers leaving a two-year-old boy in a van. The boy died of heat stroke, and the workers have been charged with injury to a child. People around the table discuss other incidents of kids left in cars and whether it might be worth developing a related topical story or sidebar about the problem.

Executive Producer of Special Projects Nann Goplerud arrives and joins the meeting. Reporter Brad Hawkins pitches one story on the Dallas Symphony Orchestra's fundraising attempts and another on bad roads in Dallas. They tentatively decide on the orchestra story. The reporter leaves to set it up.

A reporter discusses a possible update on a drug bust some months earlier by a handful of Dallas police detectives. Not only had the officers set up innocent people to arrest, but the drugs they planted weren't even real drugs. They decide on another story for now.

Reporter Brad Watson pitches several education stories, one on problem buildings in schools, one on President Bush wanting to cut after-school programs at community centers. Either one will take some setup time, and a discussion ensues over whether Brad can be spared for the day. David says yes because they have two network packages coming in. Brad leaves to get to work on the story.

Other reporters and photographers offer story ideas, and decisions are made on which to cover and by whom. Reporter Gary Reaves offers two stories left from his Jerusalem trip that he can build by tomorrow evening. David calls to see whether they're already promoting another story Reaves is working on. They are, so Reaves will complete that story first, then turn to the other two.

Nicole Block, the dayside assignments editor, offers stories on Sammy Sosa's corked bat and on an off-duty Dallas County sheriff's officer shooting a man after an argument over the man's parking in a handicapped parking spot. Was the motorist armed? If not, it changes the complexion and approach to the story. They'll get more information from the desk this morning, but they're leaning toward covering it. The problem now, however, is that every reporter is assigned. Nicole asks whether Hawkins is married to the symphony story. After more discussion on the cop shooting story, they decide to cover it and shoot for a package. After some debate, they pull Watson from his education story. The Sosa story they decide to give to sports.

Jack Beavers has been noting each story assignment on the board. He will now enter it all into the computer, and the assignments desk will take over the task of overseeing the logistics. His role in the morning meeting ends today at 9:37. Beavers will now turn to other issues involved in setting up coverage, broken up by various news managers meetings he must attend throughout the day and into the evening.

David Duitch moves to his office, looking ahead to the tasks involved in running a major-market news operation. He is ultimately responsible for WFAA's on-air news product, which means he must be kept abreast of every issue in the newsroom. He is also responsible for the financial aspects of the newsroom and serves as liaison between the news department and the rest of the station.

Nann Goplerud moves to her office to continue her day. During the morning, Nann will look over upcoming projects and return e-mails and phone calls. She'll attend the afternoon meeting at 2:00, and from 3:00 on will approve reporter's package scripts. This will be punctuated by a 4:00 news managers' meeting to discuss the next day's stories, gathering with other managers to watch and critique the Five and Six newscasts, and ending the day with a meeting to discuss coverage the following day.

After the morning meeting, Connie will stay on to discuss the day's story lineup with the Five and Six producers. She'll play a more hands-on role throughout the day, making decisions on how stories should be covered and how newscasts should be arranged and approving all copy written by producers and writers. Like Nann, David, Jack and other key personnel, she will also attend the news managers' meetings throughout the day. At the moment, though, she's working with the producers to figure out what the evening newscasts are going to look like.

Now we turn to each of the two key positions responsible for developing content—the writing—for each day's newscast.

Wednesday: A Producer's View

Toward the morning meeting's end, the reporters and photographers have mostly gone, the managers are still there, and the Five and Six producers have arrived. The producers and the assistant news director begin to "run the list," or go over what stories are available for the evening's newscasts. They discuss which stories to "slate" or "place" (include in a newscast's lineup) and negotiate the "split." WFAA tries to use different stories where possible for the Five and the Six to give each newscast something different to offer. The split refers to which stories are parceled out to one show or the other. Numerous factors go into this decision, including the news of the day (some stories may need to run in both), the demographic makeup of a newscast audience (looking at the perceived interests of that audience), and how promotable certain stories might be to a given audience, to name three concerns.

By 10 a.m., the Six producer Katharyn DeVille is at her desk. Like many others, DeVille's desk is home to a computer, two televisions, an assortment of reference books, and printouts she'll need to consult for today's work. She begins to fill in a tentative rundown with the stories she'll run on her show. She builds from a skeleton, a template that already has the news blocks and scheduled commercial breaks built in.

She briefly checks the log from the traffic department. This department is in charge of "trafficking" the programming, which means slating what programming and commercials go where. Katharyn needs to find out how much commercial time has been sold for her newscast so she knows exactly how much time she has available for news. Not counting sports (about three minutes most days), weather (about three minutes), and time set aside for the newscast's open, close, teases (vignettes running just before a commercial break that promote stories later in the newscast), stingers (also known as bumpers, which are teases appearing during the commercial break) and transitions, she normally has 12 minutes for news. However, today the sales department has "oversold the show," meaning it has sold more than the typical amount of commercial time. This is good for the station's bottom line, but it means Katharyn has only a 10 1/2-minute "news hole" available. She'll have to slate fewer stories than normal or keep the stories shorter, or both. She'll figure that out as she goes.

As she's building her show, she stays aware of certain "kill points" through the newscast. These are points at which she must act if she sees her show is "heavy," meaning it's running long. This can happen even with the best planning.

Certain elements can run longer than expected and things can go wrong, all of which eats up precious seconds during the show. Katharyn builds in certain pad elements at those kill points that she can drop if the show is looking heavy. Transition cross-talk from news to sports or weather as well as the "goodbye" at the end of the newscast are good places to trim. Teases and stingers can be sacrificed during the show to cut time if absolutely necessary, but most producers are loath to cut there (and most news managers agree with that perspective)—teases constitute the key promotional tool for a producer's own newscast and, thus, are considered sacred. If need be, a producer can drop a story during the show, but that also makes producers queasy—and it's extremely problematic if the killed story is one that's been teased earlier in the newscast.

Before filling in the rundown on her computer, Katharyn scans various wires to see whether there's anything else interesting or important that she should include. She'll do this periodically throughout the day until she leaves her desk to produce the newscast itself. Katharyn's six o'clock newscast will carry primarily local and regional news, unlike the Five and Ten shows, which will carry more national and international stories in the mix. As she builds her show and scans wires, she'll be looking for stories with more local appeal. On this day, for example, Martha Stewart is indicted. It's a national story. With the limited time she has available, Katharyn won't slate the story for her show, but the Five and Ten producers will. Katharyn will also check to see what ABC's World News Tonight will be running. She might be able to tie in one of her stories to the network's newscast, which would make for a better transition from one show to another.

Throughout the day, Katharyn will also discuss story status with those reporters and writers filing stories for her show. At 10:42 this day, reporter Brad Watson stops by her desk to tell her he's not certain how his story on the cop shooting will turn out. He doesn't know what visuals will be available, whether the story will be a package or a vosot, or if management will even decide to run it. News managers, producers and reporters are constantly keeping each other apprised of the latest developments and decide together what direction the story should take, what format the story should take and, sometimes, whether it should be covered at all.

At 10:49, Brad Hawkins appears at Katharyn's desk to discuss what's available for his story on the symphony orchestra. He offers a live tag to the story, which sounds appealing to Katharyn, so she agrees and notes it on her rundown. Every element has to be specified in the rundown—what it is, what the format is, how long each element runs, and so forth. Any and all information needed by anyone involved in the show has to be spelled out.

Katharyn turns to her rundown and begins entering information. WFAA-TV uses a computer program called iNews, developed by Avid. With this program, as with any other news program, the rundown looks like a spreadsheet. Column headings along the top give critical information about each of the story elements, each of which is listed in the rows going down the page. Katharyn is most concerned with the first two blocks of the newscast, which are designated for news.

She begins to fill in her show with the stories she's planning on using. Throughout the day, she will adjust her rundown depending on how the stories develop. If something is discovered about a story that makes it more newsworthy, she may move it higher in the rundown to place it closer to the beginning of the show. Because everything is still fluid at this point in the day, no page numbers are assigned to the stories. The order may change, and it often does, several times before the show airs.

The computerized system affords certain advantages to the producers. As stories are edited and filed by the writers and reporters, those stories will be placed on the system's on-air server and attached to the corresponding story slug cell in the producer's rundown. This way, once a story is filed, Katharyn can simply click on the slug cell of a story row and see the story itself. In addition, at WFAA, all video, whether shot by an in-house photographer or taken from a satellite feed, is digitized and downloaded into a separate server called the daily server. This system enables Katharyn to view and listen to any raw (unedited) or edited video available and check times on the stories. And she can do it all from her desk.

A note comes in to Katharyn through her computer. Reporters and producers can communicate with each other by sending text messages among computers and pagers. The note's not good. The story on layoffs at DFW airport is falling through. She sends a message back to see whether a package can still be salvaged, perhaps with a live tag from the reporter to make up for the lack of video. Katharyn still needs more stories for her show. Also, she's slated the story on the cop shooting toward the bottom of her A block (called the 10-block at WFAA), but she doesn't want to end the block that way. She looks over a story on the Dallas mayor losing a bet with the mayor of San Antonio. The Spurs beat the Mavericks in the NBA playoffs, so a Spurs flag now has to fly over Dallas' city hall. Not a bad story to end a segment on, but Katharyn thinks it would work better as a segue to sports. She looks over a few other possibilities.

She wants to follow up on the death of the two-year-old boy left in a van at a daycare center. She led her newscast with it the day before, but nothing new so far has developed in the story. She knows that both this story and the cop shooting story are "fishing expeditions"—neither one is a certainty.

Katharyn keeps searching the wires and feeds for other story possibilities. It's 11:36 a.m. She begins to turn to potential graphics for her newscast, both full-screen graphics and over-the-shoulder boxes. Katharyn will decide on what she wants, then look to see whether something already exists that might serve. If not, she'll file an order with the graphics department, giving detailed instructions on what she'd like to see. If a frame of video can be lifted from videotape and used for a graphic, she'll include the location of that video in her instructions. Once she decides on the graphic, she'll give a number and title to the graphic so it can be called up later during the show. She'll actually file the request during the early afternoon as a compiled "box list" once her lineup is more set.

She finds a story on an indicted police officer who's suspected of using union funds to put a down payment on a pickup truck. She likes the story and decides to end her first block with it. It's lighter than but related to the cop shooting story. She'll look for a picture of the officer to use as a box.

Katharyn says it's important for a producer to think graphically, looking for ways to help tell the story visually. Katharyn originally pursued a career in reporting, working as an associate producer at the same time. Because of her producing skills, her news director at the time pushed her toward producing full time, and she found she enjoyed it. "I like being the puzzle master, taking all the pieces and putting them together. I like the writing. And I like the flow of the stories, coming up with the transitions and connecting the stories together. For me, this job puts it all together."

She sees a text message on her computer. The daycare death story looks like it's coming through, so she moves it up in her newscast. The phone rings. A reporter is covering a story on Collin County's police department's position on continuing to use the Ford Crown Victoria as a squad car. Several cars' gas tanks have exploded on impact, often killing or injuring the officers inside, and Dallas is canceling their use of the Crown Vic. But Collin County is not looking at giving them up yet. Katharyn searches for previous scripts, puts in a request for file tape, and sends those scripts to the reporter in the Collin County bureau.

Katharyn is trying to wrap up as many loose ends as possible, knowing that everything can change in an instant. She plans to finalize her rundown by 1:45, in time for the 2 p.m. meeting. However, a story on Dallas water rates is dragging on. Discussion on the issue in city council still has not started, and the reporter's unsure of when the council will take it up. She knows if the assignments desk folks run across any potential stories, they'll send her a message, but she sees nothing so far she finds appealing.

Later in the day, she'll also have to deal with the WFAA Web site. She will send the Web editor what stories from the Six she'd like the Web site to tease. Also, the Web editor will be rewriting stories from WFAA for the Web site, so Katharyn will check to see which of those Web stories she'll have her anchors tease with the phrase, "For more information on this story, go on-line to wfaa.com."

Two to three writers are available to write for the Five and the Six, but Katharyn prefers to write her stories herself, if she has time. At 1:11, she's on the phone with Brad Watson. The shooting apparently was provoked by the man in the car, who wrestled pepper spray away from the cop and sprayed him. The man gunned his engine and the cop thought he was in danger and fired his gun. If the man had been unarmed and been shot simply for arguing with the cop, that would have warranted a major story. Given the circumstances, however—the guy assaulted the cop and posed a threat—Katharyn and Brad decide the story should be a vosot.

Katharyn talks with the sports producer to verify sports stories for possible transitions and teases, then continues scanning other stories for possible inclusion in her show. It's 1:47. Katharyn is satisfied with her lineup and prepares for the 2 p.m. meeting.

At 2:00, the producers for the Five, Six and Ten, all news managers (news director, three executive producers, assistant news director, managing editor, nightside assignments editor, newscast director and video coordinator), the promotions director and the nightside reporters and photographers who have just come in assemble, along with a phone bridge that brings in the other bureaus. David begins the meeting with another caution on the showing of the body bag and the bereaved mother on the previous night Ten newscast. All agree greater sensitivity should be shown. The Five and Six producers go through their latest rundowns with a brief description of each story. The reporters give status on potential stories that would likely air on the Ten.

Katharyn is concerned with the status of the childcare death story. There are still questions over whether the owner and employee involved will surrender and when. Reporter Don Wall is waiting at the Lancaster police department, where it occurred. Rather than have Don shoot a standup that could "go stale" if the two women turn themselves in, they'll send a live truck so that Don can give the story a live tag with the latest.

At 2:31, Katharyn, back at her desk, learns the Dallas water rates story is doubtful. The council still has not gotten to it. She drops the live shot planned for the story. Plus, the story on the shooting at a Fort Worth shopping mall has no sound (meaning, no sots). Katharyn discusses the situation with news director David Duitch, who wants her to drop it. Now she needs another story and goes searching again. She sees a story on the hold list for the Ten that she likes, and the Ten producer lets her have it. Katharyn adds it to her lineup and also learns she will have the story on the layoffs at DFW airport after all. She slates it in.

Katharyn adjusts her lineup one more time, then decides which stories will be teased and where and begins writing the teases. She double-checks the times on the various stories. The computer program keeps a count of the story times she's entered and tells her she's actually a bit heavy. She's not concerned—yet. Not all the stories are edited, which means the estimated times can change. Plus, she can find places to trim if necessary.

At 2:54, she will set a space on the on-air server for every story with video. Her rundown will let her know the status of each story. Right now, the word "unavailable" appears in the "Status" column next to most of them. The "unavailables" will be replaced with story information as they are finished, filed and attached to her lineup.

At 2:58, Katharyn begins to build her box list, looking for visuals she'll need for her graphics. It's now that she will place her requests to the graphics department. The phone rings, and it's reporter Don Wall discussing how the story will be formatted. He wants the anchor to pitch to Don live in the field. Don will pick up the story, then cue a vosot. Don will keep talking over the vo portion, then cue the sot, which will then wipe to a package Don is working on. At the end of the package, Don will pick up with a live tag, then toss back to the anchors. Katharyn notes this, knowing she will need all of the roll cues when Don has them ready.

Five minutes later, Don lets her know some information has changed. He will have to drop a line from his package voice tracks.

Katharyn returns to her boxes. Once each one is set, she attaches it to the corresponding script embedded in her rundown. She assigns a number to each new box to be built and submits that number with the request to the graphics department. The request comes in the form of a detailed memo explaining the visual effect that she wants.

She then turns to her supers (superimposed titling at screen's bottom), which, like the boxes, will be attached to the corresponding scripts. Any super information that appears must be entered by the story's writer. For each of her stories, teases, transitions and the like, she sets up "shells," dummy pages into which the script copy will be placed.

At 3:43, Katharyn is still waiting on several elements and has a few extra minutes. She begins writing one of the stories for her newscast, a vo, then realizes she needs another box. She quickly files the request, then returns to finish the story, referring to wire copy for background.

Three minutes later, word comes in that the Dallas city council is now discussing the water rates story. She may have it for her show after all. She finishes the story she's writing, then turns to assigning which anchors will read what stories. She has already decided the look of each shot for each story in her show: whether one anchor is on camera or both, whether a single anchor will have a box, whether the anchor toss to a live reporter will be in a double box, and so on. This information is typed into a set column beside the corresponding show element. Typically, if one anchor takes the lead story one night, Katharyn will assign the other to read the lead story the next night. Also, the anchor who does not lead the newscast will generally lead the second block. As she is filling in her rundown, she refers to her completed scripts and dummy pages, marking each director's cue in the left column of the script (roll cues, supers, etc.) with an asterisk. This will shift that cue into a special director's column that does not show up on the TelePrompter, keeping the anchors' prompter scripts uncluttered. With a few minutes to spare, she reads a story she had assigned to one of her writers and makes a few changes.

She then turns to the Five rundown. Part of her job as the Six producer is filling in teases for her newscast that the anchors will give at the end of the Five. She goes with the DFW layoffs, the daycare death folo (follow-up story), and the Crown Vic stories. Don Wall calls with roll cue information. The producer and director will need to know when to roll the vo, when to roll the sound bite, the outcue of the sound bite that will cue them to roll the package and the outcue of the package to cue them to return to Don live on camera. Katharyn enters it all into her computer.

Katharyn begins to see that stories are being completed, and the actual times are close to the estimated times. She may have to drop the cop ndicted story. However, she sees that two packages are coming in well under time, saving her 30 seconds.

Assistant news director Connie Howard recommends a change in Katharyn's lineup. Katharyn notes it, then sees that this could cause a problem with the anchor flow. She makes another adjustment, then reassigns the anchors. A message comes in from Graphics. They can't find a frame of video she's called for. She locates it, memos them back, then turns to writing her remaining teases. It's 4:44, one hour and 16 minutes from air.

Katharyn begins reading through "interior" or "verbatim" scripts—those written for the reporters' packages. This gives her a better idea of the stories themselves. She may also adjust the anchor intros written by reporters to flow better from one story to the next. At this point, she's trying to tie up all loose ends. As scripts are completed, they'll go through Connie or Nann for approval. Once approved, it's noted in that producer's rundown. Also, Katharyn is trying to nail down final times on edited pieces. She makes a note of the stories and times she's still missing. Twelve stories are not yet edited, and it's 5:25—35 minutes before air.

As times come in, the computer readjusts. Katharyn also prefers quickly adding up times by hand. At this point, her show still looks heavy by about 30 seconds. She begins to note mentally those padded elements—teases, stingers, and so on— she will likely trim should she have to. With each element, she can pick up five to eight seconds, and she may have to decide what to trim on the fly—while the newscast is actually underway.

At 5:32, two more stories come in. Katharyn is now going over anchor intros and reviewing her rundown. A minute later, two more stories change to "Ready" status in her rundown. With each completed story, Katharyn replaces the estimated time with the exact time, which continues to shift the time situation for the newscast. By 5:39, all stories are complete and all times are in. Katharyn gives one last scan of the wires to make certain she hasn't missed anything, then contacts a member of the technical staff to find out remote and IFB assignments.

All live shots are brought into the station via a microwave link, either from one of the station's local live trucks or from a satellite source. A station as large as WFAA can handle as many as 22 remotes at the same time, including nine live shots the station's own trucks can carry. Each incoming signal is routed to a numbered line, which will then appear on one of the screens mounted in the control booth from which the newscast is directed. Once in the booth for the newscast, the producer and director will verify which routing line carries which live signal. When it's time for that particular live shot, the director will call for that routing line to be put on the air.

In addition, someone in the director's booth must be able to communicate with the reporter and videographer in the field. They do this through a system called interruptible feedback, or IFB. This system allows the people in the field to hear what's going out over the air through their earpieces. This way, the reporter can talk with the anchor, hear the stories and listen for cues. The IFB system also enables people in the booth to "interrupt" that "feedback" to speak directly to the reporter or videographer, and do so without that communication going over the air. The IFB communication links are also routed to the booth over a numbered line. The producer and director will need to know the remote number and the IFB number before the show hits air.

By 5:54, Katharyn is in the control booth with the rest of the newscast crew. In front of her is a computer, through which she'll monitor her rundown throughout the newscast. She dons a headset. Sitting to her right is the director, whose station also has a computer screen. He also wears a headset. The director has printed out all script pages for the show and has marked them up—noted camera changes, effects, supers and so on—and laid them in a neat stack in front of him. To his right sits the assistant director. In front of the AD is an intimidating array of switches, knobs, levers and row upon row of lighted buttons. Behind the director is the associate producer, who handles live traffic, meaning she is the one who will communicate with the reporters and videographers doing the live shots and with the engineers monitoring them. Farther to the right, behind a glassed-in booth, is the audio technician, who ensures the correct sound is coming into the newscast and at the correct volume levels. The board at which she sits is an enormous series of sliders, switches, buttons and meters. Laid out across the front wall of the main control room a few feet away from the producer, director and AD is a series of 87 television monitors—one set of 16 for the producer and the remainder for the director and assistant director—each labeled with a color-coded LED display beneath. In the center, in prominent display, are two clocks—one digital, the other analog.

Katharyn goes over graphics with the assistant director and sees that she is still missing one, and another has a misspelling. The graphics department is notified and begins to make the correction. These two new graphics come a few minutes into the show, so no one is too concerned. The show begins, and Katharyn follows her rundown on the computer screen in front of her.

As the newscast progresses, Katharyn moves her cursor down each element in her show. Beside each element is the "Backtime," which tells her exactly what time the clock on the wall must show at the start of that given element. This way, she can gauge whether her show is on time, running short, or running long. The computer also follows along, letting her know how heavy or light the show is running as of that element. Toward the end of the first block, the computer tells her she's heavy, and she verifies this through a quick mental check of the times. The last story coming into the commercial break—a reporter's package—has an anchor tag. While the package runs, Katharyn calls to drop the tag into the break. Without hesitation, the director calmly states "kill the tag into break," which is then communicated to the anchors by the floor director in the studio. The anchors return on camera and toss immediately to the break. No one viewing the newscast at home would know that it hadn't been planned exactly that way.

But the show is still showing heavy. Katharyn calls to kill the "stinger" tease slated to run during the break, and the crew responds without missing a beat. The second block continues, the live shots go well, but time is still extremely tight. Katharyn calls "straight toss to weather," which means no transition cross talk among the anchors. At this point, even an extra five seconds could create a problem. The word goes out to the anchors on the set, and they move quickly to weather, but coming into the break after weather, the show is still a few seconds heavy. Katharyn has a bit of pad time in the goodbye, and tonight she'll need it. During the break, the sports producer comes in to run the sports segment. He will sit where the associate producer sat earlier. Katharyn lets him know that sports has exactly 2:45, because the show has only 3:00 total after the break. The sports producer assures her that's not a problem.

And it's not. As the sports segment is wrapping up, there are :30 left in the newscast. The director calls "dead roll bed." This means the closing music (music bed), which lasts 30 seconds, is rolling, but with the volume at zero. This enables the director to call for the volume to come up at the appropriate time as the show is closing, with the assurance that the music will sting (a crescendo-like conclusion to the music) when the newscast does. The sports anchor wraps up and "quick tosses" to the anchors, who thank the audience and say goodnight as the music is coming up, followed by the closing visuals for the newscast. The show ends exactly on time.

Katharyn says "nice work, thanks," then heads back to the newsroom. The show is in the archives. She and the news managers will spend the next 10 minutes or so discussing and critiquing the newscast. Katharyn believes this one went fairly well. Katharyn will leave the station about 9 1/2 hours after arriving. Tomorrow morning, she will return to the station to begin again.

(You can see Katharyn DeVille's rundown in Figures 19.1a and 19.1b. You can see the script pages for her newscast in Figures 19.2a–g).

Thursday: A Reporter's Perspective

At 8:47, Brad Watson walks into the Channel 8 newsroom, drapes his overcoat over a wall to his desk cubicle, and logs onto his computer. Brad already has been working for hours. He begins each day at 5:30 a.m. with a cup of coffee and the Dallas Morning News, after which he fires up his home computer and goes online. Brad will read the Web sites of the New York Times, Washington Post and Fort Worth Star-Telegram. As a general assignments reporter, Brad has to have a broad sense of what's going on in the world and be able to cover any topic competently. He'll read stories to stay informed on what's affecting Dallas–Fort Worth, Texas, the nation and the world. He may need to draw from the information he gleans to cover a story he's assigned that day.

In addition to covering general assignments, Brad is also the education reporter at WFAA. So, once finished with the four newspapers listed above, Brad turns to state/legislative sections of the Houston Chronicle and the Austin American-Statesman. Austin is Texas' capital, and the American-Statesman covers the legislature essentially as local news. Many legislative decisions have a direct effect on the educational systems in Texas, so checking these sections is a must. Finally, Brad will log into Education Week's Web site to read a daily com-

6/4/03 17:22:13, USER Katharyn Deville   [WFAA]SHOW.SIX.RUNDOWN 1 SLUG
0:26 over

Page	Ancr	Story	From	By	Video/Format	Tape	Time	OK	*	P	Backtime
		NEWS 8 AT SIX	X6366	DeVille	WED 03.06.04		0:00				5:58:56
		macie/jeff/riba					0:00				5:58:56
		PRE-SHOW					0:00				5:58:56
6-PREA	macie	TZ: Daycare Folo 6p		kdev	vo/wipe		0:20	kdevil	*	P	5:58:56
6-PREB	jeff	TZ: TSA Layoffs 6p			vo/wipe		0:00				5:59:16
6-PREC	macie	TZ: Plano Crown Vics 6p			vo		0:00				5:59:16
--------	--------	_PRE-NEWS BREAK--					0:30		*		5:59:16
--------		-ID/News Open-----	hit:	00:16	DDR------		0:20				5:59:46
6-01	j/m	HELLO: Daycare 6p		hall	vo/2sh		0:20			x	5:59:40
		_					0:00				6:00:00
6-02	macie	PITCH WALL	U-50	dw/hall	box/map		0:15			x	6:00:00
6-02a	DON	Daycare Warrant 6p	2bfed	dw/hall	live/vo		0:30	kdevil	*	w	6:00:15
6-02b	DON	Snd Daycare Warrant 6p	2bfed	dw/hall	dissolve sot	0:10	0:00	kdevil	*	P	6:00:45
6-03	DON	Daycare Folo 6p	here	wall	WIPE/sovt	1:15	0:00	kdevil	*	P	6:00:55
6-04	DON	WALL PITCHBACK	U-50	wall	live tag/dbl		0:20	kdevil	*	w	6:02:10
6-05	macie	Tag: Daycare		kdev	1sh/webon		0:10	kdevil	*	w	6:02:30
		_					0:00				6:02:40
6-06	jeff	Deputy Shooting 6p	here	watson	box/map/vo		0:18	kdevil	*	P	6:02:40
6-06a	jeff	Snd Deputy Shooting 6p	here	watson	dissolve sot-vo	0:11	0:15	kdevil	*	P	6:02:58
		_					0:00				6:03:24
6-07	macie	Cop Indicted	gfx	kdev	box/still/cam tag		0:30	kdevil	*	w	6:03:24
		_					0:00				6:03:54
6-08	jeff	Collin Co Crown Vics 6p	frisco	sstoler	box/map/sovt	1:35	0:20	kdevil	*	P	6:03:54
6-08a	jeff	Tag: Collin Co Crown Vic	JEFF!!	sstoler	1sh		0:10	kdevil	*	w	6:05:49
		_					0:00				6:05:59
6-09	macie	TSA Layoffs 6p	fw	douglas	box/sovt	2:10	0:15	kdevil	*	P	6:05:59
6-09a	macie	Tag: TSA Layoffs		douglas	1sh		0:10	kdevil	*	w	6:08:24
		_					0:00				6:08:34
		_BUMPER #1			ACR-coming up --4		0:00				6:08:34
6-19a	j/m	TZ: DSO Fundraising 6p		kdev	vo/wipe		0:30	kdevil	*	P	6:08:34
6-19b		_TZ: Spurs Flag 6p			vo/wipe		0:00				6:09:04
6-19c		_TZ: Sports 6p	spx		vo		0:00				6:09:04
6-19d	TROY	TZ: WX TEASE			TROY IN WX CTR		0:10				6:09:04
--------	--------	_BREAK ONE---------	--------	--------	--------		2:10		*	P	6:09:14
6-21	----	Stinger #1	twrcam		ddr/towercam		0:05	kdevil	*	w	6:11:24
		_					0:00				6:11:29
6-22	jeff	Dallas Water 6p	here	hein	box/vo		0:20			x	6:11:29
6-22a	jeff	Snd Dallas Water 6p	here	hein	dissolve sot/cam tag		0:20			x	6:11:49
		_					0:00				6:12:09
N6-23	macie	DSO Fundraising 6p	here	hawkins	box/sovt	1:25	0:10	kdevil	*	w	6:12:09
6-23a	BH/ma	Live Tag: DSO $	U-51	hawkins	live tag/dbl		0:15			x	6:13:44
		_					0:00				6:13:59
6-29b	TROY	WEATHER TZ			STUDIO/TWRCAM		0:30	kdevil	*	w	6:13:59
--------	--------	_BREAK TWO--------					2:40		*		6:14:29
6-30	TROY	_WEATHER			WX CENTER		3:00	kdevil	*	w	6:17:09
6-30a	--------	_Weather Video	twrcam		LIVE		0:00				6:20:09
6-30b	--------	_Weather cg info			ACR		0:00				6:20:09
		_					0:00				6:20:09
6-31	macie	10tz:		rob	box/vo		0:15			x	6:20:09
6-32	jeff	10tz#2:		rob	wipe/vo		0:15			x	6:20:24
6-33	jeff	Spurs Flag 6p	here	hall	box/vo		0:17	kdevil	*	P	6:20:39
		_					0:00				6:20:56
		_sports tease			ddr/next/1		0:00				6:20:56
6-39a	3SHT	_PITCH TO RIBA			2SHOT/3SHOT		0:20	kdevil	*	w	6:20:56

FIGURE 19.1A

6/4/03 17:22:13, USER Katharyn Deville
0:26 over

[WFAA]SHOW.SIX.RUNDOWN 4 SLUG

Page	Ancr	Story	From	By	Video/Format	Tape	Time	OK	*	P	Backtime
6-39b	RIBA	_TZ: Sports II		sports	nats		0:00				6:21:16
====	====	BREAK THREE ====	====	====	===============		3:00				6:21:16
6-40	-------	Stinger #3	twrcam	---------	ddr / live		0:05	kdevil	*	w	6:24:16
40a	RIBA	SPORTS			video list		2:45				6:24:21
6S-01		sammy sosa 6p			vo'		0:00				6:27:06
6S-02		cork talk 6p			sot'		0:00				6:27:06
6S-03		finals 6p			LIVE - vo'		0:00				6:27:06
6S-04		nba talk 6p			sot - LIVE		0:00				6:27:06
6-63	2-SHT	_GOODNIGHT_____	d-roll	27:06	off 27:36		0:30	kdevil	*	w	6:27:06
		_NEWS CLOSE_____			ACR		0:00				6:27:36
----------		END BREAK-----------	--------	------	------------		2:24				6:27:36
		_					0:00				6:30:00
-------		------------------	-----	-----	-------------		0:00		-		
		breaking news-1 6PM					0:00				
		breaking news-2 6PM					0:00				
		breaking news-3 6PM					0:00				
		breaking news-4 6PM					0:00				
		sports-1 6PM					0:00				
		sports-2 6PM					0:00				
		sports-3 6PM					0:00				
		sports-4 6PM					0:00				

FIGURE 19.1B

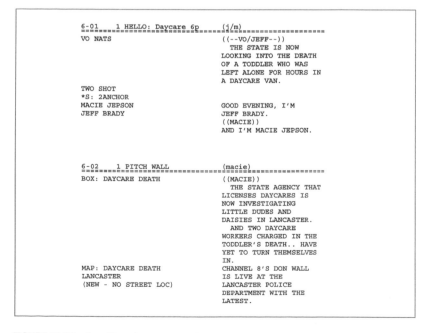

```
6-01   1 HELLO: Daycare 6p    (j/m)
============================================================
VO NATS                       ((--VO/JEFF--))
                                 THE STATE IS NOW
                              LOOKING INTO THE DEATH
                              OF A TODDLER WHO WAS
                              LEFT ALONE FOR HOURS IN
                              A DAYCARE VAN.
TWO SHOT
*S: 2ANCHOR
MACIE JEPSON                  GOOD EVENING, I'M
JEFF BRADY                    JEFF BRADY.
                              ((MACIE))
                              AND I'M MACIE JEPSON.


6-02   1 PITCH WALL           (macie)
============================================================
BOX: DAYCARE DEATH            ((MACIE))
                                 THE STATE AGENCY THAT
                              LICENSES DAYCARES IS
                              NOW INVESTIGATING
                              LITTLE DUDES AND
                              DAISIES IN LANCASTER.
                                 AND TWO DAYCARE
                              WORKERS CHARGED IN THE
                              TODDLER'S DEATH.. HAVE
                              YET TO TURN THEMSELVES
                              IN.
MAP: DAYCARE DEATH            CHANNEL 8'S DON WALL
LANCASTER                     IS LIVE AT THE
(NEW - NO STREET LOC)         LANCASTER POLICE
                              DEPARTMENT WITH THE
                              LATEST.
```

FIGURE 19.2A *(continues)*

```
6-PREA  1 TZ:  Daycare Folo      (macie)
==========================================================
TAKE VO
*S: PRESHOW                      ((MACIE))
NEXT AT 6:00
(WALL) #1 DAYCARE IN
HOLD - SHOW CENTER PLZ           NEXT ON NEWS 8 AT SIX:
                                 THE LANCASTER DAYCARE
                                 CENTER WHERE A TODDLER
                                 DIED.. IS NOW FACING A
                                 NEW INVESTIGATION.
                                 WE'RE LIVE WITH THE
                                 LATEST.
WIPE VO                          ((JEFF))
PLEASE PULL FROM
(DOUGLAS) TSA LAYOFFS            ALSO: LOCAL AIRPORT
                                 SECURITY WORKERS ARE
                                 LAID OFF.
WIPE VO                          ((MACIE))
BLAINE TO FEED FROM
FRISCO                           AND.. HEAR WHAT COLLIN
                                 COUNTY POLICE
                                 DEPARTMENTS ARE
                                 PLANNING TO KEEP THEIR
                                 OFFICERS SAFE IN SQUAD
                                 CARS.
ON CAM 2-SHOT                    ((JEFF))
                                 NEWS 8 AT SIX IS NEXT.



6-04    1 WALL PITCHBACK         (DON)
==========================================================
LIVE TAG: WALL
*S: LIVEON
*S: 8LIVE2
DON WALL
LANCASTER
*S: 8LIVE1
LANCASTER
*S: 8LIVE

                                 (WALL TAGS - TOSSES
                                 BACK IN DBL BOX)


*S: DBL
DAYCARE DEATH
WFAA-TV
LANCASTER
```

FIGURE 19.2A *(continued)*

```
6-05    1 Tag: Daycare           (macie)
==========================================================
1SHOT                            ((MACIE))
                                 THANKS DON..
*S: WEB1                         TO LEARN MORE ABOUT
HOT CAR DANGERS                  THE DANGERS OF HOT CARS
                                 AND PREVENTING
                                 INJURIES, LOG ONTO
                                 W-F-A-A DOT COM.
*S: WEB1
CHOOSING A DAYCARE
*S: WEB1                         YOU'LL ALSO FIND
NEWS LINKS                       INFORMATION ON CHOOSING
                                 A PROPER DAY-CARE
                                 PROVIDER. JUST CLICK ON
                                 NEWS LINKS.
```

FIGURE 19.2B *(continues)*

```
6-06    1 Deputy Shooting 6      (jeff)
================================================================
BOX: FATAL SHOOTING           ((JEFF))
                                    TONIGHT - THE DALLAS
                              SHERIFF'S DEPARTMENT
                              SAYS A DEPUTY WAS
                              JUSTIFIED IN KILLING A
                              CARROLLTON MAN LAST
                              NIGHT.
MAP: FATAL SHOOTING                THE SHOOTING HAPPENED
                              IN NORTHWEST DALLAS AT
                              A GROCERY STORE THAT
                              HIRED THE DEPUTY FOR
                              SECURITY.
NATS/VO
*S: LOC1                            INVESTIGATORS
DALLAS                        SAY THE MAN ATTACKED
                              THE DEPUTY AFTER THE
                              DEPUTY TOLD HIM TO MOVE
                              HIS TRUCK FROM A
                              HANDICAP PARKING SPACE.
WIPE SOT                          [---WIPE SOT---]



6-06a    1 Snd Deputy Shooti    (jeff)
================================================================
SOT SOUND FULL                [---SOT----]
WATSON TAPE @ 17.43.21
*S: SOT2                      <AS THE VEHICLE STARTED
SGT DON PERITZ                TO PULL AWAY AT THAT
DALLAS SHERIFF'S DEPT         POINT THE OFFICER FELT
                              HE WAS ABOUT TO BE
                              RUNOVER FELT HE HAD NO
                              OTHER OPTION STATED
                              THAT HE DREW HIS WEAPON
                              AND FIRED ONE TIME
                              STRIKING THE DECEDENT
                              IN THE HEAD KILLING HIM
                              AT THE SCENE.>
NATS CONT.                    [--VO
CASTILLO MUG                  CONTINUES/JEFF---]
                                  THE DEAD MAN IS
                              FRANCISCO CASTILLO.
                                HIS CRIMINAL RECORD
                              INCLUDED TWO
                              CONVICTIONS FOR BEATING
                              HIS WIFE AND AN ARREST
                              FOR COCAINE POSSESSION
                              WHEN HE THREATENED AN
                              OFFICER.
DEP WILLIAMS MUG                  DEPUTY ERNEST
                              WILLIAMS IS ON LEAVE
                              WHILE THE SHOOTING IS
                              INVESTIGATED.
                                  IT WILL BE REFERRED
                              TO A COUNTY GRAND JURY.



6-07    1 Cop Indicted          (macie)
================================================================
BOX: OFFICER INDICTED         ((MACIE))
(DPD BADGE)                   A 20-YEAR VETERAN OF
                              THE DALLAS POLICE
                              DEPARTMENT IS UNDER
                              FEDERAL INDICTMENT..
                              ACCUSED OF MISUSING
                              UNION MONEY.
                              SGT. RICK WILSON USED
                              TO BE TREASURER FOR THE
                              DALLAS POLICE
                              PATROLMAN'S UNION.
STILL: FEDERAL                THE INDICTMENT SAYS
INDICTMENT                    WILSON DIVERTED UNION
                              DUES FOR PERSONAL USE..
SGT RICK WILSON               AND CHARGED A
DALLAS POLICE                 $24-HUNDRED DOLLAR DOWN
                              PAYMENT FOR A NEW
ACCUSED OF                    PICKUP ON A UNION
> DIVERTING UNION DUES        CREDIT CARD.
> USING A UNION CREDIT        IF CONVICTED, SGT
CARD                          WILSON COULD GET UP TO
                              10 YEARS IN PRISON AND
                              A HEFTY FINE.
ON CAM                        WILSON IS NO LONGER
                              UNION TREASURER.. AND
                              HE'S BEEN ON
                              ADMINISTRATIVE LEAVE
                              FROM THE D-P-D SINCE
                              FEBRUARY OF 2002.
```

FIGURE 19.2B   *(continued)*

```
6-08    1 Collin Co Crown V    (jeff)
==================================================
BOX: SQUAD CAR SAFETY        ((JEFF))
(CROWN VIC)                      POLICE DEPARTMENTS
                             ACROSS NORTH TEXAS ARE
                             DECIDING WHETHER TO BUY
                             NEW FORD CROWN
                             VICTORIAS AS PATROL
                             CARS.
                                 CITY ATTORNEY
                             MADELEINE JOHNSON SAYS
                             DALLAS WON'T BUY ANY
                             UNTIL FORD MAKES THEM
                             SAFE FOR OFFICERS.
MAP: SQUAD CAR SAFETY            NOW.. POLICE IN
(PLANO & ALLEN)              PLANO SAY THEY'RE
                             TAKING A WAIT AND SEE
                             APPROACH, WHILE ALLEN'S
                             DEPARTMENT IS GIVING
                             THE CONTROVERSIAL CAR A
                             VOTE OF CONFIDENCE.
SOVT SOUND FULL              [------SOVT------]
*S: LOC1
ALLEN
*S: SOT2
ROBERT FLORES
ALLEN POLICE
*S: LOC1
PLANO
*S: SOT2
CHIEF GREG RUSHIN
PLANO POLICE
TRT:
OUT-Q: WHAT TO GET.




6-08a   1 Tag: Collin Co Cr    (jeff)
==================================================
1SHOT                        ((JEFF))
                                 POLICE IN MCKINNEY
                             ARE PLANNING TO BUY 11
                             NEW CROWN VICTORIAS.
                                 WHILE THEY BELIEVE
                             IT'S STILL THE BEST CAR
                             FOR THE JOB, THEY'LL
                             ALSO FINE TUNE THEIR
                             TRAINING PROGRAM TO
                             PREVENT REAR END
                             COLLISIONS AND PROTECT
                             THEIR OFFICERS.




6-09    1 TSA Layoffs 6p       (macie)
==================================================
BOX: TSA LAYOFFS             ((MACIE)) DOZENS OF
                             PASSENGER SCREENERS AT
                             DFW AIRPORT ARE TURNING
                             IN THEIR UNIFORMS THIS
                             WEEK AFTER BEING LAID
                             OFF.
                                 THE TRANSPORTATION
                             SECURITY ADMINISTRATION
                             IS CUTTING THOUSANDS OF
                             JOBS NATIONWIDE.
                                 BUT ONE LAID-OFF
                             SCREENER TELLS NEWS 8'S
                             JIM DOUGLAS OF ALLEGED
                             SECURITY LAPSES CAUSED
                             BY "UNDERSTAFFING."
SOVT SOUND FULL              [------SOVT------]
*S: LOC1
KELLER
00
*S: 8RPT
JIM DOUGLAS
JDOUGLAS
05
*S: SOT2
DAVID GOODSELL
FORMER AIRPORT SECURITY
SCREENER
20
*S: FILE
1:08
OUT: STANDARD
RUNS: 2:10
```

FIGURE 19.2C   *(continues)*

```
6-09a   1 Tag: TSA Layoffs      (macie)
=======================================================
1SHOT                           ((MACIE))
                                REPRESENTATIVES WITH
                                THE TSA SAY EMPLOYEES
                                WERE SELECTED FOR
                                LAYOFFS BASED ON JOB
                                PERFORMANCE.
                                    BUT THEY SAY THEY
                                CANNOT COMMENT ON
                                ALLEGED PROBLEMS THAT
                                WERE NEVER REPORTED OR
                                INVESTIGATED.
```

FIGURE 19.2C *(continued)*

```
6-19a   1 TZ:  DSO Fundrais     (j/m)
=======================================================
2SHOT-                          ((JEFF))
                                THE DALLAS SYMPHONY
                                ORCHESTRA HIT A SOUR
                                NOTE... TRYING RAISE
                                MONEY FOR ITS PROGRAM.

NATS (:02) - VO CONTINUES
*S: TEASE
DONATIONS DOWN
KD-- SYMPHONY                    (PAUSE FOR NATS :02)
PERFORMING SOT IS UNDER          NEXT ON NEWS 8.. WE'LL
"(HAWK) DSO$ HANDOUT"            TELL YOU WHY.. AND
AT TC ABOUT 15:00               WHAT'S HELPING GET THE
                                ORCHESTRA'S FINANCES
                                BACK IN TUNE.

NATS/VO
*S: TEASE                       ((MACIE))
SPURS TOWN?                      ALSO AHEAD.. NO YOU'RE
                                NOT SEEING THINGS..
                                WE'LL TELL YOU WHY THE
                                SAN ANTONIO SPURS FLAG
                                IS FLYING OVER DALLAS
                                CITY HALL.

NATS/VO
*S: TEASE                       ((JEFF))
CORK CONTROVERSY                 AND THE LATEST ON SAMMY
                                SOSA'S CORK
                                CONTROVERSY... LATER IN
                                SPORTS.


6-19a   2 TZ:  DSO Fundrais
WIPE WX CENTER
*S: TEASE                       (TROY TEASES WEATHER)
TROY'S FORECAST



6-21    1 Stinger #1            (----)
=======================================================
STINGER/TOWERCAM                (STINGER/TOWERCAM)



6-22    1 Dallas Water 6p       (jeff)
=======================================================
*S: 1ANCHOR
JEFF BRADY
BOX: WATER RATES                ((JEFF)) DALLAS CITY
(DALLAS)                        COUNCIL MEMBERS ARE
                                LEANING TOWARDS A HIKE
                                IN WATER RATES.

NATS/VO (USE WATER BROLL,
LEAK BROLL IN SERVER.)
*S: LOC1                            TODAY THE COUNCIL
DALLAS                          DISCUSSED A DALLAS
                                WATER UTILITIES
                                RECOMMENDATION FOR A
                                13-POINT-8 PERCENT
                                INCREASE.
                                    DALLAS HAS SOME OF
                                THE LOWEST RATES IN THE
                                COUNTRY, BUT OFFICIALS
                                SAY REPLACING AN AGING
                                PIPELINE SYSTEM AND
                                RISING COSTS MAKE A
                                BUMP IN PRICES
                                UNAVOIDABLE.
WIPE TO SOT
```

FIGURE 19.2D

```
6-22a   1 Snd Dallas Water      (jeff)
==================================================================
SOT SOUND FULL              [---SOT----]
*S: SOT2                    <WALNE: 4:36:09 I'M NOT
ALAN WALNE                  SURE THAT 13.8 PERCENT
DALLAS CITY COUNCIL         IS THE NUMBER THAT HAS
                            TO BE, OR WHATEVER. I
                            WILL TELL YOU THOUGH,
                            THE REALITY IS, WE'RE
                            GOING TO HAVE TO HAVE A
                            WATER RATE INCREASE. >

CAM TAG                     COUNCIL MEMBERS WILL
                            NOT DECIDE ON THE
                            AMOUNT OF THE INCREASE
                            UNTIL THEY SET THE CITY
                            BUDGET LATER THIS YEAR.




N6-23   1 DSO Fundraising 6      (macie)
==================================================================
BOX: DONATIONS DOWN         ((MACIE)) DONATIONS ARE
(DALLAS SYMPHONY)           DOWN ACROSS THE FINE
                            ARTS AND THOSE
                            ORGANIZATIONS ARE ALL
                            COMPETING WITH ONE
                            ANOTHER AGAINST THE
                            BUDGET CLOCK.
                              CHANNEL 8'S BRAD
                            HAWKINS REPORTS ON THE
                            FIGHT FOR FUNDING.
SOVT SOUND FULL             [------SOVT------]
*S: LOCDATE2
LONDON
FRIDAY
*S: SOT2
ANDREW LITTON
DSO MUSIC DIRECTOR
*S: SOT2
FRED BRONSTEIN
DALLAS SYMPHONY ORCHESTRA
PRES
*S: SOT2
JUDY CONNER
DALLAS MUSEUM OF ART
OUT: **NON STD** (MUSIC
ENDS, APPLAUSE)
TRT: XX:XX




6-23a   1 Live Tag: DSO $       (BH/ma)
==================================================================
LIVE: BRAD
*S: LIVEON
*S: 8LIVE2
BRAD HAWKINS
DALLAS
*S: 8LIVE1
DALLAS
*S: 8LIVE

                            (BRAD TAGS & TOSSES
                            BACK IN DOUBLE BOX)

DBL BOX
*S: DBL
DSO DONATIONS
WFAA-TV
DALLAS




6-29b   1 WEATHER TZ            (TROY)
==================================================================
TROY                        WEATHER TEASE
ON CAM
*S: WXTEASE
TROY'S WEATHER
```

FIGURE 19.2E

```
6-30   1  WEATHER              (TROY)
=================================================================
                             { TROY DOES WEATHER }




6-31   1 10tz:                (macie)
=================================================================
BOX: TONIGHT AT 10:00        ((MACIE))
                                 TONIGHT AT 10 -- THE
                             NEW HILLARY CLINTON
                             BOOK IS ALL THE TALK
                             TODAY... BUT THE EARLY
                             LEAK OF ITS CONTENTS
                             COULD BE COSTLY.
TAKE NATS                        PLUS -- SAMMY
*S: PROMO10                  SOSA'S CORKED BAT...
CORKED BAT CONTROVERSY       THE CONTROVERSY IS
                             SENDING RIPPLES THROUGH
                             MAJOR LEAGUE BASEBALL.
                                 AT 10 -- WHAT
                             ATHLETES HERE IN NORTH
                             TEXAS ARE SAYING ABOUT
                             IT.




6-32   1 10tz#2:             (jeff)
=================================================================
WIPE NATS--                  ((JEFF))
*S: PROMO10                      PLUS -- A LOOK AT A
HEART DISEASE DETECTION      NEW PROCEDURE THAT IS
                             HELPING SOME NORTH
                             TEXAS DOCTORS DETECT
                             HEART DISEASE SOONER
                             THAN EVER.
                                 JANET SAINT JAMES
                             WITH THE BREAKTHROUGH
                             TECHNOLOGY TONIGHT --
                             AFTER THE N-B-A
                             FINALS... ON THE NEWS 8
                             UPDATE AT 10.




6-33   1 Spurs Flag 6p       (jeff)
=================================================================
BOX= LOST BET                ((JEFF))
                                 THE MAYOR OF DALLAS HAD
                             TO PAY A LOST BET..
                             PUBLICLY TODAY.
NATS/VO
*S: LOC1                     FLYING HIGH IN FRONT OF
DALLAS                       CITY HALL, ... A FLAG
                             SPORTING THE LOGO OF
                             THE SAN ANTONIO SPURS!.
                                 THE MAVERICKS LOST TO
                             SAN ANTONIO IN THE
                             MAVS/SPURS SERIES.. AND
                             THIS IS HOW DALLAS HAD
                             TO PAY UP FOR TALKING
                             BIG.
SOURCE:
SPURS FLAG AT CITY HALL
02:08:06:26
```

FIGURE 19.2F

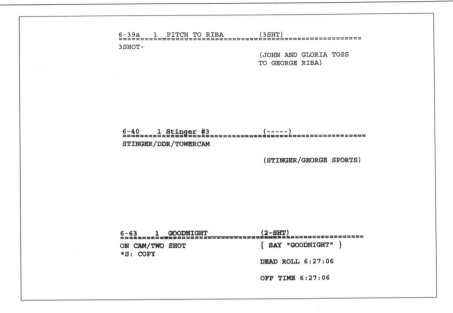

FIGURE 19.2G

pilation of education stories taken from major newspapers around the country. Daily preparation is critical to doing a competent job as a journalist.

Back in the newsroom, Brad has a couple of story ideas for packages, either of which he thinks he can turn (complete) today. After checking some on-line sources and jotting down some notes, he grabs his breakfast and heads to the morning meeting. About this time, the voice of Dayside Assignment Editor Nicole Block intones over the newsroom public address system, "It's nine o'clock, time for the meeting."

Managing Editor Jack Beavers is already at the white board by the conference table. One by one, newsroom workers move toward the conference table. The other bureaus have already linked into the speakerphone in the table's center.

The bureaus weigh in first, beginning with discussion of funding for an arts hall in McKinney, a Dallas–Fort Worth suburb. News director David Duitch gives preliminary approval to cover the story, then asks whether any of the bureaus have any "pacers"—stories to be read by anchors (readers, vos or vosots) that will add variety to the reporters' packages and break up, or "pace," the newscast. One possibility involves the Tarrant County health office placing mosquito traps to deal with the West Nile virus.

Other stories from bureaus are discussed, then the meeting turns in-house. Don Wall's story the previous day on the daycare death is ongoing. The workers at the daycare center have still not turned themselves in, and neither the police department involved nor the Dallas County sheriff's office knows when that will happen. They don't know who the accused women's attorneys are, so a discussion ensues over whether it's worthwhile to stake out some location in hopes of getting video of the women turning themselves in. Another issue involves the health of the women: one suffered a nervous collapse after the death, another suffered complications from a heart condition and had to enter the hospital for surgery.

Those around the table discuss whether it's worth doing another vignette on the problems with leaving kids in hot cars—several incidents have occurred recently, although none of the others resulted in death. Nann Goplerud mentions they've done two such features this year already. The discussion then turns to the bond set on the women. A justice of the peace signed the arrest warrants on the women, who were charged with injury to a child, a second-degree felony in Texas. The justice of the peace then set the bond at a million dollars apiece. Brad Watson states flatly that the bond is absurd and way out of line with the charge. The justice of the peace setting the bond, Luis Sepulveda, is a former political activist who has never practiced law and has no legal degree. Several wonder aloud what his motivation for the high bond is. The police involved said the two workers pose neither a flight risk nor a danger to the community.

Don Wall continues, pitching a story on invasive plants in a local lake and another story on contaminated well water in an outlying community. They'll come back to Wall.

Brett Shipp pitches the latest in the story on the Dallas police officers who planted fake drugs on people then busted them for drug possession and sales. Another possibility involves updating the move by Dallas police to end their use of Crown Victorias for squad cars, but the mayor is in Denver today. Perhaps they can talk with the city attorney if they need sound.

Other reporters in turn make pitches on stories. The table turns to Brad Watson. He generally covers education and has several possibilities, including a story on a charter school that may have to close, an issue that's come up in the voucher system, and summer school enrollments. Other story possibilities come in from various people. A story on a makeup artist who deals with cancer patients. A family that moved into a filthy, roach-infested apartment that was supposed to be cleaned and ready for move-in. A follow-up on the DFW airport layoffs. Any local tie-in to the Martha Stewart indictment?

David Duitch is shaking his head. He still doesn't see a solid lead story for the newscasts that evening, which is a problem. Perhaps the DFW airport layoffs will do, especially considering the airport is supposed to be one of the economic engines of the area.

Brad Watson then begins to pitch the million-dollar bond angle of the daycare death story as a possible piece. He repeats that the amount is absurd. "These women are not monsters, they're not criminals, they made a mistake. A bad one, but murderers get lower bonds than this. Parents of kids who die of heat in cars have been getting no-billed [a grand jury decides not to charge]." After more discussion, Brad is assigned to do the story. He'll call Sepulveda and see what he has to say. Brad will also try to track down a list of typical bonds set for various cases. Brad goes to his desk to see what he can do with the story. It is 9:32 a.m.

He consults the contacts list he has stored in his computer, then puts in a call to a public relations firm that helps set up reporters with attorneys. The firm understands that reporters typically need a quick turnaround time for getting information and on-camera interviews. Brad tells them he needs an attorney who can talk about what bond levels are appropriate for certain criminal charges. They'll check for him and get back. Brad hangs up, thinks for a second, then looks at his personal address book. "I'm going to cover my bets here," he mutters as he punches numbers in his phone. He's calling the office of Marcus Busch, a friend of his who is a former prosecutor and now works as a defense attorney. Brad tells him what he needs, then asks if he can help with an interview. Busch says yes, and Brad gets more background. What he needs is a list of recommended bond amounts for various charges, which he can get from the chief magistrate's office. Busch supplies the number. They set up the interview. It's now 10:02.

It turns out Busch knows the justice of the peace and had a case before him. The lawyer doesn't think too highly of him or his tactics and will have plenty to say. Brad will interview Busch, then possibly another lawyer, then Sepulveda, the justice of the peace who set the bond. At 10:06, Connie Howard, the assistant news director, comes up and says they have an unconfirmed report that the women have turned themselves in. Both Connie and Brad agree that when the women are formally arraigned—brought before a magistrate judge who will read the charges and set his or her own bond amount—the bond on both will be lowered substantially. Brad tells her where he is on the story, and asks if they have any video of the women turning themselves in. Connie says no, that Don Wall is on his way there now. Brad muses that he hates being late on a story. He and Connie discuss whether the story is worth pursuing today, given the fact that the bond will be lowered as soon as the women appear. They discuss holding the story as an issue story for another day and moving on to something else for now. Because it's summer, much of the reporting staff is gone on vacation, and the newsroom needs a story out of each reporter every day. Brad calls the attorney public relations firm and Busch to cancel the interviews. It is 10:11.

Brad shakes his head as he hangs up the phone. If the bond holds, they might still do the story today. Plus, it might be a day or two before the women are arraigned, in which case they'd sit in jail until the bond could be reset. He thinks for second, then declares, "There still may be legs to this story." He goes back to his contacts list, then pulls down a phone book. Before opening it, he goes on-line and scans today's related stories by the Dallas Morning News and the Fort Worth Star-Telegram. Brad calls the chief magistrate's office to get the bond guidelines. The magistrate is out until Monday, Brad's told, and no one else can talk to him. Brad hangs up. "Go around," he mutters, thinking of who else might have the information he needs, "figure out how to go around." Brad's also frustrated they don't have shots of the women turning themselves in. "We're hurting for video there," he says. He flips through the phone book and finds the court of a judge he knows personally. "This judge is a good source," he says, "pretty friendly people. Sometimes the approach you need is like moving water—traveling the path of least resistance." Brad's told he should talk with the presiding district judge, and gets the number. Brad makes the call, is told the presiding judge is out, but they can supply a copy of the bond guidelines. Brad gives them the station's fax number. The time is 10:29.

Brad verifies the level of the charge. It is a second-degree felony, which he notes. This will be important to the story. Brad checks one of the monitors overhead when he sees a competing station running a story on the deaths. He sees no video of the women surrendering on the competition and is somewhat relieved. "I hate it when we're not ahead of the story."

Brad walks to the assignments desk to discuss the surrender with Nicole, the dayside assignments editor, and Connie, the assistant news director, asking whether they know who the women's attorney is. At that moment, the desk gets word from the field that the early reports were wrong—the women have not surrendered. They also learn that the women can turn themselves in anywhere in the state, so staking out any location would be fruitless. However, there's a call in to the public information officer at the sheriff's department. He'll check to see who the women's attorney is and will let the newsroom know once they've surrendered. The sheriff's office will do what it can to let a crew get tape of the women being transferred to the county lockup or the magistrate.

The story may be worth pursuing yet. The challenge is how to track down needed information and cobble together some visuals and sound to tell the story. Brad also won't sit back and wait on the sheriff's department to supply the name of the women's attorney. He knows that, all too often, the reporter who complacently relies on one source to supply certain information winds up learning that information as it is broadcast on the competition's newscast. To stay on top, one has to be proactive.

Brad is perplexed and thinking. The police have shown they're patient and will wait for the women to bring themselves in, especially considering the health issues involved. Brad's trying to decide how to approach the story, how to get information and visuals. If he can track down the family of one of the women, perhaps he can get the name of the attorney, who might share when and where they'll surrender. No one in the newsroom has any leads. He begins to brainstorm, thinking out loud. "This is a needle in a haystack." He looks blankly at the wall, nodding. "Prominent Black attorneys . . . if I'm not well off financially, and I'm an African-American woman on the south side of Dallas, and I'm in serious trouble, and this is a high-profile case . . . what attorney do I call?" Brad names a few major Black attorneys located in South Dallas, opens the phone book and looks up the number of the first attorney he named, State Senator Royce West. West isn't in, so Brad asks he return his call, leaves a number, and hangs up.

WFAA is connected with the Dallas Morning News (both are owned by Belo). Brad calls the Morning News reporter covering the story to see whether he knows the attorney's name. He doesn't, but Brad and he share some ideas and questions together and discuss Brad's angle on the million-dollar bond.

It's 11:13. Brad reads the Morning News story once again, then goes to earlier versions WFAA has done on the story. He's searching for anything that might jog an idea that might lead him to the information he needs or another angle he might pursue.

Nicole Block, the dayside assignments editor, calls across the newsroom to Brad. She's gotten a hold of the brother of one of the women. He says they're meeting with their attorneys and may not surrender today. Brad believes his story is now definitely worth pursuing and convinces Connie he should go with it. She agrees. The story is back on.

Brad tries to set up a photographer and knows he needs to put in a call back to Marcus Busch, the defense lawyer friend he'd cancelled with earlier. Before he has a chance, Brad's phone rings, and it's the sheriff's public information officer saying there's no word on the surrender yet and he doesn't know who the attorney is. One of the newsroom's field producers, P.J. Ward, stops by to discuss the story, and they fill each other in.

Brad's still awaiting the fax on the recommended bond levels from the judge's office. He calls Justice of the Peace Luis Sepulveda to set up an interview. While Brad is on hold, Nicole calls from the desk to say she now has the name of the women's attorney. It's not the high-powered South Dallas attorney he tried to call earlier, but a man named Craig Watkins. Brad nods to her just as Sepulveda gets on the line. Brad is pleasant and tells him simply that he'd like to come out and talk about bonds in serious cases such as this. Sepulveda tells him he'd be happy to talk, and they set the time. Brad then calls the Morning News reporter and leaves a voice mail about the name of the attorney. P.J. will get an interview with Watkins, the women's attorney, and Brad calls attorney Marcus Busch to see about resetting the interview for later in the day. Brad learns that the photographer is available now, so he leaves the station with photographer Mike Coscia at 11:37 to see Justice Sepulveda.

At 11:46, they pull up in an unmarked sports utility vehicle to the justice of the peace courthouse in South Dallas. The judge seems happy to see them; they chat for a second and then decide the interview would best be conducted in the courtroom, which is empty. While Mike is setting up his tripod, camera and lights, Brad engages in small talk and gets background information: details of the case in question, when Sepulveda was elected, what he ran for before and when (Sepulveda's run for several offices), and what goes into setting bond on various types of cases. Brad asks what training Sepulveda gets as a justice of the peace and verifies he never practiced law and lacks a law degree. Sepulveda talks proudly about how much money his court is earning in fines and court costs. Mike signals Brad he's rolling, and Brad gets to the tougher questions, eventually asking the purpose of setting the bond so high. Sepulveda says he was responding to the seriousness of the crime, because a child was involved. Brad continues to ask the question phrased in different ways, looking for the justice to answer the question directly. Sepulveda continues referring to a child being involved but never refers to the classification of the crime or the criteria on which a judge is supposed to base a bond amount. Apparently sensitive to criticism that had already come in, Sepulveda continues to state that the seriousness of the crime and his responsibility to the community determined what he thought the bond should be. Finally, however, Sepulveda acknowledges that the magistrate who arraigns the two women will lower the bond amount. He also acknowledges that he wanted to send a message, and it's good that a high bond might force someone accused of injuring a child to stay in jail for a long time. He admits that he set the bond to get the attention of the women charged as well as the community. That statement of unpolished truth is the sound bite Brad needs for his story.

Brad and the justice continue chatting as Mike gets additional edit shots. Finally, to get one more series of video of the judge, Mike and Sepulveda return to the judge's office. At 12:30, Mike and Brad are walking out the door of the courthouse. Brad calls to see whether P.J. got the interview with Craig Watkins, the accused women's attorney. P.J. is at the interview now, so Brad feeds an additional question he needs answered—relating to how Watkins characterized the bond and his reaction to it—to be passed along to P.J.

At 12:40, Brad and Mike get back to the newsroom. Brad begins musing over visuals. He has long since been structuring the story in his mind, thinking in terms of visuals, natural sound, interview sound bites and the information—all of which he'll draw from to piece together his story. In terms of visuals, he decides he'll probably begin with the judge. The surrender would be great visually, but it's unlikely. He's also thinking about a live tag for the story. He knows he'll be light on visuals, so he's looking creatively to fill that gap in his story.

Brad loads the tape into one of the five download stations around the newsroom. On the computer screen, he selects a "VTR [videotape recorder] bin" into which to dub the tape, types in how long the interview will run, slugs the bin, and starts the download. All videotape shot at WFAA uses something called time code. Time code is similar to the counter readout on a home videocassette recorder. The difference is that time code gives a specific hour, minute, second and frame address to each frame of video shot (each second of video has 30 frames). Providing the time code location for a given tape will enable anyone to find requested visuals or sound bites when editing the story.

Back at his desk, Brad learns that P.J. has gotten the interview with Watkins, the women's attorney. Brad will fold a sot from that interview into his piece, along with the interview from Marcus Busch he will shoot later this afternoon. From Busch, he'll be looking for a more circumspect assessment of the high bond level. Brad checks the incoming faxes and sees his bond guidelines have come in. Brad glances over the guidelines, writes a few notes, then grabs a bite to eat.

At 1:31, he returns to his computer. He runs a search on some information he needs, then returns to the Ft. Worth Star-Telegram Web site and sees an updated version of the daycare deaths story. They, too, are following the high bail bond angle. Brad's instincts were right. He returns to the list of bond guidelines and begins thinking about a full-screen graphic he might build showing some comparisons. For a second-degree felony with no prior convictions, which applies to the two accused women, the recommended bond is $2500. "A million dollars," Brad mutters, shaking his head. He checks with the videographer to make sure they are still on for the afternoon interview with the attorney, then stops by the desks of the Five and Six producers to discuss the story. Brad needs to know in which show the story is being slated, so he talks with news director David Duitch. Duitch wants the story to run on the Ten, the newscast with the biggest audience.

Having the story running on the Ten gives Brad more time to build the story, but it also changes the complexion of the piece. Because he won't be working that late, he drops the idea of a live tag and instead begins to think in terms of a standup bridge. Brad's phone rings. It's Royce West, the high-powered South Dallas attorney he took a chance on calling earlier, the one Brad thought might the women's attorney but wasn't. As it turns out, this lawyer is involved—but he's representing the family of the dead boy. "Talk about a shot in the dark," Brad comments, a bit stunned as he hangs up the phone. It's 2:01.

Brad and Mike head out the door to talk with Busch. Brad is thinking out loud. "I want to have this story edited by six." He is organizing the piece in his mind. "We've got limited video. We'll need to hit the high points, get to the point quickly, say what it means to the audience." He talks about the whole justice of the peace system in Texas. "In smaller jurisdictions, you've got people with tremendous power, who may or may not have any legal training, and have virtually no legal supervision. They exercise power as they see fit. It's like frontier justice. Someone accused of a minor crime could sit in jail for days before being arraigned because of the high bail some J.P. can set."

Brad's also musing about his hunch paying off in calling Royce West, the high-powered lawyer whom he thought might be representing the two women but is representing the family of the dead boy instead. This lawyer is well known for his litigation skills. "There's a good chance these women will get no-billed, this probably won't go to (criminal) trial. But they probably have insurance, so . . . get out the checkbook."

Brad thinks the piece through. He'll start with Sepulveda, then to a sound bite with him; some file of the daycare center with some background copy; a bite with Watkins, the women's attorney, over the bond being excessive; then go to a full-screen graphic of the bond guidelines; perhaps then juxtapose Busch, who can talk about the purpose for bonds and how this one is way out of line. It will be a sound-driven piece (relying on strong sots more than visuals), but Brad thinks it should work.

At 2:19, the news van pulls up to Marcus Busch's office. Mike sets up the camera gear and lights and arranges chairs for the interview. Brad chats about the issue with Busch and his assistant, discussing the point that it's rare for a justice of the peace, who simply signs the arrest warrant, to set bond at all. That's generally the job of the magistrate during arraignment once the accused is brought in.

They sit and the interview begins. Busch talks about the purpose of bonds, the outlandish bond set in this case, the abuse of power. They finish, but as Mike begins to get edit shots, the lawyer comments that it's not the justice of the peace's place to make a statement. The justice of the peace is supposed to process the warrant and follow the guidelines. It's the role of trial judge or jury to make the statement. Brad hears a potential sound bite in the comments and asks if Busch would want to say that again on camera. He does. Brad is satisfied with the interview, and they break down the equipment. As the van is pulling out of the parking lot, the clock reads 2:56.

On the way back to the station, Brad comments that "ultimately, as reporters, we have to come up with a product. You have to be tenacious, and you have to be flexible. If something doesn't work, change it. Find something that does.

"That goes for the writing. We have to find ways to take this information and synthesize it down into simple, declarative sentences. And find a good way to structure the story, then structure the segments of the story. And find a way to turn that idea into a story today."

Brad tells Mike they need to stop by the criminal courthouse in downtown Dallas to shoot a standup bridge. They swing into the circular drive out front and park. Mike pulls the gear out of the van and begins to look for a good way to frame the shot. He sees a location that will place the reporter in the foreground of the frame and a recognizable part of the building in the background. As Mike puts the camera on a tripod and puts in his earpiece, Brad is sitting in the van sketching out his standup. He emerges, puts on a mic, checks his hair to make sure it's relatively tame, then gets the signal from Mike that the camera is rolling. Brad looks into the camera and gives an audio slate ("standup bridge, take one, on three, two, one) as Mike checks the audio meters on the side of the camera. Brad then nails three good takes, each with a slightly different delivery. He's satisfied with the reads, and Mike's satisfied with the quality of video and sound, so they break down the equipment and reload it into the van.

"It's like others have said," Brad says, "you have to create twice. Once in your head, then again on videotape. You have to be creative, but most importantly, you have to turn the story [get it finished]. Look at the elements, and put them together and make something. You need a beginning, middle and end, and you need to make the point."

At 3:36, Brad and Mike walk back into the station. Brad loads the latest tape and sets it to download. He now has four taped sources from which to work: the morning interview with Sepulveda, the interview P.J. did with Watkins, the interview just completed with Busch that also has the standup, and file tape of the daycare center. Brad stops by the Ten producer's desk to find out how much time he has. He's given 1:45, a very good amount of time for a ten o'clock show.

"Time is critical," Brad comments. "If you take even 10 seconds longer than allotted, that can throw off the timing of the entire show. A huge amount of human and financial resources have gone into this newscast, and one reporter not staying within time can screw up everything."

Back at his desk, Brad is rechecking his information sources in his computer. He wants to make sure he misses nothing, looking for what might turn out to be that critical nugget of information that might boost his story just a bit more. He prints off what he has, then reads through quickly, underlining key facts and making brief notes. He reviews his reporter's notepad, then begins the process of logging tape. On his computer screen, he finds the first tape with Sepulveda, opens the file and begins to view it. The visuals fill the top half of the screen. With every good sound bite he hears, he clicks to the bottom of the screen where he's keeping notes, writes the time code for the beginning of the bite, then transcribes the sot in its entirety, noting the outcue's time code at the end. For those bites he doesn't like, he paraphrases the content into his notes. He might need to use some of that information for his audio tracks. Brad continues through the tape, giving incue and outcue time codes and transcribing the bites he may use. Eventually, he ends up with four potential sots, of which he will use one or perhaps two in his package.

Brad does the same with the Watkins interview tape, then checks the file tape of the daycare center. At 4:47, reporter Don Wall walks up and asks whether Brad would like to use video of the million-dollar bond that Sepulveda signed. Don got the video two days earlier and hands Brad the tape. Brad's interested and thinks he can use it in his story, so he downloads the tape into the system. Now he has some additional video he can write to.

At 4:51, Brad turns to the full-screen graphic on recommended bonds that he'll build for his story. He needs a good set of comparisons and decides on three, all of which are based on no prior convictions: second degree felony ($2500), felony with deadly weapon with no assault ($25,000), and capital murder ($500,000). This, he thinks, will give a good sense for the audience. He types in the copy along with the source of the information to appear on the screen, adds some additional instructions, gives it a slug, and sends the request to the graphics department.

Brad logs the final tape, then turns to the anchor introduction. Having been an anchor himself, Brad is acutely aware of the need to write an ear-catching anchor intro to the story. If the intro doesn't bring the viewer in—recall what the role of a good lead is—the audience will never make it to the story. Brad always writes the anchor intro first.

He enters the necessary information along the top: story slug, writer and video format. The date and newscast are filled in automatically, as he is writing on a script page that will be attached to the Ten producer's rundown. The computer will also fill in the time automatically, based on the number of words and lines and the anchor read rate already set in the computer. Once he has written the introduction, he will need to fill in the supers needed for the story and at what point the director should bring them up. Brad returns to logging, this time of the video of the million-dollar bond. It's 5:09.

With all the tape logged and the information spread out in front of him, Brad begins scripting his package. He's already mentally shifted some elements, rearranging the story in a way that he believes works better. Brad likes to have something turn every 10 seconds or so. That means that after 10 seconds of audio tracks, for example, he wants to get to a sound bite or some natural sound up full. No one element should run more than about 10 seconds—it gives better variety, gives better pacing and keeps the story interesting.

Brad sets up the justice of the peace's position, gets to a sound bite, then uses the last phrase of the bite to move into the next segment of his package. Brad stops. It occurs to him that he needs to know what setup will take place in the show before his package, meaning what related stories will be run and how. This will likely shift the way he writes the story. He finds out that certain details about the women turning themselves in will be discussed earlier in the newscast. With that in mind, he continues.

As Brad completes each section, he goes back and reads it aloud, then revises and simplifies what he's just written. He writes in active voice, he writes in the positive, and he writes in present tense whenever appropriate. Brad continues, going back to check notes, pausing to think, copying and pasting sots from his log sheet, pausing to think, writing a section, reading aloud, revising and reading aloud again. With each section, he clicks into the left-column area of the script and gives editing instructions, noting what shots or sots he needs and where they can be found. Once he's completed the script, he goes back through one last time to see how the story flows. He's satisfied and runs back through his editing instructions to fill in any missing information. At 6:09, he is ready for script approval. The Ten producer is available and reads through and likes the story. Including the anchor intro, the piece runs exactly the allotted 1:45. The producer likes that, as well.

At 6:14, Brad takes the printout of his script and walks into one of the two soundproofed audio booths. It's a small room with an easel, a microphone on a small boom, a computer and a record deck. Audio tracks can be laid on tape or delivered directly into the daily server in the computer system. Brad will do both. He loads a tape, brings up the audio levels and does a mic check, then reads through his script aloud a few times. Once he's ready, he starts the computer and the tape deck and begins.

Each segment of the script is designated a "cut," and every attempt at laying that segment is called a "take." If you stumble during one take, you can do more and mark which take works on your script. Brad looks at the first segment of his script and delivers the words, "High Bonds [the slug] tracks, cut one, take one, going on three, two, one," and then begins to read the first segment of his script. He works his way through each section in turn, giving the cut a slate and countdown. Once completed, he goes back and listens, is satisfied and pops out the tape. He takes the script and the audio tape to the editor building the story, who has the option of taking the audio from the tape or from the server. Brad explains certain elements, then walks back to his desk. "It's a little like a sausage factory, not always pretty to look at, but what comes out in the end is generally pretty good." After checking something for tomorrow, Brad grabs his coat to leave the building. It's 6:26 p.m. Tomorrow morning, Brad Watson returns to begin work on the next story. (You can see Brad Watson's script in Figures 19.3a and 19.3b.)

Page	Ancr	Story	From	By	Video/Format	Tape	Time	OK
		daycare bond		bwatso	script		1:45	■

sovtr s: dallas
tape 1 @ 00.09.33
s: watson reporting

dallas county justice of the peace luis sepulveda dispenses justice.. and in setting the one million dollar bond for the women charged in the lancaster day care death.. a message.
[-----]

s: luis sepulveda/dallas co jp
tape 1 @ 00.06.23

it's common sense here there's a child that's dead. that's not going to see his parents anymore it's severe it's just simple. somebody needs to grab the attention here that there is something here wrong.
[-----]

tape 3/arrest warrant document

the judge's bond grabbed attention.
he set it when police requested arrest warrants for day care director onetha conners and employee jimmy smith.

file of day care from friday

police charged them with injury to a child.. a second degree felony.
but their attorney says the bond is excessive since they have ties to the community.. and no prior convictions.
so they won't surrender until this weekend.
[-----]

s: craig watkins/women's attorney
tape 4 @ 00.03.55

and i don't want to have to have them sit in jail for a week before we go before a judge try to get their bonds reduced to a reasonable amount.
[-----]

s: watson/dallas
tape 3 @ 00.08.06

when compared to what state criminal district judges in dallas county recommend for bond amounts.. sepulveda's bond is extremely high.
[-----]

graphic still

a second degree felony like this.. is 25-hundred dollars.
a felony with a deadly weapon other than aggravated assault.. 25,000.
and capital murder.. a half million.

tape 1@ 00.09.18

the constitution protects citizens against excessive bail.
attorney marcus busch is a former prosecutor who's handled high profile defense cases.
he says the bond amount should – make sure a defendant comes to court.. not

FIGURE 19.3   (*continues*)

2 [WFAA]PEOPLE.WATSON.SCRIPTS SLUG daycare bond   6/5/03 18:55:44, USER Brad Watson

s: marcus busch/attorney
tape 3 @ 00.06.57

a statement.
[-----]
there is no message that this jp needs
to send to anyone if there ultimately is
going to be a message sent in this case it
will be done by a district judge or a jury.
[-----]
sepulveda says he expects a district
judge to reduce the bond.
but these defense attorneys say
citizens shouldn't see their rights reduced
because of a judge's personal opinion.
brad watson, channel 8 news.

FIGURE 19.3   (*continued*)

Finding a Job 20

Okay, so now you are filled with the skills and talent to write brilliant television news stories. Even if you're not graduating for another two years, you need to start thinking about and planning out your job-search strategies now.

As part of your strategy, you should attempt to find a mentor (or perhaps two or three) who is in the business now and can help guide you. He or she may not know everything, but a healthy personal relationship with a working professional can pay off enormously as time goes on.

About News Directors

First, keep in mind that news directors (and everybody else in television news, for that matter) are incredibly busy. Second, a news director (or whoever does the hiring in that shop) will be swamped with piles of tapes and resumes from hopeful applicants like you—sometimes numbering well over a hundred for on-air positions—and will need to trim down those numbers significantly. As a result, he or she is looking for any excuse to get rid of an applicant on first glance. That's the simple reality. Don't provide that excuse.

Cover Letter and Paper Resume

In your cover letter and resume, remember that you are selling yourself. Although you don't want to sound full of yourself, pitch yourself in strong fashion. Be straightforward and honest in the cover letter and resume, but the only way for them to know who you are, how good you are and what potential you have is for you to tell them. Begin by listing all of your skills, experience, education, knowledge, activities and attributes, then construct your letter and resume from there. Tailor the letter and resume to the specific job for which you're applying. This is your first chance to impress and sell yourself to your potential news director. Keep in mind, also, that this is the news director's first exposure to your writing. Make it count. Write simply, and write well. If you blow it here, they'll never get to the brilliant crafting of words in your tape. So how to do it?

Cover Letter

Start with the letter. Be simple, direct and to the point. Let them know what you bring to the table and how passionate you are about this industry. Don't be cute and don't use a gimmick, such as delivering your materials in a pizza box or stuffing the envelope with confetti. Introduce yourself and state that you're interested in the position. Tell what job you're applying for and why you're interested, and show that you have some understanding of the station and the market (do your homework). What are your goals and aspirations? What makes you stand out? State those things, but don't come on like a used car salesman or a motivational speaker. Tell what you can offer the newsroom, but don't tell the news director what great things you're going to do for the station's news product or bottom line.

Keep it to a page or less. Show you can write concisely. Do not go into deep detail, just introduce, state it and get out.

Before you ever write your letter, however, make certain you have all the information straight. You can check for some basic information in the *Broadcasting and Cable Yearbook* (discussed later) or the station's Web site. However, most Web sites won't list the news director's name, and the Yearbook is out of date (in terms of personnel, which can change rapidly) by the time it hits the shelf. You can, however, get the telephone numbers of the stations, which is a start. Use those to inquire about and double-check other information you need.

This begins with the addressee. Do not write a letter that begins, "Dear News Director:" You can kiss any job that might have been yours goodbye. Even worse is, "To Whom It May Concern." If you can't show the reportorial enterprise to figure out who the news director (who might be hiring you) is, you're certainly not a good enough reporter to work at his or her television news operation.

Taking this a step further, once you research who the news director is (by calling the station), make sure you have the correct spelling of his or her name and his or her correct title (these can vary), verify whether the news director is a man or woman (you can't tell from the first name), ensure you have the correct address of the television station, ensure that you have the correct call letters . . . see a trend here? Double-check your facts and make absolutely certain you have no errors of any sort in your letter. Read through it, put it aside and do it again. Have one or two other people read through it to look for problems. Make certain it is absolutely error free. As mentioned, the reality is that, given their busy schedules and the sheer volume of tapes, resumes and letters they receive for most job postings, these news directors are looking for any excuse to pitch out applicants and trim down the pool. Any error of any sort gives them that perfect excuse. Make it easy for them to accept you; make it hard for them to reject you.

Take a look at the sample letter in Figure 20.1.

The Paper Resume

Make your resume one page and one page only. Make it clean (I'm talking about typeface, point size, formatting the document, etc.). Use professional-qual-

Hillary Hopeful
9876 College Drive
Denton, TX 76213

17 May 2005

Ms. Pat Smythe, News Director
KXYZ-TV
1234 Gittinah Jahb Lane
Sherman, Texas 76543

Dear Ms. Smythe:

I am writing to apply for the reporter/producer position in your newsroom. I believe that my skills, experience and education make me an excellent candidate for the job.

I have just completed a bachelor's degree in journalism with a minor in political science from the University of North Texas. While working on my degree, I learned to report, write, shoot and edit stories in both linear and nonlinear formats. In addition to my course assignments, I spent two semesters enterprising and building packages for NTTV News, the campus cable newscast. I also produced newscasts and anchored for NTTV.

My internships at WFAA in Dallas and KTVT in Fort Worth proved invaluable to my training. At both stations, I was able to assist the producers and assignment editors in writing and editing stories, setting up interviews, ordering graphics and trafficking live shots. I often went out with field crews and built practice packages and live shots, and I benefited from critique of my work by the producers, reporters and videographers with whom I worked.

I am industrious, creative and resourceful. I have a passion for news, I possess good news judgment, and I work well with people. I know how to enterprise and develop stories. I know good writing and delivery and how to use visuals and sound to tell a story. In addition, I already am familiar with the Sherman market and your news product. I believe I can make a positive contribution to your news team. I hope you agree.

I have enclosed my resume and tape. Thank you for your consideration.

Sincerely,

Hillary Hopeful

FIGURE 20.1

ity paper. In the heading, you should put your name and contact information, then list the following categories.

Objective

There are various schools of thought on this. Some believe the "Objective" is unnecessary, others think it's essential. It's probably a good idea to err on the side of caution, so go ahead and include it. State, in one sentence, what you want to do in this business. Watch superlatives such as, "To become the most outstanding, award-winning producer the world of television news has ever known." That's a turn-off. State it strongly but simply, without a lot of modifiers. Also, don't state that you intend to work in a major market news operation within three years. That tells the news director you're unrealistic, you're not willing to invest yourself at a current job and you're looking to be gone within a week of walking in the door. What is your immediate goal in this career? What skills do you want to build? That's what you write.

Experience

Include any and all experience that relates to the field. Do not list waiting tables at the local Chili's as part of your "experience." The prospective news director really doesn't care whether you can handle a five-table station on a Friday night. He or she only wants to see the experience and skills that relate. So, what to include?

On campus. You can list any campus TV or radio work. This is why it's important to get involved with on-campus media, even if you're not getting course credit for it. The course credit is secondary. The experience (and the fact you can list that experience on a resume) is the overriding factor. If you do a lot of volunteer work for campus media, or enterprise some projects, programs or stories, it will build your experience and skills level. It will also show a news director that you're really interested in doing this job. Get involved in campus media, and on your resume, you'll list the roles and jobs you filled and for whom and any programs you developed and produced while there. A former student of mine, working with a classmate, created a sports program that ran on campus cable. He shot, edited and reported stories and alternately anchored and produced the program. He combined tape from that endeavor with stories he produced for my television news class and wound up with a job as a sports anchor/reporter/producer for a medium-market station in the south. The initiative paid off for him. It might for you, as well.

Internships. Do at least one internship, and more if you can. A word here about internships. They are critical. First, they provide a level of real-life, hands-on experience that is very difficult to gain in a university situation. Second, an intern-ship will show the student whether he or she even wants to be in this business in the first place and what role in the newsroom he or she is most attracted to. Many students go into internships thinking all they want is to be on the air, then find that what they really enjoy is producing or editing or doing some other job. This is important to learn early.

Third, internships will provide you with contacts—a whole host of them. Even in an entry-level market, an internship will enable you to meet (and, hopefully, positively impress) folks who may know other folks or who may go on to other stations and meet other folks. Internships can lead to jobs—it's just that simple. Plus, it will provide a very nice line on your resume under "Experience."

Something else about internships. Many internships are structured carefully to provide the students good hands-on experience. Often, however, an internship is unstructured. Don't go into an internship thinking they will provide you with "The Step-by-Step Guide to Becoming a Brilliant Television Journalist." Instead, politely and humbly look for ways to learn while making yourself useful. Ask for jobs to do. Work the phones. Do research. Ask a lot of questions (at the appropri-ate time). Ask to write stories. Look for ways to pitch in. Take initiative. Sit with producers and go out with field crews. Work hard. Create the learning experience. You'll get more out of it, and you'll impress those around you. Two good things.

Also, there are pros and cons about large-market versus small-market intern-ships. As we'll discuss later in more detail, there are 210 markets in the U.S. that are sized according to the number of television households in that market. The larger markets will expose you to more sophisticated procedures and equipment as well as (presumably) top-level talent in the various roles. You can learn much by watching and asking questions. The smaller market stations may not be state-of-the-art or have major-market, 15-year veterans working there, but you'll get the chance to get a lot more hands-on work in a small market. Some believe medium-sized markets (from about market 50 to market 120 or so) are the best. Also, stay away from unionized newsrooms, if possible. There's nothing wrong with unions, but strict union rules will often keep you from getting the kind of hands-on expe-rience that can be so beneficial in an internship.

In every experience-gathering situation, work hard and show the people around you you're willing to do any job. Also, in terms of getting as much hands-on experience as you can, see if they'll let you practice standups and live shots or write stories for the newscast, and have a reporter or producer critique the work. Do everything you can.

Part-Time or Full-Time Jobs. Obviously, if you've worked at a local televi-sion station, radio station or newspaper, you would list that. That also goes for in any related field, such as working in promotions, public relations, publicity or audio-video communications for a local firm.

Skills

List all related skills that you acquire, but make certain you can perform the skills you list. If you can shoot and edit, list it. If you know linear editing as well as nonlinear, list it. If you've worked with a newsroom computer system at your internship, list it. By now you know how to write and script a story for virtually any television story format, so find a way to succinctly state that. Sell yourself.

Education

State the university you attended (or still attend), the year you graduated (or intend to graduate), the degree completed (or being sought), and the sequence/emphasis, if applicable. For example, I graduated from the University of Texas at Austin with a "Bachelor of Journalism/Broadcast News Emphasis." If you've won awards, scholarships or honors of some kind, list them. If your GPA is above 3.0, list that. Otherwise, leave it out. Also, you can list any student organizations to which you belonged, especially those related to the field.

References

References matter. List references from people you've met and worked under in the newsroom from your internships and campus news experience as well as television news professors. First, ask them whether you can list them as references, then make certain the contact information is current. You'll want three references, and you'll list them at the bottom of the resume. Give the name, some sort of title that shows how you know this person and a current phone number. Do not state "References upon Request." If the news director wants to call your references, he or she will want to pick up the phone now and track them down.

Last Thoughts

Tailor the resume to the job. If you are interested in both producing and reporting, and the job that's open is for a producer, tailor your resume to reflect that. Push the producing experience and skills. Create a resume for that particular job.

In general, list your strongest aspects first. If you have good professional experience, such as experience working in your campus television newscast, or (better still) an internship, or (best of all) a part-time or full-time job in a newsroom, list the professional experience ahead of your education. If you have little experience that you can list, put your education higher. The idea is to sell your best qualities as high as you can on the resume. And, as with the cover letter, make absolutely certain your resume has no typos, misspellings, or any other problems. Recontact your references occasionally to ensure they still know you're out there and to ensure you have the latest contact information. Take a look at the sample resume in Figure 20.2.

Hillary Hopeful
9876 College Drive
Denton, TX 76213
940/555-1212
hhopeful@aspirations.com

Objective: To work and gain experience as a television news reporter and producer.

Experience

Reporter/Anchor, NTTV News (January 2005–May 2005)
    Enterprised, reported, shot and edited general assignment stories and anchored shows for campus cable newscasts.

Intern, WFAA-TV, Dallas (January 2005–May 2005)
    Assisted producers writing and editing stories, ordering graphics and trafficking live shots. Assisted assignment editors setting up interview and researching stories. Accompanied and assisted field crews; built practice packages and live shots.

Producer, NTTV News (August 2004–December 2004)
    Produced newscasts for campus cable news.

Intern, KTVT-TV, Fort Worth (May 2004–August 2004)
    Assisted producers writing and editing stories, ordering graphics and trafficking live shots. Assisted assignment editors setting up interview and researching stories. Accompanied and assisted field crews; built practice packages and live shots.

Reporter, NTTV News (January 2004–May 2004)
    Enterprised, reported, shot and edited general assignment stories for campus cable newscasts.

Anchor/Reporter/Producer, KNTU-FM (August 2003–December 2003)
    Reported, wrote and voiced general assignment stories, and wrote, produced and anchored newscasts for campus radio station.

Newsroom assistant, KRLD-AM (May 2003–August 2003)
    Took phone interviews, scanned and rewrote wire copy, other duties as assigned.

Reporter, North Texas Daily (August 2002–May 2003)
    Researched and wrote stories for campus daily newspaper covering general assignments and science/medical, religion, and agriculture beats.

Skills: Ability to enterprise, research, report, write, shoot and edit television news stories. Ability to produce and anchor for television and radio newscasts. Competency in linear and nonlinear formats. Knowledge of newsroom computer programs, live shot operations. Competency in online research.

Education: Bachelor of Arts, University of North Texas (May 2005)
Major: Journalism/Broadcast News emphasis. Minor: Political Science. GPA: 3.61
Awards: Top Broadcast News student, March 2005. Shuford Scholarship, 2004-2005.
Organizations: SPJ, RTNDA (president-2004–2005), AWRT.

References

Dr. Eric Gormly, television journalism professor, UNT (940-369-0000)
Natasha Newswoman, executive producer, WFAA (214-555-1212)
Phyllis Slocum, NTTV newscast supervisor (940-565-0000)

FIGURE 20.2

The Resume Tape

News directors want a sense of whether you can do the job and get your work onto tape. The resume tape is critically important to nearly every position for which you might be applying (exceptions might be writing or, to a lesser extent, producing). You need to know that, generally speaking, a tape must pique the news director's interest within about the first 15–30 seconds or you're done—hit the stop button, punch eject, tape goes back in the box and sails across the news director's office to land on the "reject" pile. End of story. You have to hook that news director immediately. We'll discuss how to do that shortly.

First, some logistical considerations: The tape format should be VHS. Although no newsroom shoots in this format, every news director has a VHS player in his or her office. This has taken over as the standard format for resume tapes, so dub your resume reel onto VHS cassettes.

Label the spine and the face of the tape with your name, address, telephone number and e-mail address. Use whatever address and telephone number will be current when your tape is under review. If you're graduating from college in a month and a half and moving back in with the folks until you find a job, don't list your campus apartment—list the folks' contact numbers and let them know. If you're keeping a cell phone, that number can work well. As already mentioned, if that information changes, let people know. Use a professional-looking label that's been printed from a computer (do not scrawl a label by hand).

Tape a rundown (on a 3 x 5 index card) with contact info inside the box (or to the outside of the jacket, if the box is cardboard). The rundown should include the story slug, the time it runs, and what you did on the story (report, shoot, edit, etc.). Use a plastic box that is labeled on the spine and face, and use a box that stands out (red or blue is better than black, black plastic is better than cardboard, cardboard is better than no case at all). Put the tape, resume and letter in a padded envelope (the bubble wrap variety, not the kind with the dusty, shredded paper padding) and send it off.

Warning: Do not send the only tape of your work. You likely won't get it back. Make a dub, and consider it expendable.

What Should Go on the Tape?

That depends on the job you're looking for. All tapes, however, should follow this basic formula: Ten seconds of black should be at the head of the tape, followed by 10 seconds of a slate. A slate is a screen of titling showing your name and phone number. Do not put color bars or tone at the beginning of the tape. News directors hate that.

After the slate, edit a second or two of black, then your tape content. If you begin with a montage (more on that in a moment), edit your vignettes back-to-back, then leave a second or two of black and lay your first story. Lay a second or two of black between each story. More black follows your last video, followed by another 10 seconds of your slate, followed by black.

Do not include a bio on your tape. News directors hate tapes that begin, "Hi, I'm Nancy Needajob, and I want to tell you a bit about myself." It's one of the fastest ways to get the tape punched out of the machine.

Once you've edited your tape, checked it, and dubbed a copy (or multiple copies) to send out, rewind the tape so that it's cued to the beginning your first slate. Do not make the news director hunt around for the start of your tape. If the search proves too time consuming, your tape will soon be flying toward that dreaded reject pile. The key is to look for ways to make it easy for the news director to see and like you and your work. Don't make it hard. Jobs are too tough to get, and the competition is too fierce.

Let's take a look at each of these elements and what the various types of tapes should include.

Reporters and Anchors.

1. Slate.

2. Montage. A montage is a series of vignettes edited together in succession. These should come from your standups or live shots (if you have any). Make each about five to eight seconds, with a total time of about 40 seconds. Although a few news directors don't care for the montage, the vast majority of them want to see and hear you at the top of the tape.

3. Packages. Include three to four. Use packages that show a range of stories, and include a live shot if you have one. An on-set introduction to one of your packages wouldn't hurt, either. Treat your tape the way you would a newscast. Put your very best story up top, and put a good, solid piece at the end.

4. Anchoring. Include a few minutes of anchoring, preferably a mix of readers and vosots. Be aware, however, that few if any stations will hire an anchor straight out of college. If you're looking at an on-air career, focus on developing good reporting and live-shot skills. However, it's not a bad idea to show that you could step in to anchor if need be.

5. Slate. End the tape with the same slate you began with.

The tape should be 12 to 15 minutes long, maximum.

What News Directors Are Looking For: A good look on camera (professional dress, professional hair, professional look all around), a good sound (good voice and delivery, smoothness, enunciation, pronunciation, energy and flow), and good on-camera presence (good eye contact, confidence, a relaxed and engaged style). They want to see good, memorable interactive standups (you're doing something rather than just standing there), they want to hear good writing (personalizes and humanizes the story while it offers context and interesting detail, and writes to video), and they want the story to carry good pacing and variety with good use of natural sound and a good variety of sound bites.

News directors want to see strong, creative visuals (including graphics) and natural sound that capture the story. They want to see creativity and resourcefulness in enterprising stories. They want to see stories they haven't seen before, they want to see a fresh approach or angle to stories, and they want to see stories that deal with life outside of campus.

Go for big-time stories that have a major market look and sound, and deal with major market subject matter. Put together stories and standups that pop out and have good movement to them. Do not be cute, gimmicky, or clichéd. Be natural.

Videographers.

1. Slate.
2. Four to five good stories. Use stories that show a range of work, a range of skills, a range of different types of shots. You might include a straight news story, a news-oriented feature or two, a spot news piece (if you have one), and a live shot (if you have one). But show your best work, no matter what the story type, and start the tape with the strongest package (in terms of visuals and natural sound) you have.
3. Slate.

What News Directors Are Looking For: They want to see high-quality shooting and editing. They'll be looking to see whether you capture great shots and shoot a good variety of shots. Do you get in close, do you know how to build sequences, are your shots steady, in focus and well framed? They'll want to know whether your sound quality and lighting are both good. Are you creative and resourceful, and can you tell a good story through visuals and natural sound?

Producers.
If you have a tape of a newscast.

1. Slate.
2. A newscast.
3. Slate.

What News Directors Are Looking For: They want to see quality writing, writing from a personal or human perspective and writing to video. Do you make good use of production values (visuals and other graphic support, use of good camera shots), do you have good story placement and flow, and is the story variety and pacing good? They'll look for good use of anchors, for teases and transitions that work, and for a good sense of timing on the show.

Some will want only the producer's elements in the tape. In other words, they will want you to edit down the packages, extracting everything from after the first sentence to before the last sentence. They'll want the same of any commercial/public service announcement breaks. Find out what they want in the tape, and if you're going on the road armed with tapes (discussed under Strategies later), make sure you have one of each to show and leave.

Also, include a critique of your show—what you think went well, what went not as well as you'd like and how you'd do it differently. Discuss the news philosophy of the show—is it conservative, tabloid, middle-ground, something else—and discuss how that influenced your choices.

Finally, tape every show you do. Some news directors will call and ask for the last show you produced.

If you don't have a tape of a newscast. If you've reported any stories, send a tape of those. Many of the same principles apply: Do you write well, do you write well to video, do you understand good visuals and natural sound, can you tell a story from a human, personalized point of view? Take a look at the section on tape under reporters and follow that, but without the standup montage at the beginning. State in your cover letter you don't have a newscast, but you do have stories you've reported. Also, list those skills on your resume under "Writing." If you can write well to visuals and natural sound, and if you understand good use of sound bites and pacing, say so. News directors will be looking for many of the same elements in your stories that are listed under "Producers" above: They want to see quality writing, writing from a personal or human perspective and writing to video.

If you don't have any tape at all, you're not out of the running. The news director will be relying on your paper resume and references. Also, have some writing samples available if they want them, but don't include them in your initial packet of materials.

A final reminder about producing: On-air applicants face enormous competition. Producers face a lot less, and a good producer can write his or her ticket. Also, a producer holds perhaps the most secure position in the newsroom—not a bad thing.

The Search Itself

The hardest job to get is the first one. It also may take the longest to land. The key is developing good proactive strategies and knowing where to look, as well as working the contacts you develop.

Generally speaking, you'll be looking at entry-level markets—markets that are sized 100 or below. That's on average—be advised that some markets in the 125–100 range consider themselves second-level markets. Also, it's not unheard of for a graduate with a good tape and good references to land a job in a 90s market. Writers and producers may be able to get into a larger market initially. But the point here is don't count on Dallas, Los Angeles, New York or Chicago right out of journalism school. In fact, it's a bad idea to get a job in too large a market too early. You're going to make mistakes, and it's best to make them in the smaller markets, learn from them, develop your skills and judgment further and then move on. Otherwise, you could get washed out of a good-sized market and have to step a ways down to continue your career. People who work in television news go through what is, in essence, a series of informal apprenticeships. You enter a market, spend a couple of years, learn everything you can, then look to a larger market.

So how do you find out about these entry-level markets, and how do you decide where to target? If living in a particular region of the country is essential to you, then look in that region and find the entry-level markets there. Often, in fact, it's best to look at an area within a day's drive of where you're living now for that first job. Get out a map, and consult the *Broadcasting and Cable Yearbook* (which also has maps of the markets, listed state by state). You should be able to find a copy in your school or public library.

A brief word about market sizes. Areas of the country are divided up into markets that are set geographically according to what's called the DMA, or designated market area. This is determined largely by population centers and the "reach," or range, of the broadcast signal there. The "size" of the market depends on the number of television households in that market. As I mentioned earlier, there are 210 markets in the United States. The largest is New York. The smallest is Glendive, Montana. You can find a listing of all the Nielsen markets (Nielsen is a rating service that catalogs this information) either in the *Broadcasting and Cable Yearbook* or on-line at http://www.nielsenmedia.com/DMAs.html. Several other industry sites list the markets, as well.

At this point, you have various strategies you can follow. One is to look for jobs that are posted, another is to contact a placement service, and two others are to plan site visits and network for contacts. We'll start with job listings.

Where to Look for Available Jobs

Bulletin boards around your journalism or radio-TV-film departments or the departmental Web sites often post good entry- or second-level jobs. Stations you might have identified as good potentials will generally post jobs on their Web sites.

Many of the trade magazines, such as Broadcasting and Cable, Electronic Media, Quill (the Society of Professional Journalists publication, which comes free with a membership and includes Jobs for Journalists for an additional fee), RTNDA (Radio-Television News Directors Association) Communicator and other industry publications advertise news positions in their classified ads sections. They're also a good way to keep up with industry news.

In addition, an array of Web sites that list available jobs in television news has popped up. News directors use these heavily, so they should prove to be valuable resources for you. I've included a list of them in Figure 20.3. Do keep in mind that Web sites come and go with great regularity.

Once you've found a job you're interested in, put together your packet and send it in.

Incidentally, if the ad states "No calls," do not call. In fact, if you do call in spite of this warning, you've just given the news director that dreaded excuse to pitch your tape onto the reject pile. To ensure they received the tape, send it with a tracking number through one of the parcel services or the post office. If the ad does not state "no calls," you can do so, but do it advisedly. And call with legitimate questions.

JOB SITES

This is a compilation of sites that can be helpful for those searching for a job in television news. It's not an exhaustive list, but it provides a good base for your search. Some of these sites also carry industry news and helpful links.

NO FEE:
Electronic Media: www.emonline.com
TV Newz.com: www.tvnewz.com
Talent Dynamics: www.talentdynamics.com
N.A.B.: www.nab.org (great job site)
N.A.T.S.A.: www.emmyonline.org
+ Shoptalk: www.tvspy.com
Broadcast Image: www.broadcastimage.com/jobs/
RTNDA: www.rtnda.org (organizational student membership is $50)
I.R.E.: www.ire.org/jobs/look.html
JournalismJobs.com: www.journalismjobs.com/
TVNewsWeb.com www.tvnewsweb.com/briefing/jobshop.shtml
TVNEWSWEB: www.tvnewsweb.com/jobs.shtml
MEDIA BISTRO: www.mediabistro.com/joblistings/

FEE CHARGED: (Although these do cost some money, the investment can be worth it.)
TVJobs.com: www.tvjobs.com
Medialine: www.medialine.com
Media Headhunter: www.mediaheadhunter.com
Medialand: http://www.medialandjobs.com
PlanetMedia: http://www.planetmedia.net/

VIDEOGRAPHER-ONLY SITES:
NPPA: http://www.nppa.org/default.cfm (free, but must sign up for user account)
B-Roll Net: http://www.b-roll.net/
Photog Lounge: http://www.photogslounge.net/

SALARY INFORMATION:
SALARY SURVEY: http://www.rtnda.org/research/salaries.shtml
COST OF LIVING: http://www.homefair.com/homefair/calc/salcalc.html
http://cgi.money.cnn.com/tools/costofliving/costofliving.html

FIGURE 20.3

If you do not receive word back for a while, don't panic. It can take weeks to narrow down the pile of candidates to a short list (three to five) that the news directors want to look at more closely. You may be on that list and not get a call for weeks. You may be the top finalist and not get a call for weeks. However, if you think you might be under consideration for one position and get a job offer somewhere else, it behooves you to pick up the phone and let the news director know. Politely state that you've been made an offer elsewhere, and you wanted to know the status of the search there. If you're under consideration there, they'll want to know. If you're not, it won't matter anyway.

While you're culling the classifieds and Web sites, you want to be actively engaged in following other strategies, as well. Do not simply send out tapes and wait by the phone. Be proactive. Here's how to do it.

Placement Organizations. One approach is to use a placement organization. These services are free to you—television stations pay them to act as headhunters to find good talent. These companies, who often consult the station's on-air product as well, have built a business around supplying good potential reporters, producers, videographers, anchors and news managers to client stations. They build a pool of talent and try to match that talent with the stations. Take advantage of all of them. They can be quite effective. They typically also do critique and coaching, although most do charge a fee for this.

Talent Dynamics in Dallas, Broadcast Image in San Antonio, and Frank Magid and Associates in Cedar Rapids, Iowa, are the three largest agencies. All have Web sites, and all perform their placement services for free (to you, that is). In addition, many smaller firms and consultants, such as Don Fitzpatrick Associates in San Francisco (Fitzpatrick also runs ShopTalk and tvspy.com), do a good job of working with television news placement. Contact these firms and ask how to send in materials. Then do it.

Networking. Be aware that many, many jobs come from contacts and referrals. I said this before, and I'm saying it again: Meet and stay in contact with as many people as you can (professionals, instructors, former classmates). They can help keep you informed of anything that comes open. Also, you will get a good word to others from the people you impress. Go back and review the first chapter of this book. These are the qualities people are looking for. You never know who might be in a position to mention your name or get you that first job, so if you work hard and develop good skills and a good attitude in every endeavor, you've done everything you can to show yourself in the best light. It pays off.

Tactics

Keep a Rolodex of any contacts you make. On the business card or beside the entry, note where and when and under what circumstances you made the contact.

Drop a note about a week after the initial contact and every few months or so after that. Don't make a pest of yourself, but stay in touch with people to keep yourself fresh in their minds.

During your job search, it's important to keep running files on whom you've contacted for jobs, for inquiries, dates of the contact and so on. Also, as mentioned earlier, update your own contact information if it changes—to everyone. If you have 12 tapes out and you're moving to a new address, let all the contacts know. That also serves as a good excuse to reestablish contact.

While we're on the subject of networking, go out of your way to join the student chapters of every professional organization you can: Society of Professional Journalists, Radio-Television News Directors Association, National Association of Black Journalists, National Association of Hispanic Journalists, Native American Journalists Association, Asian American Journalists Association, American Women in Radio and Television, and the list goes on. These organizations enable you to meet not only classmates who can help you later but working professionals, all of whom can begin to spread your network a lot further. Make those contacts, and make them count. Also, keep up with what's happening in the industry. One way is to read RTNDA Communicator and other industry publications. Another is to subscribe to on-line Listservs, such as tvspy.com. Several of the Web sites that post jobs are also good sources for industry news.

Go to the conferences that news directors attend, the most important of which is the RTNDA. Meet these folks, chat with them, have a cup of coffee with them, make sure you leave them with a positive impression. Have resumes handy, but don't offer one unless asked. You might ask whether you can see their operation some time soon, or whether he or she might be willing to visit at some future time to view and critique your work. Then, follow up.

In addition, know that news directors talk with each other. If one sees a good candidate but doesn't have a position, he or she may pass that candidate on to someone who does. News directors also talk with journalism professors, many of whom spent substantial time in the business. Many small-market news directors stay in touch with the universities to get the best talent coming out of school. The grapevine is alive and well in this industry, especially considering that the industry is not really all that large. This is why networking is so important, as is treating people well and not burning bridges. Impress people and get your name out there.

Incidentally, all of these guidelines also figure prominently as you move up the ladder in market sizes. Show professionalism always. Treat others with respect. Show a great work ethic. Don't burn bridges. It will always pay off in the end.

Cold Calling

This consists of finding a region, market or station you're interested in and taking the first bold step. Keep in mind, however, there's an art to this. You don't simply call and say, "Yeah, I'm graduating and I was wondering if you've got any openings for producers or reporters." Wrong approach.

Instead, call the news director (we're talking small markets, here—medium- to large-market news directors won't have the time and won't hire you anyway) between 10 a.m. and noon and see whether they'd be willing to sit with you at some point, answer some questions you have about the business and perhaps look at your tape and critique it.

If they have time, they'll usually consent to meeting with you. Chances are they'll tell you they don't have a job. That's fine—your primary purpose is to put your face and voice in front of them. Plus, an opening may come up next week or next month, or someone they know may have something available. Also, they may or may not want to critique your tape, but that's fine as well. Simply meeting with them puts you ahead of most of the others.

You'll want to give at least one week's notice, and preferably two or more. Try to keep the search within an easy day's drive of your home. If possible, try to line up two or three meetings over the same two-day period, and don't schedule them too close together. Book an inexpensive motel, reconfirm the meetings two days out, get there the evening before the first meeting and check out the stations' newscasts. Also, get a local newspaper and read it. The news directors are a lot more impressed when you know their news product and people as well as the current issues in that community.

Use all of these strategies. Be proactive about hunting down these jobs, and do not give up. If you have something to offer in this business, eventually you'll get in front of a news director who will realize that and hire you.

Professionalism

We've discussed the need for professionalism in everything you do. It's important that you look, sound and act professional in every contact, be it in a story, on a job interview or at a conference. Men should wear a moderate to conservative jacket and tie (unless you're doing a standup in a cow pasture or covering a flood), and women should wear the equivalent. Wear your hair in a relatively conservative way. The only piercings acceptable are those in women's earlobes (the only male on-air correspondent who can get away with a pierced ear is Ed Bradley, and he's earned the right), and have no visible tattoos.

An additional word about professional presentation as relates to e-mail and voice mail. First, set up an e-mail account that's separate from the university and that you can take with you. Go with a firm that looks like it will be around for a while. Many major Web sites offer free accounts. With regard to your e-mail address: Please put some care and thought into what address you choose. It needs to be professional sounding and absolutely cannot be cute or suggestive in any way. "Newsbabe@hotmail.com" or "buffed_and_blonde@yahoo.com" simply will not cut it. If you have such an address, change it now. It is far better to go with your name or something else simple and professional sounding. Also, check your e-mail. It sounds basic, but I actually know of cases in which students had messages from potential internship and job sources that went unanswered because the students never bothered to check their e-mail.

While we're on the subject of professionalism in presentation, please be aware of your voicemail or answering machine message. A student of mine, looking for a job, had the following message with her roommate on their answering machine (I've changed the names):

Marcie: This is Marcie,
Janice: and this is Janice,
Both: and if you're some cute, hunky guy, leave a message and we'll get back right away. Otherwise, leave a message and we'll get back whenever.

Imagine what would have been going through the mind of a prospective news director should he or she have called. I would be surprised if the first inclination were not to hang up the phone, pitch the applicant, and move on. Don't doom yourself. Be professional in everything.

Interview

Okay, so you've finally gotten a call, you're one of the finalists for a job, and they want to do an interview. What now? Don't panic, but do remember that first impressions count big. Again, come dressed professionally, be confident without being cocky, be engaged, and maintain good eye contact.

Prepare for the interview. Ask a lot of questions that they might ask you. List them out, then try to answer them. As you think about what questions they might ask, consider how you might bring your strengths into the answers, even if they're asking for weaknesses. Why should they hire you? How have you handled rough situations? Know the answers and some examples, and have a sales pitch ready.

Also, come with questions for them. Save them until the appropriate time in the interview, but have them ready. First, you are interviewing them as much as they are interviewing you. You'll need to find out some things about the station, its news operation, how things run and the hierarchy of the newsroom. Second, if you come in prepared with questions, you show an interest in that job and that newsroom. You show that you can jump in where appropriate and take control. However, do your research first. If they get peppered with a lot of questions that are easily answered through a glance at their Web site, they may start wondering.

Show a good disposition. Maintain poise, confidence, assertiveness, interest, relaxation and maturity. They want to know how you handle yourself. News directors look for certain traits in their hires: whether he or she takes initiative, works well with others and has a sense of mission and purpose. They want to hire people who are optimistic, driven, energetic, curious, motivated and honest and have a passion for the work. Take the opportunity to allow them to see some of those traits in your responses to their questions, in your questions to them and in your overall demeanor.

During any conversation with the news director or anyone else at the station, do not complain or gossip about anything or anyone. Know that some will actually bait you to see if you'll go for it. Here's the setup: the news director (or someone else in the newsroom) complains and gossips about someone with whom you've been in contact, and you complain and gossip right back. Problem is, unbeknownst to you, the person you're complaining about is the news director's best friend. You've just gossiped yourself out of a job. And complainers in general are marked off the list before they've even finished the interview. If you're asked about an unpleasant situation or person, find a mature, diplomatic and positive way to express your feelings or position.

Also, know that a lot of news directors love to spring current events quizzes on job applicants during the interview. I know of people who have actually lost out on jobs (not to mention internships) because they blew a current events quiz. Don't let that happen to you.

Whether to Use an Agent

As a beginning television journalist, I'd advise against it. There are many good, honest, hardworking agents out there. There also are quite a few who are not. Often, unethical agents will scope around for all the young, good-looking talent they can find, then approach the nearly or recently graduated folks to sign them on as clients. Typically, an agent will take 10% or more of your gross salary for a period of years, and many charge an initial fee on top of that. You sign the contract, then the agent forgets about you, focusing instead on the $300,000- or $600,000- or $1.1-million-a-year anchors. Some may distribute your tapes with an introductory cover letter, but that's not typical and may not even help.

So, for the most part, you are forced to find the jobs on your own. That's what they're counting on. If you're able to land a job, suddenly they reappear and start demanding their percentage for "representing" you. The agents figure that if they sign a lot of good-looking clients with initiative and good skills, enough clients will find the jobs themselves to pad the agent's annual income by a nice sum.

Plus, an agent not only might fail to help you but actually could hurt you in landing an entry level job. Many if not most small-market stations won't deal with an agent and might even disqualify a candidate who is represented by one. Having said all that, I'll repeat there are many very good agents out there. You just don't need one at an entry level. In fact, I know of reporters in top-10 markets who have never had an agent and don't intend to retain one.

Negotiating

You've been offered a job. Obviously, you want as much as you can get, but you want to be careful that you maintain a positive, sincere and somewhat humble approach. If your new news director thinks you're a demanding, high-maintenance prima donna as you're coming in the door, you may be in for a tough ride.

And with an entry-level position, you won't have a great deal of negotiation room anyway. You might be able to squeeze a few dollars more, or negotiate for moving expenses, a clothing allowance (if it's an on-air position), a better shift, certain holidays off, an early-out clause on a contract or something else. In any of these points, however, if the news director states that this is absolutely all that he or she can offer, believe them. There's a good chance the terms were set by the station manager and the news director's hands are tied. Try to get the best deal you can, but accept what you can get and make the best of it while you're there.

Salaries

Salaries for beginning television journalists are insultingly low. It's a matter of supply and demand. Plan on $21,000 to $24,000 a year on your first job. Some new hires get less. But hey, consider it an extension of your college days. Basically, this is a postbaccalaureate education for which you're being paid an assistantship. Find someone with whom to share an apartment, eat a lot of macaroni with tuna, and trim expenses everywhere you can. Plus, you don't have to worry about not being able to afford a social life. In your first job in television news, you won't have time to date, anyway. However, the financial picture does start improving as you move up in market sizes, and producers often don't stay in their first jobs more than eight months to a year. Just find a way to do it and do it. It's only a year. Or two.

Commitment and Contracts

Plan on giving the first job a year and a half to two years, unless you're a producer, in which case you'll move up more rapidly. You can break the two-year rule once, but if you're hopping from one position to another every six to nine months, people won't want to hire you. Always give everything you can to the job you currently hold.

Some entry-level stations are requiring contracts of some of their employees, especially the on-air positions. If the contract is for two years or less and you really like the station and the market, do it. You're going to need that time to develop anyway. More than a two-year commitment is asking a bit much for an entry-level job, though.

Subjectivity and Hiring Decisions

News directors are pretty consistent in the skills they're looking for. They want people who know how to write, shoot and edit. They want people who make good use of language and are good storytellers. They want a professional look and sound. They want people who can think clearly and logically, can stay organized, are focused and work hard. They want people who are well rounded and have a broad base of knowledge. What they don't want is someone whose chief aspiration is "to be on TV."

Keep in mind, however, that the candidate one news director can't stand and marks as a loser, another news director loves and sees as the next Peter Jennings or Leslie Stahl. The point is, keep looking and don't give up easily. Finding a job is a full-time job. Get yourself out there, and start now. It can take time to land that first position. Again, do everything in your power to present yourself well to everyone with whom you work. A lucky break will help and is often necessary. However, you should keep in mind some wisdom my mother passed on to me many years ago: You make your own breaks.

She's right.

Summary

As a television news journalism student, you need to begin thinking now about the job search. You must start looking at ways to develop the skills, experiences and networking contacts you'll need to land a job in this business. The cover letter and resume are essential in the job-search process. As the first introduction to you, they must sell you as a prospective newsroom employee and must be free of any errors. Any mistakes in either could end your chance of a job. Both the letter and resume must contain certain information in a certain format.

The tape is just as critical, and even more critical for certain jobs. Review the suggestions for the content and content order needed for a tape in each given newsroom role.

Review job search strategies. There are four: searching for posted positions, working with placement organizations, networking and cold calling. Each requires a different approach, and all are necessary to provide the best chance of landing a job.

Professional presentation is essential, in both your approach to applying for a job and in the interview. News directors are looking for certain traits in their workers. Know those traits and adopt them.

Exercises

1. Research the television stations in a given market. The market size must be 125 or smaller. Give pertinent information such as the call letters, addresses, the region of the country, market name and what cities are included, the market size and the news director's name (spelled correctly) and exact title.

2. Write a resume. On a separate sheet, state what additional experience and skills you will want to add before graduation.

3. Look for available jobs in publications and on-line. Focus on a particular region and on a particular position. Come in with a list of available jobs and how you learned about them. Research one of them and write a cover letter you would send to that station.

4. Come up with interview questions a prospective news director might ask.

5. Set up to conduct mock interviews.

6. Set up a strategy for networking, and write it out. What additional work will you need to do before graduating to get your networking off to a good start? What will you continue doing?

Index

Page numbers in italics represent pages that contain figures.

A

Abbreviations, in news story, 35, 50

Accuracy, 17
attribution, 44–45, 50
fairness, 43, 50, 95, 106
in news story, 42–43, 95, 106, 107, 120, 121, 146, 158, 192, 194, 266

Acronyms, in news story, 37–38, 50

Active voice
n conversational writing, 59–60, 65
in live shots, 292
in news story, 94–95, 106, 107, 121, 142, 146, 157, 192, 194, 361
in writing leads, 84, 120

Adjectives
vs. adverb use, 26–28, 31
in conversational writing, 60–61, 65
as parts of speech, 18, 31
worthless adjectives, 274

Adverbs
vs. adjective use, 26–28, 31
in conversational writing, 60–61, 65
as parts of speech, 18–19, 31

Alliteration, 64

Anchor cues
in package scripts, 235, 239–240, 244, 266
in reader scripts, 112–114, *113,* 131
in scripts with full screen graphics, 132
in scripts with sots, 175, 183
in scripts with sots, back-to-back, 181, 183
in scripts with vo and sots, 192
in scripts with vo/nat full, 159, 160, 161
in scripts with vo or vo/nat, 147, 150, 161

Anchor position, in the newsroom, 323, 326, 327, 328

"Ask-back" in live shot, 279

Assignment editor position, in the newsroom, 322, 326, 327, 328

Assistant news director position, in the newsroom, 322, 328, 334–335, 341

Associate producer position, in the newsroom, 324, 328

Attribution
before information rule, 47–48
of coming from someone else, 45–47
in crime stories, 47
of knowing to be true, 44–45
levels of, 49
libel, 47
in news story, 50, 95, 106
of opinions, 44
of other news sources, 45
problem words and phrases, 41–42
rcliable sources, 47
"rings true" concept, 46–47
of seeing for yourself, 44–45
suggestions regarding, 47–49
summary regarding, 50
"trial balloon" pitfall, 48–49
unidentified sources, 48

Audience hook, 75, 96, 131, 142

Audio slate, 254

"Axis" factor in shot framing, 228–232, *229–231,* 233

B

"B-roll," in package scripts, 236, 266

Back timing, of newscast production, 311, 318, 342

Balance
in news story, 15, 43–44, 50, 95, 106, 165, 178–179

Bliss, Ed, 274

Broadcasting and Cable Yearbook, 266–267

C

Camera shot. *See also* Live shot
script format, 112
in scripts, with vo and sots, 188
in scripts with graphics, 123, 125
in scripts with vo/nat full, 159
in scripts with vo or vo/nat, 149

CG (character generator), 149

Character generator (CG), 149

Chief photographer position, in the newsroom, 323, 328

"Chyron" (superimpose), 149

Clauses, 20, 31

Clichés
in leads, 84, 87, 96
in news story, 40–41, 50
in standups, 254

Clustering of story flow, 302–303, *304,* 305,
320

Conjunctions
as parts of speech, 19, 31
starting sentences with, 26, 31

Continuity, in production, 298

Contractions, in news story, 38, 50

Conversational writing
active *vs.* passive voice, 59–60, 65, 94–95,
106, 107, 121, 142, 146, 157, 192,
194, 361
editing and rewriting, 63, 65
exercises, 65
false present tense, 65, 273–274
present tense, 61–63, 65, 94, 106, 120, 121,
192, 266, 361
reading aloud, 63, 64–65, 72, 106, 121,
146, 157, 195
rhythm, 64
short, simple sentences, 13–14, 54–56, 65,
94, 104, 106
small, simple words, 14, 15, 53–56, 65
strong, compelling words, 60–61, 65, 94,
106
summary regarding, 65
television sentences, 53, 56, 65

Copywrited information, 45

Credibility. *See also* Attribution
accuracy and, 42–43, 50, 95
good grammar, 17

Criticism, 7

Cronkite, Walter, 12

Curiosity, 6

"Cutaway" interview shot, 232, 233

D

Dead air, 190

Deadlines, 5–6

"Debrief" in live shot, 279

Defamation, 47

Delayed lead, 77, 91

Dependent clause
in conversational writing, 58

in leads, 84
in news story, 94
as part of sentence, 20, 31

Designated market area (DMA), 376

Direct video references, 139, 141–142, *143,*
144–146

Director cues
in package script, 243–244
in scripts with full screen graphics, 132
in scripts with graphics, 108, *109–110,*
111–112
in scripts with sots, 175, 183
in scripts with sots, back-to-back, 181
in scripts with vo and sots, 188, 190–192,
191
in scripts with vo/nat full, 159, 161

Dissolve camera shot, 315

DMA (designated market area), 376

"Donut," within live shot, 276

Double out cues, 175

E

Educational requirements, 7–8

Ego, 7

End script
format, 104, 114
in scripts with full screen graphics, 126
in scripts with vo and sots, 192–193
in scripts with vo or vo/nat, 150

Executive producer position, in the newsroom,
322, 326, 327, 328, 334–335

F

Fairness, in news story, 15, 43, 50, 95, 106,
165, 178–179

False tense, 62–63, 65

Flow, of producing the newscast, 302–303,
304, 305, 320

Flow of news stories, 302–303, *304,* 305,
320

Focus of new story, 73–75

"Font" (superimpose), 149

Front timing, of newscast production, 311,
312

Fs/gfx (full-screen graphic). *See* Full-Screen
Graphic (fs/gfx)

Full-Screen Graphic (fs/gfx)
defined, 101. *See also* Scripts, combining
elements in
lead scripts, 120
scripts from wire copy and, 115, 119, *119*

Future tense, in news story, 61, 65, 94, 142,
146, 192

G

"Gee whiz" journalism, 290

General assignment reporter position, in the newsroom, 325, 328

   newscast production example, 336, 343, 352–361, *362–363*

General assignment reporters, 12

Getting a newsroom job. *See also specific newsroom position*

   about news directors, 365

   cover letter, 365, 366, *367,* 384

   exercises, 384

   interview, 381–382

   professionalism, 380–381, 384

   resumé, paper, 365, 366, 368, *371,* 384

     education, 370

     experience, 368–369

     objective, 368

     references, 370

     skills, 370

   resumé, tape, 372–373, 384

     for reporters and anchors, 373–374

     for videographers, 374–375

   the search, 375–376

     cold calling, 379–380, 384

     tactics, 378–379

     where to look, 376, *377,* 378, 384

   summary, 384

   using an agent, 384

     commitment and contracts, 383

     negotiating, 382–383

     salaries, 383

     subjectivity and hiring decisions, 383–384

Good *vs.* well, in sentence, 28–29

Grammar, parts of a sentence

   clauses, 20, 31

   objects, 19–20, 31

   phrases, 20, 31

   predicate, 19, 31

   subjects, 19, 31

Grammar, parts of speech, 17–18

   adjectives, 18, 31

   adverbs, 18–19, 31

   conjunctions, 19, 31

   nouns, 18, 31

   prepositions, 19, 31

   pronouns, 18, 31

   verbs, 18, 31

Grammar, rules of

   adverb or adjective, 26–28, 31

   ending sentences with prepositions, 26, 31

   exercises, 31

good *vs.* well, 28–29, 31

I *vs.* me, 23–24, 31

   phrase, placement of, 30, 31

   pronoun as object of prepositional phrase, 25, 31

   pronouns and noun-pronoun agreement, 24–25, 31

   reflexive pronouns, 23–24, 31

   spelling, 30–31

   starting sentences with conjunctions, 26, 31

   subject-verb agreement, 20–22, 31

   summary regarding, 31

   that *vs.* which *vs.* who, 29–30, 31

Graphics. *See* Scripts, with full screen graphics

Gross, Terry, 232

H

Hyphens, use of, 37–38

I

Independent clauses, sentence structure, 20, 31, 58

Initials, in news story, 37–38, 50

Initiative, 6–7

"Insert package," 276

Interior script (package script), 246, 267

Internet

   job search, *377*

   as research tool, 4

   source reliability caution, 224

Internships, 368–369

Interviewing. *See also* Reporting

   asking questions, 225–226, 227, 232–233

   "axis" factor, 228–232, *229–231,* 233

   background factors, 228, 232

   backlighting factors, 228, 233

   contact cultivation, 223–224

   "cutaway" shot, 232, 233

   framing the shot, 227, *228,* 233

   lighting, 232, 233

   listening, 226, 233

   microphone control, 227

   in package script, 250–251, 250–253

   prearranged interview, 225, 232

   research and background interview, 224, 232

   for segment of longer program, 224

   sound quality, 227, 233

   for soundbites, 224, 225, 226, 232

   spot interview, 225, 232

   strategy, 225–226

   summary, 232

   "talking ear shot," 227

Interviewing (*continued*)
   technical notes, 227–232, *228–231*
   tripod use, 232, 233
   yes-or-no question avoidance, 225, 251

K
"Key" (superimpose), 149
"Kill points" in newscast planning, 335–336
Koppel, Ted, 232

L
Language skills, 7
Leads
   "continues" trap, 81
   hard lead, 75, 96
   latest lead, 80–81, 106
   length of, 72–73
   in scripts with fs/gfx, 120
   soft or summary lead, 75
   story focus and, 73–75
   suspense and delayed leads, 76–77
   throwaway lead, 76
   umbrella or multiple lead, 75–76
   viewer's questions, 106, 120
   weak leads, 81–84, 96
   which way to lead, 77–80
Libel, 47
Live shot, 102
   ending with, 279–280, 283
   exercises, 283–284
   format selection, 277–279, 283
   live with interview, 275, 283
   live with package, 276, 280, *281–282,* 283
   live with sot, 275, 283
   live with vo, 276, 283
   live with vosot, 276, 283
   newscast production example, 341
   sound bites in, 275, 278
   straight-up live, 275, 283
   summary, 283
   timing, 275, 276–277, 283
   writing and scripting, 276–277, 283
      active voice, 292
      flexibility, 289, 290
      insert package *vs.* voice over format, 290
      mastering live shot, 291–292
      organization, 289
      package *vs.* live shot writing, 287–289
      roll cue, 289
      storytelling art, 286
      tight writing, craft of, 292–293
      Beverly White's philosophy on, 286
      words matching visuals, 287

      writing as relating to reporting process, 286–287
Live shots, 318–310, 320
Log sheet
   scripts with vo and vo/nat, 140, *140, 143*
   scripts with vo/nat full, 157
"Lower third" (superimpose), 149

M
Metaphor, use of, 64

N
Names, in news story, 37, 50
Nats to Sound, 102
Natural sound (SOT under), 161, 165
Natural sounds. *See* Scripts, combining elements in; Scripts, with vo/nat full; Scripts, with vo or vo/nat
Networking, to get a job, 378, 379
News anchor position, in the newsroom, 123, 132, 160–161, 323, 328. *See also* Anchor cues
News director position, in the newsroom, 322, 326, 327, 328, 332, 333–335
"News hole" concept, of production, 297–298, *298, 300,* 301, 319
News operation example
   beginning of day, 332–335
   managing editor responsibilities, 332–335
   news director responsibilities, 332–335
   newsroom layout, 331–332
   producer responsibilities, 335–343, *344–352*
   reporter responsibilities, 336, 343, 352–361, *362–363*
News story, assembly process (sequential order)
   read wire copy, 93, 96
   understand wire copy, 93, 96
   find and mark key facts, 93, 96
   think before you write, 93–95, 96
   write, 95, 96
   test the story, 95–96
   exercises, 97
   summary regarding, 96
News story, beginning. *See also* Leads
   leads, 72–84, 96
News story, end
   final points, 92–93
   importance of, 91–92
   punch line, 91
   transitions, 92
   variety, 92

News story, general
  diagram of, 69–70, *70*
  exercises, 97
  first steps of writing, 71–72
  newsworthiness elements, 70–71
  summary regarding, 96
News story, middle
  answer viewer's questions, 85–86, 96, 120
  clichés, 87, 96
  unnecessary names and places, 88–91
  unnecessary time references, 87, 95
  unnecessary words, 87, 96
Newscast director position, in the newsroom, 123, 327
  package scripts, 243–244
  scripts with on cam, vo/nat under, vo/nat full, sot and fs/gfx, 216
  scripts with sots, 175, 183
  scripts with sots, back-to-back, 181, 183
  scripts with vo and sots, 188, 192
  scripts with vo/nat full, 157, 159
Newsroom. *See also* Getting a newsroom job; specific newsroom position
  content positions, 323–324, 328
  exercises, 329
  management positions, 322–323, 328
  organizational chart, *321*
  production positions, 324, 328
  specialty reporting positions, 325, 329
  summary, 328–329
  typical day in, 326–328, 329
Newsworthiness, of stories, 302, 320
Non-standard out, of package script, 239
Nouns
  in conversational writing, 60–61, 65
  as parts of speech, 18, 31
  pronoun agreement with, 24–25, 31
Numbers, in news story, 35–37, 50

O
Objects, as parts of a sentence, 19–20, 31
One-shot camera shot, 314, 315
Onomatopoeia use, 64
Opinions, in news story, 44
Out cues
  in live shot, 279
  reporter out, package script, 239
  in scripts, with vo and sots, 192
  in scripts with sots, 175, 183
  in scripts with sots, back-to-back, 183

P
Pacing a newscast production, 305–307, *306,* 320
Package scripts, 102
  anchor cue, 244
  anchor introduction, 235, 266
  anchor tag, 239–240, 266
  "B-roll," 236, 266
  components of, 236–239, 267
  concept/story idea and research, 249–250
  director cues, 243–244
  exercises, 268–269
  formatted introduction, 243–244, 266
  formatted tag, 244, *245,* 246
  interviews, 250
  left column, 246, *247–248,* 267
  page numbering, 246
  personalization, 259, 267
  putting it all together, 254–255
  reporter standups, 239
  reporter tag, out, sig out or sign off, 236, 239, 244, 266
  reporter tosses, 235–236, 266
  right column, 246, *247–248,* 267
  script format, 240, 243
  script timing, 240
  shooting the interviews, 251–252
  shooting the story, 251
  standups, 236
    doing the standup, 253–254
    standup bridge, 252–253, 266, 359
    standup close, 253, 266
    standup open, 253, 266
  summary, 266–267
  video, 236
  visualization, 250
  voice track, 236, 266
  voicing, 255
  writing process of (sequential)
    gather information, 255, 267
    understand the story, 255–256, 267
    note key facts, 257, 267
    catalog story elements, 257–258, 267
    think before writing, 258–260, 267
    write script, 260, *261–265,* 267
    test script, 260, 267
  writing the package, reporter's approach to, 246, 249
  writing to shots and bites, 255
Pad video, 151, 315, 317, 336
Paraphrasing, in news story, 39, 54–55
Parts of a sentence. *See* Grammar, parts of a sentence

Parts of speech. *See* Grammar, parts of speech
Passive voice
in conversational writing, 59–60
in news story, 94–95, 106, 107
in writing leads, 84
Personalization, of news story, 259, 267
Personification use, 64
Photographer position, in the newsroom, 324, 326, 327, 328
Phrases, as parts of a sentence, 20
Placement organizations, to get a job, 378
Potter, Deborah (interview), 271–274
Power of observation, 7
Predicates. *See* Verbs
Prepositional phrase, object of, 25, 31
Prepositions
ending sentences with, 26, 31
as parts of speech, 19, 31
prepositional phrase, 25, 31
Present tense
in news story, 61–63, 65, 94, 106, 120, 121, 142, 146, 157, 192, 194, 266, 361
Print news, *vs.* television news, 11–12
Prioritizing a newscast production, 302, 320
Prioritizing news stories, 302, 320
Producer position, in the newsroom, 295, 323, 326, 327, 328. *See also* Producing the newscast
in live shot, 279–80
newscast production example, 335–343, *344–352*
script timing, 155
scripts with vo and sots, 204
Producing the newscast, *300. See also* News operation example
building the show, 315, *316,* 317
continuity, 298
excitement of, 319
exercises, 320
filling the rundown, 309, *310*
flow, 302–303, *304,* 305, 320
live shots, 318–310, 320
mechanics of producing, 297
"news hole" concept, 297–298, *298, 300,* 301, 319
newsworthiness, 302, 320
pacing, 305–307, *306,* 320
prioritizing, 302, 320
producer responsibilities, 295, 319
"reach" concept, 305–307
skeleton rundown, *300,* 301–302
skeleton rundown (sequential)
page column, 299, 301
slug column, 301

video column, 301
budget time column, 301
time (running) column, 301–302
backtime column, 302
"story budget," 297, 319
summary, 319–320
"tease" portion, 297, 307, 309, 311, 313–314, 320, 336
timing, 307–308, *309,* 320
back timing, 311, 318
front timing, 311, *312*
transitions, 305, 320, 336
"typical structure," 295, *296,* 297
variety, 305–307, *306,* 320
visual look, 295, 314–315, 320
Professionalism, 7
Pronouncers, in news story, 39, 40, 50
Pronouns
I *vs.* me, 24–25, 31
and noun-pronoun agreement, 24–25, 31
object of a prepositional phrase, 25, 31
as parts of speech, 18, 31
reflexive pronouns, 23–24, 31
Pseudopresent tense, 62–63
Pull to the anchor camera shot, 315
Punch line conclusion, 77, 91
Punctuation, in news story, 38, 50
Push to the anchor camera shot, 315

Q
"Q/A" in live shot, 279
"Quick out" cue, 181
Quotes
in leads, 83–84
in news story, 39, 50

R
rdr/sot (reader/SOT), 175
"Reach" concept, of newscast production, 305–307
Reader scripts, 101. *See also* Script formatting; Scripts, with full screen graphics
format, 108
script timing, 105
what viewers hear, 104
what viewers see, *107,* 107–108
writing the script, 105–107
Reader/SOT, 175
Reading aloud
conversational writing, 63, 64–65, 72
finished story, 92–93, 106, 121, 146, 157
Reflexive pronouns, 23–24, 31
Remote, 102
Reporter on-set, 102

Reporter positions, in the newsroom, 325, 326, 327, 328, 329, 333–335, 336, 339–340

    newscast production example, 343, 352–361, *362–363*

    tag or out, 236, 239, 244, 266

Reporter tosses

    in live shots, 275–276, 283

    in live shots, ending, 279–280

    package scripts and, 235–236, 266

Reporting. *See also* Interviewing

    gaining skill at, 4

    general assignment reporters, 12

    organization focus, 272

    standups, package scripts and, 239, 266

    vs. writing, 272

Responsible writing, 44. *See also* Attribution

    accuracy, 42–43, 50, 95

    attribution, 44–49

    balance, 15, 43–44, 50, 95, 106

    exercises, 50

    fairness, 15, 43, 50, 95, 106

    summary regarding, 50

Resumé. *See* Getting a newsroom job

Rhythm, of conversational writing, 64

"Roll cue"

    for sot in live shot, 275, 278, 283, 289

Rules of grammar. *See* Grammar, rules of

Rundown (sequential), of a newscast production, *300*

    page column, 299, 301

    slug column, 301

    video column, 301

    budget time column, 301

    time (running) column, 301–302

    backtime column, 302

S

Scripts. *See* Package scripts; Reader scripts; Script copy; Script formatting; Scripts, *specific subject, type*

Script copy

    format, 112

    with full screen graphics, 125, 132

    in scripts, with vo and sots, 192, 207

    in scripts with vo/nat full, 160

    with vo or no/nat, 150

Script formatting. *See also* Television newswriting

    anchor cue, 112–114, *113,* 132

    camera shot, 112

    cleanliness, 112, 114, 132

    date, 103, 111, 132

    director cues, 108, *109–110,* 111–112, 132

    end script, 104, 114

    format, 111, 132

    header information, 103

    left column, 104, *109–110,* 111–112, 132

    more, 104, *109–110,* 112

    newscast, 103, 111

    of package script, 240, *241–242,* 243, *245,* 246

    page number, 103, 108, 111

    parentheses, 104, 112

    right column, 103–104, *109–110,* 112, 114, 132

    run time, 103, 104–105, 111

    script copy, 112, 132

    slug, 103, 111

    top of page, 108, 132

    writer's initials, 103, 111

Scripts, combining elements in

    on cam, sot and full-screen graphic, 214, 216, *217*

    on cam, vo/nat under, vo/nat full, sot and full-screen graphic, 216, *218–219*

    on cam, vo/nat under, vo/nat full and sot, 212, 214, *215,* 216

    exercises, 220

    summary, 216

    vo/nat under and full-screen graphic, 211–212, *213,* 214, 216

Scripts, with full screen graphics

    anchor cue, 125, 126, 132

    building and using, 114, *115, 116,* 131–132

    camera shot, 123, 125

    date, 123

    director cue, 123, 125, 132

    end script, 126

    exercises, 133

    format, 122–123, 123, 131–132

    information for, 115, *117,* 131–132

    left column, 123, *124,* 125, 132

    newscast, 123

    page number, 123

    right column, *124,* 125–126, 132

    run time, 123, 131

    script copy, 125

    slug, 123

    summary regarding, 131–132

    top of page, 123, *124,* 132

    variety in, 126, *126–131*

    what viewers see, 121–122, *122,* 132

    when to use, 115–117, 131–132

    writer's initials, 123

    writing story for, 117–121, *118, 119,* 131–132

Scripts, with sots. *See also* Scripts, combining elements in; Scripts, with sots, back-to-back; Scripts, with vo and sots
    adding sots, 177–178, 183
    anchor cue, 175, 183
    cautions, 175, 183
    director cue, 175, 183
    exercises, 184
    finding sots, 165–167, 183
    introduction of, 170–171, 183
    left column, 175, *176*
    out cue, 175, 183
    placing of, 171–173
    rating of, 167–168
    right column, 175, *176, 177*
    script timing for, 174, 183
    the sot, 177
    "sot" under, 165
    summary, 183–184
    the super, 175
    tagging of, 174, 183
    trimming of, 168–169, 183
    writing out of, 173
    writing to, 165, 183
Scripts, with sots, back-to-back, 177–178, 184. *See also* Scripts, combining elements in; Scripts, with vo and sots; Scripts, with vo/nat full
    anchor cue, 183
    director cue, 181
    exercises, 184
    introduction of, 178–179
    left column of, *182*
    out cue, 183
    placement of, 180
    right column of, *182,* 183
    script timing for, 180–181
    the sot, 183
    summary, 183–184
    super of, first, 181
    super of, second, 181, 183
    tag, 180
Scripts, with vo and sots
    adding a sot, 195, 200
    anchor cue, 192
    back-to-back sots, *200,* 200–203
    camera shot, 188
    cautions, 200–201
    date, 188
    director cues, 188, 190–192, *191*
    end script, 192–193
    example of, 194–195, *195, 196–199*
    exercises, 207
    format, 188, 207

    left column, 188, *189,* 190–192
    newscast, 188
    old rules regarding, 187–188
    out cue, 192
    page number, 188
    right column, *189,* 192–195
    script copy, 192
    shot notation, 188, 190
    slug, 188
    the sot, 192
    summary, 207
    the super, 161, 188, *190,* 192, *193*
    tag, 192
    tagging sots with vo, 203–204, *204, 205–206,* 207
    top of page, 188
    writer's initials, 188
Scripts, with vo/nat full, 155, 157, *158*
    anchor cue, 159, 160, 161
    camera shot, 159
    date, 157
    director cue, 159, 161
    exercises, 162
    format, 157, 161
    left column, *158,* 159
    newscast, 157
    page number, 157
    right column, *158,* 159–160
    running time, 157
    script copy, 160, 161
    slug, 157
    summary, 161–162
    the super, 159, *160,* 161
    timing, 160, 161
    top of page, 157, *158*
    writer's initials, 157
Scripts, with vo or vo/nat. *See also* Scripts, combining elements in; Scripts, with vo and sots; Scripts, with vo/nat full
    anchor cue, 147, 150, 161
    beginning and ending of, 151, *153, 154*
    camera shot, 149
    cautions, 155, *156*
    date, 147
    direct video references, 139, 141–142, *143,* 144–146
    director cue, 149, 161
    end of script, 150
    exercises, 162
    format, 147, 161
    left column, *148,* 149–150
    log sheet, 139, *140, 143*
    logging tape, 139, 141–142, 144–146
    newscast, 147

pad video, 151
page number, 147
right column, *148,* 150
running time, 149
script copy, 150
sequences, 139, 146–147
shot notation, 151, *152*
slug, 147
summary, 161–162
the super, 149–150, 151, 161
timing, 146–147, 155
top of page, 147, *148,* 149
"wallpaper video," 139
what viewers hear, 138
what viewers see, 146–147
write to vo, 138–139, 161
writer's initials, 149
Segues, 303, 305, 337
Sequences, in vo, 139
Set piece, 102
Shot notation, 151, *152*
　in scripts, with vo and sots, 188, 190
Shot sheet, shot-sheeting, 139
Sign off
　in package scripts, 236, 239, 244, 266
Sig(signal) out
　of live shots, 279–280
　of package scripts, 236, 239, 244, 266
Simile, use of, 64
Skeleton rundown (sequential), of a newscast
　production, *300*
　page column, 299, 301
　slug column, 301
　video column, 301
　budget time column, 301
　time (running) column, 301–302
　backtime column, 302
Slug (story's title)
in package script, 243, 244
in scripts with graphics, 103, 111, 123
in scripts with vo/nat full, 157
in scripts with vo or no/nat, 147
sot (sound on tape), defined, 101–102, 165,
　　183. *See also* Scripts, with sots; Scripts,
　　with sots, back-to-back; Scripts, with vo
　　and sots
Sound bites. *See also* Interviewing
　attribution and, 49
　defined, 101
　in live shots, 275–276, 278
　in news story, 39, 357, 358, 360, 361
　in package script, 232, 236, 250–251, 255
　quote, 39
　in scripts with sot, 165

in scripts with vo and sots, 188, 192–193
transitions to and from, 188, 192–193
Sound on tape (sot), defined, 101–102. *See
　　also* Scripts, with sots; Scripts, with sots,
　　back-to-back; Scripts, with vo and sots;
　　sot
Specialty staff positions, in the newsroom,
　　325, 329
Spelling, 30–31
Sports staff position, in the newsroom, 325,
　　329
Standups
　definition of, 236
　doing the standup, 253–254
　in package scripts, 236, 252–254, 266
　reporter standups, 239
　standup bridge, 252–253, 359
　standup close, 253, 266
　standup open, 253, 266
Station. *See* Newsroom
Station manager position, in the newsroom,
　　322, 328
"Stepping on a bite" concept, 190
"Story budget," of newscast production, 297,
　　319
Story flow of newscast, 302–303, *304,* 305,
　　320
Studio wide-shot camera shot, 314
Subjects
　as parts of a sentence, 19, 31
　verb agreement with, 20–22, 31
Super(impose)
　in newscast example, 340
　in scripts, with vo and sots, 188, 192
　in scripts with sots, 175
　in scripts with sots, back-to-back, 181, 183
　in scripts with vo and sots, *190,* 192, *193*
　in scripts with vo and vo/nat, 149–150, *150,*
　　161
　in scripts with vo/nat full, 159, *160,* 161
Superlatives, in news story, 42
Suspense lead, 76, 91
Symbols, in news story, 35, 50

T
Tag
　in newscast production example, 342
　of package script, 239–240, 244, *245,*
　　266
　reporter tag, 239, 244, 266
　of scripts with sots, 174, 183
　of scripts with sots, back-to-back, 180
　of scripts with vo and sots, 192, 203–204,
　　204, 205–206, 207

"Take S-O-T up full" sot cue, 181
"Talking ear shot," 227
Tape editor position, in the newsroom, 324, 326, 328
"Tease" portion, of newscast production, 297, 307, 309, 311, 313–314, 320, 336, 338, 339, 340
Technology. *See also* Internet
in television newswriting, 5
Television newswriting. *See also*
Conversational writing; Grammar, *specific topic;* News story, *specific topic;* Responsible writing; Television newswriting, rules of
auditory *vs.* visual processing, 12–15
challenges of, 3, 7, 272–273
criticism and ego, 6
education requirement, 4–5, 8
exercises, 8, 15
health maintenance, 6, 8
initiative requirement, 6–7
organization focus, 272
people, 6
picture *vs.* story, 272, 273
power of observation, 5
pressure of, 5–6
vs. print news, 11–15
professionalism, 7
reporting *vs.* writing, 272
revision, 272
rewards of, 4, 7–8
roles in newsroom, 5
skills required, 4, 5, 7–8
summary regarding, 7–8
time factor, 12
verbs, focus on, 273–274
writing, importance of, 274
Television newswriting, rules of. *See also*
Conversational writing; News story, *specific topic;* Responsible writing
clichés, 40–41, 254
contractions, 38
initials and acronyms, 37–38
names, 37
numbers, 35–37
problem words and phrases, 41–42
pronouncers, 39
pronouncers, guide to, 40
punctuation, 38
quotes, 39
symbols and abbreviations, 35
That, in a sentence, 29–30
Three-shot camera shot, 314
Throwaway lead, 76

"Thumb-sucker," 275
Time code, on videotape, 357, 360
Time factor, of newswriting, 12
Timing
of live shot, 275, 276–277, 283
of news cast, 12
of newscast production, 307–308, *309,* 320
back timing, 311, 318, 342
front timing, 311, *312*
of package script, 240, 266
producing the newscast, 301–302
of reader scripts, 105
script formatting, 103, 104–105, 111
of scripts with full screen graphics, 123, 131
of scripts with vo/nat full, 157, 160
of scripts with vo or vo/nat, 146–147, 149, 155
total running time, 240, 266–267
"Toss question" in live shot, 279
Total running time (TRT), 240, 266–267
Transitions
news story end, 92
in newscast production, 305, 320, 336
soundbites, to and from, 188, 192–193
Trax (voice track), 236, 266
TRT (total running time), 240, 266–267
Two-shot camera shot, 314

U
Usage. *See* Conversational writing

V
Variety, in newscast production, 305–307, *306,* 320
Verbatims (package script), 246, 267
Verbs
in conversational writing, 57–58, 60–61, 65
in leads, 84
newscaster-ese errors, 273
as parts of speech, 18, 31
in scripts, 106
subject agreement with, 20–22, 31
Videographer position, in the newsroom, 324, 328
Videotape. *See also* Scripts, with vo
functions of, 137
limitations of, 137
VO-Bite (VOB), 102
vo/nats (video and natural sound). *See* Scripts, with vo or vo/nat
vo/sot, 102
VO (voice over), defined, 101, 161
VOB, 102

Vocal delivery, 4
Voice over (VO), defined, 101, 161
Voice track, 236, 266
vosot, 102

W
Wallpaper video, 139
Weather staff position, in the newsroom, 325, 329
Well *vs.* good, in a sentence, 28–29
WFAA-TV, Dallas. *See* News operation example
Which *vs.* that *vs.* who, in a sentence, 29–30
White, Beverly (interview), 285–293
Who *vs.* that *vs.* which, in a sentence, 29–30
Wipe camera shot, 315

Wire copy services
attribution to, 46
lead culled from, 73, 78–79, 80–81
news story written from, 93
reader scripts, 105–107
scripts from, combining elements in, 211–212
scripts with fs/gfx from, 115, 119, *119*
scripts with vo and sots, 193–195, *195, 196–199*
scripts with vo/nat full from, 157–161
scripts with vo or vo/nat from, 141–142
Word usage. *See* Conversational writing
Writing. *See* Television newswriting
Writing for the ear. *See* Conversational writing